FUNDAMENTAL RIGHTS

AUSTRALIA
The Law Book Company Ltd.
Sydney: Melbourne: Brisbane

CANADA AND U.S.A.
The Carswell Company Ltd.
Agincourt, Ontario

INDIA
N. M. Tripathi Private Ltd.
Bombay

ISRAEL
Steimatzky's Agency Ltd.
Jerusalem: Tel Aviv: Haifa

MALAYSIA: SINGAPORE: BRUNEI
Malayan Law Journal (Pte) Ltd.
Singapore

NEW ZEALAND
Sweet & Maxwell (N.Z.) Ltd.
Wellington

PAKISTAN
Pakistan Law House
Karachi

FUNDAMENTAL RIGHTS

*A volume of essays to commemorate
the 50th anniversary of the
founding of the Law School
in Exeter*

1923–1973

Edited by

J. W. BRIDGE
D. LASOK
D. L. PERROTT
R. O. PLENDER

With a Foreword by

Rt. Hon. Lord DENNING of Whitchurch
Master of the Rolls

*London
Sweet & Maxwell
1973*

Published in 1973 by
Sweet & Maxwell Limited
of 11 New Fetter Lane, London
and printed in Great Britain by
Richard Clay (The Chaucer Press) Ltd.,
Bungay, Suffolk.

SBN 421 19130 9

FOREWORD

THE Faculty of Law at the University of Exeter have done well to publish this volume.

In the fifty years since the Law School was founded, Exeter has grown exceedingly both in stature and in numbers. The quality is well shown by these essays. There are twenty-one of them. They cover much more than the title "Fundamental Rights" would imply. The essays are not confined to conventional subjects like freedom from arrest and arbitrary detention. Under the cloak "fundamental rights" this book deals with many other topics of great interest. Family Law is prominent with the rights of spouses and of children, born and unborn. The right of privacy and of fair comment receives full treatment. The right to walk and to ride, and—a new one—the right to outdoor recreation, are all considered. There are valuable discussions on rights in the European Community.

The great merit of the essays is that they deal with topics which are not to be found in the textbooks. Where else would you find a discussion on magistrates giving reason for their decisions? Or of free movement in the European Communities? As I have read through the book, I have said to myself, time and time again: "This is a book which I must keep beside me. Here is a storehouse of reasoning on the topics of the day."

All the contributions are by present members of the Faculty —professors or lecturers—and two or three former lecturers of the University of Exeter. They show a range of knowledge, and a depth of research, which is worthy of the highest praise. They prove beyond doubt that the Faculty of Exeter is in the van of legal scholarship in this country. It is a fitting way of commemorating the 50th Anniversary. The students should be grateful to be taught by such a team: and I am pleased to commend their book.

DENNING
M.R.

PREFACE

On December 7, 1923 Holdsworth delivered in Exeter his lecture entitled "Legal Education—its Debt to Bracton." The occasion was the inauguration of a Department of Law within the University College of the South West. In the course of his address Holdsworth commented that the new Department was inheritor of a great tradition, since it was situated in the county where Bracton lived and wrote. He might have added that Exeter's tradition of legal scholarship does not depend on the works of Bracton alone. By the thirteenth century the city was already reputed for its jurists— a tradition possibly established by Leofricus. Since Bracton's death Devon has counted among its many notable lawyers Carey, Wadham, Fortescue, Hody, Pollard, Drewe, Harris, Glanville, Lushington, Giffard, Prideaux, Hooker (Master of the Temple), Whyddon, Dodderidge and Follett.

Nevertheless, most of us continue to regard Bracton as the most eminent of the Devon lawyers. Holdsworth, on another occasion, described Bracton's influence on the fundamental constitutional precept whereby the law is counted supreme—governing King and subject alike.[1] Indeed, the crisis that led to the granting of Magna Carta led also to Bracton's celebrated statement:

> *"Ipse autem rex non debet esse sub homine sed sub Deo*
> *et sub lege, quia lex facit regem."*[2]

The same theme was later taken up by Fortescue, whose treatise *De Laudibus* has been described as "the herald of the age in which the lawyers would be prepared to stand up to the King and later to Parliament in defence of the legal rights of Englishmen."[3] It is therefore appropriate that the fiftieth year of regular legal education in Exeter should be commemorated by the publication of this book of essays on Fundamental Rights.

The University College of the South West was replaced by the University of Exeter in 1955. The Faculty of Law has succeeded to the functions and premises of the old Department. Each of the following essays is contributed by a present or former member of the teaching staff of that Faculty. The first deals with some jurisprudential issues raised by the use of the term "fundamental right." The remaining contributions describe the legal bases and limitations of facilities which the authors regard as rights of a fundamental nature.

The editors have attempted to refrain from that exercise of value judgment which is necessary to admit or reject the contributor's claim that the subject of his essay forms part of a body of fundamental rights. Equally they have abstained from any effort to enclose, within the covers of this volume, a comprehensive survey of all such rights: the subject is vast, and even a large compendium must remain fragmentary. In these respects each contribution will stand or fall on its own merits. But all the essays, however diverse their contents, form part of a central theme. Some of them describe traditional liberties (such as freedom from arbitrary arrest). Others are concerned with more novel rights (such as the right to outdoor recreation). In each case, the writer contends that the liberty which he examines is, in some sense, fundamental. More than this, the authors have in all cases attempted to confine their attention to those rights which are of topical importance. It is in this sense that the volume represents a collaborative effort. The editors hope that if the essays are read as a whole they will contribute to an understanding of the central theme of the book, particularly in a jurisdiction in which a constitutionally-defined *corpus* of fundamental rights remains conspicuous for its absence.

The editors wish to express their gratitude to the Rt. Hon. Lord Denning of Whitchurch, Master of the Rolls, for kindly consenting to contribute a Foreword and to the publishers for undertaking the publication of this book.

JOHN BRIDGE

DOMINIK LASOK

DAVID PERROTT

RICHARD PLENDER

Exeter

   Michaelmas Term, 1973

1. *Some Makers of English Law*, 1938, p. 19.
2. The King himself ought not to be subject to man but subject to God and to the law, because the law makes him King.
3. Potter, *Historical Introduction to English Law*, ed. Kiralfy, 1958, p. 285.

CONTENTS

1. THE LOGIC OF FUNDAMENTAL RIGHTS

D. L. PERROTT

I—Introduction

THIS essay is intended to analyse uses of the phrase "fundamental right," and to consider when such uses are appropriate, and how they may be justified, in serious discourse about the nature and content of legal systems. In section two of this essay, the concept of "a right" *per se* is discussed, and some different meanings of sentences containing the word "right" are distinguished. Section three deals with the question of what may be involved in describing a right as "fundamental." Section four considers some traditional claims of Natural Law theory to supply an objective justification for calling some rights fundamental, and argues that the Human Reason theory of Natural Law establishes not a *content* of Natural Law (and not therefore a set of "natural" fundamental rights) but rather *certain areas of necessary legal concern* in which Positive Law, of largely, though not entirely, optional content, necessarily exists. A modification of the concept of fundamental rights to take account of this argument is finally suggested.

II—Rights

In discussing the concept "fundamental right" it will probably be helpful to begin by considering the ordinary usage of the word "right," and then to consider the usage in which the word "right" is qualified by the word "fundamental."

Bentham, Hart and Ross[1] have taught us that a fruitful approach to the problem of extracting the meaning of words like "right" is to place the word in question in some sentences of the kind in which it is characteristically used, and then to ask: what is the meaning of the whole sentence, *i.e.* what would have to be the case if the whole sentence (if it were put into propositional form) could be said to be true? Let us then take some such sentences, *e.g.*:

> "Parents have a right to choose their child's education and school."
> "A married couple has a right to decide how many children they shall have."
> "A pregnant woman has a right to an abortion if she wants one."
> "I have a right to know where you have been" (Father to teenage daughter returning home at 3 a.m.).

When sentences of the above type are uttered, it is clear that some sort of claim is being made on behalf of the person said to have the right (the rightbearer); attention is being drawn, as it were, to some advantageous

1

position which the rightbearer is supposed, by the utterer, to have in the particular game of norms or values being played, which position the utterer feels is in some danger of being ignored or disputed. But these sentences are nevertheless initially[2] ambiguous in at least two kinds of ways.

One kind of ambiguity results from the fact that it is not clear initially whether the right asserted is considered to be a legal right, or a moral or some other normatively structured non-legal type of right, or whether the assertion is intended as a way of stating some value or recording some preference held by the utterer.

A second kind of ambiguity arises from doubt as to the precise relationship envisaged between the rightbearer and any duties which are being asserted to exist (whether any, and if so, what kind of, duties *are* being asserted is ambiguity of the first kind); *e.g.* when someone says "X has a right," etc., is it being said that someone owes a duty to do something for X, or at X's request; or that X himself has no duty not to do something; or that X by his actions may cause others to acquire new, or lose existing, duties; or that X is not in a position where others, by their actions, can cause X to acquire, or to lose, duties, etc., *i.e.* has X, in Hohfeldian terminology, a *right* (strictly so called), or a *privilege*, or a *power*, or an *immunity*, etc.? Sorting out this kind of ambiguity is the task of the analysis which Hohfeld perfected,[3] and since Hohfeldian analysis of rights and duties works best in relation to legal rights and duties, what further needs to be said on this will follow in the next subsection.

Legal rights

"Rights," in the sentences under discussion could be intended to mean "legal right," in which case, *e.g.* the sentence "Parents have a right to choose their child's education" probably means something like: "A legal system exists, under one or some of the rules of which a legal duty is imposed upon someone to see that the question of what kind of education a child receives is, or may be, determined by reference to (possibly *inter alia*) the wishes of the parents, such that the parents have some legal remedy available to them should they not be consulted, or should their wishes, if known, not be given the proper weight."[4]

Even some such formulation as this is still riddled with ambiguities,[5] even if we leave out of account those irrelevant to this discussion (*e.g.* the meaning of "kind of education," or of "wishes"). It does not tell us whether the parents' choice is conclusive, or, if not, what other factors are relevant, and, in the latter case, what weight should be given to conflicting factors. It does not tell us what should happen if the two parents should disagree, or if both refuse to express any wishes. It does not tell us whether there is a positive duty to ascertain parental wishes in advance, or merely a duty to take account of parental protests if and when they arise. Most importantly, it does not tell us who bears the duty and who is to do the ultimate determining. However, it does express the necessary minimum content of any such sentence as "Parents have a (legal) right to choose their child's education," as legal rights are ordinarily understood.

But since we are talking about a *legal* right the matter is greatly simplified by the fact that it is generally relatively easy to discover whether the "right" does exist, and what its more or less precise content is, should those questions be disputed. Thus, such ambiguities as are noticed above are not, in practice, serious, *i.e.* inimical to rational discussion, since they can usually be easily resolved as and when that becomes necessary, by reference to the relevant statutes, cases and legal opinions.[6] Even very intractable ambiguities can always, in principle, be litigated to the ultimate appellate court of the relevant system, where an authoritative resolution will be obtained.

Indeed, the *relative* ease and certainty with which such difficulties can be resolved in relation to the assertion of *legal* rights is practically part of the definition of the "legalness" of such rights.

Paradoxically, this legal sense of "right" is not necessarily the most interesting or important in the discussion of "Fundamental Rights." This is because, when someone asserts that something is a fundamental right,[7] he is, typically, unlikely to be very impressed, or inclined to withdraw his assertion, if some lawyer can show that the right in question is not mentioned, or at least, not supported, in any statute, judgment or legal opinion of the legal system. He will, typically, reply: "If that right is not a *legal* right, then it *ought* to be; meanwhile it is certainly some sort of right, (probably) involving *higher* obligations than merely legal ones." There is no legal or logical guarantee that in any given legal system all rights which even the vast majority of those subject to that system would regard as fundamental are recognised and protected by that system.

Before going on to consider what other sorts of rights, apart from legal ones, might be asserted, the second kind of ambiguity mentioned on page two must be considered. Hohfeld (and others) pointed out that at least four different meanings of the legal usage of "right" could be distinguished according to the nature of the relationship between the *propositus* right-bearer, and any duties, or other legal relationships, being asserted; he marked the distinctions with the labels "right" (strictly so called), "privilege" (or "liberty"), "power" and "immunity." This is not the place to discuss, still less to explain or justify Hohfeld's analysis; a brief example will have to suffice. If someone asserts, *e.g.* "A pregnant woman has a (legal) right to an abortion," this might be intended to mean (for any legal system):

(a) "A surgeon has a legal duty to perform an abortion on the woman (i) if she asks for one, or conceivably (ii) whether she asks for one or not" (one might say, without logical absurdity, that a woman who was seriously mentally defective had a legal "right" to be given an abortion, in this sense, although incapable of consenting to the operation, and, perhaps, invariably demanding that no doctor should ever come near her).

or (b) "A pregnant woman has no legal duty not to have an abortion . . ." *i.e.* if she can persuade any surgeon to perform one on her. This is even consistent with the surgeon having a duty not to operate; the law might be such that the offence of abortion could only be committed by the person performing the operation, or by qualified, or by non-qualified, surgeons.

or (c) "A pregnant woman can, if she follows the proper procedure (*e.g.* a formal application through the Ministry of Health), alter her, and her surgeon's, existing legal duty *not* to abort her, so that the surgeon would acquire a duty to perform the operation if she were to request it, and her request would become legally permissible."

or (d) "A pregnant woman (now) has no legal duty not to have an abortion . . . even if the father of the foetus forbids it" (assuming that a previous law, which made it an offence for a woman to have an abortion after the father had expressed his disapproval, has just been repealed).

Meanings (a), (b), (c) and (d) above correspond to what Hohfeld called a "right" (strictly so called), "privilege," "power" and "immunity." It will be observed that in (a) something is said about the *existence* of the *surgeon's* duties; in (b) about the *existence* of the *woman's* duties; in (c) about possible *alterations* in the woman's and surgeon's duties; and in (d) about the woman's *freedom from* possible alterations in her duties.

The point to be made here is that while Hohfeldian discriminations are an essential tool in any serious analysis of particular propositions about particular rights and duties, the present discussion would become both unwieldy and tedious if these discriminations have to be worked through for each of the different kinds of right, or more accurately, different kinds of assertions about rights here distinguished.

It is suggested that this difficulty can be avoided by noticing that seven of Hohfeld's eight[8] "fundamental legal conceptions" can be reduced to, or expressed in terms of, the eighth, namely the legal duty.[9] Or to put it another way, three of Hohfeld's four basic legal relationships can be reduced to the fourth, namely the right (strictly so called)—duty relationship. If this be accepted, it will be sufficient if the subsequent discussion proceeds mainly in terms of this relationship, bearing in mind that what is said, therefore, about rights (strictly so called) could in principle be expanded to apply to "rights" in the senses also of privileges, powers and immunities by performing the necessary logical operations on the expressions used and vice versa: assuming, that is, that rights are being discussed in the context of some rule-system capable of yielding duty-imposing *and* power-conferring rules.

Moral rights

"Right" in the sentences under discussion could be intended to mean "moral right,"[10] in which case, *e.g.* the sentence "A married couple have a right to decide how many children they shall have" probably means something like: "A system (or code) of morals exists, under some of the rules of which a moral duty is imposed upon someone not to prevent, or attempt to prevent, or even perhaps, not effectively to discourage, a married couple from having the number of children that they want." (Or, of course, it could mean "A married couple have no moral duty to limit the size of their family" if the "privilege" meaning of right is intended, etc.)

It must be noticed that this involves, *pari passu*, the same kind of initial ambiguities as to the content and functioning of the right claimed as were mentioned in the discussion of legal rights. More seriously, this also involves the possibility of genuine lasting doubt as to whether the asserted moral duty, moral rule or moral system does exist, and of what it means to say that a moral rule or moral system does exist. It is notoriously more difficult to show (if it is strenuously denied) that a given moral rule or system exists, or to explain what is meant by such a claim, than that a given legal rule or system exists, and what is meant by *that* claim.

Moreover, not only are there no obvious and easy ways of resolving these difficulties. There is a further difficulty: assume the existence of a given moral system is granted and the contents of all its primary (*i.e.* duty-imposing) rules are known. There may still, in a given case, be a prima facie conflict between the requirements of different primary rules of the system.[11] How is such a conflict to be resolved? Legal systems provide for such problems, and for the above-mentioned existential types of difficulties in advance, by special rules for dealing with them. Moral systems notoriously do not; indeed this is the source of virtually all interesting moral problems. Lastly, even if the existence and content of a given moral right-duty relationship be granted by the relevant parties, there is, in the nature of things, no effective remedy available to the right-bearer for breach of such a duty (unless it were *also* a legal duty of course).

For all these reasons, very little attempt is made in practice seriously to maintain or demonstrate claims of the kind "parents have a *moral* right to choose their child's education," or "to determine the size of their family" once such claims encounter strenuous argumentative resistance, (apart, that is, from technical philosophical or theological writings, or unless the claimant is arguing from the basis of a religious moral system which in its degree of coherence and organisation approximates to a legal system, such as canon law, or Judaic or Mohammedan religious law). In face of the considerable difficulties involved, such assertions tend to collapse fairly quickly into assertions of value or preference of the kind discussed next; if, indeed, they were not mere muddled attempts at that kind of assertion in the first place.

Rights and values

"Right" in the sentences under discussion could be merely intended to mean, or rather refer to, some value-word, such as "good" or "desirability," in a slightly elliptical way. Hence the phrase "right of parental choice" in this kind of sense means something like "the desirability" or "the value of parental choice," and such assertions as "I have a right to know where you have been" mean, roughly, "It would be a good thing if you had to tell me," or "It is highly desirable that you should tell me where you have been"; or more subjectively, "I like to know where you have been." This kind of meaning of "right" has the advantage that it does not necessarily commit the speaker to deducing this value from a whole system of rules or values, as the legal and moral meanings discussed above do. He may be merely stating his unsupported (though not therefore illegitimate) preferences, or some immediate deduction from them, or at least some deduction from values which are held generally, for whatever reason.

There is always something slightly suspect about this kind of usage of words like "right." Such usage looks like an attempt, conscious or not, to dignify a quite proper subjective value judgment with an appearance of normative objectivity by exploiting the ambiguities inherent in such usage. In practice, these value or preference usages of "right" can be divided into two categories, bare subjective value or preference, and justified value or preference.

In stating a bare subjective value or preference the speaker is expressing a basic attitude, for which no reasons can or need be given; it is in that sense irrational (not a pejorative here), *i.e.* it cannot be argued about. If a man says "I just *like* smoking" it is silly to try to prove to him that smoking is not enjoyable and irrelevant to try to prove that smoking is harmful. The father in our example may mean "I like to know where you have been because I just like things better that way." While no doubt true, this is, argumentatively, a blind alley.

Perhaps many claims that something is a "fundamental right" are, on analysis, mere statements of basic political preference of this form. As such, they must, in a democratic polity, be paid careful attention. But, being unarguable, they provide no reason why anyone else should agree with them or accept them; the man who "just likes" smoking can never *convince* one who dislikes it that smoking is not nasty, or *a fortiori*, that it is not harmful. Moreover, one who believes the preference or value is actually pernicious would be foolish in framing deliberate policies to give such bare statements of preference too much weight. We should not encourage children to smoke merely because many adults enjoy the practice.

In stating a justified value or preference, on the other hand, the speaker is asserting that something is of value, or to be preferred, because it leads to, or tends to produce, some end or goal which everyone, or the generality of people agrees to be of value or to be preferred, and that this is why he himself values or prefers it. (If the end in view is not thought to be valued by the generality or at least, if it is, is not valued by the speaker for that reason, then either it will be valued by the speaker in itself, *i.e.* as a bare subjective valuation, or else it will probably be valued by him because of its assigned place in some organised system of values or norms to which he subscribes in which case what was said concerning moral rights will apply.)

Where a statement of value is justified by reference to an end considered generally to be of value which the first value is said to promote, there is a real possibility of sensible argument, supported by empirical evidence, and sometimes capable of definitive resolution. Even here, however, some confusion is still possible. First, it must be made clear precisely what is the end or goal that people are said to value or prefer generally. Secondly, two empirical questions must be distinguished: (a) whether the stated end or goal is in fact valued or preferred generally, (b) whether the particular thing in question really does lead to or tend to produce that end or goal.

Of course, even if the speaker can explain and justify his statement in these ways, his opponent may well still reply that general acceptance as a value is no guarantee of "genuine" value, or that in the instant case some other value, which may be equally generally accepted, is in conflict with the speaker's justifying value, and overrides it by virtue of being a more important value, *i.e.* our debaters are back with the problems similar to those mentioned in discussing moral rights.

Thus, our father may mean that he has a right to know (*i.e.* she should tell him) where his daughter has been because knowing helps fathers to protect daughters from harmful influences, and such protection is generally considered a good thing, indeed, perhaps a duty. The daughter may well consider that her father's idea of protection is obscure, that she does not need protection, that if she did her father's knowledge of her past whereabouts could not materially promote it, that only middle-aged parents of teenage daughters tend to hold such views, and that anyway it is more important to promote her own privacy and independence than her protection. Such arguments, therefore, even when cogently presented, and empirically supported, on both sides, will again often be inconclusive.

Two further comments on value-based right-assertions are necessary. First, the distinction drawn here between assertions of moral rights and assertions of value-based rights is not to be taken as suggesting that in practice a clear line can always be drawn between the two, as it can be, usually, between both these kinds of assertions and assertions of legal rights. Relatively well-organised and consistent moral systems tend to shade into relatively unorganised and inconsistent sets of values and preferences, and the precise logical relationship between the two poles of this continuum is still a matter of inquiry.[12] But the distinction does mark a difference of emphasis and approach in the justification of right-assertions.

Secondly, it would seem debatable whether the "rights" which are forms of, or derived from, value or preference assertions have, in the Hohfeldian sense, duties in others correlative to them; or alternatively, whether they really describe the absence of what could be called a duty, when they are expressed in the "privilege" form. In general it seems reasonable to suppose that we often conceive of people as having an independent duty to encourage, or at least permit, the promotion of what we regard as valuable where this is a justified value judgment. Where it is a bare subjective value or preference, however, we would probably feel in our more reflective moments some unease about saying that others generally have a duty to promote these *in themselves*. This question clearly requires a full analysis of when it is appropriate to use words like "duty," "obligation," etc. in this area of values and preferences. For the moment, what does seem clear is that "rights" which are forms of, or derived from value or preference assertions, cannot be rights in the Hohfeldian senses of "power" or "immunity,"[13] since *they* require the existence, as part of a coherent system of rules, of secondary, power-conferring rules,[14] and by definition such rules and systems are absent from these value-areas. (In practice, they are often absent from moral systems too, but given that these are rule-systems, there is no overriding *logical* reason for their absence.)

III—Fundamental Rights

Having discussed what is, or may be, meant by sentences containing the word "right" *per se*, we may now consider the meanings of the phrase "fundamental right" by asking, what is intended by describing a "right" as "fundamental," and under what circumstances is such a description appropriate or justified. Clearly, answers to these questions will vary with the kind of right-assertion being made.

If the fundamental right being asserted is intended to be a legal right, these questions can usually be answered relatively easily. Such rights are properly called fundamental when they are expressed in, or guaranteed by, laws which are basic or pre-eminent laws of the legal system[15] in question, *e.g.* rights which are specified in a written constitution, or in judgments of a superior court interpreting the constitution, or in enactments of a legislature designed to render the constitution more specific in a certain area. Where the "constitution" is unwritten, or, even if written, may be changed by simple legislative majority, there will still be rules and conventions, with their associated judgments and enactments, which are regarded as "constitutional," *i.e.* as of primary importance to the structure and content of the whole legal system, and rights expressed or implied by such rules, conventions, etc., may be properly called fundamental, even if legally their existence is somewhat insecure. For example, in English law, the right to vote is contained in an enactment rendering specific an area (composition of the legislature) of a substantially unwritten constitution; the right to issue a writ of habeas corpus is provided by ancient, unwritten rules of law (albeit statutorily qualified from time to time) which, though *structurally* less obviously "constitutional" of the system than, say, rules about the composition of the legislature, have been found as a matter of practice and history to be presupposed at various points by, and necessary for the proper working of, the constitution.

By analogy, some other legal rights may be called "fundamental" where, although the rules containing them are not at all "constitutional," in the sense that they are, or closely appertain to, the rules that Kelsen would call part of the "*grundnorms,*" or Hart, the *basic* rules of "recognition, adjudication and change" of the legal system, nevertheless these rights are legally basic in the sense that their existence and content is essential to the existence and content of many other lesser legal rights of the system. For instance, in English law, the right to organise or join a strike, or to form a company, are of this kind. It will often be politically very difficult (in a democracy) to remove or even vary legal rights which are fundamental in these senses, even if owing to the character of the constitution, or the right's position in the legal system, this is legally straightforward. Fundamentality, then, in these senses, and in relation to legal rights, refers to the technically important or influential position which the rule specifying the right holds within the whole hierarchy of legal norms constituting the legal system in question.

A legal right may also be called fundamental in the quite separate sense that it is conceived as embodying in legal form a right which is also a moral right or a value judgment, and which is considered fundamental *qua* moral right or value, in one of the senses of "fundamental" appropriate to describe moral rights or values, to be discussed next. For instance, in English law, a person might reasonably claim that, say, a woman's legal right to have an abortion (in certain circumstances), or to live in the matrimonial home after desertion by the husband-owner, were fundamental (in this sense) although these rights are not particularly significant in the structure of the whole legal system, *i.e.* not fundamental in the "legal" senses of "fundamental" discussed above.

Turning to moral rights, similar considerations apply *pari passu*. Moral rights are properly called fundamental when the moral principles that give rise to them are considered to be fundamental principles of the moral system in question, *e.g.* the right of an individual to determine what constitutes, and to pursue, his own happiness, provided he does not cause thereby equivalent unhappiness to others, in a utilitarian system; the right of an individual to be regarded as an end-in-himself in a Kantian system; the right of an individual not to have his interests sacrificed to the common good unless he would have agreed to that in advance, in a Rawlsian Social Contract-determined system[16]; and the more specific rights that are clearly and immediately derivable from such general rights. But it is usually more difficult to say whether a given moral right is fundamental than whether a legal right is. This is because, since it is inherently more difficult to establish the existence and content of a suggested moral system than of a legal system, as noted above, *a fortiori* it is more difficult to show that any given principle of the system is a fundamental principle of the system. For this reason, the assertion that a moral right is fundamental in the above sense often tends to collapse, (again, outside technical philosophical discussion) under pressure, into an assertion that the moral right is fundamental in the sense that its existence, and attempted implementation, is regarded as vitally important by the speaker or perhaps, by people generally, *i.e.* into a value or preference claim.

Alternatively, the assertion that a moral right is fundamental sometimes means, particularly in a juristic context, that a moral right exists, and that, whatever its status in the hierarchy of the moral system, it is a right suitable for legal recognition as a legal right (not all moral rights are, of course, suitable for such treatment, *e.g.* the moral right to have all promises kept, absent a morally acceptable excuse), and indeed ought to be legally recognised as a fundamental legal right, in the "legal" senses of "fundamental" discussed above, if it is not already so recognised. A current example would be the assertion that women should not be discriminated against in the allocation of employment on grounds of their sex alone. The "ought" in "ought to be legally recognised" in such cases may be justified by a variety of arguments variously related to the relevant moral systems, value systems or bare value judgments of the person making the assertion, or sometimes, where the justification is a technical legal argument, to the legal system in question. By its characteristic of relating actual moral existence and potential legal existence, this usage is more than usually productive of ambiguity, but provided the meaning is made clear, the use of "fundamental" in this sense is unobjectionable.

If the right-assertion is of a bare value or preference, the right may be appropriately called "fundamental" if the value or preference is regarded as particularly important or overriding by the speaker.

Prima facie there might seem some difficulty in arranging what are by definition bare, unsupported value or preference judgments in some sort of order of importance. But a person could hold that if forced to choose between realising his value A and his value B, he would in fact choose to realise A, without committing himself thereby to some further value *which justified* his commitment to A in the first place; *i.e.* his valuing or preferring of A to B would itself be a bare value judgment, without justification or consequences. He might, *e.g.* say, "I would rather smoke twenty a day than live to be a hundred, but there is no reason why, nor for why I value smoking."

Those values or preferences which a person would choose to pursue, if forced to choose, rather than all, or most, of his other values or preferences, would be appropriately called "fundamental" *for him*, and he could equally call "fundamental" (*for him*) the "rights" in right-assertions based on, or stating such values or preferences. But there would be no reason, of course, why anyone else should concur in that description.

If the right-assertion is of a justified value or preference, the right may be appropriately called "fundamental" if realising the value or preference in question would tend to produce the justifying end or goal with a high degree of probability, if a sufficiently large proportion of individuals in the relevant society did in fact value or prefer that end or goal, and if further their valuation of or preference for that end or goal was for each of them "fundamental" in the subjective sense discussed in the preceding paragraph.[17] By sufficient success in meeting these criteria, this kind of value-based fundamental right-assertion would achieve a respectable objectivity.

Alternatively, as with the "moral" senses of "fundamental," a value- or preference-based right might be described as "fundamental" in the sense that, whatever the quality of the value or preference in question, it was suitable for recognition in the form of a legal right, and indeed ought to be so recognised as a "fundamental" legal right in the "legal" senses discussed above. Again, the "ought" in such assertions may be variously justified, by reference to moral systems, value judgments, or occasionally, to the legal system in question.

IV—*Natural Law and Fundamental Rights*[18]

Within Western philosophy there has been a long and venerable tradition of using the concept of "Natural Law" in the definition and identification of fundamental rights. Roughly speaking, the idea has been that, apart from the actual positive law systems that obtain at different times and in different places, there exists a set of ideal norms or principles of a higher obligation, which are the same for all men at all times, which are concerned with the same problems that positive law attempts to solve, and to which positive law systems are, at best, an approximation, morally speaking, dictated by the circumstances of a particular time and place. This set of norms, therefore, is conveniently called Natural Law, and, on this view, the "natural" rights granted to individuals by the rules of Natural Law are properly also called "fundamental." To use a modern idiom borrowed from linguistics, they are the "deep structure" of which the positive legal rights generated by particular legal systems are the more-or-less successful surface manifestations.

This Natural Law usage of the phrase "fundamental rights," in terms of the analysis attempted in section III of this paper, expresses either a *legal* right meaning or a *moral* right meaning depending upon the form of Natural Law theory adopted. It is characteristic of Natural Law theories, of course, that they tend to deny that a purely logical distinction between legal and moral rules is always possible. But faced with the question, 'Is a rule that is contrary to Natural Law, but is in all other respects a valid rule of a positive law system, nevertheless a valid, (albeit bad) positive rule of that system?" Natural Law theorists divide fairly readily into two groups. Some answer the question in the affirmative, others in the negative. For the former, Natural Law is merely a moral system, in the senses discussed in sections II and III. For the latter, it is a genuinely legal system, or more accurately, any positive law system must be conceived of as having Natural Law built into its constitution or fundamental laws by necessary implication, as an overriding constitutional requirement. For these theorists, a "natural right" is necessarily a fundamental *legal* right of the kind discussed in section III and for them the ambiguities there mentioned, between moral and legal fundamentality, do not really exist.

Forced to take sides in this ancient debate, the writer would adhere to the former group, while suspecting that the question is not well formulated. An attempt to specify what is involved in comparing positive law with Natural Law, may suggest a modified method of linking the fundamentality of fundamental rights with what has been called "the core of good sense in the doctrine of Natural Law."[19]

It is a commonplace that there has been very little stability of content or emphasis in Natural Law thought throughout its long history. It has been politically conservative or radical, religiously committed or secular, has stressed now natural obligations, now natural rights. And as we have just noted, it has been in two minds over the question of the technical validity of conflicting positive law. Perhaps the one common thread that has run throughout this history is the idea that the question was at least a sensible one, *i.e.* that in principle it is possible to compare any given rule of positive law with the relevant principle of Natural Law, and discover whether there was conformity, neutral compatibility or conflict between the two, which is to say that Natural Law has always been conceived of as the standard by which positive laws are measured, even if there has been disagreement over the consequenses of measuring. Indeed, Natural Law is of little use as a concept unless we *can* compare our particular laws and institutions with it and *ascertain their conformity or contradiction.*

But for the comparison to yield such ascertainment, the principles of Natural Law must be specific and detailed enough to make such a comparison genuinely possible. They need not be stated at quite the same (low) level of abstraction as the piece of positive law under investigation, but equally they cannot be much more abstract, else alternative interpretations, one supporting, one condemning, the positive law, may become possible. So they must say fairly definite things about when we may kill each other, use available materials, whom we may sleep with, which promises we must keep, which injuries to others we must pay for, etc. But then (it is the crucial problem for all Natural Law theories) how are we to determine the content of these fairly precise instructions, and how can we feel sure that a suggested example really is a genuine, properly formulated, piece of Natural Law? Principles formulated at a level of abstraction likely to command universal assent are almost certainly *too* abstract to permit any informative comparison with the relevant areas of positive law.

Traditionally, two kinds of answers have been given to the question of how to identify the source and content of Natural Law rules. (Sometimes, as in Aquinas, both kinds of answer have been combined in a unified theory). We are said to be able to discover what are the principles of Natural Law, because either they are statements of what God requires of us, of which He has adequately informed us, or alternatively, they are those principles which our ordinary human reason, given the chance, forces us to realise to be necessary.

Of these two, the first kind of answer strikes the writer as *logically* more satisfactory. Of course, it will be factually unacceptable to the non-religiously inclined, and downright unintelligible to some atheists. But, if it were granted, for the sake of argument, that the proposition "God exists" is meaningful, that God does in fact exist, and that He has informed us of His wishes for us, there would be no particular logical difficulty about conceiving His instructions to be highly specific, at least in some areas, and indeed this is the way that *e.g.* many highly logical Christians, Jews or Moslems do conceive of Natural Laws. The objections to this approach, therefore, turn on questions of theology and religious philosophy, not of legal philosophy or general logic, and no more will be said here on this point.

Human Reason, on the other hand, seems, on analysis, far less likely to be capable of yielding sets of principles specific enough to do the job. What our human reason tells us, it is here argued, is not what the specific principles of Natural Law *are*, but for which *areas* of human behaviour we must have, and try to enforce, *positive laws* (and not merely moral principles) although, within wide limits, any of a large variety of possible laws will serve.

Human reasoning is, broadly, either inductive, deductive or analytical (*i.e.* by analogy). The last could not by itself yield Natural Law principles (analogous to given positive law principles, presumably) without some criterion of success, *i.e.* means of evaluating the suggested analogy for "naturalness," universitality, etc., and this would have to be supplied by induction or deduction.

Inductive reasoning, in this context, would presumably consist in some comparative survey of the world's positive law systems, to see if there were any positive law rules which appeared in identical form, at the same level of abstraction, *and at all times*, in all or most of the systems. But, even if research revealed the existence of such rules, their ubiquitousness would not by itself justify calling them Natural Law. They might, although widespread, be very bad rules. Surveys carried out at various points before the eighteenth century might well have revealed, for example, that slavery, or an inferior legal status for women, were well-nigh universal institutions. Alternatively the widespread rule might be a very trivial or arbitrary one; conceivably one day all the world may have to drive on the right of the road, or obtain two witnesses for a valid will, but we would probably not call such rules Natural Law. What such research does tend to reveal, of course, is not the existence of identical rules or even institutions in all or most systems, but that all systems do have (widely differing) rules about the same areas of human behaviour, *i.e.* regulating physical violence, the use of materials, sexual and supportive relationships, the keeping of promises and compensation for injuries, etc.

Deductive reasoning also leads us to conclude that there are what may be called *Natural Areas of Legal Concern* rather than Natural Law principles with a specific content. The strict proof of this is rather long, and beyond the scope of this paper, but perhaps, for the moment, the following observations will suffice. When our deductive reason is seriously applied to determining the necessary content of a morally tolerable legal system it either yields a purely formal principle or set of principles, devoid of particular content (as in Kant) or else identifies (as in Hobbes) specific areas of human behaviour which are too important to the survival of the society and of individuals in the society to be left to the somewhat haphazard, because indeterminate and (relatively) ineffective, control of merely moral rules and sanctions. That is, for these matters we need the precision of formulation and power of sanction (together with the procedures for rule —recognition, adjudication and rapid change that such precise and powerful tools render necessary)[20] that are characteristic of legal, as opposed to moral or value, systems. For each of these areas, once a basic value-choice is made as to the goal to be achieved, the choice fixes certain very wide parameters which the legal rules must satisfy. For example, if we assume, (with Hobbes and Hart), that maximum survival of the individual is the basic goal,[21] the rules must tend to decrease his chance of being killed, and increase his chances of being fed, and (in high latitudes) kept warm, until he dies of old age. Obviously this can best be achieved in a legally regulated society where individuals help each other on a reciprocal basis.

Not all killing can be permissible, but equally not all killing can be prohibited, otherwise the individual runs an unnecessary risk from attack by enemies from outside, or maniacs from inside, the society. These are the parameters, and they determine that what is needed is a legal rule which clearly distinguishes illegal killing from justifiable killing, *i.e.* which defines murder. But a number of different definitions of murder may be equally acceptable.

Similarly, the individual will need to use materials (for food, clothing and shelter) to survive. Not all taking and using of materials without the permission of anyone can be permissible (else, as Hobbes observed, no one would bother to expend labour on material production; alternatively, there would be constant violent strife). But not all taking and using without the permission of everyone could be prohibited (else, as Locke observed, man would have starved in spite of God's Plenty). These are the parameters for what we call property. There must be legal rules specifying when a man may use materials without asking anyone's permission, and when he can only use them, if at all, after first having obtained someone's permission, and in the latter case, specifying who has authority to grant the permission. But within this framework, an infinite variety of property laws is possible, based on private ownership or corporate possession, capitalism or communism, with highly developed land law, and little personalty law, as in Medieval English Law, or the reverse situation, as in some African tribal systems, and all the various admixtures and combinations of these. They may all tend to produce individual survival equally well, or at least we may have no way of identifying those which produce it best.[22]

Similarly, since sex is potentially such a disruptive force, we need legal rules telling us when we can make love with someone and when we cannot, or at least cannot without someone else's permission, and in that case, whose permission. But this leaves a wide variety of sexual arrangements possible. As a separate issue, if we are to survive successfully into old age, we need to see that children are now born and reared successfully to adulthood, so they may support and protect us then. So we need rules telling us which adults have the primary responsibility of bearing and rearing which children, and which adults have the secondary rearing responsibility, etc., *i.e.* we need laws about who is related to whom. To fix the primary responsibility on the biological mother and father is a convenient, but not a logically dictated, pattern; other arrangements are logically perfectly feasible. And so on: we need laws that distinguish the trivial promises we need not keep from the ones we must take seriously; that distinguish the harms we cause to others that we must compensate for, from those the others must bear the risk of themselves.[23] The precise content of the rules, within limits, does not matter very much;[24] what does matter is that legal discriminations should be drawn, and then generally adhered to. We *do* need to decide which side of the road to drive on; the choice of sides is, within limits, arbitrary.

V—Conclusion

If the argument of section IV is correct, that "the core of good sense in the doctrine of Natural Law"[25] is that our deductive reason tells us, and our inductive reason confirms, that for any conceivable society (above a certain low level of size and complexity) there are "Natural" areas of legal concern, *i.e.* areas of human behaviour that *must* be patterned by positive legal discriminations, and regulated by positive law rules, a modified approach to the question of basing the fundamentality of some fundamental rights in the concept of Natural Law may be suggested. By this approach, a right is properly to be called "fundamental" (along with the other kinds of occasions on which that usage is justified, as discussed in section III) when it is contained in or specified by a rule of positive law which, within its own positive law system, is a basic rule relating to a "Natural Area of Legal Concern" (as defined in section IV). In this sense widely differing rights relating to the same subject matter from different legal systems could all be equally called fundamental. Conversely, rights derived from rules regulating areas of merely optional legal concern (*i.e.* where legal regulation was not logically entailed by the existence of society —*e.g.* anti-trust, or Customs and Excise legislation) could not be "fundamental" in this sense.

NOTES

1. See Hart, *Definition and Theory in Jurisprudence* (1953), p. 8; Ross, *On Law and Justice* (1958), pp. 172–174.
2. Often, of course, it is possible to resolve the ambiguity immediately, or very quickly, from the context of the utterance, or by questioning the utterer. We are here concerned with the meaning to be extracted from the sentence itself.
3. Hohfeld, *Fundamental Legal Conceptions* (1919) (reprinted, ed. by Cook, 1964).
4. I am obviously indebted to Hart, *Definition and Theory in Jurisprudence* (1953), p. 16, for this type of formulation. The version there propounded by Hart is oversimplified, as it fails to deal adequately with the difficult question of what it means to "enforce" a legal duty, and to say that the right bearer has some "choice" in the enforcement. My present formulation has much the same oversimplification, slurred over by the words "legal remedy available," but since this paper is not primarily concerned to analyse the notion "*legal* right" exhaustively, but only to identify it as one kind of right among others, perhaps this will do for the present.
5. See note 2.
6. For some English law resolutions of this particular example see *e.g.* the Education Act 1944, s. 76, and *Cummings* v. *Birkenhead Corporation* [1972] Ch. 12.
7. Unless, by "fundamental right" he means, quite narrowly, a right specifically mentioned and guaranteed in a (written) constitution or by a fundamental law; see *post*, Section III.
8. The four not yet mentioned are the correlatives of right, privilege, power, and immunity, namely duty, no-right, liability and disability. Right and duty are often said to be "imperfect" correlatives, *i.e.* there are duties without any correlative rights. There is general agreement that the other three pairs are perfect correlatives.

9. This may be proved as follows: Hohfeld's eight fundamental legal conceptions can be reduced to four relationships, namely (i) Right–Duty, (ii) No-right–Privilege, (iii) Power–Liability, and (iv) Immunity–Disability. But (ii) and (iv) are merely the negative forms of (i) and (iii) respectively. And (iii) may be reduced to (i), since Power is defined as the ability to alter legal relationships of these four kinds. But to alter (ii) is to alter (i) negatively, and to alter (iv) is to alter (iii) negatively. So, to alter (iii) is to alter (i) or (iii). But for (iii) to alter (iii) either involves an infinite regress ("an ability to alter an ability to alter an ability . . . etc.") or an escape by substituting (i) ("an ability to alter . . . a Right–Duty relationship") in the definition of (iii). Therefore Power is always, ultimately, an ability to alter (i). And within (i) there is general agreement that Right may always be defined in terms of Duty, even if the converse is disputed. Therefore, seven of the eight conceptions can be defined in terms of the eighth, the most fundamental of all, Duty.

10. "Morality" here should be given a wide interpretation, to include *e.g.* religious morality, political theory, etc. It *may* also be taken to include obligations conceived as arising from value-judgments, provided the values in question are conceived of as ordered in some kind of value-system. Values not, or not necessarily, systematically conceived are here treated in the next subsection. The precise relationship between morals and values, or between normative and evaluative propositions, and the extent to which each is expressible in terms of the other, are, of course, matters of considerable philosophical debate, beyond the scope of this paper, but see *e.g.* Findlay, *Axiological Ethics* (1972), for an excellent brief discussion. See too, on the logic of moral rights, Hart, "Are There Any Natural Rights?" (1955), *Philosophical Review*, 175.

11. *e.g.* A married couple might see themselves as having a moral duty both to have (some) children, and not to cause seriously defective children to be born to them. If the couple know they are both carriers of, say, phenylketonuria, the problem of whether they should risk pregnancy is of this kind.

12. See note 10.

13. And cannot give rise to correlative "liabilities" or "disabilities," in the Hohfeldian senses, therefore.

14. See Hart, *The Concept of Law* (1961), pp. 77-96.

15. The rules and principles of public international law are here regarded as constituting a legal system, along with particular municipal law systems, and as including similarly certain rules and principles which are basic or constitutional, in the sense of being of primary importance to the structure and content of the whole system.

16. See Rawls, *A Theory of Justice* (1972), especially Chap. 1.5 and 3.30.

17. Alternatively, some or all of the individuals constituting that large proportion of society might value or prefer the end or goal simply because it was valued or preferred generally, *i.e.* because of acceptance of a principle of valuing what is generally valued. But probably such a principle is itself only accepted either because of a bare value or preference judgment (*i.e.* in favour of a democratic choice of value-principles) or because the principle is generally accepted, which produces circularity or infinite regress, and which again can only be avoided by retreat into some bare subjective value ("I *just prefer* a democratic choice of fundamental principles"). Ultimately, all Social Contract theories demand of the reader some such bare value judgment or preference.

18. For a very different approach to this question, see Hart, "Are There Any Natural Rights?" (1955) *Philosophical Review*, 175.

19. Hart, *The Concept of Law* (1961), p. 194.

20. Hart, *Concept*, pp. 89-96.

21. Hobbes, *Leviathan*, Chap. 14; Hart, *Concept*, pp. 187–188. Survival is here taken as the example of a basic goal because it is a familiar one, and good arguments can be made to support the choice. Other basic goals could be chosen, *e.g.* "leading the good life" or "producing the greatest happiness of the greatest number," but substantially the same kind of argument as here follows, about identifying Natural areas of legal concern, could also be made, *pari passu*, with respect to these alternatives.

22. Because other factors, having nothing to do with the legal system, are also crucially important, *e.g.* climatic conditions, the level of technological progress, etc.
23. And of course, we need constitutional laws, to enable us to operate these other laws with precision and flexibility.
24. *i.e.* With regard to what Reason, or Logic, dictates. Of course, it matters enormously from an evaluative or emotional point of view.
25. See note 19.

2. THE RIGHTS OF THE UNBORN

D. LASOK

I—Introduction

IN a dramatically painful way the plight of the thalidomide children has focused attention on the legal position of the unborn. Their "rights" have lingered for a decade in a legal limbo attributable in no small degree to the uncertainty of the law. After considerable publicity resulting in a contempt action[1] a Private Member's Bill[2] to reform the law emerged and the Government announced the setting up of a Royal Commission[3] to investigate the problems of compensation for personal injuries. Broadly speaking, three problems are to be tackled: the definition of the rights of the unborn, the product liability and the assessment of damages in personal injury claims. Within the context of "fundamental rights" we shall address ourselves to the first problem suggesting that, being the key problem of the three, it is "fundamental."

In one sense the problem of handicapped persons is a matter of social welfare in addition to family responsibility and here society bears the burden as long as it subscribes to the doctrine of sanctity of life and social justice. The alternatives would be the return to the Tarpeian Rock and other methods still used in some societies said to be uncivilised.

In another, less general, sense this may be a problem of civil law and civil justice based on individual responsibility for conduct said to be unlawful. Whilst in the field of social justice we are concerned with social services and benefits obtainable through administrative processes, in the field of civil justice we are concerned with remedies enforceable through civil processes. Here it is necessary to define the wrongful or illegal act, the wrongdoer and the victims and the consequences or sanctions, assuming that there is a causal connection between the act and the injury complained of.

In defining the civil remedies the law, depending upon the legislative techniques adopted in the given system, may proceed either from a general principle which postulates protection of a fundamental value (e.g. the integrity of the human person) or from specific, narrowly defined claims. This, basically, is the difference between the civil law and the common law systems. In the former the codes of law are constructed round a set of doctrines or general principles of law, in the latter the legislation and the courts endeavour to deal with specific problems in a casuistic manner. The nature of our system was well summarised by Scarman L.J.,[4] who said that "our statutes are elaborate to the point of complexity; detailed to the point of unintelligibility; yet strangely uninformative on matters of principle." This, of course, need not be so if we had not curtailed the dynamism

18

of common law through the rigid application of *stare decisis* and the ever increasing intrusion of Parliament.

Turning to the problem of the unborn: we are destitute in this country of a general principle of law which would ensure protection of the unborn and we have not as yet developed specific remedies to that end. Hence the problem of the thalidomide children.

II—Definition of Legal Personality

The main difficulty in defining the rights of the unborn stems from the doctrine of legal personality which implies the capacity of being the bearer of rights and duties. More precisely, in the case of the *nasciturus*, the difficulty lies in the determination of the point of time at which his existence as a legal entity attracts the protection of the law. This is partly a matter of biology and partly of social policy. Assuming that the rules of law ought to follow closely the laws of the physical world so as to avoid fictions and uncertainties, the legal determination of the commencement of a human person must take cognisance of biological facts. According to the biological process when the male sperm unites with the ovum thereby fertilising it, conception occurs and the miniscule embryo acquires at once all the characteristics not only of a human being but of a unique human being. This was hardly known to the Romans or the medieval theologians who speculated on the relationship of body and soul though they spoke of the *nasciturus* not merely of a human foetus. However the mystery of life has not been solved entirely even to this day and whilst we are certain of the pattern of the biological process we can only retrospectively ascertain what had occurred at the probable time of conception. Given the actual contact of the sperm with the ovum it is still a matter of chance (or perhaps an Act of God) whether an embryo will result and develop. In other words the commencement of life (or conception) is a matter of fact which the law ought to acknowledge retrospectively by giving effect to the biological evidence for the definition of the inception of human personality.

Biological evidence, again, testifies to the fact that an embryo, though existing within his mother's body, is an entity quite different from the mother. The mother's natural function is clear and immutable: to participate in the formation of the embryo, to sustain and nurture its growth and, at the completion of the period of gestation, propel it into a totally independent biological existence. In a sense the nasciturus *is and is not* part of the mother's body. He has a separate but not an independent existence. There is, therefore, force in the argument that the legal personality of the *nasciturus* is conditional upon his being born alive for only then does he become both a separate and independent entity.

III—The Theory of Legal Personality

The Romans, who gave a limited protection to the unborn, were denied the biological knowledge of today. More importantly they laboured under the limitations of their theory of legal personality. Their concept of the legal *persona* was derived from the dramatised ritual of legal proceedings and from the notion that the law, not nature, designates the bearers of legal rights and duties. They recognised the humanity of slaves but denied their legal personality and treated them as objects rather than subjects of law. The legal status of the *nasciturus* depended, therefore, not only on his independent existence but also on an express recognition of the law. The fiction that *nasciturus pro jam nato habetur quotiens de commodis ejus agitur*[5] reflects the social policy of affording protection not to the embryo as such but to some of its interests provided it could claim these interests through the instrumentality of the legal process. To enable its champion to wear its mask in the legal battle, it must be seen alive. The formula was general and rather vague but in practice it was restricted to the protection of the property rights of the unborn. It applied in the field of succession and the institution of the *curator ventris* was designed to safeguard his material interests but not his person. Although, according to the Digest[6] abortion was punishable the unborn had no remedy *ex delicto*. Tort to a person consists of injury to some value inherent in the human person (*e.g.* health, reputation, integrity of the body) and protected by the law. Where there is no personality there is, in logic, no subject to be injured (and protected) and, therefore, no remedy.

The relationship between the remedy and the subject of the law was well exemplified in the law of slavery. A slave could not claim compensation for his injury because he had no procedural capacity (the *orator* could not wear his mask) and, being a mere human chattel, he had no legal personality. However his master could claim compensation in view of the loss sustained by him as a result of his slave's injury. The master had both a procedural capacity and property interest in the slave.

Modern legal systems, modelled upon Roman law, have inherited the Roman concept of legal personality as emanating from the law even though they have accepted the principle that a human person is prima facie endowed with legal personality. The child born out of wedlock being a *filius nullius*, suspension of civil and public rights, the institution of "civil death" in consequence of punishment for crime so prominent in the past and the effects of the so-called Nuremberg laws in Nazi Germany reflect the theory that legal personality is a gift of the law, not of nature. The Codes of Civil Law determine the legal position of the *nasciturus* either in terms of legal capacity (*i.e.* legal personality) or specific rights which, having accrued to the unborn, become enforceable in his name on the condition that he is born alive.

The Codex Juris Canonici of the Catholic Church (Can. 747,985(4)), consistent with biological science and Christian theology[7] recognises the legal personality of the unborn as from the moment of conception. A similar, though less extreme provision can be found in the Swiss and Austrian Codes of Civil Law. According to Article 31(1) of the Swiss Code the legal personality of a physical person commences after the completion of the birth but Article 31(2) provides that the child has capacity before birth on condition that he shall be born alive. The Swiss Code thus recognises a conditional legal personality of the *nasciturus* which embraces both rights and duties accrued before birth (*e.g.* the duty of maintaining parents[8]). Similar is the interpretation of Article 22 of the Austrian Civil Code.[9]

By contrast the German Civil Code (Para. 1) provides that "the legal personality of a human being begins with the completion of the birth" and so does the Italian *Codice Civile* (Article 1(1)) but adds that "the rights accorded to the *nasciturus* are conditional upon his being born alive" (Article 1(2)). There is a subtle difference between the Swiss and Austrian Codes on the one hand and the Italian on the other. The former speak of "legal capacity of the child before his birth," the latter simply gives effect, retrospectively, to rights which have accrued to the child *en ventre sa mère*.

It is interesting to note that the *Code Napoléon*, in spite of its preoccupation with civil status and enjoyment of civil rights, is deficient of any general rule defining the legal personality of the human person. As far as the unborn is concerned the Code is content with safeguarding his rights of intestate succession (Article 725) and property rights by will or gift (Article 906) on the condition that he is born alive. From these scanty provisions the courts and writers have deduced the theory of legal personality of the unborn which has been incorporated in Article 148 of the Draft prepared by the Commission for the Reform of the Civil Code.[10]

Of the modern Marxist Codes the Civil Code of Czechoslavakia of 1963 follows the Swiss-Austrian line whilst the Codes of the Soviet Union (1964) and Poland (1964) have been modelled upon the German of Napoleonic pattern.

In the light of the foregoing there emerges a distinction between the "legal personality" and the specific "statutory rights" approach. The "legal personality" approach stems from the assumption that there can be no subjective rights protected by the law unless there is a subject (bearer) of such rights. The *nasciturus* is regarded as a person and, therefore, is a bearer of rights and duties, within the scope of his personality. It follows that the Codes of Switzerland and Austria accord a germane right of action to enforce subjective rights vested in the *nasciturus* before his birth. The "specific statutory rights" approach is limited in scope and application. It tends to regard the *nasciturus* as part of the mother's body and endeavours to avoid the problem of the definition of the legal personality of the unborn. However, recognising the existence of the unborn at least as a potential subject of law and recipient of benefits, precautions are taken to safeguard the interests of the unborn.

Clearly the shortcomings of the latter approach are only too obvious in our modern technological age which through the use of mechanical power and chemical substances has greatly increased the range and magnitude of risk to which not only the living but also the unborn are exposed. Moreover the advance of medical and biological sciences has made it possible to link prenatal injuries with definite causes in cases which in the past might have been attributed to "bad luck" or an Act of God.

In spite of the shortcomings of the "specific statutory rights" approach attempts have been made to face the problem. We shall consider now how this has been done in the civil law and the common law systems.

IV—Civil Law

The French Code, as we have noted, did not adopt the Roman formula but the writers and the courts, in the spirit of Roman law, extended the protection of the rights of the unborn enshrined in Articles 725 and 906. Of course the phraseology of these articles implies that the rights of the unborn are to be protected in exceptional circumstances. This puts a limit upon any extensive interpretation of the Code. It follows that duties arising from family obligations (*e.g.* duty to maintain his parents and certain relatives) cannot be imposed upon the unborn, though the divorce courts have to take into account the existence of the unborn when ordering financial provision for the upkeep of the children of the family. The problem of the loss of support arising from accidental death of a parent has been dealt with by the legislature under the Workmen's Compensation Law of 1898[11] and the courts have awarded maintenance to posthumous children.[12] In this sense the rights of the unborn are being protected but any extension of this protection to cover injuries sustained by the child *en ventre sa mère* in consequence of a wrongful act directed against the mother would have to overcome the principle of the restrictive[13] interpretation of the exceptional provisions of the Code (*i.e.* Articles 725 and 906) as well as the reluctance to consider the unborn to be "another person" (*autrui*) envisaged in Article 1382 of the Code.

Perhaps considerations of social security and state responsibility will pave the way as demonstrated by the *Conseil d'Etat* in the *Saulze* case decided in 1968.[14] Having contracted German Measles in the course of her duties as schoolteacher Madame Saulze gave birth to a child suffering from serious disabilities. Damages were awarded to her and the child on the grounds that the child who had been conceived must be recognised as a person entitled to the benefit of the principle of state responsibility.

Far more significant is the evolution of German Law which has overcome the limitations of the legal personality theory and deduced the rights of the unborn from an extensive interpretation of the specific provisions of the Civil Code. Older literature[15] whilst recognising the succession and property rights of the unborn, denied him the right to compensation for wrongful injury. He was regarded as being part of his mother's body and, having no legal personality, could not claim to have been injured. Indeed a tort against the unborn was "conceptually impossible" (*begrifflich ausgeschlossen*). The battleground for the rights of the unborn was not in the area of bodily harm resulting from prenatal injuries but a rather esoteric corner of German affiliation proceedings. According to German law no affiliation order can be made if it is shown that the mother had sexual intercourse at the relevant time with another man than the alleged father of the child. As such a defence (*exceptio plurium concumbentium*[16]) could be engineered without any risk either to the accused or his accomplice the child could be said to be wrongfully deprived of his remedy *i.e.* his right of support. The courts, though aware of the subterfuge, refused at first to grant a remedy for "wrongful birth" for such a tort was quite unthinkable,[17] but in the course of time they were persuaded to grant a remedy where the defence was proved to be false.[18] The authority for this remedy was paragraph 826 of the Civil Code which, in general terms provided remedy for damage brought about by an immoral act.

The real breakthrough came in 1949 when the Supreme Court of Schleswig-Holstein[19] awarded damages to a child born with a venereal disease which was transmitted to her by her mother. Her father, from whom the disease originated, was liable for having negligently caused "injury to her health." The authority for this decision was paragraph 823 (1) which provides that "whoever intentionally or negligently causes unlawful damage to life, body, health, property or any other right of another person, is liable to make good the resulting damage." Although the Federal Court had reversed this judgment on the ground that no "injury to health" could have arisen at the time of the conception, it nevertheless in a subsequent case, upheld the right of the unborn. The case which revolutionised the German thinking involved a woman who, in the course of a blood transfusion, was infected with a venereal disease and passed it on to her child conceived subsequent to the transfusion. The court granted her child a remedy against the hospital administration and the Federal Court affirmed the judgment.[20] The decision was criticised[21] mainly on the ground that the unlawful act was not directed against the child as the child was not even conceived at the time of the infection but most writers agreed with the principle that the child was entitled to a remedy. Justice was achieved by a rather astonishing interpretation of paragraph 823(1) cited above.

In the field of compensation for industrial injury the Federal Social Tribunal denied compensation to a child born physically handicapped as a result of an accident sustained by her mother at work. The Tribunal considered that the child at the time of her injury or birth was neither insured nor employed in an occupation covered by the insurance scheme.[22] The same Tribunal took a more equitable view of the child's claim when in another case[23] it awarded social security benefits for prenatal injuries sustained in the course of the mother being raped and ill-treated although, strictly, there was no remedy exactly corresponding under the social security legislation. This decision was followed by another one[24] in which benefits were awarded to a child born with a venereal disease inflicted upon his mother who was raped in a concentration camp during the Nazi lawlessness. No doubt in these decisions humanitarian considerations prevailed over legal formalism but even so these cases mark a progress towards the recognition of the rights of the unborn.

Finally, in a recent case[25] the Federal Court, on the authority of its own controversial decision[26] decided that a spastic child was entitled to damages in view of the fact that her disability was due to prenatal injuries sustained in the course of her mother being injured in a road traffic accident. The court had no hesitation in applying Article 823(1) considering the unborn a human being entitled to the protection of the law though the problem of the causal connection had to be solved.

In the light of the above the 2,000 thalidomide children in Federal Germany had a right provided, of course, a causal connection between their deformity and negligence or unlawful conduct of the manufacturers of the drug could be proved. After a long and bitter struggle the manufacturers set up a trust as compensation to thalidomide children without, however, admitting liability.[27]

Polish law, which, as we have observed earlier, was formulated on the German pattern, developed in a similar way.[28] In 1952 the Supreme Court decreed that a posthumous child was entitled to compensation, for the accidental death of his father according to Article 162(2) of the pre-war Code of Obligations (now Article 446(2) of the Civil Code of 1964) on the assumption that the child was entitled to be maintained by his father as from birth.[29] The basis of the liability is a provision similar to paragraph 823(1) of the German Civil Code to which the Polish law adds a claim for the loss of support. The relevant article refers to the victim of an unlawful act which in the terms of the Code implies a "person," that is, a child born alive in the case of a *nasciturus*. The Supreme Court did not consider itself bound by the theory of legal personality but proceeded from the assumption that a child born in to this world, being entitled to maintenance of his father, was entitled to redress from the person who unlawfully deprived him of his maintenance. In a similar case[30] the Supreme Court based its decision on two grounds: on the principle of "socialist humanism," which means that an unborn child had to be treated in the same way as his brothers and sisters, and on the principle of the analogous interpretation of the relevant provisions of the Civil Code. Thus the child was accorded a legal personality in the field of obligations because his rights were protected in the Code of Family Law (Arts. 75, 142, 182) and the Law of Succession (Civil Code, Art. 927(2)). The grounds, though not the judgment, were criticised by learned writers mainly because, as in German law, a person is a subject of law only from his birth and also because Polish law has not accepted the Roman fiction of *nasciturus pro jam nato habetur*.

However the most dramatic was the decision of the Supreme Court in which a child, injured in the course of unsuccessful abortion, was awarded damages from the hospital in which the operation was performed.[31] On that occasion the Supreme Court reviewed the legal position of the *nasciturus* and held that "a child is entitled to compensation for injuries sustained whilst in the womb of his mother in spite of the fact that the act which caused these injuries was committed before his birth and was directed against his mother." The grounds of this decision were the analogy to cases cited above and the somewhat extravagant contention (bearing in mind the admissibility of abortion) that "according to the principle of socialist humanism expressed in Article 4 of the Constitution of the Polish

People's Republic the life and health of a person is subject to a particular protection of the people's state and law."

In 1967 the Supreme Court awarded damages to a child born with defective hearing and speech caused through injury sustained by his mother at work. However, the court adduced a different ground as it held that "an unborn child cannot be in a worse position than a child suffering injury at the time of his birth or thereafter."[32] Reflecting on the legal status of the unborn the Supreme Court held that "an unlawful act directed against a pregnant woman which affects the normal developments of the foetus and results in a disability of the child, is an unlawful act against the child, provided the child is born alive."

In conclusion Polish law accords the *nasciturus* a kind of legal personality as it brings him under the rubric of Article 415 of the Civil Code which provides that "whoever through his own fault causes damage to *another* is bound to repair it."

V—Common Law

The common law, neither burdened nor blessed with a theory of legal personality, was free to develop legal remedies available to individuals on the assumption that all human beings are subjects of the law. No legislation was needed to that effect. However this probably contributed to the lack of theory or concern with the legal position of the unborn. Even the thalidomide tragedy made practically no impact until recently, whilst an isolated plea,[33] years ago, to deal with the matter under the common law spectrum remained without response. It seems that, at least in England, the *nasciturus* has been regarded as part of his mother's body.

Where property interests of the unborn are concerned an infant *en ventre sa mere* is, in English law, presumed to be born though there is no fixed rule of construction to that effect.[34] Under an old statute[35] a guardian like the Roman *curator ventris* could be appointed to look after his interest as such an infant is capable of inheritance on intestacy or by will. Moreover a life interest in land can be given to an unborn child with a gift over to his issue[36] and where such land is held on trust for the unborn the High Court has powers to make an order releasing the land from the contingent right or an order vesting the estate in the appropriate person.[37] A posthumous child can also obtain compensation for the death of his parent under the Fatal Accidents Acts[38] but his statutory remedy is merely an extension of the protection of interests of the unborn as a dependant person. The same principle applied under the Workmen's Compensation Acts.[39]

The real test of the extent and efficacy of the law with regard to the unborn as a person lies the field of tort. Two questions have to be considered—whether the law protects the unborn by recognising his right to personal safety and whether it accords him a right of action in his own name in respect of prenatal injury sustained in the course of an unlawful act against his mother. The problem has not been discussed as much as it deserves. Apart from Winfield's paper[40] we have only cursory remarks by text writers, whose opinions are divided. Whilst some[41] maintain that there is no valid reason why an action should not be brought by an infant for prenatal injury, others[42] are less certain or seem to think the opposite. It is interesting to note that the discussion is about the remedy, not about the right.

Case law has done no better. In an Irish case[43] the four judges refused to award damages to a child who sustained prenatal injuries in a railway accident on the ground that the defendant railway company owed no duty of care to the child of whose existence or presence it was unaware and that, of course, there was no contractual liability to the child.

In *Dulieu* v. *White and Sons*[44] the court was hardly concerned with the problem as it considered merely a claim for damages for shock sustained by a pregnant barmaid who was injured when a coach drove into her bar and, as a result she gave premature birth to a mentally defective child. She claimed only for herself no doubt so advised by her counsel who is reported to have said "I do not allege the injury to the unborn child as a cause of action but merely in aggravation of damages."

In one case at the Liverpool Assizes[45] the matter came nearly for a decision. A pregnant woman was injured when walking under a ladder which fell upon her due to the defendants' negligence. Her child was injured too and died a few days after birth in consequence of his injuries. The defendants, faced with a claim under the Law Reform (Miscellaneous Provisions) Act 1934 paid £100 into court and the action was not proceeded with.

The law has since advanced a little by imposing the duty of care to a person who is not known to be present in the area of potential danger created by a wrongdoer[46] and by expanding the notion of one's legal neighbour[47] but not as far as the unborn. Yet it seems logical that an unborn child is a "neighbour" in the sense used by Lord Atkin in *Donoghue* v. *Stevenson* and, therefore, should be entitled to damages for disabilities suffered in a prenatal accident. Astute insurance companies, no doubt aware of the state of the law, by showing extra generosity to pregnant women injured in accidents keep them out of court whilst lawyers, having little interest in legal developments abroad, remain satisfied with the settlements achieved for their clients.

In South Africa it was held that a child had an action to recover damages for prenatal injuries though the court found that there was no causal connection between cerebral palsy suffered by the child and the injuries sustained by his mother.[48] Quite recently the Judicial Committee of the Privy Council, confining itself to the question of territorial jurisdiction, decided that a thalidomide child could bring an action in New South Wales because the act or omission complained of took place in New South Wales.[49] In another Australian case[50] the court held that a child *en ventre sa mère* was a *persona juridica*, entitled to the protection of the law like the "neighbour" in *Donoghue* v. *Stevenson* and, therefore, capable of recovering damages for prenatal injuries sustained in a road traffic accident.

The true spirit of the common law revealed itself on the other side of the Atlantic long before the Australian case was heard. The tendency of the older American cases was to deny the remedy to the unborn in respect of prenatal injuries apparently on two grounds: that an unborn child had no existence apart from his mother and that there was a risk of spurious claims in such cases in view of the difficulty in proving causal connection. No lesser judge than Holmes decided to keep the common law stagnant for a while when he refused a remedy in a case where a pregnant woman, having fallen owing to disrepair of the pavement on which she was walking, prematurely gave birth to a child who died a few minutes after the accident.[51] This precedent was followed and the American *Restatement*[52] too denied such a cause of action. Several cases in the thirties followed suit but attracted a great deal of adverse publicity especially the decision of the Illinois Court of Appeals in *Smith* v. *Luckhardt*.[53] In that case the action of a deformed and mentally defective child claiming damages for injury sustained as a result of negligent medical treatment of his mother was dismissed but such was the criticism of this decision that in *Bonbrest* v. *Katz*,[54] the trend was reversed. By 1949 a remedy for what became known as the "prenatal injury" was firmly established.[55] Further cases followed suit and even Massachusetts turned against Holmes.[56] We can say today that in most of the U.S. jurisdictions a child born alive is capable of bringing an action for prenatal injuries and that an action for his wrongful death will lie if he dies as a result of his injuries.[57]

Whilst the rights of the unborn in respect of prenatal injuries were being formulated a new tort, that of "wrongful life" was suggested in the state of Illinois. In *Zepeda* v. *Zepeda*[58] the plaintiff sued his father for being inflicted with the stigma of bastardy. Whilst the court recognised that it was wrong for the defendant to persuade, through deceit, the plaintiff's mother to have intercourse with him it refused to devise a new cause of action. The Illinois Court of Appeals, affirming the judgment, confirmed the anomalous position that the child had a right but no remedy. This conclusion was reached for reasons of public policy as mental anguish and economic disadvantage could not be pleaded against the gift of life.

Other cases pleaded on the *Zepeda* lines were unsuccessful. For instance, in *Williams* v. *State*[59] a child born to a mentally defective mother as a result of rape whilst in a mental institution was unsuccessful in her claim for negligence against the State of New York.[60] In *Pinkney* v. *Pinkney*[61] a child born out of wedlock was denied a remedy for wrongful life in Florida. It now remains to be seen whether a new tort "wrongful life" advocated by many writers will enrich the American law though the mind boggles at the thought that the gift of life should give rise to an actionable wrong.

Although the English law remained static, the settlement involving some of the thalidomide children in 1968 and the negotiations for a trust in 1972, though without admission of legal liability on the part of the manufacturers of the drug, imply readiness to concede the rights of the unborn. If the common law were to reflect the enlightened opinion of the people the *vox populi* demanding justice for the thalidomide children would indicate to our courts that the unborn is entitled to the protection of the law and should he be injured by a wrongful act he must have the capacity to sue in his own name if born alive. In our system no legislation seems necessary to solve this problem.

In the light of the evolution of the law outlined above it is clear that advanced legal systems in their peculiar ways recognise the rights of the unborn. If such rights are recognised, logically, the personality of the unborn must be recognised too as it is difficult to imagine the existence of legally enforceable rights without their bearer being a *persona juridica*. Because the protection of the unborn in modern legal systems gives a new dimension to the Roman adage *nasciturus pro jam nato habetur* it must be regarded as a fundamental right within the concept of fundamental rights envisaged in this essay.

VI—A Right to Live?

Having established a legal protection of the rights of the unborn it seems an almost superfluous and absurd question to ask whether he has a right to live. There can be nothing more fundamental than the right to life. The right to life has been enshrined in modern Constitutions and various declarations like the American Declaration of Independence (1787), the United Nations Declaration of Human Rights (1948) or the European Convention for the Protection of Human Rights and Fundamental Freedoms (1950) but, in the case of the unborn, it begs the question. Moreover it has a hollow sound in the face of widespread legalised abortion.

The Romans forbade abortion and so did the laws based on Christian ethics. The history of abortion in this country is the history of legislation on what was considered by the common law to be "a great misprision"[62] and was, towards the end of the eighteenth century made a statutory offence.[63]

The defence against the charge of child destruction or attempt to procure abortion that the act was done in good faith for the purpose of preserving the life of the mother was, by statute,[64] converted into a permissive rule and this one extended to a rule of social convenience. In spite of the biological knowledge of today the unborn is for the purpose of the abortion law, considered to be part of his mother's body and his "right to life" depends, in practice, upon her permission.

"Termination of pregnancy," does not consist of the removal of an unwanted piece of jelly (as suggested by a high-ranking churchman) but of a deliberate destruction of a human being. Whatever form the operation takes there can be no mistake that abortion consists of the extraction of the whole or parts of a human being at some stage of development towards a unique person. Putting aside Press reports of fully formed and moving babies being incinerated and the lucrative business of abortion clinics, the ethical and legal question which society has to face squarely, is whether the gains on the side of the protection of the rights of the unborn can be allowed to be negated by licence to kill.

NOTES

1. *Att.-Gen.* v. *Times Newspapers Ltd.* [1972] 3 W.L.R. 855; *The Times*, February 17, 1973 (C.A.); *The Sunday Times*, February 18, 1973; [1973] 2 W.L.R. 452.
2. Dangerous Drugs and Disabled Children Bill presented by Mr. Ron Lewis, M.P.; talked out on February 10, 1973.
3. *The Times*, November 30, 1972.
4. BBC Third Programme, *The Listener*, January 9, 1969, pp. 44–46.
5. As far as his rights are concerned the unborn is regarded as already born.
6. Digest I, 5, 26.
7. Stevas, *The Right to Life*, 1963, pp. 31 *et seq.*
8. Egger, *Kommentar zum Schweizerischen Zivilgesetzbuch. Das Familienrecht*, 2nd edn. 1948, II, 2, pp. 304 *et seq.*
9. Ehrenzweig, *System des ost. allg. Rechts*, 2nd edn. 1951, I., p. 157.
10. Mazeaud, "Leçons de Droit Civil," ed. by De Juglart, *Les Personnes*, 4th edn 1970, pp. 464, 465.
11. Now Art. 454 of the Code of Social Security of 1956.
12. *e.g.* civ. 24 April 1929 (D.H.1929, 298).
13. No such difficulties hindered the Quebec Court in awarding damages for prenatal injuries under Art. 345 of the Quebec Civil Code; see *Montreal Tramways* v. *Leveille* (1933) 4 D.L.R. 337 followed in Ontario in *Duval* v. *Seguire* (1972) 26 D.L.R. (3d) 418.
14. *The Minister of National Education* v. *Dame Saulze*, November 6, 1968; *Review of International Commission of Jurists*, 1969, No. 1, p. 43.
15. Staudinger-Engelmann, *Kommentar Zum BGB*, 9th edn 1929, II, 3; §823 Anm. II A, I and IV.
16. The defence of several possible fathers.
17. Staudinger-Engelmann, *op. cit.*, a.a. O. §1717, Anm. 3b, y.
18. See Heldrich, "Der Deliktsschutz des Ungeborenen," *Juristenzeitung*, 19, 1965, p. 594, note 9.
19. *Ibid.*, note 11.
20. Decision of December 20, 1952; (B.G.H.Z.), *Federal Court Reports*, vol. 8, p. 243.
21. Especially by Esser, "Zur Methodenlehre des Zivilrechts," *Studium Generale* 12 (1959), pp. 97 *et seq.*
22. Decision of June 23, 1959, quoted by Heldrich, *op. cit.*, p. 595.
23. Decision of October 24, 1962, *ibid.*, p. 595.
24. *Ibid.*, p. 595.
25. Decision of January 11, 1972, quoted in (1972) 27 *Juristenzeitung*, June 9, 1972, pp. 363 *et seq.*
26. Note 20 *supra.*
27. Siöström and Nilsson, *Thalidomide and the Power of the Drug Companies*, Penguin, 1972, pp. 207 *et seq.*
28. Szpunar, "Szkoda Wyrządzona przed urodzeniem dziecka," *Studia Cywilistyczne*, vols XIII–XIV, 1969, pp. 372 *et seq.*
29. Decision of October 8, 1952, noted in *Nowe Prawo*, 5 (1953), p. 70.
30. Decision of April 4, 1966, noted in *Nowe Prawo*, 12 (1966), p. 1613.
31. Decision of January 8, 1965, noted in *Państwo i Prawo*, No 10 (1967), p. 636.
32. Decision of May 3, 1967, noted in *Państwo i Prawo*, No. 10 (1968), p. 151.
33. Lasok, "The Legal Personality of the Nasciturus," *The Law Journal*, February 15, 1963.
34. *Blasson* v. *Blasson* (1864) 2 D.J. & S. 665; in *Re Salaman: D. Pass* v. *Sonnenthal* [1907] W.N. 100; *Villar* v. *Gilbey* [1905] 2 Ch. 364; C.A. [1906] 1 Ch. 583; H.L. [1907] A.C. 139.
35. Tenures Abolition Act 1660.
36. Law of Property Act 1925, s. 161.
37. Trustee Act 1925, s. 45.
38. *The George and Richard* (1871) 3 A. & E. 466. *Hannam* v. *Wates Ltd and Another*, *Daily Telegraph*, December 16, 1972 (£1,760 awarded to an illigitimate child born six months after her father's death).

39. *Williams* v. *Ocean Coal Co.* [1907] 2 K.B. 422; *Schofield* v. *Orrell Ciery Co. Ltd.* [1909] 1 K.B. 178.
40. Winfield, "The Unborn Child," (1942) 8 Camb. L.J. 76.
41. *Winfield on Torts*, 7th edn, p. 72; *Salmond on Torts*, 14th edn, p. 622, *Bowen on Negligence*, 4th edn, p. 73; *Clerk and Lindsell on Torts*, 13th edn, p. 163.
42. *e.g. Charlesworth on Negligence*, 4th edn, p. 73; *Underhill's Law of Torts*, 12th edn, p. 44; Street, *The Law of Torts*, 5th edn, p. 470.
43. *Walker* v. *Great Northern Railway of Ireland* (1891) 28 L.R. Ir. 69.
44. [1901] 2 K.B. 669.
45. Noted in (1939) 83 S.J. 185.
46. *Farrugia* v. *G.W.R.* [1947] 2 All E.R. 565.
47. *Donoghue* v. *Stevenson* [1932] A.C. 562.
48. *Pinchin N.O.* v. *Santam Insurance Co. Ltd.*, 1963, (2) S.A. 254 (W), noted in *The South African Legal Journal*, IV Vol. LXXX (1963), p. 447.
49. *Distillers Company (Bio-Chemicals) Ltd.* v. *Thompson* [1971] A.C. 458 (P.C.), noted in *Quis Custodiet?*, No. 34, 1972, p. 35.
50. *Watt* v. *Rama* [1972] V.R. 353; Victoria Supreme Court, now subject to appeal to the Privy Council, *The Sunday Times*, January 14, 1973; Wadsworth, "Is the Unborn Child a Person at Law?", *Quis Custodiet?*, No. 36, 1972, pp. 88 *et seq.*
51. *Dietrich* v. *Northampton*, 138 Mass 14 (1884).
52. *Restatement* Torts (1939), sec. 869.
53. 19 N.E. (2d) 446 (1939).
54. D.D.C., 65 F. Supp. 138 (1946).
55. *Williams* v. *Marion Rapid Transit Inc.*, 152 Ohio St. 114 (1949); 87 N.E. (2d) 334.
56. *Bliss* v. *Possanesi* 326 Mass. 461 (1950); *Cavanagh* v. *First National Stores Inc.*, 329 Mass. 174 (1952); *Torigian* v. *Watertown News Co. Inc.*, 352 Mass. 441 (1967).
57. Prosser, *Handbook of the Law of Torts*, pp. 174, 175.
58. App. 2d. 240, 190 N.E. 2d. 849 (1963); 379 U.S. 945 (1964).
59. 18 N.Y. 2d. 481, 223 N.E. 2d. 343 (1966).
60. *Quaere*: would such a claim succeed in Germany, assuming that negligence of the institution could be proved?—see p. 23.
61. 198 So. 2d 52 (Fla) (1967).
62. *Institutes* III, 50.
63. First by a statute of George III, later by the Offences against the Person Act 1861, ss. 58 and 59 and the Infant Life (Preservation) Act 1929, s. 1. Seaborne Davies, "The Law of Abortion and Necessity" (1938–39) 2 M.L.R. 126 *et seq.*
64. Abortion Act 1967, s. 1.

3. CHILDREN'S RIGHTS

CHRISTINA SACHS

FROM many points of view it may well be doubted whether such things as children's "rights" actually exist. The fact that other people, *i.e.* parents and persons placed *in loco parentis* by the law, owe duties to children does not necessarily mean that children have corresponding rights or that there should be a definition and machinery of enforcement of such "rights." Moreover the young and the helpless enjoy the special protection of society, since the society in a paternalistic manner, no doubt imitating the natural parent-child relationship, extends its care to children, even to the extent of overriding parental claims. Does this mean that children have rights against the society, or rather does it mean that society, mindful of the welfare of the child, has devised a protective system on the pattern of that which nature has thrust upon progenitors?

Recently, perhaps as a symptom of ferment or perhaps a new trend in our society the idea of "children's rights" within the context of "civil liberties" has been advanced.[1] These claims, made on behalf of children, include[2] a right to be protected from the influence of Christianity; a right to choose their own home, their school and their friends; freedom from restraint and punishment; a right to love and happiness; a right to a better life for handicapped children; a right to sexual education and sexual freedom; a right to a new democracy in education; freedom from being indoctrinated; freedom from compulsory education; a right to be educated without any form of let or hindrance devised by adults; a right to be educated for a job; and, to cap it all, a right to be treated as children. If translated into legal rights these claims would single out children as a group enjoying special privileges the exercise of which can hardly be within their competence. A new machinery, no doubt operated by adults, including a children's ombudsman would be necessary and this in realistic terms would result in yet another form of paternalism.

Clearly the rights which children have or claim may in most cases be similar to civil rights claimed by citizens in general, but what distinguishes children from the rest of the society is the doctrine of the welfare of the child. Originated in Chancery and statutes, this doctrine has been subject to extensive judicial interpretation and application over the years resulting in a body of case law which reflects, no doubt, the judicial thinking of the time. Whilst in the past it reflected a notion of "parental rights" the present trend seems to have moved to the other extreme towards an emphasis on the rights of the child and parents' duties. An examination of the interpretation of welfare of the child may show how far this view has gone posing the question whether it has yet gone far enough or too far. As the legal position of children *vis-à-vis* their parents, strangers and the society develops in the shadow of the doctrine of child's welfare the doctrine itself can be regarded as one of general principles of law and can be said to be fundamental to our system.

I—The Age of Majority

The Report of the Committee on the Age of Majority[3] considered the position of "infants" as they were then known and made a number of recommendations (one of which was that they should be known as "minors"[4]). The most significant recommendation was that the age of majority should be reduced to eighteen, which was in fact done.[5] This was followed by a reduction of the minimum voting age to eighteen,[6] and finally by the reduction of the age for jury service to eighteen at the same time as the abolition of the property qualification.[7] This report was interesting in the willingness to admit that there is generally a responsible and increasingly mature attitude of young persons, who until then had for centuries been regarded as incapable of accepting adult responsibilities. The Committee took what even at the present day may be regarded as a somewhat controversial view "(1) there is undeniably a great increase in maturity towards that age; (2) the vast majority of young people are in fact running their own lives, making their own decisions and behaving as responsible adults by the time they are eighteen."

Further, judicial pronouncement in the case of *Hewer* v. *Bryant*[8] shows a recognition of the reality of the situation. In discussing the parental right in regard to custody Lord Denning said ". . . even up till [the eighteenth birthday] it is a dwindling right which the courts will hesitate to enforce against the wishes of the child, the older he is. It starts with a right of control and ends with little more than advice."

The Family Law Reform Act 1969, section 8 recognises the capacity for responsible and capable decision in a young person in allowing a minor who has attained the age of sixteen years to give an effective consent for surgical, medical or dental treatment without having to obtain a consent for it from his parent or guardian.

II—The Child in Adoption

From the broader viewpoint the Adoption Act 1958 directs the court to consider whether an adoption order will be for the welfare of the infant[9] which includes the duty on the court to give "due consideration to the wishes of the infant having regard to his age and understanding." The question of the conflict between the rights of the parents and the child may arise over the question of consent to adoption and the court's power to dispense with parental consent. The court may dispense with any consent required by section 4 (1) (*a*) of this Act (this includes the consent of a parent) if it is satisfied that the person whose consent is to be dispensed with is withholding the consent unreasonably.

It is interesting to note that although it is now generally considered that adoption is an arrangement which can be of benefit to a child, nevertheless formal adoption was not brought into the English law until 1926. In earlier years the view seemed to be that in adoption a parent was being deprived of its natural rights and that therefore this should not be done unless the parents clearly agreed to the arrangement or unless they had behaved in some clearly culpable fashion. A recent case articulating that attitude is *Re W*. in the Court of Appeal[10] where Sachs L.J. said "The conduct of a mother in disregarding the welfare of her child can, however, be shown to be culpable. . . . Exceptionally prolonged and repeated vacillation can be regarded as culpable conduct, at any rate if it affects the child. The standard by which the mother's conduct and reasonableness is to be assessed is [that] . . . of the mother in her particular circumstances." He goes on to say towards the end of his judgment "The plain fact is that the conduct of the mother has not been established to be culpable either as regards the welfare of the child nor in any other relevant direction. She has not been shown to be unreasonable. . . ."

These statements and the general tenor of the judgment show the emphasis being placed on the mother's rights and the need to show something blameworthy in the mother's conduct in order to establish unreasonableness on her part. The House of Lords decision in this case shows that this approach, even bearing in mind the statutory wording, does not take sufficiently into account the welfare of the child. This case shows a shift of emphasis towards the consideration of the welfare of the child playing the predominant role in the question of dispensing with consent. There the mother who withdrew her consent was not found to be culpable or insincere but probably inadequate to cope with the difficulties which having the child in her own household would bring. The House of Lords rejected the need for something approaching culpable behaviour. Lord Hailsham[11] said:

> "It is clear that the test is reasonableness and not anything else. It is not culpability. It is not indifference. . . . It is reasonableness and reasonableness in the totality of the circumstances. But although welfare *per se* is not the test, the fact that a reasonable parent does pay regard to the welfare of his child must enter into the question of reasonableness as a relevant factor. It is relevant in all cases if and to the extent that a reasonable parent would take it into account. It is decisive in those cases where a reasonable parent must so regard it."

He cited with approval the words of Lord Denning in *Re L. an Infant*[12]: "In considering whether she [*i.e.* the mother] is reasonable or unreasonable we must take into account the welfare of the child."

From this it can be seen that the current judicial view is leaning towards the child and its welfare, and that a parent can be deprived of rights, without indulging in any blameworthy behaviour at all. It is sufficient if they are unreasonable, which in this context may amount to not having regard to the welfare of their child. One of the recommendations of the Law Commission's Working Paper on adoption was that the long-term welfare of the child should be the first and paramount consideration in resolving conflicts over adoption.

Another difficulty in the broader view of the welfare of the child in the adoption situation is one raised by the National Council for Civil Liberties in *Children Have Rights*,[13] namely the right of the child to know if it is in fact an adopted child, and further who its natural parent or parents are. At present there is no such right in English law although there is a right in Scots law for an adopted child at the age of seventeen to see the original entry relating to his birth. Once again, the Home Office Working Paper[14] has considered this point and come down in favour of the view that the courts should be left with the responsibility to grant permission for access to the original birth records.

The problem is a real and very difficult one. Ideally the adoptive parents should tell the adopted child of the situation and provide background information as far as they can. The Working Paper accepts this:

> "The importance of telling a child that he is adopted has long been recognised. There is a growing recognition that he needs to know about his origins—about his parents for instance . . . —for the proper development of a sense of identity and in order that he and his adoptive parents may have a fuller understanding of him as an individual with his own unique combination of characteristics. . . . There is a growing acceptance that having children by adoption is different from having natural children and that failure to recognise this fact openly is damaging. Fulfilment of these needs is not easily reconciled with some aspects of the present legal concept of adoption as a completely new start, affording confidentiality for all concerned. We believe that a much more open approach towards adoption should be encouraged by those most closely affected, by social workers and by public opinion."

III—The Child in Wardship and Custody Proceedings

This is a context in which one can see clearly the erosion of the so-called "rights of the parents" in favour of the child, under the interpretation of the concept of the welfare of the child. Under the Guardianship of Minors Act 1971 the court is directed by section 1: "Where in any proceeding before any court . . . the custody or upbringing of an infant is in question, the court, in deciding that question shall regard the welfare of the minor as the first and paramount consideration. . . ." This provision was similar to the provision of the Guardianship of Infants Act of 1925. However, the interpretation over the years cannot be said to be similar.

In the case of *Re Carroll*[15] the Court of Appeal appeared to overrule a first instance decision based on the welfare of the child and to lay great stress on parental rights. Scrutton L.J. said "In the present case unless the mother is of so bad a character that her wishes as to religion and education may be disregarded . . . the mother has a legal right to require that the child shall be brought up in her religion. . . ." He referred to the judgment of the Lord Chief Justice in the Divisional Court, where reference had been made to the change of attitude in the law, particularly with regard to the real interest of the child, and said "Except that the mother's wishes have been put on an equality with the father I can see no such change." This view that the welfare of the child was really a serious issue only in the case of a dispute between parents, and did not apply as between parents and strangers was also given some credence by the case of *Re Thain*,[16] where a father successfully reclaimed custody of his daughter and the weight of the decision was placed on his parental right. It was suggested that the Guardianship of Infants Act had introduced no new principle but merely declared the existing one used by the Chancery division. If this were really so, then surely a case such as *Re Agar Ellis*[17] should not have been decided as it was (later described by Lord Upjohn as "dreadful") with its assertion of the father's rights as being the important factor. Danckwerts L.J. as he then was in *Re Adoption Application 14/61*[18] gave a reasonable interpretation of *Re Thain*, which was approved in *J.* v. *C.*[19]:

". . . the desire of the father to have the care of his child . . . is one of the factors which may affect the welfare of the child; and it may be that the proper view of the welfare of the child is that the child should be committed to the care of the father rather than to that of other persons. . . . The mere desire of a parent to have his child must be subordinate to the consideration of the welfare of the child. . . ."

Nevertheless, reasonable as this interpretation is, it is very doubtful whether it represents the views of the judges at the time or the interpretation made by subsequent judges.

The case of *Re Carroll* was in fact overruled in the House of Lords in the case of *J.* v. *C.*, the *Spanish boys' case*. In this case the expression "welfare of the child" was interpreted in such a way that it took effect to leave a child in the custody of foster parents, rather than give custody to the natural parents who in the words of the case were "unimpeachable."

Lord McDermott summarised the interpretation and position in regard to the problem:

"1. Section 1 of the Act of 1925 applies to disputes not only between parents but between parents and strangers and strangers and strangers.
2. In applying section 1 the rights and wishes of parents whether unimpeachable or otherwise, must be assessed and weighed in their bearing on the welfare of the child in conjunction with all other factors relevant to that issue.
3. While there is now no rule of law that the rights and wishes of unimpeachable parents must prevail over other considerations, such rights and wishes recognised as they are by nature and society, can be capable of ministering to the total welfare of the child in a special way and must therefore preponderate in many cases."

This view has been reinforced in a recent case *Re O., a Minor*[20] which concerned the future of a nine-year-old Ghanaian girl, born and fostered in England whose parents wished to return to Ghana with her. The child had been made a ward of court. The Official Solicitor on the child's behalf suggested that it was best for her to return to Ghana. The President of the

Family Division pointing out the difficulties that this kind of arrangement, frequently made by visiting West Africans, gave rise to, ordered that the child should remain a ward of court with care and control given to the foster parents. This was despite the fact that this had the effect of keeping her from her natural parents and her native culture. The President said that the court had to consider the girl's best interests and to promote her overall welfare both in the long term and the short term. The girl should stay where she had always been, despite the blood tie, race and colour. His Lordship could not bring himself to send her to Ghana, and he as well as the girl would feel a rankling sense of injustice if he were to do so. An interesting feature of the case was that the President had interviewed the child personally and received a letter from her and despite her relatively tender years, she had clearly made a great impression on him as to her wishes, and this had influenced his decision.

IV—The Child Born out of Wedlock

The particular aspect to be considered here is the question of how far it is in the interests of a child born to a mother within a marriage, but whose paternity is in doubt, to have blood tests carried out in order to assist in clarifying the situation. For many years the judicial view has been that it was very much against a child's interest to be bastardised because of the results of such a decision. The child would be deprived of the normal property rights of a legitimate child and would also suffer the stigma of illegitimacy. Since the passing of Part II of the Family Law Reform Act 1969, which assimilates the property rights of the illegitimate child to those of the legitimate child, that particular difficulty has been removed, although of course problems of maintenance rights remain.

In addition there is the problem, still as yet unsolved as regards blood tests that such tests cannot positively establish paternity, only settle negatively at most that a particular man could not be the father. This was also felt to lead to the result that, should a blood test establish that the mother's husband was not the father, then unless there was one known alternative candidate, the child was put into a disadvantaged position because all the test had done was to deprive him of his legitimacy, and had not improved the position. It was this view that prevailed with the courts until recently when the Official Solicitor, on behalf of the child opposed the ordering of blood tests.[21]

It is of course, significant that in that case the decision in the House of Lords was reached after the passing of the Family Law Reform Act 1969, which as well as dealing with the property position, also empowered the courts to order blood tests in certain cases (Part III of the Act), reflecting the view that such tests are now regarded as more reliable, within their limitations. It can further be argued that with the increase in illegitimate births and a general relaxing of the strict moral views which society at one time took, the stigma of illegitimacy is not what it once was. The case is significant because the House of Lords now establishes the modern view on the topic with, once again, importance attached to the welfare of the child in the situation. Lord Reid in his speech drew attention to the conflicting arguments:

". . . On the one hand it is said that with rare exceptions it is always in the child's interest to have a decision that it is legitimate. On the other hand, it is said that the value to a child of a finding of legitimacy is now much less than it used to be, and that it is generally better for the child that the truth should out than that the child should go through life with a lurking doubt as to the validity of a decision, when evidence which would very likely have disclosed the truth has been suppressed. In former times it was plainly in the child's interest to have a finding of legitimacy even where the presumption of legitimacy had been used to overcome evidence which without it would have pointed the other way. An illegitimate child was not only deprived of the financial advantage of legitimacy but in most circles of society other than those considered disreputable, it carried throughout its life a stigma which made it a second class citizen. But now modern legislation has removed almost all the financial disadvantages of illegitimacy and it has become difficult to foretell how grave a handicap the stigma of illegitimacy will prove to be in later life. . . . No one can foretell what view the child will take about evidence having been suppressed. Some will resent that. Others will accept the decision at its face value."

Thus the view of the courts now seems to be that the welfare of the child will generally demand that the truth of the situation be reached by the best means possible *i.e.* at the present time by means of blood tests. So that in the light of such information orders relating to the child will be made on the best evidence available. As Lord Denning has pointed out elsewhere, once the issue has been settled, there is nothing to stop the parties from subjecting themselves and the child to blood tests and then finding out what the situation is, and it is hardly likely to raise the courts in public estimation, if decisions are made on incomplete evidence.

Another aspect of the illegitimate child situation is that of the rights of the putative father in respect of the child. The problem has been considered judicially in *Re Adoption Application 41/61*[22] which concerned the right of the putative father to apply for custody of his child and thus to intervene indirectly in adoption proceedings. The relevant remarks relating to the question of the child's welfare in such a situation are contained in Diplock L.J.'s judgment:

"The alternative arrangements which the putative father proposes for the future custody and maintenance of the child can be considered in the adoption proceedings in which he is already represented; and if they appear to the judge to be better for the welfare of the infant than the proposed adoption (which is the only relevant consideration) he can refuse to make the adoption order,"

and further

". . . where the welfare of the infant is the first and paramount consideration, a comparison of what the proposed adopters and the applicant in the other proceedings can provide for the infant's welfare is essential to the decision in such other proceedings . . . this comparison can conveniently be made only by the judge in the adoption proceedings. In these, the putative father has ample opportunity to put his case in favour of his proposals for the infant's future welfare. . . ."

Another and very striking case relating to the claims of the putative father in the context of the welfare of the child and which gave rise to considerable publicity at the time was the case of *Re C. (M.A.) An Infant*[23] the so-called *Blood Tie Case*, where the basic problem stated simply was whether it was for the welfare of the child to be removed from a settled and satisfactory prospective adoptive home to his natural father's house to be brought up by his natural father and his wife, contrary to the wishes of the mother who wanted the child adopted. The majority view in the Court of Appeal was that the blood tie of the child with his natural father was of great importance and warranted this removal. Harman L.J. took the view that adoption is a second best and a step not to be taken where the real parent is available and can make suitable arrangements. Still more is this so where the father himself has a home to offer. Russell L.J. said:

"I am not, however, persuaded that, regarding the welfare of the infant as the paramount consideration the judge has in weighing all . . . matters decided wrongly. I myself do attach great weight to the blood tie. If a father (as distinct from strangers in blood) can bring up his own son as his own son so much the better for both of them, whether or not by the accident of events the legitimate relationship exists."

A further interesting and relevant feature of this case was the somewhat sceptical attitude of the Court of Appeal to expert evidence of a child psychiatrist, and the suggestion that such witnesses might be partial advocates, rather than impartial experts. This scepticism was, no doubt, reflected in *Re O. (A Minor)*[24] where the views of a psychiatrist instructed by the Official Solicitor were disregarded.

V—The Child of a Broken Marriage

In the context of matrimonial breakdown, an important aspect of the situation is the consideration of the welfare of the children of the family which is being broken up, and this factor has in recent times been well in mind in framing legislation relating to divorce, nullity, etc. Section 17 (1) of the Matrimonial Proceedings and Property Act 1970 is the current statutory provision which in effect provides that the court must be satisfied about the arrangements for the welfare of any children of the family (which expression has been given an extended definition) in so far as this is possible, before a decree absolute can be made. For this purpose, a report is frequently made by the court welfare officer which it is hoped will help to ensure that the welfare of the child is considered and catered for as far as possible, although as the Law Commission Report[25] shows, this hope is by no means always fulfilled. The provision was proposed in the Report of the Royal Commission on Marriage and Divorce in 1956 and was mentioned both in *Putting Asunder*[26] and the Law Commission's *Field of Choice* report:

". . . the procedure . . . would have the merit of ensuring that in every divorce case the interest of the children would be an issue before the court and that issue would be recognised as one which is just as important as the question of divorce. . . . If the interests of the children were thus placed in the forefront, the parents themselves would . . . be led increasingly to recognise their responsibility towards their children."

The court also has power to include in a decree absolute a declaration that either party to the marriage in question is unfit to have the custody of the children of the family.

Another development that can be distinctly seen in the field of matrimonial disputes as they affect children is the move away from the view that an adulterous parent could never have custody and sometimes even access to the child, and affirmation of the view that an award of custody of a child is not the reward of a "virtuous" spouse. For example in the case of *S.* v. *S.*[27] a mother who was clearly open to criticism in personal character was not deprived of access to her children, because she was a good mother.

Recently cases have suggested that a parent may be deprived of even access notwithstanding that he is blameless, if as a matter of fact the child's welfare will not be served by allowing such access. So, in *B.* v. *B.*[28] a father was refused access to his teenaged son because the court found that the boy disliked the visits to his father and was getting no benefit at all from them. It was not alleged against the father that he was an unsuitable person to come into contact with the boy. Davies L.J. quoted from Willmer L.J. in *S.* v. *S.* that normally it was the basic right of every parent to have access to the child or children.

". . . that of course is true. But there are exceptions to every rule, and it was only towards the end of last term that in this court we had a case where a mother was refused any access to, I think it was, five children of the marriage, including two quite young ones, because the mother, on the evidence was an unfit person to have access to the children. There is no suggestion in the present case . . . that the father is in any way an unfit person to have access to this boy. But putting it rather the other way round, on the evidence the boy is not, in his frame of mind, a suitable person to have access to his father. . . . It cannot do him any good and might very well do him harm."

And further stressing the point relating to the welfare of the child—

"It would not be proper for this court to make an order for access to reward the father or to punish the mother. We have got to consider what is best for this boy."

The courts have also in recent years set themselves against any statement of principle in regard to custody disputes with regard to children in the matrimonial situation, of saying that a child should prima facie go to one parent or the other. *i.e.* a young girl to her mother, a boy to his father. They have reiterated in various cases the view that the welfare of the child is the paramount consideration and that in viewing this they must take into account the whole background of the child's life and all the circumstances of the case—*Re C.*[29] As succinctly put by *Megarry J.* in *Re F.*[30]: "In matters of discretion, it may at times be impossible to do much more than ensure that the judicial mind is brought to bear with a proper emphasis on all that is relevant to the exclusion of all that is irrelevant."

VI—Children in Trouble

There is of course the problem of the welfare of the child in the situation of the deprived and delinquent children. There are several statutory provisions—the Children and Young Persons Act 1933, the Children Act 1948 and the Children and Young Persons Act 1969, designed generally to promote in broad terms the welfare of such children, and which contain provisions requiring the welfare of the child to be considered within the situations that may arise. Dispute has arisen particularly on the Children and Young Persons Act 1969 and how far its measures are operating effectively, but the issues raised on this issue are a topic in themselves and fall outside the scope of this essay.

VII—Conclusion

To quote from the words of the judges of the Chancery Division to the Latey Committee:

> "Any legal system must lay down some age at which people who are not mentally defective are free to live their own lives at their own risk; free, for instance to associate with whom they please, to live where they please and subject to the sanctions of the criminal law to live how they please. Whatever age is fixed there will inevitably be numbers of people over the age who many of their fellow citizens will consider to be unfit to enjoy such freedom. The law must choose the age which accords best with the needs of the great majority. Moreover the age which is appropriate to the conditions obtaining at one period, may not be fitted to the conditions obtaining at another. . . ."

Until that age is reached children must be protected in some way by some person or persons or by some agency, who should ideally be paying regard to the children's welfare in determining what should be done for children in the particular situation. The real problem is how is the welfare of the children to be served and who is to judge whether the welfare of children is in fact being served.

The current attitude of the judiciary in the contexts mentioned above shows the paternalistic view of the courts, admittedly considering recently more clearly the welfare of the child, but with the unspoken premise that they know best what is good for the child. That this view is not accepted by all can be seen for example from the discussion papers of the National Council for Civil Liberties: *Children Have Rights*. This voices a minority but growing view that the problems relating to children should develop from mere consideration of their welfare into an admission that they have rights, which agencies, parents and other individuals should assist them in attaining, without the paternalistic or "authoritarian" attitude evidenced at present.

The difficulty and argument is bound to arise in a situation where personal views, prejudices and conflicting ideologies all enter into the assessment as to what should best be done where children are concerned, but it seems reasonable in the modern approach to bear in mind children's own views on the topic, and to see that these are in fact articulated by them or on their behalf. Who should speak on behalf of children is yet another question.

It is certainly a matter open to doubt as to whether judges or lay magistrates are in fact suitable persons to assess and be the final arbiters of what is for the welfare of a child. Indeed it may be questioned how far a legally trained person is qualified to reach these decisions. It is a strong argument that the court should either be advised by or be partially constituted by persons with some other kind of training, so that the welfare is considered from other than a solely judicial angle.

It is of course also a matter for question as to whether a court is the right forum for the decision of some of these matters, although probably essential in some of the situations involving children. The re-arrangement of the High Court divisions recently so that there is now a Family Division to ensure that all matters relating to children are dealt with in the same Division is a step in the right direction, and the proposals that there should be a family court, incorporating the present jurisdictions of the inferior courts relating to children and the family will probably be the next development along the road towards "children's rights."

NOTES

1. *Children Have Rights*, No. 5, National Council for Civil Liberties.
2. *Rights of Children*, National Council for Civil Liberties, 1972.
3. The Report of the Committee on the Age of Majority, July 1967, Cmnd. 3342.
4. *Ibid.*, para. 134.
5. Family Law Reform Act 1969, s. 1.
6. Representation of the People Act 1969, s. 1.
7. Criminal Justice Act 1972, s. 25.
8. [1970] 1 Q.B. 357.
9. Adoption Act 1958, s. 7.
10. [1970] 2 Q.B. 589.
11. [1971] A.C. 682.
12. *Re L (An Infant)* (1962) 106 S.J. 611.
13. *Children Have Rights (op. cit.*, note 1, No. 5).
14. Working Paper of the Departmental Committee on the Adoption of Children (appointed by the Secretary of State for the Home Department and the Secretary of State for Scotland 1970).
15. *Re J. M. Carroll (An Infant)* [1931] 1 K.B. 317.
16. *Re Thain* [1926] Ch. 676.
17. *Re Agar Ellis* (1883) 24 Ch. D. 317, but see the case of a Jehovah's Witness mother ordered by the Court of Appeal to hand over their children to her husband whom she divorced on the ground of his adultery, *The Sunday Times*, April 15, 1973.
18. *Re Adoption Application 41/61* [1963] Ch. 315.
19. *J.* v. *C.* [1970] A.C. 668.
20. *Re O (A Minor) The Times*, December 4, 1972, approved by the Court of Appeal, *The Times*, February 26, 1973.
21. *S.* v. *S. and W.* [1970] 3 All E.R. 107 (H.L.).

22. [1963] Ch. 315.
23. *Re C. (M.A.) (An Infant)* [1966] 1 W.L.R. 646.
24. See note 20.
25. *Arrangements for the Care and Upbringing of Children,* Law Commission Working Paper No. 15, by J. G. Hall.
26. Royal Commission on Marriage and Divorce 1956, para. 372 (Cmnd. 9678); *Putting Asunder,* The Report of a Group appointed by the Archbishop of Canterbury 1966; Law Commission, *Reform of the Grounds of Divorce, The Field of Choice* (Cmnd. 3123).
27. *S.* v. *S.* [1962] 1 W.L.R. 445.
28. *B.* v. *B. (B. (An Infant) intervening)* [1971] 1 W.L.R. 1486.
29. *Re C.* [1970] 1 W.L.R. 288.
30. *Re F.* [1969] 2 Ch. 239.

4. FREEDOM FROM UNWANTED PUBLICITY

C. J. F. KIDD

I—Introduction

WRITING in 1890, the authors of the most famous and influential article on a right of privacy, Samuel Warren and Louis Brandeis, defined the purposes of such a right as being,

> ". . . to protect those persons with whose affairs the community has no legitimate concern, from being dragged into an undesirable and undesired publicity and to protect all persons, whatsoever their position or station from having matters which they may properly prefer to keep private made public against their will."[1]

It was the opinion of Warren and Brandeis that the law in both the United States and England was at that time developing such a right of privacy. The development of tort liability demonstrated a gradual extension of rights protected by legal remedies, and the right "to be let alone"[2] they considered to be the latest of such rights. As evidence of this they cited nineteenth-century English cases in which the courts had prevented the publication of private correspondence and other matters against the wishes of their authors. In particular they examined *Prince Albert* v. *Strange*[3] a case which was decided by the old High Court of Chancery in 1849. It was a case in which the Prince Consort successfully sued for an injunction to restrain the defendants from publishing a catalogue of etchings drawn by the Prince and Queen Victoria for their private use and not intended for general publication. The judgment of Knight Bruce V.-C. had, in places, come near to suggesting that the injunction was being granted as part of a general law protecting the public disclosure of matters of private concern. After considering such cases Warren and Brandeis submitted that an embryonic right of privacy did exist at common law and that such right should be recognised and extended. They wrote that,

> "[the] principle which protects personal writings and any other productions of the intellect or of the emotions, is the right to privacy, and the law has no new principle to formulate when it extends this protection to the personal appearance, sayings, acts and to personal relations, domestic or otherwise."[4]

It is the purpose of this essay to examine the developments in the law since that article was published. Because the article was intended to point the way of development of the law in the United States we shall consider that law first. Then we shall come nearer home to briefly consider the protection given to privacy by the law of France. Lastly we shall consider the present position in English law and some of the proposals that have been made for legislative change in such law. In all cases our concern will be primarily with freedom from undesired publicity, the freedom to have one's private life kept private and not to be exposed to the public gaze. Above all we shall have regard to the manner in which courts in these jurisdictions have attempted to achieve the difficult and delicate reconciliation between two potentially conflicting but vital interests: the interest of the individual in the preservation of his privacy, and the interest of the community as a whole in freedom of speech, in particular the freedom of the press and other sections of the communications media to impart information to the public.

II—Privacy in the United States

The Warren-Brandeis article exerted a considerable formative influence upon the development of the law in the United States. There has been a gradual increase since 1890 in the number of states recognising a right of privacy so that today the position is that a large majority of them accept such a right. In the words of Fortas J. in the leading case, *Time Inc.* v. *Hill*,[5]

> "[a] distinct right of privacy is now recognised, either as a common law right or by statute, in at least 35 States. Its exact scope varies in the respective jurisdictions. It is, simply stated, the right to be let alone; to live one's life as one chooses, free from assault, intrusion or invasion except as they can be justified by the clear needs of community living under a government of law."

This right is not merely an appendage to some other pre-existing law such as defamation but one which is *sui generis*. A publication can be true and yet be a breach of privacy. It may involve no transgression of the laws protecting confidential information but still amount to a transgression of the law protecting privacy. In those few states which do not at present possess such a right the lack of it is a matter of topical concern.[6] Time and again American courts have traced the right of privacy back to the Warren-Brandeis article.

To attempt a detailed discussion of the nature of the American right of privacy would be beyond the scope of the present essay. For this the reader is referred to the vast American literature upon the topic particularly to the writings of Dean William L. Prosser.[7] We can only hope to present a rudimentary outline of the American right. Our best starting point is probably the definition given in the American *Restatement of Torts*.[8] In 1939 the *Restatement* expressly recognised a right of privacy. It stated such right as follows: "A person who unreasonably and seriously interferes with another's interest in not having his affairs known to others or his likeness exhibited to the public is liable to the other." The *Restatement* treated the right as one which is recognised only in a comparatively advanced society. This is because the essence of the cause of action in many cases is not so much any financial loss which might ensure from such an interference but the emotional distress or embarrassment which it might cause. As is well known courts have been notoriously reluctant to countenance claims in respect of mental distress unaccompanied by any physical or financial symptoms. However, American courts permit such claims. In this respect they have travelled further than English courts which are still rather suspicious of claims other than those in respect of actual physical or pecuniary damage.[9] This, by the way, is one of the obstacles which will have to be surmounted if English law is to develop a similar right of privacy. American courts can award substantial damages in respect of distress and embarrassment caused by a breach of the right of privacy. Indeed they are empowered in some instances to award punitive damages in such a case.[10]

How have American courts attempted to resolve the conflict between privacy and freedom of speech? This is a conflict which assumes particular importance in the United States because of the First Amendment to the Constitution. There stated as one of the fundamental rights guaranteed by the Constitution we find a firm prohibition upon any law which abridges "the freedom of speech or of the press." As can be expected, the First Amendment has exerted a considerable influence not only upon the development of the American law of privacy but also upon the law of defamation. Indeed, as will be seen later, its influence upon the latter has been such that it can be said that United States laws confer less protection against defamatory statements than does English law. In the field of privacy it was recognised by Warren and Brandeis, as it has been ever since, that the right to privacy must give way to the right to investigate and comment upon matters of proper public interest and concern. Persons whose affairs are or become, either voluntarily or not, a matter of legitimate public interest must sacrifice a substantial area of that privacy which would otherwise be protected by the law. The candidate for political office, the film or pop star striving after publicity, the man of commerce whose business activities might affect the lives and well being of thousands, the criminal whose activities attract an undesired publicity—all these and others have attracted the public limelight and in so doing their private lives must often be subordinated to the interest of the community in freedom to discuss and receive information upon such matters. We are all familiar with the intimate financial disclosures that are now expected as a matter of course from aspiring American candidates for high political office. Speculation upon such matters appears indeed to go further in the United States which recognises a general right of privacy than it does in England which does not at present recognise such right.

Now to illustrate this conflict by reference to some of the leading American cases. First, the case, *Elmhurst* v. *Pearson*[11] which exemplifies the comparatively wide area in which free comment is permitted upon matters of public concern. It concerned an action for breach of privacy in which the plaintiff had been one of the accused in a notorious sedition trial. During the course of the trial he had obtained work as a waiter in an hotel his duties being performed during periods when he could be absent from the courtroom. The defendant, a radio broadcaster, commented upon this fact during a radio broadcast. His broadcast contained a statement that the plaintiff, as a waiter at that hotel, was in a position to overhear private conversations between prominent government officials who frequented it. As a result of this broadcast and the consequent publicity, the plaintiff claimed, he had been dismissed by the hotel. However, the plaintiff's action failed for reasons explained by the Court of Appeals for the District of Columbia. In the words of the court, "it is well settled in the jurisdictions which entertain [actions for invasions of privacy] that one who becomes an actor in an occurrence of public or general interest must pay the price of publicity through news reports concerning his private life, unless these reports are defamatory." In the present case the plaintiff's "misfortune in being a defendant in the nationally discussed sedition trial made him the object of legitimate public interest" and therefore the defendant had the right to comment as he did.

Also in *Sidis* v. *F-R Publishing Corporation*[12] the *New Yorker* magazine was held to be entitled to publish what was described by the court as a "ruthless exposure of a once public character." The plaintiff had been a famous infant mathematical prodigy who, in later life, had become an eccentric recluse trying to avoid the public limelight. The article about which the plaintiff complained dissected his later life in intimate but true detail. Despite the "ruthless exposure" of the plaintiff's secluded existence and despite the mental distress thereby caused him, the later life of a former infant prodigy was still, said the court, a matter of public concern. The plaintiff had once been a public figure and the public had a legitimate interest in knowing whether or not he had fulfilled his early promise.

On the other hand a Californian court came to a different conclusion in *Melvin* v. *Reid*.[13] In that case it was held that a film company had invaded the privacy of the plaintiff, a woman who had some years previously lived the life of a prostitute and had been acquitted in a murder trial, when they produced a film portraying her earlier unsavoury life. Eight years before the film was produced the plaintiff had abandoned her "life of shame, had rehabilitated herself, and had taken her place as a respected and honoured member of society." Many of her present friends had learned for the first time of her earlier activities by the release of the film. In these circumstances, held the court, the defendants had no right to rake up the details of the plaintiff's past life. Society's interest in the rehabilitation of the character outweighed any public curiosity in knowing about the past indiscretions of the rehabilitated.

Finally we turn to what is probably the most famous of American cases on privacy, *Time Inc.* v. *Hill*,[14] a decision of the United States Supreme Court in 1967, which involved a straight confrontation between the individual's desire to be let alone and the freedom of speech provisions of the First Amendment. James Hill, the plaintiff, sued in a New York court under a statute of that state protecting the right to privacy. He alleged that an article in *Life* magazine falsely portrayed an experience suffered by himself and his family when they had been held hostage in their own house by three escaped convicts. The article complained of was one describing a play, *The Desperate Hours*, which was a fictionalised account of a family being held hostage by escaping convicts. However, *Life* magazine had portrayed it as a re-enactment of the Hills' experience, an experience which had been much in the news three years earlier. In true life the Hill family had not been treated violently by the convicts. In the play the fictional family had been treated in a brutal and insulting manner. Also ever since their true life experience the plaintiff had discouraged all efforts to keep the family in the public eye. The family desired nothing more than to be able to live in peace and to forget the entire episode. Now their three-year-old ordeal had been sensationally revived in an exaggerated manner. The question for the courts was whether this entitled them to damages for breach of the privacy statute which allowed a civil action for the un-authorised use of a person's "name, portrait or picture" for "advertising purposes, or for the purpose of trade" without that person's written con-sent. It was claimed by the plaintiff that the article in *Life* magazine had been published in order to advertise the play and to increase the magazine's circulation.

In the New York courts the defendants, the publishers of *Life* magazine, were held liable. At first instance the jury had found the defendants liable and this liability had been upheld on appeal. They then appealed to the Supreme Court claiming that their constitutional guarantees of freedom of speech and of the press had been denied by the findings of the New York courts. Their appeal was allowed by a majority of the court. It was the opinion of the majority that the subject matter of the article, the opening of a new play linked to an actual incident, was a matter of legitimate public interest. As such it was protected by the First Amendment. That protection would be lost only if a false story was published with knowledge of its falsity or in reckless disregard of its truth. The verdict of the jury could not be upheld because of a failure by the trial judge to instruct them that they could reach a verdict for the plaintiff only if the defendants had published the story with that knowledge or recklessness.

In the opinion of the minority of the court the defendants had displayed recklessness in publishing the article by failing to make a reasonable in-vestigation of the facts of the story. By their conduct in publishing such a story they had unlawfully invaded the privacy of the Hill family. Important as the rights guaranteed by the First Amendment were there were also, in the words of Fortas J., other "great and important values in our society . . . which are also fundamental and entitled to this Court's careful respect and protection." Among these was the right to privacy. The majority opinion had given too little protection to the privacy of the citizen against abusive intrusion by the organs of the press. There are suggestions also in the minority opinion that they did not regard the revival of the experiences of the Hill family as a matter of "current public interest." The defendants had published an article, "which irresponsibly and injuriously invades the privacy of a quiet family for no purpose except dramatic interest and com-mercial appeal."

This division of opinion (five judges against three and one partial dissent by Harlan J.) in the *Hill* case does demonstrate the difficulty faced by courts in drawing a line between privacy and freedom to publish. At what point do the affairs of the individual become a matter of legitimate public interest and concern? Given that those affairs are a matter of public interest how much licence to expose and comment upon them is possessed by the communications media? The majority opinion in the *Hill* case confers a comparatively wide area of freedom. Publication of material of legitimate public interest, even if such publication in untrue, is protected by the First Amendment so long as the publisher neither knows of its falsity nor acts with recklessness as to its truth or otherwise. It would also appear from the majority opinion as with other cases that American courts tend to construe the concept of matters of public interest with considerable latitude in favour of the publisher.

It is interesting to note that the same freedom exists in United States law in the case of an alleged defamation of a public figure. In *New York Times Co.* v. *Sullivan*,[15] for example, the Supreme Court held that a public figure cannot successfully sue for defamation unless the defendant in publishing a false statement about him was actuated by malice. In this context "malice" was explained as meaning that the defendant must be shown to have published the statement knowing of its falsity or with a reckless disregard for its truth.[16] This case was heavily relied upon by the majority in the *Hill* case. Public figures in the United States would certainly seem to be more exposed to character assassination than their counterparts in England.

To summarise the protection given by United States law to freedom from undesired publicity, the cases appear to demonstrate the following principles:

 (i) The right to privacy which exists in the large majority of States confers a general right to be let alone untroubled by unwelcome publicity.
 (ii) However, this right is subordinated to the constitutional rights guaranteed by the First Amendment in the case of discussion of matters of legitimate public interest.
 (iii) In the case of a true discussion on a matter of public interest then, apart from official secrets with which we are not here concerned, there is virtually unfettered freedom to publish and comment upon such a matter.
 (iv) In the case of an untrue story on a matter of public interest freedom to discuss such a matter still exists, but it is subject to the limitation that the defendant neither knew of its falsity nor acted with a reckless disregard of its truth.
 (v) If the matter given publicity is not a matter of legitimate public interest it constitutes an invasion of privacy if,
  (a) the plaintiff has not consented, expressly or impliedly to such publicity, and
  (b) if the publicity is such that it would be objected to by the reasonable man.[17]
 (vi) In such a case it matters not, for purposes of liability whether the matter published by true or untrue. Truth is no defence to an action for breach of privacy.

(vii) Also in such a case there is no need to prove special damage. Emotional distress or embarrassment is sufficient and can lead to an award of substantial damages.

(viii) The cases also suggest that the spoken word alone is insufficient to give rise to an action for breach of privacy. There must be a publication in some permanent or quasi-permanent form. Broadcast statements are sufficient for these purposes

III—Privacy in France

Our discussion of the French law of privacy will be brief. France like some other Member States of the EEC, in particular Germany, recognises a right of privacy. In fact French law appears to be highly developed in the protection it confers against undesired publicity.[18]

French case law reinforced by legislation[19] seems to go further than United States law in that the concept of public interest has received a narrower interpretation by French courts. A number of cases have been brought by French celebrities in recent years which illustrate this point. One of the most recent was a case brought by the film star Gunther Sachs in 1971.[20] A periodical had published an article about him based on previous press material when he had been married to Miss Brigitte Bardot. Although the article complained of was based on matters which had already been disclosed to the public it was still held to be an invasion of his privacy especially since the article tended to show Mr. Sachs in a bad light. The publicity given to him several years previously could not be revived and used against him in his present life although he was still a celebrity. This is a decision the implications of which would seem to pose a potentially difficult problem to the writer of contemporary French history or biography. However, the principle of this case does not apply to the communication of information which has been obtained from published official sources such as, for example, the story of a trial gathered from the official transcript. Nor does it apply to the publication of facts which are a matter of common knowledge.[21] Also if a person expressly or impliedly authorises publication of details of his private life he would have no cause of action.

The French citizen also appears to possess something approaching a proprietary right in the use of his family name. However, he only has a cause of action if he can show that he has suffered damage as a result of unauthorised use of his family name and that the defendant has been at fault in the sense that he intended such damage. This was made clear in an unsuccessful action brought by one Jacques Goldfinger in 1968 against the producers of the James Bond film, *Goldfinger*.[22]

In all cases of alleged invasions of privacy in French law the plaintiff has to prove "fault" on the part of the defendant. This is because the present law of privacy has its origin in Article 1382 of the French Civil Code which confers, in broad terms, a remedy against any one who commits a "fault" causing damage or injury to another. In the case of privacy "fault" seems to include an intention to invade privacy or negligence in so doing.

One last comment must be made about the French Law in relation to remedies for a breach of privacy. Not only has a French court the power to award damages in such a case but it can, in addition, make orders for "any appropriate measures," in particular seizure of an offending publication. These powers were added to French law by legislation in 1970.[23] Thus a French publisher incurs not only the risk of damages for an invasion of privacy but also the potentially more serious step of judicial seizure of his publication. All in all the French citizen in his private life would seem to receive a fairly high level of legal protection against the activities of the publicity media. And, unlike American law this protection applies to public figures as well as the French man in the street.

IV—The Position in English Law

In English law there has been a different story. Although the genesis of the claim of Warren and Brandeis that a right of privacy exists was the old English case, *Prince Albert* v. *Strange*,[24] the subsequent development of English law has not fulfilled the hopes and expectations of those two authors. There is at present no general right of privacy. It is now clear that the old cases cited by Warren and Brandeis were illustrative of a developing law protecting against breaches of confidence. As we shall see later in this essay this development has continued. Indeed it shows signs of being capable of further growth so as to include within its scope more of the area protected in other jurisdictions by a right of privacy. However, the development of this area as with other areas of English law falls short of conferring a legally protected right of privacy.

In the area of privacy which concerns us in this essay, freedom from undesired publicity in the communications media, the individual, whatever his station in life, has at present comparatively little legal protection. If a published statement is false and lowers the reputation of the individual he has a remedy in defamation. However, this remedy is frequently more apparent than real. Costs in defamation proceedings are notoriously high and legal aid cannot be granted to the impecunious in such proceedings. For these reasons defamation does sometimes appear to justify its reputation as "the rich man's tort."

Most important in our context, however, is the fact that the tort of defamation does not protect a person against public disclosure of true information about himself however much damage and suffering such a disclosure might cause him. It is this fact that most distinguishes the present English law from the laws of the United States and France which we have already considered. Disclosure of true (or of course untrue) information about an individual's private life is only protected in those countries if such disclosure is upon a matter of legitimate public interest. In England, however, the past long-forgotten indiscretions of a now respected member of the community can be resurrected and laid bare to the public gaze by the exposure journalism of a newspaper more interested in furthering its circulation than in the public interest. The rehabilitated prostitute who, as we have seen, obtained a remedy in the Californian courts in *Melvin* v. *Read*[25] would obtain no remedy in similar circumstances in an English court. Gunther Sachs in the circumstances of his case would not obtain in English law the satisfaction granted him in French law.

It is true that in such a case the law of criminal libel provides that truth is not a defence unless the publication can be shown to be for the public benefit. However, this is at present mainly of theoretical rather than of practical importance. Prosecutions for criminal libel are very rare indeed and then are only brought if the libel is of a nature which is likely to provoke a breach of the peace. Even then such proceedings, in the circumstances outlined above, would not provide the criminally libelled person any compensation in respect of the damage which the publication might have caused him.

Also the defamation laws provide no protection against the unauthorised use of a man's name or picture unless such use lowers his reputation. In *Correlli* v. *Wall*,[26] for example, Miss Correlli, a famous novelist of the time, complained of the defendant's having published and sold without her consent coloured postcards depicting bad portraits of her in imaginary incidents of her life. She sued for an injunction on two grounds. First she claimed that the publication libelled her. Secondly she claimed that as a private person she was entitled to restrain the unauthorised publication of a portrait of herself, especially when, as she maintained, it was a bad representation of her. Swinfen-Eady J. refused her an injunction on both grounds. He held that the portrait was not libellous and that, since no authority in support of the plaintiff's second line of argument could be found, no such right as had been claimed existed.[27] In the famous case, *Tolley* v. *Fry*,[28] the result was different. The plaintiff did recover damages in respect of the unauthorised use of his name to advertise a chocolate product. However, this was only because the House of Lords upheld a verdict that the advertisement in question was libellous. It bore a defamatory innuendo meaning that the plaintiff, a famous amateur golfer, had prostituted his amateur status by permitting his golfing reputation to be used for financial reward. If the use of the plaintiff's picture had not borne this defamatory innuendo then his action would have failed.

Apart from the law of defamation English law does afford a limited area of protection in certain other instances. In particular the developing law of breach of confidence is relevant to our discussion. An injunction can be granted to restrain the disclosure of information which has originated in a breach of confidence. Such a remedy on these grounds was granted in *Prince Albert* v. *Strange*[29] discussed earlier in this essay. It will be remembered that in that case the defendant was restrained by injunction from publishing a catalogue of etchings which he had compiled. The breach of confidence arose from the fact that an employee of the printer, to whom the etchings had been entrusted by the plaintiff, had breached the confidence reposed in him by passing impressions of the etchings to the defendant. The defendant himself had not been responsible for the breach of confidence but he knew that the impressions had originated in a breach of confidence. As it was put by Ungoed-Thomas J., in *Argyll* v. *Argyll*,[30] an important recent case on breach of confidence. "An injunction may be granted to restrain the publication of confidential information not only by the person who was a party to the confidence but by other persons into whose possession that information has improperly come."[31] In that case an injunction was granted to restrain the disclosure to the press by the Duke of Argyll of marital confidences made between himself and the Duchess during their marriage. The injunction also restrained the newspaper concerned from publishing those confidences. It would appear also that an injunction will lie in such a case against a publisher who acquires confidential information innocently once he gets to know that it was originally given in confidence.[32]

Since the law of breach of confidence is still in a formative stage of development there is much that has yet to be settled by the courts. Does a remedy, for instance, only lie where information has been confided by one person to another or can it apply to any confidential information, howsoever obtained by the defendant, which is known not to be intended for publication? Exactly what sort of information is confidential? Is it a defence to an action for breach of confidence that disclosure of such information is in the public interest? If so what is the public interest in such a context? Although the primary remedy in such an action is an injunction, can the plaintiff also, or in the alternative, obtain damages? Depending upon the answers which the courts give to questions such as these the law of breach of confidence could play an increasingly significant role in the protection of privacy. It is, however, impossible within the scope of this essay to discuss them in any detail. For such detail the reader is referred to the specialist articles which had been written upon the subject.[33]

However, apart from defamation and the law of breach of confidence, and apart from some other more spcialised areas of the law such as breach of copyright and the tort of passing off, English law provides no protection to the individual against undesired publicity. The vital question is, should it do so in the guise of a general right to privacy?

This is a question that has been much to the fore in recent years. Advocates of a right of privacy, and they include some very distinguished names, point to the protection given to the individual by the laws of those jurisdictions which do possess such right. If the United States, if France, and other jurisdictions can confer such a right then surely, they say, English law can also do so. They point to the occasions when the Press and other sections of the media have abused freedom of speech by invading the privacy of the individual. They point also to the growing threat to privacy posed by the development of sophisticated technological devices, computors and the like. Now is the time, they urge, to fill the gap left in English law by its lack of a right of privacy. Parliament should enact such a right leaving it to the courts, in the course of time, to construct a body of case law indicating in more precise terms its limits. In particular, the courts can and should be trusted to find a proper balance between that right and the right to freedom of expression. Besides, it is argued, in as far as English law does not recognise such a right it is inconsistent with two important International Conventions,[34] one of which has been signed and the other ratified by the United Kingdom, which, *inter alia*, recognise a right of privacy.

Three Bills were introduced in Parliament during the 1960s to create such a right.[35] The first of them, introduced in the House of Lords by Lord Mancroft, achieved a considerable degree of support in that House. In the division on its Second Reading debate 74 lords voted for the Bill and 21 against. However, in the face of Governmental opposition to the measures proposed Lord Mancroft withdrew his Bill. If enacted the Bill would have prohibited publication[36] of details of an individual's private affairs or conduct, without his consent, by any newspaper, in the cinema, on television or on the radio, ". . . if such publication [was] calculated to cause him distress or embarrassment." As with the other Bills such organs of the media would have had a good defence if such publication was upon a matter of "reasonable public interest."

Lord Kilmuir, the then Lord Chancellor, strongly opposed Lord Mancroft's Bill on the grounds that it would prove to be unworkable and that it constituted a serious danger to freedom of publication. In as far as it would constitute the courts as arbitrators upon matters of reasonable public interest it would confer upon them discretionary powers so wide as to make them virtual censors of the Press. The two other Bills were wider in their scope than that of Lord Mancroft in that they would have enacted a general right of privacy not restricting it to publication by the communications media. However, Mr. Lyon's Bill made no progress beyond its First Reading, and Mr. Walden's Bill was withdrawn after an announcement by the then Home Secretary that the whole matter was to be referred to a Committee for detailed consideration.

There has also been considerable support outside Parliament for the creation of a right of privacy. The National Council for Civil Liberties and JUSTICE, the British Section of the International Commission of Jurists, have both supported such a right. Academic writers, notably Winfield,[37] have supported it, as have some judges both inside[38] and outside[39] court.

Thus far, however, the campaign for a law of privacy has failed to achieve its object in spite of the apparent attractiveness of the arguments of the campaigners. There have undoubtedly been occasions when the media have abused their powers by invading the privacy of the individual. Examples of such abuses are given in the Report of the Younger Committee on Privacy published in 1972.[40] Even more recent examples come to mind. Complaints have lately been made on behalf of the Royal Family concerning alleged harassment of their personal lives by press photographers. In *The Times* newspaper of December 4, 1972, there is a report of an adjudication by the Press Council of a complaint lodged by Miss Evonne Goolagong, a famous tennis player, against the *Sun* newspaper. The Press Council ruled that drawings published in the *Sun* purporting to portray Miss Goolagong in the nude, and published without her consent, constituted an infringement of her privacy. The Press Council, however, is not a court of law. Its sanctions are much more limited. In fact its only sanction appears to be the moral pressure which it can bring to bear upon an offending newspaper to publish a notice in its columns of a critical adjudication upon its conduct. It has no power to prevent or stop publication of offending material nor has it any power to levy fines or order payment of compensation to a person aggrieved by an offensive publication.

Why has Parliament so far refused to enact a law protecting privacy? The main reason seems to be that stressed by Lord Kilmuir in the debate on Lord Mancroft's Bill. In other words that such a law would unduly restrict freedom of speech and expression, in particular the freedom of the Press an essential ingredient of a healthy democracy. As one would expect this is the view of the Press itself. However, it is a point of view which has attracted powerful support from other quarters. In particular two important law reform committees have supported it.

The first of these, the Porter Committee on the Law of Defamation,[41] reported to Parliament in 1948. Its terms of reference embraced reform of the law of defamation, consideration of privacy being only incidental to such terms. In a brief paragraph the Committee recommended against legislation to confer a legal right of privacy. Their opinion was that reform of abuses on the part of the media should be left to good taste and community standards of decency rather than to legal intervention. The dangers to the freedom of the Press inherent in such an intervention outweighed any possible advantages to the individual of such a course.

The second of these committees, the Younger Committee on Privacy, was appointed in 1970 after the House of Commons debate on the Walden Bill. As its name suggests it was specifically concerned with the question as to whether legislation was needed to confer further protection against intrusions upon privacy. The Committee unanimously recommended certain legislative reforms of a piecemeal nature. They recommended a restatement of the law of breach of confidence to give it greater coherence and publicity. They recommended more legal restrictions upon the use of surveillance and "bugging" devices. And thirdly they recommended the creation of a new tort of disclosing or using information obtained by illegal means. However, by a majority[42] the Committee, like its predecessor, could find no necessity for a general right of privacy. Again the Committee were impressed by the evidence of the Press and broadcasting authorities concerning the dangers to free speech which it was claimed would result from the enactment of such a right. Legislation conferring a general right of privacy would, they considered, introduce a highly uncertain area into the law. This is because a concept such as privacy is inherently vague and impossible to define in precise terms as is the concept of "reasonable public interest" with which the courts would also be inevitably concerned. Such a course would be justified in the Committee's majority opinion only if there was "compelling evidence of a substantial wrong, which must be righted even at some risk to other important values."[43] The evidence adduced to the Committee failed to show this. Maintenance of proper standards of conduct by the media in this area was better left to factors other than the law. To this end they recommended, *inter alia*, certain changes in the rules and procedures of such extra-legal bodies as the Press Council and those dealing with programme complaints in the broadcasting media designed to strengthen their powers and effectiveness.

In essence the major argument of those who oppose the enactment of a general right of privacy is that such a step would tilt the delicate balance between individual privacy and freedom of speech too much against the latter. It would be too drastic a remedy, it is claimed, to deal with the relatively infrequent occasions upon which the communications media have abused their powers by unwarranted invasions of privacy. Newspapers, broadcasters, authors and publishers might be deterred by such a legislative step from communicating information on matters of great public concern. Rather than to court this danger it is the lesser of two evils that the law should tolerate the occasional offensive intrusion upon the individual's desire to be let alone.

This argument, in view of the quarters from which it emanates, must command considerable respect. If indeed a law protecting privacy would dangerously jeopardise freedom to communicate important information it would also command considerable support. However, would this be the consequence of such a law? This question is difficult indeed to answer. On the one hand the Press supported by two law reform committees answer affirmatively. On the other hand experience in the United States and other jurisdictions which have such a law suggests that it would not have the feared consequence. The communications media in such jurisdictions do not, thus far, seem to have been deterred by a law of privacy from fulfilling their role as communicators of matters of public concern. It is only fair to note, however, that in at least some of those jurisdictions, notably the United States, this apparently satisfactory result has only been achieved because of a liberal interpretation by the courts of those publications which are matters of legitimate public interest and, as such, not unlawful invasions of privacy. Also, as we have seen, the defamation laws of a country such as the United States seem to be of more limited application than their equivalent laws in England, at least in their application to public figures. However, the fact remains that in the United States, which does possess a right of privacy, the Press, broadcasting authorities, and other sections of that nation's media do not appear to be any less free than their English counterparts. Nor do the media of such nations as France and Germany which also uphold such a right.

The answer to this question posed in the last paragraph, is surely the crux of the whole matter. If indeed the consequences to freedom of speech feared by the opponents of a right of privacy are illusory then their other arguments have, it is submitted, little to commend them. The argument that the evidence shows relatively few cases of offensive intrusions upon privacy by the media can be countered by the question: is that a good reason for denying a remedy in those few cases, cases which might cause considerable harm and distress? The argument that privacy is an inherently imprecise concept impossible of legislative definition and that it is undesirable to introduce such an uncertain law can also be effectively answered. Such uncertainty exists in several other important areas of the civil law. It exists to a large extent in the laws of negligence and nuisance to mention only two, but it has not prevented the courts constructing a coherent and intelligible body of case law in such areas. Indeed it is the very uncertainties in such laws which have enabled the courts to mould and adapt them to the changing circumstances of life. Lastly, we must mention the argument which nearly always seems to be heard whenever a new law is suggested: that the new law might involve the danger of large numbers of worthless and trumped-up claims, even claims of a blackmailing nature. Surely the rejoinder to this argument must be that, apart from the expenses involved in bringing a legal action, we can surely trust the courts of this country to give short shrift to any claims of this nature. Besides should any such possibility operate to deny access to the courts to the litigant with a genuine claim?

Having discussed the main arguments on both sides of this issue, and having considered laws protecting privacy in the United States and France, what changes in English law can we now suggest? First, at the very least, it is hoped that Parliament will find the time to support by legislative action the changes of a piecemeal nature unanimously suggested by the Younger Committee. Secondly in the area covered by this essay, freedom from un-desired publicity, one would support further legislation somewhat similar in nature to the measures proposed in Lord Mancroft's Bill. The objective of such legislation should be to give protection to the individual where such publicity takes the form either,

    (a) of an unauthorised intentional use of his name, picture or other means of identification, or
    (b) of an unauthorised publication of details of his private life.

In both cases the individual should have an action where the publicity has been calculated to cause and has caused him damage. The damage referred to should include emotional distress or embarrassment as it does in the United States. Indeed it must do so if any such law is to be effective. There must of course be a defence to such an action that the publication was upon a matter of legitimate public interest. Although, as already indicated, this defence will present the courts with difficult problems of reconciling conflicting interests it is thought that we can have every confidence in the ability of the English courts, like American courts, to surmount them. It is further suggested that cases of privacy should normally be determined by a court sitting without a jury. Jury trial should only be permitted if both parties to the case so request. This would at least partially reduce the apprehensions of those critics of a law of privacy who fear the consequences of decisions on such matters being "subject to the unguided judgments of juries." [44] Experience would tend to suggest that the absence of a jury would also lead to greater uniformity and moderation in awards of damages, again going some way towards meeting the fears of the critics.

If such a change in the law is considered to be too ambitious at present then, as a less radical alternative, perhaps the defamation law could be strengthened so as to give greater protection against harmful publicity. Two suggestions come to mind in this context. First, why not make legal aid available in defamation actions under the same conditions as it is now available in other tort actions? The justification given in support of the present position has never impressed the present writer as having much force. Would the granting of legal aid in such actions really encourage "gold digging" actions as has been traditionally alleged? Could not legal aid committees be trusted to sift the deserving from the undeserving claim? Secondly, one would suggest that truth should only be a defence to a defamation action when the defendant can justify the publication as being upon a matter of legitimate public interest. This would be to apply the rule which already applies to criminal libel. It would give some protection to the rehabilitated against damaging public exposure of past long-forgotten misdeeds. The publisher would have to justify such exposure as being in the public interest. It is submitted that such a change would have the beneficial effect of curbing some of the more unsavoury types of exposure journalism.

Overall it is submitted that none of these suggested reforms of English law would have the pernicious effect upon freedom of speech feared by the critics. As we have pointed out this has not been the experience in other jurisdictions. Indeed, far from being pernicious, such reforms would have the opposite effect. They would benefit society by encouraging greater responsibility than now occasionally exists in the exercise of that basic freedom. Freedom of speech is of fundamental importance in our society. It is, however, equally important that such freedom be not abused at the expense of the privacy of the individual. The purpose of this essay has been to suggest possible means of advancing the latter aim without doing undue harm to the former, means which it is hoped would enable the courts to achieve that delicate reconciliation between them to which we earlier referred.

NOTES

1. Warren and Brandeis, "The Right to Privacy" (1890), 4 Harv. L. Rev. 193 at pp. 214–215.
2. To use the famous expression first coined by the American, Judge Cooley in *Cooley on Torts* (1888).
3. (1849) 2 De G. & Sm. 652, (1849) 64 E.R. 293. Affirmed 41 E.R. 1171.
4. (1890) 4 Harv. L. Rev. at p. 213.
5. 385 U.S. 374 at p. 413 (1967).
6. For example in the 1972 United States election the voters of California were invited to vote in a referendum as to whether the state legislature should be advised to enact legislation strengthening the right of privacy in that state.
7. The most famous of these is his article, "Privacy" (1960) 48 Calif. L Rev. 385.
8. *Restatement of Torts*, §867. The Restatement is not, of course, a Code.

However, it does possess considerable influence as a considered statement by the American Law Institute of the general law in the United States.

9. See *e.g. Hinz* v. *Berry* [1970] 2 Q.B. 40, a case on nervous shock in which the Court of Appeal emphasised the point that damages for shock do not include grief and mental anxiety, but they do include any recognisable psychiatric illness.

10. See *e.g.* the New York Civil Rights Law, §§ 50–51.

11. 153 F. (2d) 467 (1946). United States Court of Appeals, District of Columbia.

12. 113 F. (2d) 806 (1940). 138 A.L.R. 15, United States Circuit Court of Appeals, Second Circuit.

13. 112 Cal. App. 285, (1931). District Court of Appeal of California.

14. 385 U.S. 374 (1967).

15. 376 U.S. 254 (1964).

16. *Ibid.*, at pp. 279–280. See also *Ginzburg* v. *Goldwater*, 396 U.S. 1049 (1970), concerning a highly derogatory attack, in an American journal, upon Senator Barry Goldwater the defeated Presidential candidate in 1964.

17. See *e.g. Sidis* v. *F-R Publishing Corporation, supra,* and 138 A.L.R. 46. In the *Restatement of Torts*, §867, Comment d. it is said: "Liability exists only if the defendant's conduct was such that he should have realised that it would be offensive to persons of ordinary sensibilities."

18. The earlier development of the French law of privacy is discussed in some detail by F. P. Walton in (1931) 47 L.Q. R. 219. See also a useful short summary of the present law in Appendix J. of the Report of the Younger Committee on Privacy, 1972, Cmnd. 5012, at pp. 308–310. The author is indebted to the valuable asistance he has received on French law from his colleague Mr. John Usher.

19. The Law of July 17, 1970, which added Article 9 to the introduction to the Civil Code, and which confirmed and strengthened the previous case law on privacy.

20. (1971) D. 71, 263.

21. See *e.g.* (1971) D. 71, 678.

22. (1967) D. 68, 439.

23. The Law of July 17, 1970, *supra,* note 19.

24. (1849) 2 De G. & Sm. 652, (1849) 64 E.R. 293. Affirmed 41 E.R. 1171.

25. *Supra,* p. 46.

26. (1906) 22 T.L.R. 532.

27. See also *Dockrell* v. *Dougall* (1899) 80 L.T. 556, in which it was held that a doctor, whose name had been used, without his permission, to advertise the sale of a brand of medicine, had no cause of action in the absence of any defamatory imputation in the advertisement.

28. [1931] A.C. 333 reversing the Court of Appeal [1930] 1 K.B. 467. See also *Dunlop Rubber Co. Ltd.* v. *Dunlop* [1921] A.C. 367.

29. *Supra.*

30. [1967] Ch. 302.

31. *Ibid.*, at p. 333.

32. See *Fraser* v. *Evans* [1969] 1 Q.B. 349, *per* Lord Denning M.R. at p. 361.

33. See *e.g.* P. M. North, "Breach of Confidence: Is there a new Tort?" [1972] J.S.P.T.L. 149; Report of the Younger Committee on Privacy, Appendix I, pp. 295–299.

34. The International Covenant on Civil and Political Rights, 1966, has been signed, and the European Convention for the Protection of Human Rights and Fundamental Freedoms, 1950, has been ratified.

35. By Lord Mancroft in 1961, Mr. Alexander Lyon in 1967, and Mr. Brian Walden in 1969. They are set out in The Younger Report, Appendix F, pp. 273–278.

36. "Publication" here, as elsewhere in this essay, is used in the sense it possesses in the law of defamation, *i.e.* communicating matter to persons other than the plaintiff.

37. See P. H. Winfield, "Privacy" (1931) 47 L.Q. R. 23.

38. See *e.g.* Greer L.J. in the Court of Appeal in *Tolley* v. *Fry* [1930] 1 K.B. 467 at p. 478.

39. See *e.g.* Lord Denning M.R. in the course of the Second Reading Debate in the House of Lords of Lord Mancroft's Right of Privacy Bill.

40. (1972) Cmnd. 5012.
41. (1948) Cmnd. 7536.
42. Two powerful Minority Reports by Mr. A. W. Lyon, M.P. and Mr. D. M. Ross, Q.C. argued in favour of a general right of privacy.
43. Younger Report at p. 206.
44. *Ibid.*

5. THE RIGHT TO COMMENT

A. J. E. JAFFEY

I—Introduction

THE right with which this essay is concerned is an aspect of the general right of free expression: the right to express views on matters which are of public, as opposed to merely private, concern. That this right deserves the epithet "fundamental" in a free, democratic community, goes without saying. But however fundamental, it must have its limits. We are not here concerned with any limitations imposed by the criminal law, but with limitations which arise when the right comes into conflict with another fundamental right, that of reputation. In the exercise of the right to discuss public matters inevitably statements are made which are defamatory of people who participate in public life or who offer their work for public scrutiny. The branch of the law which regulates the competing interests here is the defence of fair comment to an action for defamation. To investigate the extent of the right to discuss public matters thus requires a discussion of some of the case law on fair comment, and as with any encounter with the law of defamation, the exercise is apt to be technical, terminological and perhaps unduly analytical.

The policy underlying the defence of fair comment is that, within limits, free discussion on matters of public interest is to be permitted and encouraged, even though such discussion involves defamatory imputations which cannot be proved to be true. It is clear, however, that it is only *discussion* which is so protected. The essence of rational debate is that reasons are given for opinions which are expressed. Opinions, as opposed to prejudices, are based on facts known or believed to be true, and the expression of an opinion is a useful contribution to a discussion only if the facts on which it is based are indicated. Only then can those to whom the opinion is expressed be in a position to assess its worth. When the opinion is defamatory of someone, it is all the more important that the facts on which it is based should be indicated, so that the person defamed will know what it is that he has to answer. So what English law protects is reasoned discussion. Bare assertion, without giving reasons, is not deemed worthy of protection if it is defamatory. That this is the policy is clear from the cases, in which it has always been insisted that comment must be based on facts, and those facts must be sufficiently indicated.[1]

It is proposed to discuss, in the light of this policy, some aspects[2] of the right to make defamatory comments on matters of public interest, as defined by the law of fair comment.

II—What is a Comment?

Having regard to the policy as described above, one would conclude that a comment is an opinion expressed on the basis of a given fact or facts. It is clear that a comment is an expression of opinion, but the word "opinion" can be used in more than one sense. It may be used to denote a mere estimate, assessment or judgment, which by its nature is necessarily a matter of opinion, for it cannot be proved to be true or false (for example, a statement that a public official is unfit for his office, or that a picture is devoid of artistic merit). But in another sense, one can express an opinion as to the existence of a state of fact. The question is whether the right to comment in defamatory terms is a narrow one confined to the expression of judgments or estimates, or is broad enough to include even opinions as to matters of fact. Suppose the *"Daily Muckraker"* publishes an article designed to expose the corruption which it believes to exist in a government department. To support its case it suggests that officials X, Y and Z have taken bribes, and it sets out fully the facts which in its view lead to the conclusion of their guilt. Must the *"Daily Muckraker,"* to escape liability for defamation, satisfy the jury that X, Y and Z did indeed accept bribes, *i.e.* justify its allegation? Or, as the matter is one of public interest, can the newspaper rely on fair comment, on the ground that the accusation is the newspaper's opinion, an inference drawn from the facts stated in the article, so that it will avoid liability if those facts are true and the inference is one which the jury thinks a reasonable man might draw from those facts?[3] The newspaper's task, if fair comment is an available defence, is much lighter: a jury might well hold that the inference drawn is a reasonable one, though not prepared to find that X, Y and Z did in fact take bribes.

It is customary, in defining a comment, to draw the distinction between a comment on the one hand and an allegation of fact on the other. If a defamatory statement is a statement of fact it cannot be protected as fair comment but must be justified. So, for example, Salmond[4] says: ". . . comment or criticism must be carefully distinguished from a statement of fact. The former is not actionable if it relates to a matter which is of public interest; the latter is actionable, even though the facts so stated would, if true, have possessed the greatest public interest and importance." Gatley[5] defines a comment as "a statement of opinion on facts," and says, "If the words complained of contain allegations of fact, the defendant must prove such allegations of fact to be true; it is not sufficient to plead that he bona fide believed them to be true." Clerk and Lindsell[6] say, "The distinction cannot be too clearly borne in mind between comment or criticism and allegations of fact. . . ." The distinction is of course drawn in the cases.[7] A recent example is *London Artists Ltd.* v. *Littler,*[8] to which we shall return.

This distinction could be understood to mean that only an estimate or judgment, not an opinion as to a state of fact, can be a comment, so that the *"Daily Muckraker"* could not plead fair comment for its allegation of taking bribes. This view is expressed by Salmond[9] thus, "Comment or criticism is essentially a statement of opinion as to the estimate to be formed of a man's writings or actions. Being therefore a mere matter of opinion, and so incapable of definite proof, he who expresses it is not called upon by the law to justify it as being true, but is allowed to express it, even though others disagree with it, provided that it is honest." Weir[10] says, "The distinction between comment and fact is a real one, but it is difficult to draw; it depends on the understanding of the addressee: would the speaker be understood to be imparting information or expressing a value judgment?" This approach is to be found in the cases. For example, in *Grech* v. *Odhams Press Ltd.*,[11] Jenkins L.J. said, "the very use of the word 'dirt' might well be thought to import a moral judgment," and in *Bailey* v. *Truth and Sportsman Ltd.*,[12] Dixon J. said, "I do not deny that they might be regarded as comments as distinguished from statements of fact, that is, as the expression of the writer's moral judgment upon conduct otherwise stated or known." Lord Denning M.R. may have been using the same criterion when, in holding that it was arguable that a statement imputing to the the defendants "a Mafia take-over bid" was capable of being a comment, he said[13] the statement "might be taken to mean a take-over by people like the Mafia." While to say that a person is a member of the Mafia is an allegation of fact, to say that he is "like the Mafia" is to express an estimate or judgment of his conduct.

A reason for confining the protection of fair comment to estimates and judgments is indicated by Salmond: because an estimate or judgment in the nature of things cannot be proved to be true, the defence of justification is inapplicable.[14] It is submitted, however, that policy suggests a wider ambit to the right of discussion of public matters. The purpose of the defence of fair comment is not simply to permit defamatory expressions of opinion which by their nature are not susceptible of justification. The policy is to permit reasoned discussion of matters of public concern. It is not only the assessment of the actions of public persons which is of importance; what those actions in fact were, or can reasonably be inferred to have been, may also be of concern. Where the grounds for an allegation are sufficiently indicated to enable the person defamed to defend himself, and the public to judge its validity for themselves, there seems little reason not to extend the protection to inferences of fact as well as mere value judgments. Where, however, the grounds for an imputation are not given, so that it is a bare, unreasoned assertion, then it will not be a comment, a proper exercise of the right of public discussion, and that will be so whether the allegation is one of fact or an estimate or judgment.

Despite the distinction drawn between comment and allegations of fact, there is indeed considerable authority that defamatory allegations stating or suggesting facts can be comments. In *Lefroy* v. *Burnside*[15] Palles C.B. said, "It was contended . . . that the statement of one fact cannot be excused as fair comment upon another fact. That proposition is, in my opinion, far too wide, and I cannot concur in it; but I think that when a matter of fact is to be excused as comment upon another fact, the fact alleged and sought to be excused must be a reasonable inference from the facts alleged, and upon which it is a comment." The fullest judicial statement of the point is perhaps that of Field J. in *O'Brien* v. *Marquis of Salisbury*:[16]

> ". . . comment may sometimes consist in the statement of a fact, and may be held to be a comment if the fact so stated appears to be a deduction or conclusion come to by the speaker from other facts stated or referred to by him, or in the common knowledge of the person speaking and those to whom the words are addressed, and from which his conclusion may be reasonably inferred. If a statement in words of a fact stands by itself naked, without reference, either expressed or understood, to other antecedent or surrounding circumstances notorious to the speaker and to those to whom the words are addressed, there would be little, if any, room for the inference that it was understood otherwise than as a bare statement of fact, and then, if untrue, there would be no answer to the action; but if, although stated as a fact, it is preceded or accompanied by such other facts, and it can be reasonably based upon them, the words may be reasonably regarded as comment, and comment only, and, if honest and fair, excusable."

Thus a statement of fact may be a comment if it is put forward as an inference, deduction or conclusion from other facts stated or referred to. If, however, it is put forward "naked," as a bare assertion of fact not inferred from other facts indicated, it is not a comment.

Relevant here are the cases dealing with defamatory imputations as to motives. The question is whether a defamatory statement that the plaintiff was actuated by a particular motive or had a particular intention can qualify as a comment. If the defendant says of the plaintiff that his motives were dishonourable he is merely expressing a judgment, but if for example he says of him that his motive for a particular action was to make a profit for himself, he is of course making an allegation of fact. Despite the statements of Lord Atkinson in *Dakhyl* v. *Labouchere*[17] and Fletcher Moulton L.J. in *Hunt* v. *Star Newspaper*[18] to the contrary, the generally accepted[19] and, it is submitted, the correct, view is that such an allegation of fact as to motive, when put forward as an inference, can qualify for protection as a comment and so need not be proved to be true. Thus in *Hunt* v. *Star Newspaper* there was an allegation that the conduct of a returning officer at an election was actuated by political bias. Cozens-Hardy M.R.[20] held that the allegation would be a fair comment if in the opinion of the jury it was "reasonably made," and Buckley L.J.[21] said that such an imputation of a motive would be fair comment if based upon facts truly stated, if it honestly represented the opinion of the person who expressed it and "was not without foundation." The law thus is that an imputation of a discreditable motive, even though it is an allegation of fact, may nevertheless be a comment if it is put forward as an inference from sufficiently indicated facts, and is protected even if the commentator cannot prove the imputation to be true. It is enough that the inference was one which could reasonably be drawn.[22]

The cases holding that an allegation of fact, if it is an inference from other facts, can be a comment are not confined to allegations as to the motives actuating conduct. There are cases in which defamatory inferences as to the conduct itself have been held to be comments. In *Cooper* v. *Lawson*[23] the libel stated that the plaintiff had falsely sworn that he had the necessary property qualifications to be a surety in an election petition, and then, asking the question why, when he was unconnected with the borough in question, he should take so much trouble and risk, gave the answer that he must have been hired for the occasion. Dealing with the defamatory allegation, stated as an inference, that the plaintiff had been hired, the court, though holding that it could not be covered by justification of the allegation of false swearing because it was not a necessary inference from or "mere shadow" of that allegation, nevertheless accepted that it was a comment whose fairness it was for the jury to decide. In *Risk Allah Bey* v. *Whitehurst*[24] Cockburn L.J. went so far as to hold that if the defendant newspaper in discussing the evidence in the plaintiff's trial for murder in Belgium, in which he was acquitted, expressed the conclusion on the evidence that he was really guilty, that could be a fair comment. In *Davis* v. *Duncan*[25] it was held that an inference drawn that the plaintiff might have been drunk when he attended a public meeting could be protected by a defence of fair comment. In *Lefroy* v. *Burnside*[26] Palles C.B. accepted that an allegation that the plaintiff had improperly supplied information to a newspaper could be a comment if it was a reasonable inference from other facts.

The important, but difficult, case of *London Artists* v. *Littler*[27] must be considered against this background. Here the defendant's allegation was that the plaintiffs had plotted together to force the closure of a play staged by the defendant. It was contained in a letter to the plaintiffs which was made public by the defendant. The allegation was of course one of fact, but which could arguably have been understood to be advanced as an inference based on facts which were contained in the letter. Cantley J. held[28] that the imputation was capable in its context of being a comment. The Court of Appeal disagreed, though their precise reasons are not altogether clear. Lord Denning M.R. said[29] "Reading the letter as a whole, I have no doubt that it stated *as a fact* that there was a plot between the plaintiffs . . .," and Edmund Davies L.J. held[30] that the statements were not comments but assertions of fact. These conclusions cannot be understood to mean that in no circumstances can an allegation of fact, even if put forward as an inference, qualify for protection as a comment. It is implicit in the words of the Master of the Rolls that the allegation as to the existence of the plot could have been so formulated that it would not have been "*stated as a fact.*" So we have the notion of what is clearly an allegation of fact (that the plaintiffs plotted together) being put forward not as a fact. What does this mean? It could well mean that to put forward an allegation of fact as an inference based on other facts is not to state the allegation "as a fact." Although the terminology is confusing, the distinction is plain. The law would be clearer if the distinction was drawn, not between comment and allegation of fact, but between comment (including allegations of fact advanced as inferences from other facts) and bare assertion (including allegations which are mere estimates or judgments[31]).

The judgments of the Court of Appeal are perhaps open, however, to further interpretation. It might be suggested that although an inference of fact can be a comment, yet since a comment is an expression of an opinion, an inference of fact will not be a comment unless it is specifically put forward by the defendant as being his mere opinion, and as such open to doubt, rather than as a certainty. Thus Cantley J. held that an inference may be a comment, "provided it appears that the writer is offering the inference as no more than his personal opinion and not as an assertion of fact from his premises."[32] When in the Court of Appeal Lord Denning said that the letter "stated *as a fact*" that there was a plot between the plaintiffs, he perhaps meant that it was stated as a fact in the sense of being advanced by the defendant as being a certain and unarguable fact. (The allegation was made in the letter in different forms: in earlier paragraphs it was qualified by the words "apparently" and "in other words," but in the final paragraph the accusation was unqualified.) There is other authority for this approach. In the Australian case of *Smith's Newspapers* v. *Becker*[33] Evatt J. held that an allegation that the plaintiff doctor was a "quack" was not in its context a comment, on the ground that it would appear to the reader that the writer did not regard the description of the plaintiff as such as being open to any debate, but as a perfectly accurate portrayal of a fact. A good example of this attitude is to be found in the South African case of *South African Associated Newspapers* v. *Yutar*.[34] Here the imputation in a newspaper article was that the plaintiff, the prosecutor at a trial, had deliberately misled the court, and in the article were set out the facts from which that defamatory allegation of fact was inferred. Steyn C.J. accepted that an allegation of fact, where it is a deduction or conclusion from other facts, may be a comment. He held however that the allegation in the present case was not a comment because "it is put forward as a fact proved with a measure of irrefutability which places it to all intents and purposes beyond dispute, and the reader is told, in effect, that that is what he will himself find if he applies his mind to the statement and the facts."[35]

It is submitted that this line of thought is objectionable as being unduly restrictive of the right to comment. It is clear that a statement which is the expression of an estimate or judgment, as opposed to an inference of fact, is no less a comment because it is advanced as a certain and unquestionable judgment. For example, in the leading case of *Kemsley* v. *Foot*[36] the allegation was, without any admission of doubt or qualification, that the plaintiff's press was a low one. There seems no reason why inferences of fact should be treated differently. Of course to be a comment the statement must be so expressed that it will be understood as being wholly inference based on the facts indicated and not as bare assertion or as containing an element of bare assertion. It must not be put forward as if prefaced by the words "Take it from me because I know," nor, even if it appears to some extent to be an inference from facts indicated, should the impression be conveyed that, in addition to drawing an inference, the writer or speaker is relying on direct knowledge or undisclosed sources. The point is made thus in a frequently cited passage in Odgers[37]:

> "If he states the bare inference without the facts on which it is based such inference will be treated as an allegation of fact. But if he sets out the facts correctly, and then gives his inference, stating it as his inference from those facts, such inference will, as a rule, be deemed a comment. But even in this case, the writer must be careful to state the inference as an inference, and not to assert it as a new and undisputed fact."

It is nevertheless perfectly possible for a writer to make it clear that an allegation of fact is solely an inference based on the facts stated or referred to, and yet state the inference in terms of certainty. That after all is just what a man would do if in his opinion the inference he draws is the only and irresistible one in the circumstances; why should he be required to express doubt if he feels none? The reasonable reader will still understand the allegation to be the expression of an opinion, even though he understands the opinion to be that the allegation is definitely true. The law cannot reasonably be that the right to express opinions on matters of public interest is limited to tentative as opposed to definite opinions. If the fear is that the reader's critical faculties may be overwhelmed by the certainty with which an inference is expressed, there is the safeguard that if it is to be protected the inference must be a reasonable one.[38]

On the whole, it seems that *London Artists* v. *Littler* is best regarded as a decision that, though an allegation of fact can be a comment, the allegation in question was not one because it was not capable of being understood as put forward solely as an inference from the other facts stated in the libel. There was an element of bare assertion.[39]

The technical conclusion from the above discussion is that the distinction commonly drawn between comment and allegation of fact is a misleading one, for it is apt to suggest that the scope of the defence is narrower than it really is. The true distinction is between comment and bare assertion. In substance the discussion shows that the right to express defamatory views on matters of public interest is a broad one. Provided that the other requirements are satisfied, reasoned allegations of fact are protected. It is only mere *ipse dixits* that are not. The American law goes further. "Against the background of a profound national commitment to the principle that debate on public issues should be uninhibited, robust and wide-open,"[40] bare assertions of misconduct on the part of public officials are protected, provided only that they were made in good faith. In this country the commitment to that principle is less absolute, and it is suggested that the standpoint that it is only reasoned allegations that take priority over the right to reputation produces a wide enough right of public discussion, and one which achieves a fair balancing of the relevant interests.

III—*Comment Based on Facts Sufficiently Indicated*

As has been emphasised above, it is allegations which are reasoned that are protected, which means that the facts which are the basis of the comment must be indicated. The object of this requirement cannot simply be that unless they are indicated readers may not realise that the statement is only an opinion. Where it is a value judgment that is expressed it can necessarily only be understood as an opinion, even if there is no indication whatever of the facts on which it is based. Yet it will not be a comment in the absence of such indication. The reason for the requirement is surely as stated above, that it enables readers to assess the value of the opinion expressed and the victim to answer the criticism. The extent to which, and detail with which, the underlying facts must be indicated must depend on the nature of the allegation in the light of the purpose of the rule. Where the artistic merit of a work is criticised, it is enough that the work be identified. If however an allegation of plagiarism were to be made against an author, the readers of the review could not be in a position to judge the validity of the allegation, nor the author to refute it, unless they were given adequate references to the allegedly pirated work and the other facts from which the critic drew his inference. Generally it would seem fair that where the comment consists of an imputation as to motive, or other allegation of fact, the facts which are the basis of the comment should be given or referred to with greater precision than where a mere judgment or estimate is complained of, because the drawing of inferences of fact is, or should be, a more precise exercise than forming value judgments, or aesthetic judgments on books or other artistic works.

Kemsley v. *Foot*[41] gives rise to some difficulty here. In that case, where the allegation was that the plaintiff's press was a low one, it was held that the mere mention of that press was a sufficient indication of the facts commented on, for the plaintiff's newspapers were well known and members of the public could ascertain for themselves the subject-matter on which the comment was based. That might well be so, if in its context the word "low" was no more than a value judgment. The plaintiff, however, claimed that in its context the statement meant that he had procured the publication of statements he knew to be false.[42] The House of Lords apparently held that even on that basis there was a sufficient indication of the facts. Yet to be able to consider the merits of such an allegation the persons who read it would need to be given chapter and verse, and the plaintiff could hardly be in a position to rebut the public accusation against him if he did not know the precise facts on which it was based. It is true that the plaintiff in such a case will, if he sues, become entitled to particulars of the facts. But that is hardly to the point. If the statement is capable of being a fair comment he probably will not sue, and yet he will have insufficient information on which to defend himself out of court. In *Kemsley* v. *Foot* Lord Oaksey went so far as to say[43] that it is not a matter of importance that the reader should be able to see exactly the grounds of the comment. No doubt there must be a limit to the detail demanded, but if the requirement is relaxed to the point that the readers will not be able to judge the value of the comment for themselves, then the policy of the defence is being ignored, and there is no reason why bare assertions, without any indication at all of the supporting facts, should not be protected. It is of course not suggested that all or any of the facts must necessarily be contained in the statement; only that somehow or other—for example, by reference to notorious or well publicised facts or to a readily available book or newspaper—the reasonably knowledgeable reader, and the plaintiff, are placed in a position where they can, if they choose, follow and assess the reasoning of the commentator, if not with complete precision then at least in general terms. Nothing less than this is consistent with the policy that the right is only one of reasoned discussion.

IV—The Facts on Which the Comment is Based Must be True

A defence of fair comment will fail if the defendant cannot prove that the facts on which the comment was based are true.[44] The requirement is that the defendant must prove sufficient of the facts to be true to make the comment fair.[45] That is to say, where fairness requires the comment to be merely an honest[46] one, the jury must be able to find that an honest man could have formed the opinion on the basis of such of the facts as are proved to be true; in those cases where fairness requires that an inference drawn should be a reasonable[46] one, the jury must be able to find that the opinion was a reasonable inference from such of the facts as are proved to be true. (Of course, where any fact stated by the commentator as the basis of his defamatory comment is itself defamatory, and cannot itself qualify as comment then the only defence open in respect of that allegation is justification and it must be proved to be true.)[47]

The requirement that the facts commented on must be true is presumably based on the proposition that conclusions drawn from false premises are worthless.[48] Yet it does not follow that such conclusions should never enjoy the protection of the law. It is clear why there should be no protection if the premises are invented. It is understandable that, in adjusting the conflicting interests of reputation and freedom of expression, immunity should not be given to a person who has not taken reasonable care to see that the facts, the basis of his comment, are correct. It is difficult, however, to see why there should be liability where, although the facts are not, or cannot be proved to be, true, the commentator had reasonable grounds for his belief in them. It is an undue restriction of the right to discuss public matters to hold that the right can be abused or exceeded by a person who acts in good faith and reasonably. Where a person wishes to exercise his right to comment in defamatory terms it should be within his own power to ensure that he remains within the limits of his right. The possibility of liability for a large sum in damages even though the commentator has taken reasonable care to get his facts right is an undesirable deterrent of free public discussion. It is true, of course, that many aspects of the law of defamation are strict, and it would go beyond the bounds of the present discussion to criticise that general policy in favour of reputation. But fair comment is the point at which the private interest in reputation comes into conflict not only with the private interest of freedom of expression but also the public interest in full and free discussion of public matters. Here the strictness in other aspects of the law of defamation is out of place.

V—When is a Comment Fair?

Given that the grounds for the defamatory opinion are sufficiently indicated, what further requirement does policy demand for the comment to be protected? Malice will of course defeat the defence: rightly, because when the defendant's predominant motive is to damage the plaintiff's reputation he does not really intend to exercise his right of discussion. In addition the comment must be fair. In many cases the comment will be fair if it is honest, that is if the opinion expressed genuinely is the opinion of the commentator. That is hardly an additional requirement. In one category of case, however, for a comment to be fair it must be reasonably warranted by the facts on which it is based. This involves a further objective requirement. It is usually said that this requirement applies to imputations of an evil motive,[49] but it seems that the real distinction is between comments which are estimates or judgments, which require no more than honesty, and those which are inferences of fact, where reasonableness is also necessary. Thus the imputation of a dishonest motive, if it is the expression of a value judgment rather than the allegation of the existence of a particular motive, may require no more than honesty. In *Slim* v. *Daily Telegraph*[50] Lord Denning M.R. said that a comment imputing that the plaintiff's conduct was dishonest, insincere or hypocritical would be fair if it was the expression of the defendant's genuine opinion. In that case the conduct being commented on was before the readers, and the defendant was merely expressing his estimate of the quality of the motives actuating that conduct. Where however the existence of a particular motive is alleged, then the inference of that fact must be reasonable, as for example if the defendant were to say of a returning officer at an election that in carrying out his functions he was motivated by the desire to assist a particular party.

The same applies to any allegation of fact, as opposed to an estimate. Thus in *Lefroy* v. *Burnside*[51] Palles C.B. said, "when a matter of fact is to be excused as comment upon another fact, the fact alleged and sought to be excused must be a reasonable inference from the facts alleged." In *London Artists* v. *Littler* Lord Denning M.R., discussing the position on the assumption that the allegation of the existence of a plot was a comment, applied a different test from the one he had applied to a mere estimate in *Slim* v. *Daily Telegraph*. He said that even if the defendant honestly believed that a plot existed, still the comment was not a fair one, for he had jumped too hastily to his conclusion and ought to have made further inquiries.[52] Wigery L.J. (as he then was) expressed a similar view.[53]

The question to be considered is whether good policy justifies this requirement that an inference of fact should have been reasonably drawn. In relation to estimates and judgments the concept of reasonableness is almost as inappropriate as that of truth. A reasonable judgment would presumably be one which a jury supposes that a substantial number of people would make; yet the free expression of minority estimates and judgments is a necessity. It is a less subjective task to assess an inference of fact as reasonable or otherwise, and indeed courts and juries are constantly required themselves to draw inferences of fact, not merely as being reasonable, but even as being correct beyond reasonable doubt. Yet one may well ask why, when *ex hypothesi* the grounds for the inference are sufficiently indicated, it is not a sufficient safeguard that the readers of the statement can decide for themselves whether or not the inference is a reasonable one, to be accepted as certain, probable or possible, or an unreasonable one, to be rejected? An argument can thus be advanced that this objective requirement is an undue impediment to the right under discussion. The problem however is always to reconcile that right with the interest in reputation. Human frailties must be allowed for, and casual readers or listeners (which includes many people much of the time) tend to accept a conclusion without bothering to consider for themselves whether it is justly drawn from the premises. For that reason the requirement of reasonableness can be accepted as a desirable safeguard.

How successful then is English law in demarcating the respective spheres of the competing fundamental rights of comment on public matters and reputation? There is the danger that the traditional distinction between "comment" and "fact" can obscure the proposition that an allegation of fact, as much as an estimate or judgment, may qualify for protection. The requirement that the facts on which the comment is based must be true, not merely reasonably believed to be so, perhaps unduly favours the right to reputation. On the other hand, an under emphasis of the need for the supporting facts to be sufficiently indicated will unduly favour the right to comment. For the rest, it is suggested, the common law has selected wisely the points at which the one right must yield to the other.

NOTES

1. *Popham* v. *Pickburn* (1862) 7 H. & N. 891, 898; *Hunt* v. *Star Newspaper Co.* [1908] 2 K.B. 309, 319; *Christie* v. *Robertson* (1889) 10 N.S.W.L.R. 157, 161; Veeder (1910) 23 Harv. L.R. 419–420.
2. One aspect which, for reasons of space and because there is little to be said in criticism of the law on the topic, is not discussed is the scope of "public interest." The courts give an increasingly generous meaning to the phrase, see *e.g. London Artists Ltd.* v. *Littler* [1969] 2 Q.B. 375.
3. As to the requirement that the inference must be reasonably, not merely honestly, drawn, see Part V below.
4. *The Law of Torts* (15th edn by Heuston), p. 232.
5. *Libel and Slander* (6th edn by McEwen and Lewis), paras. 705, 706.
6. *Torts* (13th edn by Armitage), para. 1777.
7. *e.g. Popham* v. *Pickburn* (1862) 7 H. & N. 891 at p. 898; *Davis* v. *Shepstone* (1886) 11 App. Cas. 187 at p. 190; *Thomas* v. *Bradbury Agnew & Co.* [1906] 2 K.B. 627 at p. 638; *Sutherland* v. *Stopes* [1925] A.C. 47; *Grech* v. *Odhams Press* [1957] 3 all E.R. 556 at p. 557; *Silkin* v. *Beverbrook Newspapers* [1958] 1 W.L.R. 743 at p. 746.

8. [1969] 2 Q.B. 375.
9. *Op. cit.* at p. 232; see Veeder (1910) 23 Harv. L.R. 422–423, Harper and James, *The Law of Torts* (1956), Vol. 1, p. 370.
10. *A Casebook on Tort* (2nd edn), p. 407.
11. [1958] 2 All E.R. 462, at p. 469.
12. (1938) 60 C.L.R. 700 at p. 719.
13. In *Associated Leisure Ltd.* v. *Associated Newspapers Ltd.* [1970] 2 Q.B. 450, at p. 456.
14. But it may be necessary to justify a defamatory estimate or judgment, *e.g.* where the subject is not of public interest, or the facts on which it is based are not indicated. In such a case it is presumably necessary to persuade the jury to agree with the estimate or judgment. There seems to be no English authority (*cf.* Harper and James, *op. cit.*, p. 371) that a defence of justification in respect of a comment requires merely that the comment be reasonable in relation to the facts commented on. See *Sutherland* v. *Stopes* [1925] A.C. 62.
15. (1879) 4 L.R. (Ir.) 556, 566.
16. (1889) 54 J.P. 215, 216.
17. [1908] 2 K.B. 325 n, at p. 329. Lord Atkinson's position is not easy to understand. He accepted that an imputation as to a person's state of mind can be protected by the defence of fair comment, but then described the requirements for the defence in such a case in terms that apparently amount to actual justification; for the defence to succeed, in his view, the jury must find that the inference drawn by the defendant of the existence of the improper motive was correctly drawn. This approach was not adopted by Lord Lore-burn L.C. (with whom Lord Robertson concurred).
18. [1908] 2 K.B. 309 at p. 321: "To allege a criminal intention or a disreputable motive as actuating an individual is to make an allegation of fact which must be supported by adequate evidence. I agree that an allegation of fact may be justified by its being an inference from other facts truly stated, but . . . in order to warrant it the jury must be satisfied that such inference ought to be drawn from the facts." Thus he considered that because the imputation of a particular bad motive is an allegation of fact (as of course it is), it must be proved to be true. The text above shows that the other members of the court did not share this view.
19. See Gatley, *op. cit.*, paras. 725–728; Report of the Committee on the Law of Defamation (Cmd. 7536), para. 85; Paton, (1944) A.L.J. 158. In earlier editions of Salmond (see 14th edn, pp. 254–255) the contrary view was taken. In the present edition the learned editor, though he still says (at p. 240) that "such a personal attack, therefore, is to be regarded as a defamatory statement of fact, and not as a mere comment," accepts, on the authority of *Porter* v. *Mercury Newspapers* [1964] Tas. S.R. 279, that it is perhaps enough that the inference is reasonable. See also *Homing Pigeon Publishing Co.* v. *Racing Pigeon Publishing Co.* (1913) 29 T.L.R. 389; *Greville* v. *Wiseman* [1967] N.Z.L.R. 795, at p. 800.
20. [1908] 2 K.B. at p. 317.
21. At pp. 323–324. See also the views of the same judge in *Peter Walker* v. *Hodgson* [1909] 1 K.B. 239 at p. 253.
22. See note 19 above. For the South African law to this effect, based on English authorities, see *Crawford* v. *Albu*, 1917 A.D. 102, at pp. 115–116. See also *Porter* v. *Mercury Newspapers* [1964] Tas. S.R. 279 at p. 292.
23. (1838) 8 Ad. & E. 746.
24. (1868) 18 L.T. 615 at p. 620.
25. (1874) L.R. 9 C.P. 396.
26. (1879) 4 L.R. Ir. 556.
27. [1968] 1 W.L.R. 706; [1969] 2 Q.D. 375.
28. [1968] 1 W.L.R. 607.
29. [1969] 2 Q.B. at p. 392.
30. At p. 397.
31. Thus if I say of a public man that he is "a disgrace to human nature," but do not indicate the facts on which the statement is based, that is no comment, though it is an estimate of his conduct, not an allegation of fact (*pace* Gatley, *op. cit.*, para. 709). It may be that such a statement carries with it the implication that there are facts to support the opinion; but such unex-

pressed facts would not themselves necessarily be defamatory if they were expressed, and since in any event they are unknown to those to whom the defamatory opinion is published, it is not the unexpressed facts but the expressed opinion that damages the plaintiffs' reputation. The reason why such a statement is not a comment is not that it is an allegation of fact but that it is a bare assertion.

32. [1968] 1 W.L.R. at p. 607.
33. (1932) 47 C.L.R. 279, 302.
34. 1969 (2) S.A. 442.
35. At p. 454.
36. [1952] A.C. 345.
37. *Libel and Slander* (6th edn), p. 166. See also *Pearce* v. *Argus Printing and Publishing Co.* 1943 C.P.D. 137 at p. 144.
38. See part V below. An inference might be reasonable in a particular case if expressed merely as a possibility, but unreasonable if expressed as a certainty.
39. The decision that the statement was not capable of being a comment was surely near the border line. The Court of Appeal in any event held that if the statement were a comment, it was not a fair one. See below.
40. *New York Times Co.* v. *Sullivan* 376 U.S. 254 at p. 270; 11 L. Ed. 2d, 686 at p. 701, *per* Brennan J.
41. [1952] A.C. 345.
42. See p. 346.
43. At p. 361.
44. An exceptional case is where the comment is on a statement of fact which is protected by privilege. *Mangena* v. *Wright* [1902] 2 K.B. 958; *Grech* v. *Odhams Press* [1958] 2 Q.B. 285.
45. This is the effect of s. 6 of the Defamation Act 1952 as regards facts stated or referred to in the words complained of, and of *Kemsley* v. *Foot* [1952] A.C. 345 as regards facts not so stated or referred to, but relied on in the particulars of defence as the basis of the comment.
46. See Part V below as to the requirement of fairness.
47. *Truth (N.Z.) Ltd.* v. *Avery* [1959] N.Z.L.R. 274; *Broadway Approvals* v. *Odhams Press* [1964] 2 Q.B. 683, [1965] 1 W.L.R. 805 at p. 818.
48. See *e.g. Joynt* v. *Cycle Trade Co.* [1904] 2 K.B. 292 at p. 294; *Digby* v. *Financial News* [1907] 1 K.B. 502 at p. 508.
49. See notes 19 and 22 above.
50. [1968] 2 Q.B. 157 at p. 169.
51. (1879) 4 L.R. Ir. 556 at p. 566.
52. [1969] 2 Q.B. at pp. 392–393.
53. At p. 399.

6. THE RIGHT OF PRIVATE OWNERSHIP

E. Y. EXSHAW

I—Moral Justification of the Right

THE right to the private ownership of property, the most honourable of all fundamental rights in point of antiquity, is accorded scant treatment in the textbooks on constitutional law. By contrast, the philosophical and economic theories on the origin and justification of the right are legion. Even if space permitted, it is not proposed to examine these theories, but rather to consider the extent of the protection afforded by modern law to the right. Theories, often highly speculative in character, as to the origin and development of the concept of private ownership in the infancy of civilisation are irrelevant to the existence of the right in the law of today. More relevant, however, at all times, is the moral justification of the right. A brief comment on this aspect of the matter is required.

Most Christian thinking accepts that private ownership of property is essential for the full expression of personality under the conditions of this life and, therefore, regards it as one of the basic personal rights. The Anglican position may be seen in Article 38 of the Articles of Religion, which reads: "The Riches and Goods of Christians are not common, as touching the right, title, and possession of the same, as certain Anabaptists do falsely boast. Notwithstanding, every man ought, of such things as he possesseth, liberally to give alms to the poor, according to his ability." The basis of Roman Catholic teaching on the subject appears to be the principle of Aquinas: 'Sic habet homo naturale dominium exteriorum rerum quia per rationem et voluntatem potest uti rebus exterioribus ad suam utilitatem quasi propter se factis."[1] Modern Roman Catholic doctrine is largely reflected in Article 43 of the Constitution of Eire which will be considered subsequently.

II—The Legal Right

Turning now to the question of the protection of the right by law, the dictum of Lord Camden C.J. in *Entick* v. *Carrington*[2] is frequently cited as an illustration of the law as the principal buttress of the right:

> "By the laws of England, every invasion of private property, be it ever so minute, is a trespass. No man can set his foot upon my ground without my licence. If he admits the fact, he is bound to show by way of justification, that some positive law has empowered or excused him."

While this can be understood in a general sense to mean that the law will

73

protect property rights against unlawful interference, this is not the only problem today. The other problem is that of their protection against what may be called lawful invasion: that is, their usurpation by legislation. Rights in property may be abolished, restricted, regulated or terminated by statute, and, against these eventualities, there is no constitutional guarantee.

It may be asked how does the right of private ownership differ in this respect from any other fundamental right. The answer lies in the fact that, while in democracy other fundamental rights tend to thrive and flourish, there is a marked tendency on the part of a sovereign Parliament, elected by universal suffrage, to restrict property rights. It is a case of the rights of a perpetual minority being at the mercy of politicians dependent on the pleasure of the majority. Once the suffrage is divorced from a property qualification, the doctrine of Parliamentary sovereignty makes this injustice (as far as the property-owning sections of the community are concerned) inevitable.

Is the position more equitable where a non-sovereign legislature operates under a written constitution guaranteeing this and other minority rights? Naturally, the answer will depend on the strength of the constitutional guarantee which can never be absolute, but the examination of a concrete instance of such a situation obtaining in a common law jurisdiction should be of interest. The example taken is that arising under the Constitution of Eire.

III—Position under a Written Constitution

The first two clauses of Article 43 of the Constitution of Eire acknowledge and guarantee the right to the private ownership of property. They read as follows:

> "The State acknowledges that man, in virtue of his rational being, has the natural right, antecedent to positive law, to the private ownership of external goods.
> The State accordingly guarantees to pass no law attempting to abolish the right of private ownership or the general right to transfer, bequeath, and inherit property."

The next two clauses then proceed to qualify these provisions. They provide:

> "The State recognises, however, that the exercise of the rights mentioned in the foregoing provisions of this Article ought, in civil society, to be regulated by the principles of social justice.
> The State, accordingly, may as occasion requires delimit by law the exercise of the said rights with a view to reconciling their exercise with the exigencies of the common good."

What is the effect of the Article as a whole? First, attention may be drawn to the fact that the language of the Constitution is general. It does not speak with the precision of a modern statute or conveyance. The value of the guarantee may be lessened more by the terms in which it is expressed than by the operation of the qualifying clauses.

The guarantee is merely one against legislation attempting to abolish the right of private ownership or the general right to transfer, bequeath, and inherit property. Would the first part of this guarantee invalidate any law falling short of one that completely displaced the concept of private ownership in the legal system? On a fair construction of the provision, it is difficult to see what protection it affords to an individual against the compulsory acquisition of his property.

The effect of the second part of the guarantee would appear to be similar. That this is so, may be illustrated by the fact that the Succession Act 1965, enacted subsequently to the Constitution and containing provisions severely restricting the freedom of testamentary disposition and altering the rules of inheritance, has not so far been challenged in the courts on either of these grounds. Section 11 of this Act abolished all existing rules, modes and canons of descent of realty except in so far as they might apply to the descent of an estate tail. Section 111 confines the freedom of testamentary disposition enjoyed by a married person to the right to dispose of one-half of the estate at most. In the absence of children, the surviving spouse is given the right to the other half of the estate. While the right of the spouse is restricted to one-third of the estate if there are children, application may be made by or on behalf of any of the children for such provision out of the estate as the court thinks just.

The guarantee, in the form in which it is expressed, is so far from being an effective protection of the property rights of the individual that it might not have been thought necessary to weaken it further by the insertion of the qualifying clauses. However, the ironical point emerges that, if the guarantee had been an effective one, the qualification upon it might have been construed as a somewhat limited one.

By virtue of the qualification, the exercise of the rights may be delimited by legislation. This would not appear to justify any interference with the nature of the rights themselves, or the expropriation of them. In itself, it might possibly justify the restrictions imposed by the Succession Act on the freedom of testamentary disposition. However, would it justify the ouster of the claim of the person who, but for the provisions of the Act, would have been heir-at-law?

Although, on a reasonable construction, the qualification is a limited one, it is necessary to turn to the case law to ascertain its extent in actual practice.

IV—The Irish Decisions

The first case in which the effect of Article 43 was judicially considered by the High Court was *The Pigs Marketing Board* v. *Donnelly* (*Dublin*) *Ltd.*[3] The action was brought by the Board against the defendant company to recover monies payable in pursuance of certain provisions of the Pigs and Bacon Acts of 1935 and 1937. Although this legislation had been enacted prior to the coming into operation of the Constitution, Article 50 of the Constitution provided that such legislation should continue to be in force subject to the Constitution and to the extent to which it was not inconsistent therewith. The purpose of the Acts was to make provision for the control and regulation of the production and marketing of bacon, including the regulation of the price of pigs. The Board was empowered to fix the price of pigs and, where a licensed bacon curer purchased pigs at a lower price, the difference in price had to be paid by him to the Board. Although it was not the only ground upon which reliance was placed, it was argued on behalf of the defendant company that the relevant provisions of the Acts were unconstitutional as being an infringement of Article 43.

In the part of his judgment dealing with this ground of defence, Hanna J. first directed his attention to the provision in the first qualifying clause that property rights ought to be regulated by the principles of social justice. Of the phrase "social justice," his Lordship said:

> "I cannot define that phrase as a matter of law. It cannot be the old standard of the greatest good of the greatest number, for, at the present day, it may be considered proper that the claim of a minority be made paramount on some topic. As to the meaning of social justice, opinions will differ even more acutely than on the question of 'good government.' I cannot conceive social justice as being a constant quality, either with individuals or in different States. What is social justice in one State may be the negation of what is considered social justice in another State. In a Court of law it seems to me to be a nebulous phrase, involving no question of law for the courts, but questions of ethics, morals, economics, and sociology, which are, in my opinion, beyond the determination of a Court of law, but which may be, in their various aspects, within the consideration of the Oireachtas [legislature], as representing the people, when framing the law."

While one cannot help being in total agreement with this view of the chimerical nature of social justice, it is regrettable that it involved the court in holding that it was not its function to determine whether the Legislature had been acting in accordance with the principles of social justice when enacting legislation regulating property rights. The legislature, and not the courts, was to be the sole judge of this matter. Moreover, this view of the respective functions of the courts and the legislature was again repeated when his lordship came to consider what limitations of property rights by the legislature might be justified. On this point, his lordship said:

> "It has been frankly argued on behalf of the defendants that any law passed by the State which interferes with the free operation of competition in trade or interferes with the contractual or proprietorial rights of citizens, is unconstitutional. In my opinion, it is too late in the day to have that view accepted. The days of *laissez faire* are at an end, and this is recognised in paragraph 2 of clause 2, which enacts that the State can 'as occasion requires delimit by law the exercise of the said rights with a view to reconciling their exercise with the exigencies of the common good.' I am of opinion that the Oireachtas [legislature] must be the judge of whatever limitation is to be enacted. This law does not abolish private ownership in pigs or bacon, it only

delimits the exercise of these rights by the persons in whom they are vested, and if the law is contrary to the common good, whatever that may mean, it must be clearly proved, and I repeat that an Act is deemed to be constitutional until the contrary is clearly established. I have gone through our own statutes from the year 1932, and I find almost fifty statutes that seem to me to delimit the exercise of the rights of private property and of contract, not to mention the Land Acts. Accordingly, in my view, this point is also unsustainable."

His lordship, having also rejected the other grounds upon which it had been argued that the Acts were unconstitutional, held that they were clearly constitutional and within the powers of the legislature to enact.

The reference in this part of the judgment to the fact that the statutes did not abolish private ownership in pigs or bacon might give rise to the disturbing inference that his lordship would have been prepared to hold them to be unconstitutional only if they had purported to do that. However, the following sentence indicates the view that it would be the function of the court to determine whether a delimiting statute was void on the ground that it was contrary to the common good. Admittedly, the judge drew attention to the fact that the concept of the common good, like that of social justice, would be difficult to define. Consequently, a party seeking to challenge a statute delimiting the exercise of proprietary rights on the ground that it was contrary to the common good, would have to discharge an extremely severe onus of proof to do so successfully. On the whole, there is very little comfort in the decision for those who might see in Article 43 an effective protection against legislative intrusion upon the individual's proprietary rights.

A more promising view of the force of Article 43 was taken by the Supreme Court in *Buckley and Others (Sinn Féin)* v. *Attorney General and Another*.[4] The facts giving rise to the case were as follows. Because of divisions that had arisen in the original Sinn Féin Organisation, the trustees of its assets had been unable to determine what persons were entitled to these monies, and had lodged the funds in the High Court under the provisions of the Trustee Act 1893. In 1942, the plaintiffs, as members of the Organisation as it then existed, instituted proceedings against the Attorney-General and the personal representative of the last-surviving trustee, claiming that the funds were the property of the Organisation and that payment of these funds be made to them. While this action was pending, the Sinn Féin Funds Act 1947 was passed by the legislature. Section 10 of this Act provided that all further proceedings in the action should be stayed, and that the High Court, on the application of the Attorney-General, should dismiss the action and direct that the funds should be disposed of in the manner laid down by the Act.

On the Attorney-General's application to the High Court, the Court refused the application on the ground that it could not comply with the Act without abdicating its proper jurisdiction in a cause of which it was duly seized. At the hearing of the Attorney-General's appeal to the Supreme Court, the respondents also relied upon Article 43 of the Constitution. Delivering the judgment of the Supreme Court, O'Byrne J. said:

"It was contended by counsel for the Attorney-General that the intendment and effect of Article 43 . . . was merely to prevent the total abolition of private property in the State and that, consistently with that clause, it is quite competent for the Oireachtas [legislature] to take away the property rights of any individual citizen or citizens. We are unable to accept that proposition. It seems to us that the Article was intended to enshrine and protect the property rights of the individual citizen of the State and that the rights of the individual *are* thereby protected, subject to the right of the State . . . to regulate the exercise of such rights in accordance with the principles of social justice and to delimit the exercise of such rights so as to reconcile their exercise with the exigencies of the common good. . . . It is claimed that the question of the exigencies of the common good is peculiarly a matter for the legislature and that the decision of the legislature on such a question is absolute and not subject to, or capable of, being reviewed by the Courts. We are unable to give our assent to this far-reaching proposition. If it were intended to remove this matter entirely from the cognisance of the Courts, we are of opinion that it would have been done in express terms as it was done in Article 45 with reference to the directive principles of social policy, which are inserted for the guidance of the Oireachtas [legislature], and are expressly removed from the cognisance of the Courts."

This part of the judgment concluded by pointing out that there was no suggestion that any conflict had arisen, or was likely to arise, between the exercise by the respondents of their rights of property in the trust monies and the exigencies of the common good. In the opinion of the court, it was only the existence of such a conflict and an attempt by the legislature to reconcile such conflicting claims that could justify the enactment of the statute under review. Accordingly, the Supreme Court held that the Sinn Féin Funds Act 1947 was repugnant to Article 43 of the Constitution and, thus, that it was void.

This decision of the Supreme Court indicated that the role of judicial review in the protection of proprietary rights might be a much more positive one than that envisaged by Hanna J. in *The Pigs Marketing Board* case. Moreover, it was a decision of the final court of appeal, whereas the earlier decision had been one of the High Court. However, too much emphasis should not be placed on the fact that it was the decision of a full court of five judges because, in constitutional cases, this does not necessarily imply unanimity. Article 34 of the Constitution provides that the decision of the Supreme Court on a question as to the validity of a law in the light of the Constitution shall be pronounced by one judge, and no other opinion, whether assenting or dissenting, shall be pronounced, nor shall the existence of any such other opinion be disclosed.

It has been argued by some commentators that the Supreme Court withdrew from the stand it had taken in the *Sinn Féin Funds* case when, in *Foley* v. *The Irish Land Commission and Attorney-General*,[5] it held that certain provisions in section 2 of the Land Act 1946, were not repugnant to Article 43 of the Constitution.

The Land Act 1946, was part of a code of legislation, commencing in the latter part of the last century, by virtue of which public monies were advanced to tenants of agricultural and pastoral holdings to enable them to purchase the freehold in the holdings. The advances were repayable in the form of terminable annuities, and the Irish Land Commission was the body constituted to administer the scheme. As the scheme progressed, the categories of persons to whom advances might be made for the acquisition of land were extended, and advances might be made to them for carrying out improvements on the land including the erection of buildings. Section 2 of the 1946 Act provided that, where a holding was allotted to, but not vested in, a purchaser and it included a dwelling-house, the Land Commission might direct the purchaser to reside continuously in the dwelling-house. If the purchaser failed to comply with this direction, the Commission might recover possession of the holding.

In *Foley's* case, the Land Commission had instituted ejectment proceedings against the plaintiff in pursuance of the powers given by section 2. These proceedings were stayed in order that the plaintiff might test the validity of section 2 in the light of the Constitution. It is obvious that the position of the plaintiff was completely different from that of an ordinary landowner whose property is being compulsorily acquired from him under statutory powers. In the course of its judgment, holding section 2 of the 1946 Act to be constitutional, the Supreme Court spelled this out in no small degree of detail:

> "The appellant was allotted the parcel of land out of lands which had been acquired by the Land Commission at the expense of the State. . . . This involved no capital expenditure in the part of the appellant. Within a period of two years the Land Commission, again at the expense of the State, built a house on the lands for the accommodation of the appellant and this again involved no capital expenditure on the part of the appellant. . . . The object of the legislation was, not to forfeit the rights of the allottee, but to ensure, under the penalty of possible forfeiture, that the allottee should reside on the lands and work them satisfactorily."

Having earlier referred to the object of the Land Acts as being to create a peasant proprietorship of a certain standard, the judgment continued:

> "Bearing in mind the general object of the Land Purchase Acts and the manner in which these Acts are financed, we are of opinion that the imposition of the condition as to residence, with the statutory sanction for failure to comply therewith, is not an abolition of the right of private ownership within the meaning of Article 43 . . . and we are further of opinion that this limitation of the rights of the appellant is sanctioned by . . . the said Article as a delimitation of his rights, as allottee, with a view to reconciling their exercise with the exigencies of the common good and in accordance with the principles of social justice."

In effect, therefore, the Supreme Court regarded the object of the Land Purchase Acts as being in accordance with the exigencies of the common good and the principles of social justice. Although the court's examination of this question was negligible, and amounted to no more than expressing it as a conclusion, it is preferable that the judgment proceeded on this basis rather than on the basis that the legislature had determined it to be so and the court had no function in reviewing this determination.

For these reasons, the decision in *Foley's* case does not appear to qualify the decision in the *Sinn Féin Funds* case. The first qualification of this latter decision appears in the judgment of the Supreme Court in *Attorney-General* v. *Southern Industrial Trust Limited and Simons*.[6]

In this case, the validity of section 5 (1) of the Customs (Temporary Provisions) Act 1945, was challenged by the defendants. This section provided for the forfeiture of goods exported unlawfully. A completely novel approach emerged in the course of the judgment:

"Article 6 of the Constitution should be referred to. It provides:

1. All powers of government, legislative, executive and judicial, derive, under God, from the people, whose right it is to designate the rulers of the State and, in final appeal, to decide all questions of national policy, according to the requirements of the common good.
2. These powers of government are exercisable only by or on the authority of the organs of State established by this Constitution.
It is clear therefore that by positive provision, which indeed might have been considered unnecessary, that the Oireachtas [legislature] has the primary function in securing that the laws enacted by it have regard to 'the requirements of the common good' and are 'regulated by the principles of social justice.' It is necessary to state this obvious fact as it was contended that the Courts had the peculiar and exclusive jurisdiction of examining legislation to determine whether it was in accordance with the constitutional limitations."

This conclusion of the Court is not justified by Article 6. The Oireachtas [legislature] is nowhere mentioned in the Article nor, for that matter, is social justice. If applicable at all, why should the Article be more specifically referable to the legislature than to the courts or the government? The Article deals with certain matters in a general way, but the court construed it as applying to a totally different question.

Nevertheless, whatever the defect in reasoning, the proposition was advanced that the legislature has the primary function in determining the "requirements of the common good" and the "principles of social justice." A little comfort may be drawn from the fact that the court did not say that the legislature has the sole function in doing so, but the word "primary" in such a context is a strong one.

In holding section 5 (1) of the 1945 Act to be valid, the court did attempt to distinguish the case from the *Sinn Féin Funds* case on the ground that, in the latter case, there was not, nor could there have been, any case made that the common good required that the plaintiffs be deprived of their property. Thus, although the court was not prepared to undertake the function of determining the requirements of the common good in the case before it, it did not hesitate to pronounce a dogmatic opinion as to those same requirements in relation to a case decided years earlier.

The extent of this tendency of the Supreme Court to abandon the function of securing that legislation limiting proprietary rights has regard to the requirements of the common good was stated in the following manner by the President of the High Court in the case of *East Donegal Co-operative Livestock Mart Ltd. and Others* v. *Attorney-General*:[7] "Primarily, it is for the legislature to determine what limitations the exigencies of the common good require, although the constitutionality of the determination of the legislature is not excluded from review by the courts." In this case, the plaintiffs sought a declaration that section 9 of the Livestock Marts Act 1967 was invalid having regard to the provisions of Article 43 of the Constitution on the ground that it permitted the arbitrary confiscation of property in a manner inconsistent with the Article. However, the plaintiffs also challenged other vital sections of the Act on different grounds, and the question of the invalidity of section 9 does not appear to have been pressed strongly in the High Court. In fact, in the Supreme Court, it was conceded on behalf of the plaintiffs that they were not affected by this provision and, consequently, it was not necessary for the court to consider it.

The most recent case in which legislation was challenged on the ground that it offended Article 43 was *Meade* v. *Attorney-General and Cork County Council*.[8] Under the Labourers and Housing of the Working Classes Acts, cottages had been provided at low rents for persons entitled to the benefits of these Acts. The Labourers Act 1936 introduced a scheme whereby an occupier of such a cottage might purchase the freehold reversion therein from the housing authority, and the payment would be in the form of a terminable annuity. Section 98 of the Housing Act 1966 provided that, during the period of the payment of the annuity, the occupier might subdivide or allienate the cottage or plot of ground occupied with it subject to the consent of the housing authority. The section obliged the housing authority, as a condition of giving its assent, to require the payment to it by the occupier of such a sum as was approved by the Minister for Local Government.

It was this latter provision of section 98 that was challenged by the plaintiff as an unconstitutional interference with her property rights in that it imported a new term into fee simple ownership. The action was dismissed by the High Court on the ground that the amount payable to the housing authority, which was slightly less than one-third of the market value of the plot as one unit, was not unreasonable or oppressive. The effect of the legislature enabling occupiers to subdivide or sell was to enhance the market value of labourers' cottages, and it was reasonable that some of this enhanced value should be made available to reimburse housing authorities for the cost of having provided these same labourers' cottages at uneconomic rents in the first instance.

The reasoning behind this decision appears to be similar to that in *Foley's* case. The plaintiff had availed of a scheme financed by public monies and involving no capital expenditure on her part. Consequently, her position was completely different from that of an ordinary landowner.

Having availed of the benefits of the scheme, she must be prepared to be bound by any onerous conditions attached to it.

V—The Result of the Irish Decisions

The assessment of the effect of the cases made by the President of the High Court in the *East Donegal* case appears to be an accurate one. Primarily, it is for the legislature to determine what limitations the exigencies of the common good require, although the constitutionality of such a determination is not excluded from review by the courts.

Although this is the constitutional position, two points may be noticed. First, this role of judicial review has not been pursued in a very positive manner in relation to Article 43. In practice, there seems to be little difference between saying that the determination of the common good is primarily for the legislature and that it is solely for the legislature. In only one case has legislation been held to be invalid in the light of Article 43, and the facts of that case were surely unique.

Secondly, an unfavourable deduction as to the efficacy of Article 43 must be drawn from the fact that such a small number of cases have arisen under it in the thirty-five years of its existence. Smaller still is the number of cases in which the sole or principal ground upon which reliance was placed was Article 43. Furthermore, the types of case that have been argued under the Article are surely peculiar. If the Article afforded genuine protection for proprietary rights, one would have expected a deluge of cases involving questions of compulsory acquisition, the development of land, taxation, death duties, company law and many other matters.

VI—Other Considerations

In conclusion, it should be pointed out that Article 43 makes no mention of compensation. Statutes providing for the compulsory acquisition of property normally make provision for the payment of compensation, but there is no constitutional requirement that compensation must be paid, except in the case of the property of a religious denomination or educational institution. These express exceptions emphasise the position in relation to all other property.

Finally, a further element of uncertainty has been introduced into the matter by the Third Amendment of the Constitution Act 1972. The purpose of this amendment was to allow the State to become a member of the European Communities. The relevant part of the amendment reads:

> "No provision of this Constitution invalidates laws enacted, acts done or measures adopted by the State necessitated by the obligations of membership of the Communities or prevents laws enacted, acts done or measures adopted by the Communities, or institutions thereof, from having the force of law in the State."

While no Irish lawyer would be rash enough to predict the effect of this omnibus amendment, it is probable that one of the Articles of the Constitution most likely to be affected by it is Article 43.

NOTES

1. Thus has man natural authority over external things because through reason and will he can use external things to his benefit as if he had made them for himself.
2. (1765) 19 St. Tr. 1030, 1067.
3. [1939] I.R. 413.
4. [1950] I.R. 67.
5. [1952] I.R. 118.
6. (1960) I.L.T.R. 161.
7. [1970] I.R. 317.
8. 1972, High Court. Unreported.

7. THE RIGHTS OF SPOUSES IN THE MATRIMONIAL HOME

P. M. SMITH

WHILE the parties to a marriage continue to live happily together the question of individual rights in the matrimonial home will rarely, if ever, be foremost in their minds. It is in the event of that marriage breaking up when some sort of division must be made between the parties that these rights become fundamental.

The rights in the matrimonial home may be regarded as three-fold; the right to a proprietary interest, the right of occupation during marriage, and the right to maintenance after the marriage has been terminated.

I—The Right to a Proprietary Interest

For many couples the home must constitute their greatest capital asset and it is therefore not surprising that the breakdown of a marriage is increasingly attended with a bitter dispute over the property.

There is at present no doctrine of community of family property in English law. A wife consequently obtains no proprietary interest merely by virtue of her marital status, but possesses only that share in the home to which she is personally entitled.

Any dispute between a husband and wife as to the ownership of property may be determined by an application to the court under section 17 of the Married Women's Property Act 1882, either during the marriage or within three years of its termination.[1] The significant words of the section are that "the judge . . . may make such order with respect to the property in dispute . . . as he thinks fit."

The manner in which this jurisdiction should be exercised has however given rise to one of the most protracted judicial debates of modern times. There may be seen to be two distinct schools of thought which differ fundamentally as to whether a dispute concerning the property rights of spouses is to be treated differently from other property disputes.

Foremost in this controversy is Lord Denning M.R. who has consistently approached the section on the basis that disputes between spouses are not to be decided by the strict rules of law.[2] As early as 1947[3] he expressed his belief that section 17 gave the judge a wide discretion, and this he elaborated in *Hine* v. *Hine*.[4] There he maintained that the discretion "transcends all rights, legal or equitable, and enables the court to make such order as it thinks fit." This he saw as entitling the court "to make such order as appears to be fair and just in all the circumstances of the case."[5]

Two principles were formulated by Lord Denning to indicate how property disputes between spouses should be settled.

> "The first is that when you can clearly see that the parties intended that one piece of property or one amount of money should belong to one or the other in any event, that intention should prevail."[6]

This principle was not seen originally as fettering the wide "discretion" which the statute conferred, rather it served to show "the manner in which that discretion ought normally to be exercised. . . ."[7]

Such a view however was quite unacceptable to the traditional school, which contended that section 17 was procedural only, and the existence of a discretion allowing a court to establish a title to property contrary to the intention of the parties was denied in very clear terms.[8] There was no doubt in Lord Hodson's mind in *National Provincial Bank Ltd.* v. *Ainsworth*[9] that the court did not have a discretion "to vary agreed or established rights to property in an endeavour to achieve a kind of palm tree justice."

As a result of the criticisms emanating from the House of Lords, Lord Denning found himself obliged to change his position with respect to the supposed discretionary nature of section 17. "I have myself in the past preferred to give it a liberal interpretation in keeping with the width of the words used by Parliament," he explained in *Bedson* v. *Bedson*,[10] "But those who are wiser than I am have declared that it does not enable the court to vary existing rights. We have always to go back to see what the rights of the parties actually are."[11] Thus it has been generally accepted that where there is evidence of the parties having a common intention with regard to the ownership of the property in dispute, the court is *bound* to give effect to that intention.

Having said this however, it should be noted that the only common intention or agreement which is relevant to the liberal school is that which is to apply in any event come what may, even the breakdown of the marriage, for, it is argued, parties to a marriage generally arrange their affairs on the basis that any property they acquire is for the benefit of them both and their intentions regarding the property do not extend to the break-up of the marriage which is an event usually outside their contemplation when the property is purchased.[12] It follows therefore that:

> "[I]t is often of no use to ask what were their legal rights, nor even their equitable rights . . . for those rights, as often as not, arise by operation of equity on the assumption that the marriage will not break down but will continue until parted by death."[13]

The case of *Bedson* v. *Bedson*[14] affords a good example of how this argument was applied in practice. A married man purchased a shop with living quarters above, and on the advice of his solicitor the conveyance was taken in the joint names of his wife and himself. The wife later left and claimed a share in the property. Although Lord Denning did not consider himself bound merely because the conveyance was in their joint names, he found that the system of accounting used by the husband even after the disputes had arisen showed that "the parties did intend that, come what may, the proceeds of the sale of the property (when it should happen) should be shared equally"[15] and consequently (with some reluctance) he was obliged to give effect to that intention.

It is obvious that an intention of this kind must be comparatively rare, for "in many cases . . . the intention of the parties is not clear for the simple reason that they never formed an intention. . . ."[16] This is particularly true where the property is bought for their joint use,[17] for when setting up their home spouses seldom give thought to what might happen if the marriage should break up.

In the absence of such an intention, according to the liberal theory, the court is required to attribute an intention to the parties,[18] and when the property in question is a "family asset" such as the matrimonial home or the furniture in it where both husband and wife have contributed in some way to its acquisition and which is intended to be a continuing provision for them for their joint lives,[19] the court leans towards the view that prima facie they are each entitled to an equal share in the property notwithstanding in whose name the property stands or who paid for precisely what.[20] This attributed intention is summed up by Lord Denning in the second of his principles:

> "[W]hen the parties by their joint efforts, save money to buy a house, which is intended as a continuing provision for them both, the proper presumption is that the beneficial interest belongs to them both jointly."[21]

The application of this presumption of equality, dubbed by some "palm tree" justice, to a property dispute between spouses can be seen in many cases which have come before the Court of Appeal in the last two decades. There, despite the parties having made disproportionate contributions to the purchase of the house, in the absence of an intention to hold the property in definite shares, the court was prepared readily to infer from any joint endeavour an intention that each was to have an equal share. A good example is furnished by *Fribance* v. *Fribance* (*No. 2*).[22] The house was in the husband's name, and he had provided £130 towards the deposit compared with the wife's £20. The mortgage was paid off with income from sub-letting part of the premises and by contributions from the husband for the remainder. The court held that this was a joint venture, and that the beneficial interests of husband and wife were therefore equal, irrespective of the amount of money given by each.

But very considerable inroads have been made into this approach adopted by the liberal school by the cases of *National Provincial Bank Ltd.* v. *Ainsworth*,[23] *Pettitt* v. *Pettitt*[24] and *Gissing* v. *Gissing*[25] which collectively constitute a most important trilogy of House of Lords decisions. Despite Lord Denning's assertion in *Chapman* v. *Chapman*[26] that *Pettitt* v. *Pettitt* "cast no doubt on the many decisions of this court"[27] which followed his principles, it is clear when the judgments in these three cases are carefully examined that the majority view to a substantial degree adheres to a traditional interpretation of section 17.

It has now been established beyond doubt that the section is procedural only and does not permit the court to vary property rights once they are established between the parties.[28] This, as we have seen, has been fully conceded by Lord Denning. The majority of judges in *Pettitt* v. *Pettitt* did not accept that the intention had to extend to what would happen in the event of the marriage breaking up before the court was bound by it, for an action to determine property rights does not involve different principles depending on whether the marriage is subsisting or not, and rights to property once established are not affected by the later breakdown of a marriage.[29] As Lord Reid put it,[30] the property rights of spouses "must be capable of determination immediately after the property has been paid for or the improvements carried out and must in the absence of subsequent agreements or transactions remain the same." What is important therefore is the intention or agreement which the parties evidenced at the time when the house was purchased unless there is an indication of a subsequent agreement, and the court must make an order which gives effect to this intention.[31] Most commonly this will be an intention to create a common pool of their resources and to share all property equally,[32] but by the same token there may be evidence to show that an equal share was not intended. In *Re Rogers' Question*[33] a conveyance of property costing £1,000 was made to the husband alone and he was solely responsible for the mortgage repayments. The wife contributed £100 towards the purchase, but the court held that though the intention was definitely that she should have an interest in the property, the fact that she retained a further £400 in personal savings showed that she wished only to give a limited amount and did not desire a half-share. Accordingly the court awarded the wife one-tenth of the proceeds of sale and the husband nine-tenths.

It has already been remarked however that very often there is no intention which can be seen because the parties never formed one. Nor is this particularly surprising, for married couples do not normally spend "the long winter evenings hammering out agreements about their possessions. . . ."[34]

In this situation, the court is thrown back on the presumption of a resulting trust to ascertain the beneficial entitlement of the parties.[35] By this doctrine trusts are imposed on the spouse with the legal estate to give each party a beneficial interest in the property proportionate to his or her respective contribution to its purchase.[36] This is in accord with precepts which go back nearly 300 years, for as early as 1683 it was held in an anonymous case[37] that: "Where a man buys land in another's name, and pays money, it will be in trust for him that pays the money, tho' no deed declaring the trust, for the statute of 29 Car. 2, called the Statute of Frauds,[38] doth not extend to trusts raised by operation of the law."[39] Such a presumed intention is not entirely unreasonable, and it does still largely represent the "common sense of the matter" today.[40] But the same cannot be said of the presumption of advancement which traditionally has always been associated with the presumption of resulting trust, and in the realm of matrimonial property this presumption would now appear to have fallen into desuetude.[41] At one time which of these presumptions was applicable in any given case depended on which spouse took the legal title and which made the payments. A resulting trust was presumed where the property was in the husband's name and the wife made payments towards its purchase,[42] but where the conveyance gave the property to the wife and the husband contributed the funds he was presumed to have advanced his contribution to the wife as a gift.[43] In *Silver* v. *Silver*[44] Parker L.J. voiced the opinion that the presumption of advancement could easily be rebutted, but the judges in *Pettitt* v. *Pettitt* went even further to suggest that such a presumption had become outmoded and had now largely lost its force under modern social conditions.[45]

There comes a time however when a strict mathematical application of the doctrine of resulting trust is both impractical and inappropriate. Such a position is reached where the parties both make substantial contributions but the extent of each is difficult to compute precisely because of the complexity of the transactions involved. Faced with this difficulty the court may then exercise a kind of "palm tree" justice and adjudge each spouse to have an equal share in the property. This to the traditionalists is the proper place of "palm tree" justice, and it may be used only as a last resort when "the ownership of property has become so inextricably entangled or become legally incapable of solution that an equitable knife must be used to sever the Gordian knot."[46] Lord Upjohn[47] cites *Rimmer* v. *Rimmer*[48] as a good example of such a case. The home was purchased in the husband's name, the wife paying the deposit of £29 and the balance of £430 being raised on a mortgage for which the husband was responsible. During the war when the husband was in the services the wife worked and paid the mortgage and in fact ultimately paid more than the husband. The court held that the contributions of each could not easily be distinguished and that they were entitled to equal shares in the home.

Some of the criticisms made in *Pettitt* v. *Pettitt* and *Gissing* v. *Gissing* go to the very root of Lord Denning's arguments. The majority of judges were categorical that property rights of spouses are to be decided in the same way as other property disputes,[49] that is by means of the resulting trust, and not according to special principles. Indeed in Lord Upjohn's opinion "the expression 'family assets' is devoid of legal meaning. . . ."[50] There is therefore no power in the court to determine beneficial entitlement to property on the basis of what is fair, reasonable or just,[51] nor in the absence of intention either express or implied can the court make an order which reflects what reasonable spouses would have agreed had they put their minds to it; a contract cannot be made by the court which the parties themselves have never made.[52] Moreover, since each spouse is entitled to a share in the property relative to the size of their respective contributions, it is *not* the case that they are necessarily entitled to a half share.[53]

Viscount Dilhorne's verdict on Lord Denning's presumption of equality as enumerated in *Rimmer* v. *Rimmer* was unequivocal.[54] "In the light of the views expressed in *Pettitt* v. *Pettitt* the passage cited above cannot in my opinion be regarded as good law." Nevertheless, Lord Denning still continued to assert the principle that "when the parties by their joint efforts, save money to buy a house . . . the proper presumption is that the beneficial interest belongs to them both jointly"[55] though in *Wachtel* v. *Wachtel*[56] he does appear to concede that the cases establish that: "[I]f a wife contributes directly or indirectly, in money or money's worth, to the initial deposit or to the mortgage instalments, she gets an interest proportionate to her contribution." Whether or not this does indicate that he has accepted the traditional manner of finding the beneficial interests of spouses in the matrimonial home remains to be seen.

Declaration of beneficial interests in a deed

It has already been shown that once there is evidence of what the parties intended should be the beneficial entitlement of each at the time when the property was acquired, the court must give effect to that intention. There is a divergence of judicial opinion however as to the extent to which a declaration of beneficial interests in a deed is *conclusive* evidence of such an intention.

In some cases the now familiar argument has been used that any agreement or common intention even when expressed in writing is binding on the court only where it can be shown that the parties intended the property to be held as declared in the conveyance "in any event" including the break-up of the marriage.[57] *Hine* v. *Hine*[58] was such a case. A house was bought in 1950 for the sum of £2,950 of which the wife provided £2,000 and £1,000 was raised on a mortgage which the husband paid. Although the house was conveyed to them in their joint names and it was assumed by the court that as is usual the conveyance contained an express declaration of trust for them both jointly,[59] an order was made for the £2,000 to be returned to the wife and the remaining proceeds of sale to be divided equally. The court did not accept that a joint tenancy necessarily meant that the parties could each claim a half interest in the total proceeds of sale as they did not "make any agreement or have any common intention as to what would happen in the event of the marriage breaking up and the property then being sold."[60]

It is interesting to note that this terminology has been used by some judges who generally would not be prepared to upset the interests set out in a conveyance. Ormerod L.J. in *Wilson* v. *Wilson*[61] for example concluded that the words of the document left little doubt that the husband was providing for the wife in whatever circumstances might arise in the future as there was no need for a declaration that they would hold the proceeds of sale as joint tenants unless it was intended that the wife's interest should continue in any event.

It would appear that after *Pettitt* v. *Pettitt* such reasoning is no longer tenable for, as has already been indicated, rights to property do not change because the marriage breaks up and this fact does not permit the court to disturb those rights.[62]

There is a body of opinion which maintains that where a conveyance declares the beneficial interests of the parties, as is commonly the case in a conveyance to joint tenants, such a declaration is conclusive of those parties rights and the courts cannot investigate behind the deed.[63] Lord Upjohn set out the position as he saw it in *Pettitt* v. *Pettitt*[64]:

> "If the property in question is land there must be some lease or conveyance which shows how it was acquired. If that document declares not merely in whom the legal title is to vest but in whom the beneficial title is to vest that necessarily concludes the question of title as between the spouses for all time, and in the absence of fraud or mistake at the time of the transaction the parties cannot go behind it at any time thereafter even on death or the break-up of the marriage."

Yet this is the approach of a strict property lawyer, and there are no cases which have decided this point. There may indeed be something to be said for allowing the court to go behind a declaration in a conveyance, especially when it is in a standard form, where it can be shown that the declaration did not represent the intentions of the parties. The evidence would certainly have to be exceptionally strong to overcome the very heavy burden of rebutting the words of a deed, but this might be possible in a case like *Grzeczkowski* v. *Jedynska*.[65] There a wife using her own funds purchased property to let to produce a continuing income for her so that she could be self supporting. Only a small part of the property was the matrimonial home, but the building society required the property to be conveyed to herself, her husband and a friend as joint tenants, and on the break-up of the marriage the husband claimed a share on this basis. Although the conveyance took the common form and declared that the proceeds of sale were to be held by the parties as joint tenants, the court recognised that this did not reflect the intention of the parties and held that the husband was not entitled to any share in the property.

What is a contribution?

Thus far we have examined the right to a beneficial interest in the property which a spouse obtains by virtue of a contribution made to its purchase. But what constitutes a contribution which the courts will recognise as qualifying a spouse for such an interest is altogether another question.

It is trite law that a spouse who makes a *direct* contribution of cash to the purchase of property (which would appear to include a significant payment of the mortgage instalments[66]) will thereby obtain an undivided share in the property of some sort, and after *Pettitt* v. *Pettitt* and *Gissing* v. *Gissing* that share will be relative to the size of the contribution. In many cases however there may be no cash payment but a spouse may help in other ways by going out to work, paying for household expenses, working for the other without payment, doing work on the property, etc. As there is no doctrine of community of property, the dividing line between what is truly an *indirect* contribution to the purchase and what is normally expected of a good spouse is difficult to define.

Once again opinion has become stratified into the two schools of thought.[67]

It is a logical development of the concept of "joint effort" to accept that a spouse, usually the wife, who uses her resources to relieve the husband of some of his financial obligations thereby enabling him to devote more of his income to the payment of the mortgage instalments is making an indirect contribution to the acquisition of the home. This argument is not without its attraction.

> "In the present case it so happened that the wife went out to work and used her earnings to help to run the household and buy the children's clothes, whilst the husband saved. It might very well have been the other way round. . . . The title to family assets does not depend on the mere chance of which way round it was. It does not depend on how they happened to allocate their earnings and their expenditure."[68]

But after the cases of *Pettitt* v. *Pettitt* and *Gissing* v. *Gissing*, both of which were primarily concerned with indirect contributions, it is no longer possible to assert that property disputes between spouses are to be treated differently from other disputes,[69] and this necessarily precludes the existence of a special jurisdiction in the case of "family assets" to decide their rights on the basis of what might appear to be fair in the circumstances. It follows that even between spouses a beneficial interest can be created by indirect contributions only where these are treated by the parties as having been provided under an agreement or common intention.[70] This agreement may be either expressed or implied from all the relevant facts.[71] "Contributions are not limited to those made directly in part payment of the price of the property. . . . There can be a contribution if *by arrangement between the spouses* one of them by payment of the household expenses enables the other to pay the mortgage instalments."[72]

Yet an agreement there must be, and the court is not competent, as Lord Denning suggested in *Appleton* v. *Appleton*,[73] to artificially construct one which the parties might have made had they thought about it.[74] In other words, in any given case the circumstances must show that the contribution in question is in some way "referable to the acquisition of the house."[75]

Only Lord Diplock in *Gissing* v. *Gissing* made any real attempt to enumerate the circumstances which would give rise to the inference that the parties intended certain conduct to amount to a contribution. He evinced the argument that where a spouse has made an initial contribution to the purchase of the house thereby indicating an intention to have a beneficial interest of some sort, the later payment of household expenses is in the nature of an indirect contribution in the furtherance of this intention and it is purely a matter of convenience which spouse actually pays which expenses.[76] Where on the other hand there is no initial payment, a spouse may still be seen to make an indirect contribution if there is evidence of an internal rearrangement of the parties' finances on the acquisition of the house which would suggest the existence of some agreement.[77] There the line is drawn and where there is no initial payment to the purchase price or the mortgage instalments "nor any adjustment to her contribution to the expenses of the household which it can be inferred was referable to the acquisition of the house. . ." there is nothing to justify the court finding an intention to have a beneficial interest merely because a spouse contributes her earnings to the expenses of the household.[78]

In *Gissing* v. *Gissing* itself none of these conditions could be satisfied. The husband had bought a house which was conveyed to him alone and he paid all the mortgage instalments though the wife spent some £220 on furnishings for the home and for laying a lawn. For a time she had also gone out to work and paid for many items of household expenditure. The court felt bound to conclude that these payments made by the wife did not amount to an indirect contribution to the house.

Lord Denning added another most useful example in *Hargrave* v. *Newton*.[79] The wife had received a reward for money found by her which had come from the "Great Train Robbery," and this she used for household matters such as the garden, a car, a holiday etc. The Master of the Rolls held that in this case the contributions were referable as the husband could not have purchased the house without the wife's assistance.

> "Nothing would be said specifically as to her contributions being referable to the house, but they would indirectly be so. . . . If her efforts or her contributions relieved him of other expenses which he would otherwise have had to bear—so that he would not have been able to meet the mortgage instalments or the loan without her help—then she does make an indirect contribution."[80]

However in *Hazell* v. *Hazell*[81] Lord Denning appears to deny that the contribution need be referable, for when counsel insisted that indirect payments must be referable, he replied that:

> "Since the judge's decision, however, we have considered those words in *Hargrave* v. *Newton*, and I hope that in the future we shall not hear so much of them. It is sufficient if the contributions made by the wife are such as to relieve the husband from expenditure which he would otherwise have had to bear. . . . It may be that he does not strictly need her help—he may have enough money of his own without it—but, if he accepts it . . . she becomes entitled to a share."[82]

It is submitted that this cannot be right after *Gissing* v. *Gissing*.

There appears to be no good reason why a wife who works for her husband without remuneration should be treated differently from a wife who brings money into the home. In both cases it could be said that the husband is relieved of the obligation of paying particular expenses, and he is therefore more easily able to devote his resources to making direct payments towards the house.

In *Nixon* v. *Nixon*[83] for example, the wife helped the husband in his shop and market stall and it was held that this did amount to an indirect contribution to the property obtained by the husband.[84]

But it should be remarked that these were all decisions of the liberal school, which cannot be regarded as entirely satisfactory, as the same provisos should apply here as for other indirect contributions, namely that the work must be done without reward in the pursuance of an agreement or common intention, expressed or implied from the circumstances so as to be referable to the purchase of the property. Lord Denning's test in

Hargrave v. *Newton* is a good one, and had it been applied in the cases of *Nixon* v. *Nixon* and *Muetzel* v. *Muetzel* it would undoubtedly have been satisfied.

The same restrictions, it is submitted, used to apply to the indirect contribution made by a spouse who did work or spent money improving the property which belonged solely to the other. These however were not observed by the Court of Appeal.

In *Appleton* v. *Appleton*[85] the wife had bought a house with her own money. The husband, a skilled wood-carver, helped to renovate the house and it was sold at a considerable profit. The proceeds of sale were then used to buy an old cottage and again the husband worked on it. The court held that the husband was entitled to a share in the proceeds of sale of the cottage commensurate with the work done and the materials supplied.

Similarly in *Jansen* v. *Jansen*[86] a husband gave up his studies and converted his wife's house into four self-contained flats, of which three were already sold at a profit of £9,000 with one flat still unsold. Again the court held[87] that the husband was entitled to some beneficial interest in the proceeds of sale which was assessed at £1,000.

The scope of the work for which *Appleton* v. *Appleton* could be authority was limited by *Button* v. *Button*[88] where the court made it clear that the work must be substantial "of a type which a contractor is normally employed to do" and not merely of an ephemeral character. It was fully accepted by the court in *Pettitt* v. *Pettitt* and *Gissing* v. *Gissing* that such activity could never constitute an indirect contribution, and had the judges not used these cases as a vehicle for a much wider ranging discussion of the law relating to matrimonial property, both could have been dealt with on the short ground that the work done in each was not sufficiently substantial.[89]

These cases whereby a person could *earn* a beneficial interest in property by doing work on it without any agreement to that effect were criticised by Lord Upjohn in *National Provincial Bank Ltd.* v. *Ainsworth*.[90] Of *Appleton* v. *Appleton* he said that "the husband could have no claim on property which he knew to be his wife's by doing work on it, in the absence of some agreement." Nevertheless, despite this stricture, the Court of Appeal in *Pettitt* v. *Pettitt*[91] felt themselves bound by *Appleton* v. *Appleton*. The property was the wife's and she had provided the purchase money. The husband had done some decoration and improvement of the property and he claimed a beneficial interest in the house by virtue of the work he had done. The court upheld his claim, albeit with considerable reluctance as is shown by Willmer L.J. "[I]f the question were free from authority, I should for myself have been disposed to take the view that the husband's claim was quite without substance."[92]

In the House of Lords the whole basis of the decisions in *Appleton* v. *Appleton* and *Jansen* v. *Jansen* was questioned. These cases were disapproved not because work done on the property of another could not under any circumstances give rise to a beneficial interest, but rather because the work had been done without any agreement, express or implied.[93] "Some-times an agreement, though not put into express words, would be clearly implied from what the parties did. But there must be evidence which es-tablishes an agreement before it can be said that one spouse has acquired a beneficial interest in property which previously belonged to the other. . . .[94] Perhaps the legislature may have somewhat overreacted to the criticism of *Appleton* v. *Appleton* and *Jansen* v. *Jansen*, for by section 37 of the Matri-monial Proceedings and Property Act 1970, it was enacted that "where a husband or wife contributes in money or money's worth to the improve-ment of real or personal property in which . . . either or both of them has or have a beneficial interest . . . if the contribution is of a substantial nature . . ." he or she shall be entitled to a share in the property by virtue of that contribution.

This does have the effect of creating an anomaly in the law relating to indirect contributions, for only in the case of improvements to property under the statute is an indirect contribution made irrespective of any in-tention or agreement. A spouse by doing work on the property is thus *ipso facto* entitled to a share in the property.

In practice there may be considerable problems as to what exactly con-stitutes an indirect contribution. Even when one is found, it may be difficult accurately to assess each share, though some attempt must be made to do so and the court should not automatically order an equal division of the property.[95]

II—The Right to Occupation During Marriage

From a practical point of view, of probably equal importance is the right of a spouse to remain in occupation of the matrimonial home during the subsistence of the marriage. Conflicts in this respect as often as not concern wives who, having been deserted by their husbands, wish to stay in the house at least until they are properly provided for as part of their main-tenance on divorce.

At common law a wife is entitled to be maintained by her husband and the provision of a roof over her head is part of this larger right. The right of occupation is therefore personal to her as a wife, and so long as she has not forfeited it, the court will enforce this right against the husband by res-training him from interfering in her enjoyment of it.[96]

A husband is therefore not at liberty to turn his wife out of the matri-monial home even though it may be in his sole ownership. Consequently, where eviction is threatened, usually because the husband wishes to sell the house with vacant possession, the court may make an order prohibiting the husband from selling or doing any act which might lead to her eviction at least until he provides her with suitable alternative accommodation.[97] If the wife has already been evicted, the court is similarly empowered to order her restitution, again irrespective of the title to the property,[98] especially as in *Gurasz* v. *Gurasz* where the wife is having to live in unsatisfactory accommodation.

It may be appreciated that under many circumstances, particularly where divorce proceedings are pending, the tensions and pressures of continued cohabitation may be considerable, nevertheless, the court will not order one spouse to leave the house "unless the situation is impossible."[99] In *Hall* v. *Hall*, though there were suggestions of cruelty in the forthcoming divorce petition, the court felt that the house was large enough and it was not intolerable for the parties to live together sensibly as a family. But where such an order is clearly necessary, one party may be excluded from the home.[1] In *Jones* v. *Jones* the husband had brought his mistress to live with him in the home to the exclusion of the wife, and in *Gurasz* v. *Gurasz* the husband brought a friend into the home as a lodger.

Statutory rights of occupation are given to a spouse by section 1 (2) of the Matrimonial Homes Act 1967 which authorises the court to make an order "declaring, enforcing, restricting or terminating those rights or regulating the exercise by either spouse of the right to occupy the dwelling house."

Two important restrictions on the exercise of this statutory power must be noticed.

The House of Lords in *Tarr* v. *Tarr*[2] examined the words of the section to discover whether the court was able to make an order under the section excluding one spouse from the premises as had been held in *Maynard* v. *Maynard*.[3] Lord Pearson, delivering the judgment of the House, concluded[4] that the word "regulate" did not confer such a power and that accordingly the court was not able under section 1 (2) of the Act to prohibit the exercise by the property-owning spouse of his right to occupy the home. Presumably therefore, a spouse may be excluded from the matrimonial home only under the common law in exceptional circumstances.

Secondly, the protection of the Matrimonial Homes Act as amended by the Matrimonial Proceedings and Property Act 1970, section 38, is available only to a spouse who does not have any legal title to the property. It was therefore held in *Gurasz* v. *Gurasz* where there was a legal joint tenancy that the Act was not applicable, and a spouse in this position must rely on her common law rights.

It is also essential for the adequate protection of a wife that her right of occupation in the house is preserved even as against third parties. At one time it was thought that a measure of protection was afforded a deserted wife by what was termed the "deserted wife's equity."[5] This right was however put to the test and found wanting in *National Provincial Bank Ltd.* v. *Ainsworth*.[6] The husband had deserted the wife and subsequently charged the house to the bank as security for a loan. When this was not repaid, the bank brought an action for possession which the wife resisted on the ground that the bank was bound by her equitable right to occupy the house. This assertion however was not accepted by the court, which denied the existence of any such right.

The repercussions of this case were enormous for it was generally accepted that a wife should be protected against the possibility of a husband as sole owner alienating the property to a third party who without notice of her existence could evict her.

The result was the Matrimonial Homes Act 1967. In order to bind subsequent purchasers, section 2 enables a spouse who has no legal interest in the house to register his or her right of occupation as a land charge, thereby adding a new class of land charge (class F) to section 10 (1) of the Land Charges At 1925.[7] In the case of registered land, the right of occupation under the Act is not an overriding interest and the charge must be affected by registering a notice or caution under the Land Registration Act 1925.

This Act is not without its difficulties. Being a land charge, the right is dependant on registration for its validity as failure to register will render it void.[8] But when should a wife register her interest? It may be too late to leave registration until there is trouble, for by that time the house may already have been sold. One is therefore forced to conclude that registration should take place as soon as possible after marriage, but is it really feasible to suggest to a newly-married woman that of course she should register her rights of occupation in case she is deserted by her husband? It seems likely that in practice wives will refrain from registering until the first signs of domestic strife, and it may well become standard procedure for solicitors to register a class F charge on behalf of their clients immediately they are consulted on any matrimonial difficulty.

Like any other land charge, priority will be determined by the order in which the interests were registered, so that where the house is purchased by means of a mortgage (as is commonly the case) the mortgage if registered first will take priority over the subsequent class F charge. Alternatively, if a class F charge is already registered, a mortgagee on discovering its existence doubtless would be well advised to require the wife to remove her charge so as to give priority to the mortgage. The Act would therefore appear to offer little practical help against a mortgagee who wishes to realise his security. Admittedly a measure of protection is afforded by section 1 (5) which stipulates that payment of the mortgage instalments by a spouse left in occupation shall be as if made by the other spouse, but many cases can be envisaged where a wife deserted by her husband will be in no position to do this. It is indeed ironic that the wife in *National Provincial Bank Ltd.* v. *Ainsworth* would have fared little better after the Act.

As originally conceived, the registration of a right of occupation as a land charge under the Act did not extend to a spouse who had any interest, including a beneficial interest, in the property.[9] Yet, as has been shown earlier, it is not always easy to determine whether a spouse has a beneficial interest or not, and if for safety's sake a spouse did register, this might have had the effect of prejudicing a future claim to a beneficial share since registration under an Act reserved for those with no interest could be construed as showing that she did not intend to have any proprietary interest. Nor could it be said that a spouse with a beneficial interest had any less need for the protection of the Act. The case of *Caunce* v. *Caunce*[10] shows that a purchaser or mortgagee is not affected with notice of the interest by section 199 (1) of the Law of Property Act 1925, so that where a spouse's beneficial entitlement does not appear on the face of the title her rights are easily overreached. Stamp J. suggested that the presence of the wife in the house was "wholly consistent with the title offered" and a vendor need not inquire of her. This was not accepted by Russell L.J. in *Hodgson* v. *Marks*[11] who criticised *Caunce* v. *Caunce* on the ground that he did not believe that inquiry need not be made of every person on the property where the vendor appears in occupation. The question remains unresolved.

It would appear that where the house is registered land, a beneficial interest of a spouse may be an overriding interest within section 70 (1) (*g*) of the Land Registration Act and may entitle that spouse to continue in possession. This position is closely analogous with that in *Hodgson* v. *Marks* where an old lady was induced to convey her property to the lodger who later sold it. The court held that she had a beneficial interest under a resulting trust which came within section 70 (1) (*g*) and the purchaser took the land subject to her rights as beneficiary.

The difficulties of the beneficial owner were recognised when the Matrimonial Homes Act 1967 was extended by section 38 of the Matrimonial Proceedings and Property Act 1970 to permit a spouse with a beneficial interest to take advantage of the Act.

Although there are still problems associated with the Matrimonial Homes Act, one undoubted advantage to be gained from registration is that the wife is furnished with a very valuable lever in any negotiations for maintenance. But perhaps the greatest benefit which may be seen to come out of the Act is the continuation of the status quo with respect to the property until a definitive order can be made ancillary to the decree terminating the marriage.

The right of a spouse to occupy the matrimonial home, including that derived from the Act, is effective only so long as the marriage subsists and comes to an end with a decree absolute of divorce, unless the court specifically makes an order under the Act continuing it.[12]

III—*The Right to Support on the Termination of Marriage*

After the termination of the marriage, the husband (or more exceptionally the wife) remains under a two-fold duty to support his wife and to recompense her for what she may have lost as a result of the marriage coming to an end.[13]

During the subsistence of a marriage, questions relating to property are to be decided according to the established principles of property law discussed earlier, but on the dissolution of a marriage very different considerations apply, and it is *at this point* that the court has a discretion to make an order relating to property which is fair in all circumstances.

Taken as a whole, section 4 of the Matrimonial Proceedings and Property Act gives the court very wide powers to deal with property belonging to the spouses as part of the divorce, nullity or separation settlement. In part section 4 re-enacts the earlier provisions of section 17 of the Matrimonial Causes Act 1965 and enables the court to inquire into the existence of any post- or ante-nuptial settlements made on the parties and where appropriate to vary those settlements for the benefit of any children of the marriage or the parties themselves. It would appear that any joint beneficial ownership in undivided shares will constitute a settlement for the purposes of this section,[14] so that if it can be established that a spouse has acquired a beneficial interest in the house by virtue of contributions made by her to its purchase or under an agreement or common intention, the proportionate shares of each spouse may be varied "as the court thinks fit."

An even wider power is given by section 4, for as well as being able to vary post- and ante-nuptial settlements the court is also permitted to make an order transferring the property of one spouse to the other or settling it on the other. Thus a husband, though absolute owner both in law and equity, can now be made to give his wife an interest in the property to his wife on the termination of the marriage.

The judicial procedure is well illustrated by the cases of *Ulrich* v. *Ulrich and Felton*[15] and *Cowcher* v. *Cowcher*.[16] The court should first decide the "cold legal question" and ascertain the beneficial entitlement of the parties. Having done so, the court may then proceed to vary those rights under section 4 in the exercise of the very wide discretion given by the section.

In making any order under section 4, the court must take into account the criteria set out in section 5 which are relevant in the assessment of all forms of maintenance. By section 5 (1) (*f*) the court is to have regard to: "the contributions made by each of the parties to the welfare of the family, including any contribution made by looking after the home or caring for the family. . . ." This is an entirely new provision, and in *Wachtel* v. *Wachtel*[17] where the wife's contributions to the running of the home may not have been sufficient to establish a share in the home, the court held that "now the powers of transfer under section 4 enabled the court to do what was just in all circumstances" and taking into account section 5 (1) (*f*) an order could be made giving her an interest in the property even though she would not have been so entitled under section 17 of the Married Women's Property Act 1882. In *Wachtel* v. *Wachtel* the court awarded the wife a one-third share, which Lord Denning suggested should normally be the starting point in assessing a proper division.

The discretion given to the court by section 4 may thus be used to give a spouse a share in what is perhaps the parties' most important capital asset, and on the breakdown of the marriage it would seem that a spouse will no longer be prejudiced simply because she devoted her resources to her home and family and not the house. In many respects the Act appears to have taken us a long way towards a doctrine of community of property.

IV—Conclusion

The rights which a spouse possesses in the matrimonial home are therefore complex. There seems always to have been a conflict between treating the home as no more than any other piece of realty and recognising that the parties to a marriage have special needs and responsibilities. The rights of the more dependant spouse, who is usually the wife, have received considerably greater recognition from both the Matrimonial Proceedings and Property Act and recent cases. As social conditions change, it is to be hoped that the law will continue to develop, as the lives and welfare of spouses are very much tied up with the property which comprises their home.

NOTES

1. The Matrimonial Proceedings and Property Act 1970, s. 39.
2. *Fribance* v. *Fribance* (*No. 2*) [1957] 1 W.L.R. 384 at p. 387; *Jansen* v. *Jansen* [1965] P. 478 at p. 488; *Ulrich* v. *Ulrich and Felton* [1968] 1 W.L.R. 180 at p. 185; and *per* Romer L.J. in *Rimmer* v. *Rimmer* [1953] 1 Q.B. 63 at pp. 75, 76.
3. Then as Denning J. in *H.* v. *H.* (1947) 63 T.L.R. 645 at p. 646.
4. [1962] 1 W.L.R. 1124 at p. 1128.
5. *Ibid.*
6. *Ibid.*
7. *Per* Donovan L.J. in *Wilson* v. *Wilson* [1963] 1 W.L.R. 601 at p. 607.
8. See Romer L.J. in *Cobb* v. *Cobb* [1955] 1 W.L.R. 731 at p. 736.
9. [1965] A.C. 1175 at pp. 1220–1221.
10. [1965] 2 Q.B. 666 at p. 677.
11. To the same effect in *Fish* v. *Fish*, *The Times*, November 17, 1965; 109 S.J. 228.
12. *Hine* v. *Hine* [1962] 1 W.L.R. 1124 at p. 1127.
13. *Ibid.*
14. [1965] 2 Q.B. 666.
15. *Ibid.* at p. 682.
16. *Per* Lord Denning in *Fribance* v. *Fribance* (*No. 2*) [1957] 1 W.L.R. 384 at p. 387.
17. *Ibid.*; Romer L.J. in *Cobb* v. *Cobb*, *ante* at p. 735.
18. *Ibid.*
19. *Cobb* v. *Cobb*, *ante* at p. 734; *Fribance* v. *Fribance* (*No. 2*), *ante* at p. 387; *Hine* v. *Hine*, *ante* at p. 1127; *Ulrich* v. *Ulrich and Felton*, *ante* at p. 185; *Gissing* v. *Gissing* [1969] 2 Ch. 85 at p. 93.
20. *Ibid.* and Diplock L.J. in *Ulrich* v. *Ulrich and Felton*, *ante* at p. 189.
21. *Hine* v. *Hine*, *ante* at p. 1128, quoting *Rimmer* v. *Rimmer*, *ante* at p. 74. Reiterated in *Ulrich* v. *Ulrich and Felton*, *ante* (*per* Diplock L.J.) at p. 189; *Gissing* v. *Gissing* [1969] 2 Ch. 85 at p. 93; *Chapman* v. *Chapman* [1969] 1 W.L.R. 1367 at p. 1370; *Smith* v. *Baker* [1970] 1 W.L.R. 1160 at p. 1162.
22. [1957] 1 W.L.R. 384.
23. [1965] A.C. 1175.
24. [1970] A.C. 777.
25. [1971] A.C. 886.
26. [1969] 1 W.L.R. 1367 at p. 1370. Also in *Smith* v. *Baker*, *ante* at p. 1162.
27. The Court of Appeal.
28. *National Provincial Bank Ltd.* v. *Ainsworth* [1965] A.C. 1175, Lord Hodson at pp. 1220–1221, Lord Upjohn at p. 1235, Lord Wilberforce at p. 1246; *Pettitt* v. *Pettitt* [1970] A.C. 777, Lord Reid at p. 793; Lord Morris at pp. 798, 800, Lord Hodson at p. 808, Lord Upjohn at pp 812, 813, Lord Diplock at p. 819, 820.
29. *Pettitt* v. *Pettitt*, *ante*, Lord Reid at pp. 793, 794, Lord Morris at p. 803, Lord Upjohn at p. 816, Lord Diplock at p. 825.
30. *Pettitt* v. *Pettitt*, *ante* at p. 794.
31. *Re Rogers' Question* [1948] 1 All E.R. 328 at pp. 328–329; *Pettitt* v. *Pettitt*, *ante*, Lord Morris at p. 799, Lord Upjohn at p. 813.
32. *e.g. Allen* v. *Allen*, *The Times*, February 21, 1962.
33. [1948] 1 All E.R. 328.
34. *Per* Lord Hodson in *Pettitt* v. *Pettitt*, *ante* at p. 810.
35. Lord Morris in *Pettitt* v. *Pettitt*, *ante* at p. 803, Lord Upjohn at pp. 813–816; *Gissing* v. *Gissing* [1971] A.C. 886, Lord Morris at p. 898, Lord Pearson at p. 902, Lord Diplock at pp. 904–905.
36. *Gissing* v. *Gissing*, *ante*, Lord Upjohn at p. 814, Lord Diplock at p. 907.
37. (1683) 2 Ventr. 361.

38. Now s. 53(2) of the Law of Property Act 1925.
39. To the same effect is *Dyer* v. *Dyer* (1788) 2 Cox Eq. 92, approved by Lord Upjohn in *Pettitt* v. *Pettitt*, *ante* at p. 814.
40. Lord Upjohn in *Pettitt* v. *Pettitt*, *ante* at p. 816.
41. *Falconer* v. *Falconer* [1970] 1 W.L.R. 1333.
42. *e.g. Mercier* v. *Mercier* [1903] 2 Ch. 98.
43. *Murless* v. *Franklin* (1818) 1 Swans. 13 at p. 17; *Thornley* v. *Thornley* [1893] 2 Ch. 229; *Dunbar* v. *Dunbar* [1909] 2 Ch. 639.
44. [1958] 1. W.L.R. 259 at p. 265.
45. In *Pettitt* v. *Pettitt*, *ante*, Lord Reid at p. 793, Lord Hodson at p. 811, Lord Upjohn at p. 815, Lord Diplock at p. 824; in *Gissing* v. *Gissing*, *ante*, Lord Diplock at p. 907.
46. *Per* Lord Upjohn in *National Provincial Bank Ltd.* v. *Ainsworth*, *ante* at p. 1236.
47. *Ibid*
48. [1953] 1 Q.B. 63.
49. *Pettitt* v. *Pettitt*, *ante*, Lord Morris at p. 803, Lord Hodson at p. 811, Lord Upjohn at p. 813, Lord Diplock at p. 821; *Gissing* v. *Gissing*, *ante*, Viscount Dilhorn at p. 899.
50. *Pettitt* v. *Pettitt*, *ante* at p. 817; similarly Lord Hodson at pp. 809–810.
51. *Pettitt* v. *Pettitt*, *ante*, Lord Morris at pp. 799, 800, Lord Upjohn at p. 816.
52. *Pettitt* v. *Pettitt*, *ante*, Lord Morris at p. 804, Lord Hodson at p. 809, Lord Upjohn at p. 816; *Gissing* v. *Gissing*, *ante*, Lord Morris at p. 898, Viscount Dilhorne at p. 900, Lord Diplock at p. 904.
53. *Gissing* v. *Gissing*, *ante*, Lord Reid at p. 897, Lord Pearson at p. 903.
54. *Gissing* v. *Gissing*, *ante* at p. 899.
55. *Chapman* v. *Chapman* [1969] 1 W.L.R. 1367 at p. 1370; *Smith* v. *Baker* [1970] 1 W.L.R. 1160 at p. 1162.
56. [1973] 2 W.L.R. 366 at p. 374.
57. *Hine* v. *Hine*, *ante* at p. 1127; Lord Denning in *Bedson* v. *Bedson* [1965] 2 Q.B. 666 at p. 682.
58. [1962] 1 W.L.R. 1124.
59. Lord Denning in *Bedson* v. *Bedson*, *ante* at p. 682.
60. *Per* Pearson L.J. in *Hine* v. *Hine*, *ante* at p. 1132.
61. [1963] 1 W.L.R. 601 at p. 605.
62. *Pettitt* v. *Pettitt*, *ante*, Lord Reid at pp. 793, 794, Lord Morris at p. 803, Lord Upjohn at p. 816, Lord Diplock at p. 825.
63. Russell L.J. in *Wilson* v. *Wilson*, *ante* at p. 608 and *Bedson* v. *Bedson*, *ante* at p. 689; Lord Upjohn in *Pettitt* v. *Pettitt*, *ante* at p. 813.
64. [1970] A.C. 777 at p. 813.
65. *The Times*, January 18, 1971.
66. *Gissing* v. *Gissing*, *ante*, Viscount Dilhorne at p. 900, Lord Diplock at p. 908.
67. Lord Denning in *Davis* v. *Vale* [1971] 1 W.L.R. 1022 at p. 1025.
68. *Per* Lord Denning in *Fribance* v. *Fribance*, *ante* at p. 387.
69. Footnote 49.
70. See particularly Lord Morris in *Pettitt* v. *Pettitt*, *ante* at p. 804.
71. *Pettitt* v. *Pettitt*, *ante*, Lord Morris at p. 804; *Gissing* v. *Gissing*, *ante*, Viscount Dilhorne at pp. 900, 901; Lord Pearson at p. 902, Lord Diplock at pp. 906–909.
72. *Per* Lord Pearson in *Gissing* v. *Gissing*, *ante* at p. 903 (italics mine). Cited by Lord Denning in *Hazell* v. *Hazell* [1972] 1 W.L.R. 301 at p. 304 as authority that no agreement is necessary: *sed quaere.*
73. [1965] 1 W.L.R. 25 at p. 28.
74. Footnote 52.
75. Lord Diplock in *Gissing* v. *Gissing*, *ante* at p. 909.
76. Lord Diplock in *Gissing* v. *Gissing*, *ante* at p. 908.
77. Lord Diplock in *Gissing* v. *Gissing*, *ante* at pp. 909, 910.
78. *Pettitt* v. *Pettitt*, *ante*, Lord Hodson at p. 811; *Gissing* v. *Gissing*, *ante*, Viscount Dilhorne at p. 901, Lord Diplock at p. 909.
79. [1971] 1 W.L.R. 1611.
80. *Ibid.* at p. 1613.
81. [1972] 1 W.L.R. 301 at p. 304.

82. But this is not consistent with what he did actually say in *Hargrave* v. *Newton, ante.* See above.
83. [1969] 1 W.L.R. 1676.
84. Also *Muetzel* v. *Muetzel* [1970] 1 W.L.R. 188.
85. [1965] 1 W.L.R. 25.
86. [1965] P. 478.
87. With Russell L.J, dissenting.
88. [1968] 1 W.L.R. 457.
89. *Pettitt* v. *Pettitt, ante,* Lord Reid at p. 796, Lord Hodson at p. 807, Lord Upjohn at p. 818, Lord Diplock at p. 826; *Gissing* v. *Gissing, ante,* Lord Pearson at p. 903.
90. [1965] A.C. 1175 at p. 1236.
91. [1968] 1 W.L.R. 443.
92. *Ibid.* at p. 449.
93. *Pettitt* v. *Pettitt, ante* Lord Morris at p. 805, Lord Hodson at p. 809, Lord Upjohn at p. 818.
94. *Per* Lord Morris in *Pettitt* v. *Pettitt, ante* at p. 804.
95. Footnote 53.
96. Lord Hodson in *National Provincial Bank Ltd.* v. *Ainsworth, ante,* at p. 1220.
97. *Lee* v. *Lee* [1952] 2 Q.B. 489n; *Halden* v. *Halden* [1966] 1 W.L.R. 1481.
98. *Gurasz* v. *Gurasz* [1970] P. 11; *Jones* v. *Jones* [1971] 1 W.L.R. 396.
99. *Hall* v. *Hall* [1971] 1 W.L.R. 404.
 1. *Shipman* v. *Shipman* [1924] 2 Ch. 140; *Silverstone* v. *Silverstone* [1953] P. 174; *Gurasz* v. *Gurasz, ante*; *Jones* v. *Jones, ante.*
 2. [1973] A.C. 254.
 3. [1969] P. 88.
 4. At pp. 267–268.
 5. *Bendall* v. *McWhirter* [1952] 2 Q.B. 466.
 6. [1965] A.C. 1175.
 7. s. 2(6).
 8. s. 13 of the Land Charges Act, 1925 as amended by the Schedule to the Matrimonial Homes Act 1967; Law of Property Act 1925, s. 199(1)(i).
 9. s. 1(1).
10. [1969] 1 W.L.R. 286.
11. [1971] Ch. 892 at pp. 934–935.
12. ss. 1(8) and 2(2)(*b*).
13. See s. 5 (1)(*g*) of the Matrimonial Proceedings and Property Act 1970; and *Trippas* v. *Trippas* [1973] 2 W.L.R. 585.
14. *Cook* v. *Cook* [1962] P. 181, affirmed [1962] P. 235.
15. [1968] 1 W.L.R. 180.
16. [1972] 1 W.L.R. 425.
17. [1973] 2 W.L.R. 366.

8. THE RIGHT TO OUTDOOR RECREATION

J. M. COOMBES

I—Introduction

THE purpose of this essay is to examine the rights accorded by English law to members of the public to enter land and wander at large (that is, otherwise than along more or less defined tracks[1]) for purely leisure-time purposes which, nowadays, most people regard as fundamental.

At the outset it must be appreciated that at common law no general doctrine emerged under which the public were permitted to disport themselves on undeveloped or uncultivated land. In principle such an activity done without the consent of the owner of the soil was, and is, a trespass. Thus in *Attorney-General* v. *Antrobus*[2] Farwell J. declared that the *jus spatiandi vel manendi* (the right to stray and remain) was unknown to our law, a reference to the lack of any right corresponding to that given by Roman Law to people generally to wander about an open space and remain on it for any purpose they thought proper. Such a right may however be acquired as a private right by individuals. In *Re Ellenborough Park*[3] Lord Evershed M.R. said: "A *jus spatiandi* cannot be acquired by public user as an easement. . . . It does not necessarily follow from this, however, that no such *jus* could be acquired by individuals by prescription, and still less does it follow . . . that no such *jus* could be created in favour of an individual . . . by a grant."

The rigour of the common law rule excluding a public right of recreation has been mitigated by three factors which will be mentioned briefly below and discussed more fully in the sections which follow.

First, if the inhabitants of an area had by immemorial custom enjoyed recreation upon a piece of land such a custom would be recognised by the common law, for, as it was expressed in *Abbott* v. *Weekly*,[4] it was "necessary for the inhabitants to have their recreations." Consequently in that case a claim by the owner that entry by the inhabitants would constitute a trespass "et spoil son grass" failed. This species of local right, however, was never extended to the public as a whole. This will be discussed further in the section on town and village greens.

Secondly, in equity land may be held on trust to permit the public to have access to it. This will be dealt with in the section on the dedication of land for public recreation.

Thirdly, the most significant erosion of the common law doctrine has occurred by way of a variety of statutory interventions under a number of Acts of Parliament. There has been some cross-fertilisation of the second and third heads in that where statute has intervened the courts have sometimes treated the owner of the land as a trustee for the public: this will appear particularly in the section dealing with pleasure grounds provided by local authorities.

In the sections which follow an attempt is made to define the rights which have been developed in various ways over various kinds of open areas. In some cases it will be seen that the precise nature of the rights concerned has not been elucidated by the courts; and in other cases it will emerge that—as has already been indicated above—rights which are strictly in favour of a limited class are in fact enjoyed by the public without hindrance. The historical development of the rights is indicated in outline in most cases, and the treatment of common land in particular is historical since this is the only way in which the matter can be understood properly. Where appropriate a brief assessment of the present efficacy of particular rights is made. The last section deals with the seashore, where it will be seen that there is a large measure of *de facto* public enjoyment without any true right at all save in exceptional circumstances.

II—*Public Access to Common Land*

It is frequently thought that common land is not privately owned, being either publicly owned or not subject of ownership, so that in either case the public may venture on it as of right. In fact, however, common land is privately owned (though the owner might, because of the low economic worth of most of such land, be elusive, at least until registration of commons was provided for in 1965), and the public only have a right of access to certain areas under statutory provisions discussed below.

The word "common" refers to the rights enjoyed by certain holders of land to enter other land to exercise *profits à prendre* attached to their land, *e.g.* to cut turves, to cut wood, or to depasture beasts. Where a number of such landholders are entitled to go on to the same piece of land for this purpose they are said to be commoners, and the land on which they exercise their rights is common land. The origin of these essentially agricultural rights is of great antiquity. They were well established under the manorial system not long after the Conquest, and appear to have been preceded in Saxon times by a system of village communal ownership under which all members of the community could turn their animals out on uncultivated land and cut turf and bracken there.[5] When the feudal system was introduced under the Normans the ownership of entire village units, or manors, was vested in individual lords, the lords of manors, and lesser landowners holding of them continued the ancient practices on the waste grounds, now known as the manorial wastes, in virtue of their holdings rather than of communal ownership.[6] Though these wastes became known as common lands it should be observed that not all wastes were in fact subject to common rights.

Erosion of the area of common land by inclosure for more efficient land utilisation began at an early stage and continued at varying rates well into the nineteenth century. At first the lord of the manor allowed his tenants to inclose (or "approve") part of the manorial waste (as well as parts of the common fields and pastures of the manor) by licence or charter. This was regulated by the Statute of Merton 1236 under which lords of manors could approve commons so long as they left for the commoners "as much pasture as sufficeth for their tenements." This process reduced the area available not only for exercising the common rights, but also for recreational purposes, and whilst no doubt the amount of recreational use was in early times minimal, the utility of common land in this respect was at least recognised in areas near towns by the Tudor period, for an Elizabethan statute of 1593,[7] after reciting that "divers Commons, Waste Grounds, and Great Fields near adjoining to the Cities [of London and Westminster] which have heretofore been used . . . for Recreation, Comfort and Health of the people inhabiting in the said Cities . . . have of late been enclosed . . ." went on to prohibit inclosures of any part of the commons or waste grounds situate within three miles of the City of London. The fact that no right of access was given perhaps indicates that landowners tolerated technical trespassers on the wastes so long as they remained uninclosed.

Approvements under the 1236 statute were superseded by private and local inclosure Acts, largely in the period 1700 to 1844. There were over 4,700 of these Acts, of which 1385 related to waste alone.[8] There is evidence that in this era the cause of recreation was acknowledged by the Parliamentary Committees whose awards defined the areas to be inclosed and fixed compensation for loss of rights of common over the wastes. The Committees could set aside land for the recreation of the inhabitants of an area, known as recreation allotments, though this was not done in any generous measure.

Dissatisfaction with both the procedure under the private Inclosure Acts (there was no public inquiry into the rights and *de facto* enjoyments affected) and their effects (particularly the inadequacy of compensation for the extinguishment of common grazing rights on wastes and on open fields and pastures, and the injurious effects upon small holdings which depended on the common grazing) led to the passing of the Inclosure Act 1845. This provided a uniform procedure, including local inquiries by Inclosure Commissioners, in place of consideration by remote Parliamentary committees. The Commissioners embodied their recommendations in provisional orders which were effective upon the passing of confirmatory Acts of Parliament (s. 32). In practice these Acts were passed annually with very little discussion in Parliament. The Commissioners were given power to require, as a condition of inclosure, "the appropriation of an allotment for the purposes of exercise and recreation for the inhabitants of the neighbourhood" (s. 30), and indeed in their annual report to Parliament were required to state the grounds for not exercising this power in cases where no such appropriation was made. The Commissioners however did not make extensive use of this power, for in the years 1845 to 1869, when 614,800 acres of land were enclosed, only 1,742 were the subject of recreation allotments.[9] However, during the years which followed the passing of the

Act, a number of factors contributed to the promotion of the recreational cause, and, from the late 1860s, to the diminution of inclosures. First, certain provisions relating to inclosures in the 1845 Act and subsequent Inclosure Acts and Common Acts led to a check on inclosures, despite the fact that the "Inclosure Commission proceeded on the principle that its main function was to facilitate inclosures, whether public interests were involved or not."[10] The 1845 Act (s. 12) prohibited the inclosure of wastes of manors subject to rights of common without the previous authority of Parliament being obtained, and this was extended to the inclosure of "any lands" by the Inclosure Act 1852 (s. 1). Again, the 1845 Act prohibited all inclosures within fifteen miles of London and within a distance of between two and three-and-a-half miles of large towns, depending on population, without the previous authority of Parliament (s. 14). More importantly, the Commons Act 1876 declared in its preamble that under the 1845 Act the Commissioners must certify to Parliament that a provisional inclosure order "would be expedient, having regard to the benefit of the neighbourhood as well as to . . . private interests." This resulted in more attention being paid in practice to the spirit of this requirement of the 1845 Act (s. 27), which was repealed by the 1876 Act (s. 34) and effectively replaced with a provision that specifically required the Commissioners to consider whether orders would be "for the benefit of the neighbourhood" and to insert terms and conditions with a view to such benefit, including "that free access is to be secured to any particular points of view . . . that there is to be reserved, where a recreation ground is not set out, a privilege of playing games or of enjoying other species of recreation . . . and that carriage roads, bridle paths, and footpaths over such common are to be set out in such directions as may appear most commodious" (s. 7).

Secondly, there emerged organised opposition to inclosures, in particular by the Commons, Open Spaces and Footpaths Preservation Society (founded in 1865), arising from increased public awareness of the recreational value of common lands, though the economic value of the common rights themselves had very much declined. The Society supported a number of actions by commoners to remedy unlawful enclosures (the most notable being *Glasse* v. *Commissioners of Sewers*[11] in consequence of which large tracts of Epping Forest which had been enclosed without authority were disgorged) and its members promoted or actively supported some of the legislation passed in the second half of the nineteenth century to preserve commons for public use.

Thirdly, there developed the concept of regulation of commons, involving statutory schemes of regulation technically for the benefit of the inhabitants of the districts concerned, but which in fact benefited the public at large. These schemes began in London with the Metropolitan Commons Act 1866 which applied to commons in the Metropolitan Police District; the Act was amended by the Metropolitan Commons Acts 1869, 1878 and 1898. The schemes provided for the management of metropolitan commons to be taken out of the hands of lords of manors (without divesting them of their beneficial interests) and vested in local authorities. Schemes were prepared by the Inclosure Commissioners on the application of lords of manors, commoners or the local authority concerned (ss. 6 *et seq.*, Act of 1866). A scheme was inoperative until confirmed by Parliament (s. 22). Although the schemes made a slow start,[12] many areas of common land have been preserved for the benefit of Londoners under these acts.[13] Inclosure of metropolitan commons is prohibited (s. 5). Similar regulation schemes were introduced into the rest of the country by the Commons Act 1876 (Part I) by means of provisional orders, drafted by the Inclosure Commissioners and subject to Parliamentary confirmation. The Act specifically required the Commissioners to consider whether orders would be "for the benefit of the neighbourhood," and to insert terms and conditions with a view to such benefit. The Commons Act 1899, whilst leaving available the procedure under the 1876 Act, provided a shorter means of securing regulation which dispensed with the rather cumbrous procedure of provisional order and its requirement of recourse to Parliament for confirmation: instead, the urban and rural district councils which had by then been created[14] were enabled to make schemes "for the regulation and management of any common within their district" which could include any of the statutory provisions for the benefit of the neighbourhood under the 1876 Act, and provide for expenditure on improvement and for "the making of byelaws and regulations for the prevention of nuisances and the preservation of order on the common" (s. 1, Act of 1899). The schemes were confirmed by the Board of Agriculture (who had succeeded to the functions of the Inclosure Commissioners), and because of the lack of Parliamentary procedure were more widely made use of than was the Act of 1876. The standard form of scheme of regulation under the 1899 Act provides a definite right of access:

> "Clause 5. Public right of access and recreation. The inhabitants of the district and neighbourhood shall have a right of free access to every part of the commons and a privilege of playing games and of enjoying other species of recreation thereon subject to bye-laws made by the council under this scheme."

The result of these three factors was a considerable drop in the number of applications for inclosures under the 1845 Act (which is still in force). According to the Report of the Royal Commission on Common Land (1955–58)[15] there have only been twenty-nine applications since 1876, the last being in 1914.

The principal modern statute affecting public access to common land is the Law of Property Act 1925. Under section 193 members of the public "have rights of access for air and exercise to any land which is a metropolitan common . . . or manorial waste, or a common, which is wholly or partly situated within a borough or urban district and to any land which at [January 1, 1926 was] subject to rights of common. . . ." The lacuna in this provision in respect of commons wholly situate in rural districts was noted by the Royal Commission on Common Land which recommended "that all common land should be open to the public as of right" subject to the safeguard that persons committing certain injurious acts should be liable in trespass to the owners of the soil,[16] and added "anything less than this would not prove satisfactory," because of the detailed investigations necessary into the circumstances of individual proposals. This recommendation has not been implemented. However, section 193 (2) of the Law of Property Act 1925 enables lords of manors or any persons entitled to the soil of any land subject to rights of common to declare by deed that the section shall apply to the land, and provides that the section shall apply to such land when the deed is deposited with the Minister of Agriculture, Fisheries and Food; in this way rural commons can be made subject to a right of public access. In fact only 127 such deeds had been deposited by 1955, involving 12,000 acres, as against a total acreage of common land reported by local authorities in England and Wales of 1,505,002. It is arguable that a public right of access to rural commons is impliedly given by section 194, which applies to any land subject in 1926 to rights of common and declares that the erection of any building or fence, or the construction of any other work, whereby access to such land is prevented or impeded is unlawful, unless the Minister consents to it (he must take into account the same considerations as are required by the Commons Act 1876 on applications for inclosure and regulation, including the "benefit of the neighbourhood" requirements).[17] However, despite the incorporation of the "benefit of the neighbourhood" requirements, it seems fairly clear that the "access" protected is that of the commoners, not the public.[18] No implied public right appears to have been asserted in the courts, nor was it canvassed by the Ministry of Agriculture in giving evidence to the Royal Commission. It therefore appears that the greater part of the unregulated rural common lands of England and Wales was not opened to the public under the 1925 Act, and although the effect of this has no doubt been ameliorated by landowners *de facto* tolerating the public on their land, and by the inclusion of many commons in National Parks (though this does not of itself give automatic rights of access) the legal position remains the same and will so remain until the Royal Commission's recommendation is implemented.

It may also be mentioned that from time to time a public right of access to commons is given under private Acts.

A necessary concomitant of the right of access, where it exists, is that members of the public should be able to ascertain its existence and the extent of the land to which it attaches. In the case of common land this remained difficult after 1925, since under section 193 the public right depends on the existence in 1926—and the continued existence—of rights of common. The Commons Registration Act 1965 (s. 1) makes the task easier by providing for the registration of rights of common with county and county borough councils and the Greater London Council by a date ultimately set at July 31, 1970.[19] Further, although registrable rights of common not registered by the above date cease to be exercisable (s. 1 (2)), the public right of access to urban commons (which normally ceases on the extinguishment of the common rights) is preserved (s. 21).[20]

The present position in regard to public access to common land may be summarised by saying that the public may have a right of access:

(i) on urban commons, where common rights existed in 1926 and continue to subsist;
(ii) on rural commons, where a deed of declaration has been deposited
by the owner with the Ministry of Agriculture;
(iii) on commons subject to the Metropolitan Commons Acts or regulated under the Commons Acts 1876 and 1899;
(iv) on land subject to recreation allotments made under private inclosure
Acts or under inclosures under the Inclosure Act 1845;
(v) under local and private Acts.

Under (iii) and (iv) the right may not be strictly public, being confined to
the inhabitants of the area.

III—Town and Village Greens

These form a limited exception to the general lack of a public *jus spatiandi*
at common law, because the right of the inhabitants of a town or parish to go
on such greens was recognised where they had by immemorial custom used
them for exercise and recreation (*Edwards* v. *Jenkins*[21]). Indeed the recognition of such a right is not confined to greens and can attach to any piece
of land (*Abbot* v. *Weekly*[22]). Greens were frequently fragments of manorial
waste and subject to rights of common, and the recognition of the right of
recreation could conceivably have been extended under the above principles
to entire commons. Possibly the reason why it was not so extended was the
close association of recreation with the playing of games in a relatively
small area in the cases dealing with greens; large tracts of manorial waste
would be neither required nor suitable for this purpose. However, in one
unreported case at Bristol assizes in 1892 a claim by inhabitants to recreation over an area of common amounting to 64 acres—much larger than the
ordinary village green—was upheld on evidence that games had been played
over the whole of it.[23]

It should be noted that the right was accorded to the inhabitants rather
than to the public at large (as in the case of the statutory provisions relating
to regulated commons). This is well illustrated in *Fitch* v. *Rawling*[24] in
which it was held that the inhabitants of a parish may have a customary
right to play cricket on a piece of land, but a similar custom in favour of all
mankind is bad. Similarly in *Coventry* v. *Willes*[25] it was held that there
could be no custom for the public to enter land owned by the trustees of
Newmarket Heath to watch the races, though it was intimated that if the
defendant could have claimed as an inhabitant of Newmarket, he might
have been able to establish such a custom. However, there is (as in the case
of regulated commons) no practical limitation upon use by non-inhabitants.

Various statutory provisions have preserved the recreational amenities
provided by greens. The Inclosure Act 1845 prohibited the inclosure of
town and village greens, and it enabled the Inclosure Commissioners, on
an inclosure of land in a parish, to direct the allotment of such greens "to
the churchwardens and overseers of the poor of such parish, in trust to

allow the same to be used for the purposes of recreation" (s. 15). The effect of such allotments (which are separate from the recreation allotments discussed earlier) was to extinguish any rights of common over the green whilst preserving the recreational rights.[26] Land so vested in the churchwardens and overseers was later vested in parish councils in rural districts and the rating authority in urban districts and boroughs.[27]

Village greens may be included in regulation schemes under the Commons Act 1899 (s. 15), but not in schemes under the Metropolitan Commons Act 1866 unless they are in fact subject of rights of common (s. 4).

The Commons Registration Act 1965 provides for the registration of town and village greens (s. 1(1)(a)) and declares (s. 1(2)(a)) that no land capable of being so registered shall be deemed to be a green unless registered within the proper time limit (by July 31, 1970). Where no owner is registered the Act provides for the local authority to be registered as owner (s. 8).

The present position is therefore that greens are protected from inclosure and are preserved for public recreation by being vested either in the local authority upon trust for that purpose or in a private owner subject to the customary rights. The provisions for definitive registration make the ascertainment of the public right straightforward, though it is to be regretted that under the 1965 Act the public right was apparently lost in those cases where greens were not registered.

IV—National Trust Land

The National Trust was incorporated in 1894 under the Companies Acts as a non-profit making body to promote "the permanent preservation for the benefit of the nation of lands and tenements (including buildings) of beauty or historic interest and as regards lands for the preservation of their natural aspect features and animal and plant life."[28] By 1907 it had acquired some hundreds of acres of land over the country (listed in Schedule 1 to the Act of 1907), and admitted the public to the enjoyment of such land (as well as its buildings). In order to ensure the continuation of its work of obtaining similar property, "and for the permanent holding and maintenance thereof,"[28] and "for promoting the permanent preservation of buildings places or property having historic associations or . . . natural beauty," the Trust was in that year dissolved and reincorporated by the National Trust Act (s. 3). The Act declares the purposes of the Trust to be as above (s. 4 (1)), and these are specifically extended by the National Trust Act 1937 (s. 3) to include "the promotion of the access to and enjoyment of such . . . places . . . by the public." To execute these purposes the Trust has the following powers:

(a) Most importantly, it may acquire lands and buildings by purchase, gift or otherwise (s. 4 (2), Act of 1907).

In order to preserve its land (and buildings) permanently for the public, the Trust holds inalienably lands which the council of the Trust resolve are proper to be held for the benefit of the nation, as well as most of the property it owned in 1907, which the Act specifically declares shall be held for preservation for the benefit of the nation (s. 21). It seems therefore that its lands (when held inalienably) are held upon trust to permit public access, at least so far as they are unenclosed, and consist of open country. At any rate it is clear, where such lands are common lands, that they are held on such a trust to permit public access, the 1907 Act providing that the Trust shall at all times keep such property unenclosed and unbuilt on as open spaces for the recreation and enjoyment of the public (s. 29 (A)). Further, the Trust is a charitable body (see the National Trust Charity Scheme Confirmation Act 1919). Where, therefore, land consisting of open countryside is acquired by the Trust it would appear to be held on a charitable trust to permit public access (see below: Dedication of Land for Public Recreation). It may be noted that the 1907 Act was in fact the first statutory provision to secure access not limited by inhabitancy. The public right is, however, subject to extensive powers of management. For example, reasonable charges for admission may be made (s. 30), though this may not be done on common land or on any other property of the Trust to which the public had a right of access when the Trust acquired it, except for land set aside for games or sports meetings (s. 30 (2)). Again, the Trust may make by-laws to regulate activities on its land, where held inalienably for the benefit of the nation, and these may include the exclusion of offenders from its lands (s. 32). In addition the scheme under the 1919 Act empowers the Trust to grant leases of properties held inalienably, subject to the sanction of the Charity Commissioners on their being satisfied that they may properly be granted "with due regard to the purposes of the Trust"; such leases (*e.g.* to farmers) will clearly be effectual to exclude the public.

The purchasing powers of the Trust have been extensively used, the Trust being empowered to raise money by mortgage of its property (except that held inalienably) (s. 22, Act of 1907), by subscriptions from members of the public who become subscribing members, and otherwise. Likewise the power to accept gifts has been taken advantage of by testators attracted by an estate duty exemption first given in 1931 in respect of land devised and bequeathed to the Trust (s. 40, Finance Act 1931), and later extended to land so bequeathed subject to a life interest (s. 31, Finance Act 1937) and maintenance funds (s. 31, Finance Act 1949); these provisions have now been replaced by a complete exemption for all property given to the Trust (s. 121 and Sched. 25, Finance Act 1972).

A notable example of extensive acquisition by the Trust is Enterprise Neptune, launched in the 1960s, under which the Trust's holdings of cliff-land (and consequently public access thereto) have been extended by many miles of coastline.

(b) The Trust may maintain and manage "lands as open spaces or places of public resort . . . and may accept property in trust for any public purposes and may act in any trusts for or as trustee of any property devoted to public purposes" (s. 4 (2), Act of 1907). This provision enables it to manage lands which are not actually in its ownership for the benefit of the public.

(c) The Trust may make arrangements with local authorities and others for giving effect to the objects of the 1907 Act (s. 31). Under such arrangements local authorities may carry out maintenance of National Trust land within their areas.

V—National Parks

These are established under the National Parks and Access to the Countryside Act 1949 (s. 5) by means of designation orders made by the National Parks Commission (renamed the Countryside Commission by the Countryside Act 1968 (s. 1) and confirmed by the Minister of Town and Country Planning (now the Secretary of State for the Environment[29]). The purposes of these orders and the relevant provisions of Part II of the 1949 Act are the preservation and enhancement of the natural beauty of these areas and the promotion of their enjoyment by the public (s. 5 (1)). The areas concerned are "extensive tracts of country" selected for their natural beauty and "the opportunities they offer for open-air recreation, having regard both to their character and to their position in relation to centres of population" (s. 5 (2)).

Local authorites (joint boards being set up where parks overlap planning areas) are given powers and duties in relation to the development and management of the parks (ss. 8 to 13). They may, for example, arrange for the provision of camping sites and parking places (s. 12), and the improvement of waterways (s. 13). A number of these parks have been provided, notable examples being those in the Lake District, Peak District, Exmoor and Dartmoor.

Though the purposes of the parks include the promotion of enjoyment by the public, rights of access are not automatically given by the establishment of a National Park. The parks typically include not only open country but also enclosed agricultural land and villages and it would be impracticable to allow unrestricted access throughout the areas concerned. This emerges clearly in the speech of the Minister of Town and Country Planning on the second reading of the Bill[30]:

> "The national park is defined in the Bill, both implicitly and explicitly as an extensive area of outstanding beauty, suitable for open air recreation by the general public, but where the normal life of the existing community goes on . . . the ordinary rural life, such as farming, rural industry and afforestation, should continue to function. This is a small country, and we cannot afford, as can the United States, to set aside large areas solely for the purpose of public recreation or establishing a museum."

Nevertheless the Secretary of State for the Environment does have a general power to acquire land in a National Park, by agreement, for the purposes of the Act (s. 14),[31] including of course public enjoyment, and a specific power to acquire open country in a National Park, either by agreement or compulsorily, where "it is requisite that the public should have access thereto for open-air recreation" and "it is expedient that such access should be secured by the acquisition of the land by him" (s. 77). Land acquired under either power is to be transferred to other persons on trusts or conditions designed to secure the management of the land in a manner suitable for accomplishing the Act's purposes (ss. 14 (2), 77 (3)).

More importantly in practice, local planning authorities can secure a public right of access by means of access agreements and orders or by acquisition for the purpose. This is discussed in detail later. Again, the National Trust owns considerable tracts in some parks (for example the Lake District) and the public do enjoy a legal right of access in these areas on the principles above discussed.

The National Parks have proved to be among the most popular areas for recreational activity, containing some of the most attractive open country-side in England and Wales. In practice the lack of a formal right of access has not impeded public use of the open areas to any significant extent. However the conflict of interest between recreational and more utilitarian uses of land, coupled with the increasing threat which the growing pressure of the numbers using the more popular parks poses to the maintenance of their character, has given increasing cause for concern in recent years to those who wish to preserve the quiet and beauty of these areas.

VI—Provision by Local Authorities

It has been seen that local authorities have functions in relation to all the means of access already discussed. They are also instrumental in securing rights of access in a number of other ways. The more important types of area are as follows:

(a) Parks (*public walks and pleasure grounds*)

These are provided under public health legislation. Section 164 of the Public Health Act 1875 enables district and borough councils to acquire, improve and maintain land for use as public walks and pleasure grounds, and to support or contribute to the support of such walks and grounds provided by others.[32] Acquisition may be compulsory (s. 159, Local Government Act 1933).

Public access is subject to regulation by by-laws which may provide for the removal of offenders (s. 164, Act of 1875), and which normally provide for closure at night. These by-laws must be confirmed by the Secretary of State (s. 250, Act of 1933). The authority has power to close pleasure grounds to the public for up to twelve days in a year for the exclusive use of charities, agricultural shows and other public purposes and admission charges may be made when they are so closed (s. 44, Public Health Acts Amendment Act 1890). Further, parts may be set aside for particular pur-poses and exclusive use of them given (*e.g.* for sports) (s .76, Public Health Acts Amendment Act 1907).

With regard to the public right of access it seems clearly established that such a right exists, subject to the powers of regulation and of giving ex-clusive use for limited periods mentioned above. Local authorities hold the grounds as "merely custodians and trustees for the public . . . they must allow the public free and unrestricted use of it": *per* Lord Halsbury L.C. in *Lambeth Overseers* v. *L.C.C.*[33] In *Blake* v. *Hendon Corporation*[34] it was held that where land had been acquired under and was found being used by the public for the purposes set out in section 164, without such an exclusion of the public as went beyond what was ancillary to those purposes, the inference was that the beneficial ownership of the land had passed to the public. Again, in *Hall* v. *Beckenham Corporation*[35] Finnemore J. held that a park under the Act was dedicated to the public use, and that although the authority had the management and control of the park, their power to regulate the conduct of members of the public using the park was limited to the enforcement of the by-laws: "If they go beyond those [by-law-making] powers, it seems to me plain that their officer, and, therefore, the corporation themselves, would be liable to an action for assault and false imprisonment should they lay hands on someone and forcibly put him outside the park." If a public park were shut to all, no doubt a relator action for a declaration or injunction would lie at the instigation of the Attorney-General as the protector of public rights.[36]

(b) *Open spaces and disused burial grounds*

Certain lands can be transferred to local authorities (including parish councils) under the Open Spaces Act 1906 to be maintained as open spaces, defined as any land, inclosed or not, on which there are no buildings (or of which not more than one twentieth is covered by buildings) which is laid out as a garden or used for recreation and lies waste and unoccupied (s. 20). Such open spaces, and also disused burial grounds, which can be transferred to local authorities, are held upon a statutory "trust to allow . . . the enjoyment thereof by the public under proper regulation," with power to inclose it with railings and gates and to improve it generally (s. 10). The headstones can (subject to safeguards) be removed in disused burial grounds (s. 11).

The open spaces which can be transferred to local authorities to be held as above include the following:

(i) those vested in trustees under private or local Acts for preservation as a garden or open space (s. 2);
(ii) those vested in non-statutory trustees for public recreation (s. 3);
(iii) those vested in charity trustees which are no longer required for the purposes of their trust or which may with advantage to the trust be dealt with by conveying them to the local authority as open spaces (s. 4);
(iv) those owned subject to rights of user for exercise and recreation of the owners or occupiers of any houses round or near them (s. 5). This enables developers of residential estates which are laid out with open spaces to transfer them to the local authority for permanent maintenance; it also facilitates the transfer of open spaces enjoyed by the residents of a mature development to do so. In each case the authority holds the land on trust for the public to enjoy it.

In addition to the above specific powers, local authorities have a general power to acquire open spaces by purchase or gift (for example privately owned ones not subject to any rights of recreation) to be held on the statutory trusts. By-laws regulating the days and times of admission and the preservation of order may be made, subject to Ministerial confirmation (s. 15), as in the case of land acquired under the Public Health Act 1875, discussed above.

(c) *Open country subject to access agreements or orders or acquired for public access*

"Open country" consists, for the purposes of the National Parks and Access to the Countryside Act 1949, "wholly or predominantly of moun-tain, moor, heath, downs, cliff or foreshore" (s. 59). Local planning authori-ties (county and county borough councils) may make access agreements with landowners (s. 64), subject to the consent of the Secretary of State for the Environment, and, where it is impracticable to secure agreement, make access orders, subject to the confirmation of the Secretary of State.[37]

The public acquires a right of access under an agreement or order in that "a person who enters upon [the land] for the purpose of open air recreation without breaking or damaging any wall, fence, hedge or gate . . . shall not be treated as a trespasser on that land or incur any other liability by reason only of so entering . . ." (s. 60). The landowner must not carry out any work on the land whereby the area available to the public for access is substantially reduced (s. 66). The public right of access does not however extend to "excepted land" (s. 60 (5)), which includes in particular certain agricultural land (other than rough grazing land),[38] nature reserves estab-lished by agreement or acquisition by the Natural Environmental Research Council (formerly the Nature Conservancy), and land covered by buildings or used as a park or garden. Further, commercial or amenity woodlands may be excluded from the area concerned if access would prejudice the commercial use or amenity value of it (s. 79), though not if the benefit conferred on the public by access facilities would outweigh the prejudicial effect (s. 19, Countryside Act 1968).

Access agreements and orders may include provision for the construction and improvement of means of access (s. 67, Act of 1949), and maps show-ing the areas subject to public access may be displayed on the areas con-cerned. The authority must in fact keep an up-to-date map of each area and have copies available for public inspection (s. 78).

It is noteworthy that planning authorities may enter access agreements and make orders in respect of land in National Parks (ss. 64 (5), 65 (5)), and also in areas designated by the Countryside Commission as being of outstanding natural beauty (s. 88). In these cases the Secretary of State must consult with the Commission before giving his agreement or con-firmation. The Commission may indeed take the initiative and request the authority to make an access order in either of these types of areas.

In addition to the powers just discussed, planning authorities have a general power, as regards any open country in their area, to acquire land compulsorily where it appears to them that it is requisite that the public should have access to it for open-air recreation, and that it is expedient that access should be secured by acquisition (s. 76). (This power corresponds to that already observed of the Secretary of State to acquire land in national parks for public access.) The planning authority must so manage land thus acquired as to give the public access for open-air recreation to as much of the land as appears practicable (s. 76 (4)).

Common land may be subject to an access order or agreement,[39] and this is therefore a means of securing rights of public access to commons lying wholly in a rural area (see the discussion on section 193 of the Law of Property Act 1925, above).

Considerable use has been made of these powers by planning authorities in national parks and areas of outstanding natural beauty. By September 30, 1968[40] 61,347 acres had been either acquired for access or made subject of access agreements in these areas, involving twenty-three acquisitions and thirty-four agreements.[41] In the following three years[42] 14,401 acres were added, and this period shows a trend towards acquisition (fourteen cases) rather than access agreements (six cases). (There seems to be no disposition to make access orders.) It has been the clear policy of the Countryside Commission and its predecessor, the National Parks Commission, to encourage planning authorities to make use of their powers.

Outside the national parks and areas of outstanding natural beauty, however, the activity of planning authorities has apparently been relatively slight. The Ministry of Housing and Local Government reported to the Royal Commission on Common Land (1955–58) that, when county councils were required, following the passing of the 1949 Act, to carry out surveys of open country in their areas to ascertain the extent of the need for securing access by the public for open-air recreation (s. 61, Act of 1949), ten authorities had stated that they had no appreciable area of open country, and no less than forty had indicated that no action was necessary under the Act to secure public access to open country in their area.[43] And by September 1972 the County of Devon, for example, still had no areas subject to access orders or agreements outside the national parks in its area.

(d) *Country parks*

These were introduced by the Countryside Act 1968.

> "The idea of a country park," explained the Minister of State, Ministry of Housing and Local Government, when moving the second reading of the Bill,[44] "is that of a piece of countryside to be kept as a piece of real countryside where the public, townsmen mostly but not exclusively, can go for quiet enjoyment and recreation. There may be some facilities there for organised games, but this is not the primary purpose. The primary purpose is to let people enjoy the ordinary country pursuits of walking, riding, swimming, sailing, rowing, fishing and so on. Many such parks already exist, provided mostly and very well by the National Trust, in some cases by local authorities, and in others on a commercial basis by 'with-it' dukes and marquises. But they are not nearly enough."

The Act gave certain local authorities powers "for the purpose of providing or improving opportunities for the enjoyment of the countryside by the public" (s. 6). The principal power is to provide country parks, defined as parks or pleasure grounds to be used for the above purpose (s. 7), on land belonging either to the authority (which may acquire land compulsorily for the purpose) (s. 7 (4)), or to others on terms agreed with the owners. Powers of management conferred include the power to provide facilities for outdoor recreation (s. 7 (2) (c)), and powers to provide sailing, boating, bathing and fishing facilities where the park includes any waterway (s. 8). The authorities concerned are given similar powers of management of common land to which the public have rights of access (s. 9), and the Act in fact provides a procedure for taking such land out of the common land by acquiring it (compulsorily if necessary) and any commonable or other rights over it (s. 9 and Sched. 2).

The nature of the actual rights conferred on the public under these provisions is somewhat obscure. There is no clear right of access such as is given in respect of access agreements by negativing liability for trespass. It may be that land held by local authorities for the purposes of the Act is held on trust for the public as in the case of pleasure grounds; however the primary purpose of the 1968 Act in connection with country parks is to provide *opportunities* for public enjoyment, and it may be argued that this falls short of the position under the Public Health Acts, where once land has been acquired and appropriated for use as a public park, the public can only be excluded by the proper exercise of powers of regulation under by-laws. The obscurity is not removed by a provision made in relation to common land taken by acquisition (though not in relation to other country parks) that it shall be held "free from the public right of access, but shall be used for the benefit of the public resorting to the common land" (Sched. 2). This would seemingly enable an authority to deprive the public of access so that the duty to manage the land for the benefit of the public resorting to it would be nugatory. Whilst no doubt no responsible authority would contemplate acting in this manner there seems to be little point in providing a statutory basis for it to do so. It is submitted that it would have been much better if any former rights of access were preserved and merely restricted so far as necessary to enable proper management under the general powers in the Act. It would also seem better if a public right of access similar to that given over "access land" were accorded to the public in open country in country parks generally (at least where owned by the local authority), subject only to restrictions consistent with their management as country parks.

Although the Act has only been in force for a few years, a considerable number of these parks have been provided in a variety of types of countryside, including cliffland at the Seven Sisters in Sussex and Berry Head in Devon, and part of Sherwood Forest in Nottinghamshire. By September 30, 1971 a total of forty-five had been provided by local authorities (including eight existing parks recognised by the Countryside Commission as country parks) on land in their ownership, and a further nine on land owned by others.[45] The acreages of the parks vary widely, from eighteen to 3,784 at the above date. Publicity is given to the parks, *e.g.* by road signs, and they are well attended by the public.

VII—Dedication of Land for Public Recreation: Charitable Trusts of Recreational Land

In *Re Hadden, Public Trustee* v. *More*,[46] Clauson J. held that such a dedication of land is dedication to a charitable use[47]; and in *I.R.C.* v. *Baddeley*[48] Viscount Simonds said[49] in the House of Lords: ". . . in my opinion, a gift of land for use as a recreation ground by the community at large or by the inhabitants of a particular geographical area might well be supported as a valid charity." Land so dedicated is accordingly held upon a charitable trust, which may be perpetual. It must be observed by way of qualification, however, that if the purpose is specifically for sport, it will not amount to a charitable one (*Re Nottage*[50]), and if the property may be used for what has been described as "social" purposes (*i.e.* the provision of whist drives and like entertainments) the trust will not be exclusively charitable and will fail (see *I.R.C.* v. *Baddeley*; *Williams' Trustees* v. *I.R.C.*[51]), unless it is saved by the Recreational Charities Act 1958.[52]

Since a dedication is effectively the declaration of a trust it seems that a dedication must fulfil the conditions specified by section 53 of the Law of Property Act 1925 for declarations of trusts of land, namely it "must be manifested and proved by some writing signed by some person who is able to declare such trust or by his will." In *Hadden's* case the dedication was made by will by means of a direction to expend the residue of the testator's estate upon (*inter alia*) "playing fields, parks, gymnasiums or other plans which will give recreation to as many people as possible"; so that it is clear that a gift of land *in specie* is not essential and land bought with the donor's money will be subject to the charitable trusts.

The idea of a trust could have provided a basis for upholding the recreational practices of inhabitants, and perhaps the public as a whole, by application of the doctrine exemplified in *Goodman* v. *Saltash Corporation*.[53] In that case the inhabitants of Saltash were accustomed to take oysters from the bed of the River Tamar, and the court succeeded in finding a lawful origin for this by presuming that it was done lawfully under a trust in favour of the inhabitants. However, the courts were not prepared to take so benevolent a view in the case of mere recreational practices, as appears from the judgment of Farwell J. in *Attorney-General* v. *Antrobus*[54] in dealing with an alleged *jus spatiandi* claimed on this basis in favour of the public in respect of Stonehenge:

". . . the gist of the principle on which such presumptions are made is that the state of affairs is unexplained without such presumption. But the liberality with which landowners in this country have for years past allowed visitors free access to objects of interest on their property is amply sufficient to explain the access which has undoubtedly been allowed for many years to visitors to Stonehenge. . . . It would indeed be unfortunate if the courts were to presume novel and unheard-of trusts or statutes from acts of kindly courtesy, and thus drive landowners to close their gates in order to preserve their property."

It has already been seen that under the Open Spaces Act 1906, open spaces held by charity trustees may be transferred to local authorities, and a number of public parks and gardens now held and maintained by such authorities have been acquired in this way. Further, as has been seen, the National Trust is a charitable trust.

Once land has been dedicated for public recreation its devotion to that purpose may be enforced by the Attorney-General, who has a general duty to ensure that charitable trusts are carried out. It would seem that the trustees would be liable for assault if they or their servants excluded a member of the public from the land by force on the same principles as apply to parks acquired under the Public Health Act 1875.

VIII—The Seashore

The seashore or foreshore (these terms being synonomous: see Vaughan Williams L.J. in *Mellor* v. *Walmsley*[55]) is the area lying between the high and low water marks of the ordinary (medium) tides (see *e.g.* Bayley J. in *Scratton* v. *Brown*,[56] and the same judge in *Blundell* v. *Catterall*[57]).

The foreshore is prima facie vested in the Crown (except in Cornwall, where it is prima facie vested in the Duke of Cornwall), though in particular cases grants have been made by the Crown to others, who (or whose successors) are accordingly owners. It is also possible to acquire a title as against the Crown or other owner under the Statutes of Limitation. In practice, considerable areas of foreshore are leased out, particularly to local authorities in seaside resorts.

The ordinary common law denial of a *jus spatiandi* applies to the seashore as it applies elsewhere. Accordingly there is no general public right to go on the foreshore for the purposes of bathing or other recreation. In *Blundell* v. *Catterall* the defendant used bathing machines on the plaintiff's foreshore, and in an action for trespass pleaded (*inter alia*) that a "common law right to bathe exists, from the universal practice of the whole realm, which is a proof of what the common law is, the usage of a place being a custom, but that of the whole realm being the common law." But this was rejected by Abbott C.J. who declared that the practice "differs in degree only, and not in kind or quality, from that which prevails as to some inland wastes and commons." It could be argued that in some areas there is a customary right of the inhabitants to use the foreshore for recreation, and there seems to be no reason in principle why this should not be admitted, as in the case of village greens; indeed in *Blundell* v. *Catterall* Bayley J. said[58]: "In those places in which convenience has required the right and it has continued from the time of legal memory, there will be a right of custom." But since bathing is the principal recreation and has only been popular in the last few centuries[59] it seems unlikely that many claims on this basis would succeed, as a custom must be immemorial (customary rights for non-recreational purposes, *e.g.* drying nets,[60] are frequently well established).

The general position is therefore, in theory at least, unsatisfactory, for the Crown (or other person entitled to possession) could arbitrarily exclude the public from the beaches. This is in marked contrast to Roman law under Justinian: "By natural law, then, the following are the common property of all, the air, running water, the sea, and accordingly the shores of the sea. No one therefore, is denied access to the seashore. . . ."[61] Manifestly, however, the public are not in general prevented from using the foreshore in England and Wales. This seems to be due to the following factors:

(i) Where the foreshore remains in the Crown, not having been granted away or leased out, it is not the practice to object to public use for recreation. It is in fact the policy of the Crown Estate Commissioners to allow the public to use the foreshore for recreational purposes. Indeed it would be extremely expensive to enforce exclusion over several thousand miles of coastline.

(ii) Where the foreshore is owned by, or leased to, others no objection is normally taken, either because the value of the land concerned is low, or because public use can be exploited by charging for such facilities as deck chairs and boating.

In practice then, objections by the owner are unlikely in cases of pure recreational activity by the public; they are made usually when there is some attempt to exploit the foreshore commercially, as by removing materials (a recent case, involving the removal of sea coal on a commercial scale on the Durham coast is *Beckett (Alfred F.) Ltd.* v. *Lyons*[62]); or letting chairs out to the public and so reducing the owner's or lessee's own receipts (as in *Ramsgate Corporation* v. *Debling*[63]). Moreover, despite the lack of a public right, the courts have sometimes shown themselves slow to grant injunctions to restrain trespasses on foreshore which cause no injury to the owner; this being part of their policy, in exercising the discretionary remedy of an injunction, not to grant it where the matter involved is trivial. Thus in *Llandudno U.D.C.* v. *Woods*[64] where a clergyman held orderly meetings on Crown foreshore leased to the Llandudno U.D.C., Cozens-Hardy J., holding himself bound by *Blundell* v. *Catterall*, said that he could not refuse a declaration sought by the council that the defendant was not entitled, without their consent, to hold meetings there; but he refused an injunction and made no order for costs. In the course of his judgment he said: "I consider this action wholly unnecessary . . . it is no part of the duty of the council . . . to prevent a harmless user of the shore. . . . This action is an attempt to assert rights which the Crown would never have thought of putting forward. . . ." Nevertheless it must be thought that the courts are always quite so loth to enjoin trespassers on the foreshore. In *Brighton Corporation* v. *Packham*,[65] for example, a case very similar to the Llandudno one, the lessee corporation succeeded in obtaining an injunction against two preachers (the cases are perhaps distinguishable in that in the

Brighton case meetings had been held for fifteen years—the courts are more ready to grant injunctions in respect of acts often-repeated, even if trivial; and also in that in the *Brighton* case the defendants admitted in the proceedings that if they failed on the merits the case was a proper one for an injunction. It is also clear that in the *Brighton* case the court did not regard the action, which was brought in response to complaints from occupiers of neighbouring houses, as being an improper one, as did Cozens-Hardy J. in the *Llandudno* case). Again, in *Brinkman* v. *Matley* [66] where the defendant headmaster had taken boys to bathe on the foreshore of the Isle of Thanet, Buckley J., having affirmed the principle that there was no public right to bathe, granted an injunction *de cursu* without consideration of the question of triviality, and this was upheld unanimously by the Court of Appeal (including Cozens-Hardy L.J. who did not, surprisingly, refer to his own judgment at first instance in the *Llandudno* case).

In respect of certain areas of foreshore there do appear to be rights in the public (or sometimes inhabitants of the neighbouring areas) to enter for recreational purposes. The existence of such rights cannot be regarded as well established, since because of the liberal attitude of the Crown and most grantees of foreshore there has been little need to test them in the courts. Nonetheless there seems no reason why a right should not exist to the extent indicated in each of the cases below, on principles already discussed:

(i) It seems clearly established that foreshore may be included in the grant of a manor from the cases of Duke of *Beaufort* v. *Swansea Corporation* [67] and *Re Walton-cum-Trimley (Manor), ex parte Tomline*. [68] In principle, therefore, where the foreshore is part of an area of common land, it seems that section 193 (1) of the Law of Property Act 1925 will operate in the ordinary way if any part of the common is within a borough or urban district. Proof that a particular parcel of foreshore is within the grant of a manor may, however, be a very difficult matter, as it was in the cases above mentioned. In addition, it is understood that the Crown Estate Commissioners are advised that Crown foreshore cannot form part of a common or waste of a manor and in their view, therefore, no rights can arise over it under section 193.

(ii) Where the foreshore is part of a common lying wholly within a rural district, it appears competent to the owner to secure a right of public access by means of a declaration under section 193 (2) of the Act of 1925. No such declarations have been made by the Crown in respect of Crown foreshore, in accordance with the Commissioners' above view.

(iii) The foreshore may be subject of an access agreement or order, or may be acquired by the local authority for public access, under the provisions of the National Parks and Access to the Countryside Act 1949. The definition of "open country" for the purpose of that Act specifically includes foreshore (s. 59). In practice no such agreements, orders or acquisitions have been made in respect of Crown foreshore.

(iv) Tracts of foreshore were leased to the National Trust by the Crown in some cases where the Trust acquired adjacent land under Enterprise Neptune. These will be subject to a right of public access to the same extent as other National Trust land, on principles discussed above. (The terms of these leases did not specifically require that public access be given).

(v) Foreshore may be included in a country park under the Countryside Act 1968, and in fact two areas, Lepe and Calshot Foreshores on the Solent in Hampshire, had been so included by September 30, 1971.[69] So far as any land in a country park can be said to be subject to a public right of access, foreshore would appear to be subject to it.

(vi) As already indicated above in this section, a customary right of recreation for inhabitants may be capable of being proved in some areas. Such a claim would be rendered difficult in view of the Crown's policy of allowing the whole public access (see *Coventry* v. *Willes*, above).

NOTES

1. For this, see "The Right of Passage," below.
2. [1905] 2 Ch. 188 at p. 198.
3. [1956] 1 Ch. 131 at p. 183.
4. I *Levinz* 176.
5. See Lord Eversley: *Commons, Forests and Footpaths* (1910), p. 5.
6. *Ibid.*, pp. 6–9.
7. 35 Eliz. 1, c. 6.
8. Appendix II, para. 45, Report of Royal Commission on Common Land (1955–58), Cmnd. 462.
9. Lord Eversley, *op. cit.*, p. 14. These areas have now been vested in local authorities (parish councils in rural districts, and the rating authority in urban districts and boroughs).
10. Lord Eversley, *op. cit.*, p. 16.
11. (1874) 19 Eq. 137.
12. Eversley, *op. cit.*, p. 241.
13. There were 33 metropolitan commons in 1955, of which all but two were in existence by 1909; see Table III, Appendix III, Memorandum of Evidence of Ministry of Agriculture, Fisheries and Food to the Royal Commission on Common Land (1955–58), Cmnd. 462.
14. Local Government Act 1894.
15. Appendix III, para. 43.
16. Paras. 314 and 318 of the Royal Commission's Report, Cmnd. 462.
17. It is interesting to note that in practice the Minister takes a wide view of the "neighbourhood." For example, he has consented to the erection of a television transmitter on Dartmoor as it would benefit the inhabitants of Plymouth, some miles distant. (See Minutes of Evidence of Ministry of Agriculture to the Royal Commission, para. 219, p. 76.)
18. The commoners, and not members of the public, are given a remedy in the county court (s. 194(2)). It may be urged against this, however, that the public interest is represented by the right of application to the court being extended to local authorities.
19. Commons Registration (Time Limits) (Amendment) Order 1970, S.I. 1970, No. 383, art. 2.
20. Registration of the common rights does not appear to be *conclusive* in favour of public access to urban commons, since it does not establish that the common rights existed in 1926.
21. [1896] 1 Ch. 308.
22. (1665) 1 Lev. 176.
23. Lord Eversley, *op. cit.*, pp. 286 *et seq.*
24. (1795) 2 H. Bl. 393.
25. 12 *Weekly Reporter* 127.
26. *Halsbury's Laws of England*, 3rd edn, Vol 5, p. 407.
27. ss. 5 and 6 Local Government Act 1894; and Overseers Order 1927 S.R. & O. 1927 No. 55. Lands subjects to recreation allotments made in pursu-

ance of s. 15 of the 1845 Act—known frequently as "recreation grounds"— have devolved in the same manner: see s. 73 of the 1845 Act.

28. Preamble to National Trust Act 1907.
29. Secretary of State for the Environment Order, S.I. 1970, No. 1681.
30. H.C. Deb., Vol. 463, cols. 1464 *et seq.*
31. This power has in fact only been invoked once (in 1967/68) when the Secretary of State for Wales acquired about 1300 acres in the Vaynol Estate in the Snowdonia National Park.
32. Originally rural district councils were not given these powers, which were extended to them by the Rural District Councils (Urban Powers) Order 1931, S.R. & O. 1931 No. 580. Parish councils in rural districts were given the same powers by s. 5 (1) (*d*) of the Local Government Act 1894. County councils were given the powers by s. 14 of the Open Spaces Act 1906.
33. [1897] A.C. 625.
34. [1962] 1 Q.B. 283.
35. [1949] 1 K.B. 716.
36. It seems doubtful whether such an action could be taken successfully by a private individual without joining the Attorney-General; for such an action there must either be an interference with a private right of the plaintiff as well as an interference with the public right, or there must be special damage peculiar to the plaintiff flowing from the breach of the public right.
37. Compensation must be paid for any depreciation of the interests of persons interested in the land (ss. 70 *et seq.*).
38. Agricultural land is removed from the category of excepted land under s. 17 of the Countryside Act 1968 unless a specific direction is made by the Secretary of State.
39. This is clearly impied in s. 9(6)(*b*) of the Countryside Act 1968.
40. At that time there were 10 national parks covering 5,258 square miles and 25 areas of outstanding natural beauty covering 9,549 square miles.
41. 19th Report of National Parks Commission and 1st Report of Countryside Commission, H.C. 33 (1968/69).
42. 2nd, 3rd and 4th reports of Countryside Commission, H.C. 45 (1969/70), H.C. 181 (1970/71), H.C. 38 (1971/72).
43. Minutes of Evidence, Appendix 1 to Memorandum of Evidence of Ministry of Housing and Local Government.
44. H.C. Deb., Vol. 753, col. 1418.
45. 4th Report of the Countryside Commission, H.C. 38 (1971/72).
46. [1932] 1 Ch. 133.
47. The decision was founded on s. 6 of the Mortmain and Charitable Uses Act 1888, which enacted that certain requirements of the Act in relation to charitable uses should not apply to any land dedicated to the recreation of the public: "That enactment seems to me necessarily to involve that in the view of the legislature, dedication of land to the recreation of the public is dedication to a charitable use; and in face of that enactment . . . the provision of means for public recreation is a charitable object within . . . the preamble to the Act of 43 Eliz. c. 4."
48. [1955] A.C. 572.
49. At p. 589.
50. [1895] 2 Ch. 649.
51. [1947] A.C. 447.
52. See s. 1.
53. (1882) 7 App. Cas. 633.
54. [1905] 2 Ch. at p. 199.
55. [1905] 2 Ch. 164.
56. (1825) 4 B. & C. 485 at p. 495.
57. (1821) 5 B. & A. 268 at p. 304.
58. At p. 306.
59. In *Blundell* v. *Catterall* (at p. 311) Abbott C.J. says "we know that sea bathing was, until a time comparatively modern, a matter of no frequent occurrence. . . ."
60. *Mercer* v. *Denne* [1905] 2 Ch. 538.
61. *Institutes of Justinian*, Book 2, Tit. 1, Sec. 1, 1.
62. [1967] 1 Ch. 449, C.A.

63. (1906) 22 T.L.R. 369.
64. [1899] 2 Ch. 705.
65. (1908) 72 J.P. 318; 24 T.L.R. 603.
66. [1904] 2 Ch. 313, C.A.
67. (1849) 3 Exch. 413.
68. (1873) 28 L.T. 12.
69. 4th Report of the Countryside Commission, H.C. 38 (1971/72).

9. THE RIGHT OF PASSAGE

J. S. HALL

THE right to walk and ride is of immemorial antiquity and was essential for the economic and social life of the community. With changes in the function and use of property and the advent of mechanised transport footpaths and bridleways survive as one of the "fundamental rights" and this essay examines the law relating to them.

I—Authoritative Rights of Way Maps

County councils and county borough councils have prepared "rights of way maps."[1] They show footpaths by means of a purple line; bridleways by means of a green line[2]; and byways open to all traffic of which there are very few, by means of a broken green line.[3] The scale must be not less than two-and-a-half inches to the mile[4] but in most cases six-inch maps are provided. Where the map shows a footpath the map is conclusive evidence that there was, when the map was drawn up, which will be in December 1949[5] or subsequently, a footpath as shown; where the map shows a bridleway it is conclusive evidence that the public then had thereover a right of way on foot and a right of way on horse-back or leading a horse[6]; and now on a bicycle[7] and similarly with a byway open to all traffic. Footpaths, bridleways and all ways over which the public have a right of passage are legally "highways."[8] Usually if a highway is shown on the map it will still exist. "Once a highway always a highway" is an established legal maxim.[9] A footpath or bridleway is not lost merely through disuse for however long a period it may have been overgrown and impassable. It can only be stopped up or diverted under statutory authority. Usually a public path extinguishment (or division) order is made, but before it can be confirmed and become operative notice in the prescribed form must be given and any member of the public may object to the closure and make representations to a person appointed by the Minister.[10]

Thus if a right of passage is challenged the first steps should normally be to see if the right of way is on the said maps. The public have the right to inspect them; and the maps relating to the area of the respective authority are available during office hours at the offices of the county, county borough, borough, urban and rural district councils; and often at a place in each parish.[11] If a public right of way is not on the map it may be a "county road" although having the appearance of a derelict footpath.

The theory behind the new legislation, all footpaths and bridlepaths clearly shown on maps which all may see, is excellent. Its implementation cannot be thus described and in some areas its practical application has been very disappointing. Even paths which are clearly signposted as footpaths or bridleways do not appear on the "rights of way maps."

There are three main reasons for this situation. The National Parks and Access to the Countryside Act 1949, Part IV, is the parent statute which initiated the new procedure. It imposed upon the council of every county in England or Wales the duty to carry out a survey of all land in their area over which a right of way existed or was reasonably alleged to exist with a view to preparing a draft map of their area showing such rights of way.[12] Footpath officers and other personnel were appointed, *inter alia*, to carry out this obligation. However this proved to be a formidable task. The surveying of such paths is tedious and time consuming. Some councils will frankly admit that they had not been able to complete the task or investigate all assertions by members of the public that a right of way existed in the limited time available for the preparation of the draft map. Where the right of passage is disputed by the landowner the county council is usually not itself in a position to contest the issue, but must rely on members of the public coming forward to give evidence of user. An attempt by the council to ensure that the public interest is adequately represented and safeguarded usually entails lengthy and inconclusive correspondence. From the council's angle the line of least resistance was to exclude from the maps paths which they had not had time to survey or in respect of which there was any doubt. All too often it was taken. Bridleways fared particularly badly in this respect both because farmers are more reluctant to see people crossing their land on horse-back than on foot and also because the Ordnance Survey maps, except in the most recent edition, did not differentiate between the two types of path indicating both by the letters "F.P." thus tending to give the misleading impression that bridlepaths were only footpaths.

Secondly, although after the draft map was issued it was available for public inspection for at least four months[13] and representations could be made by any member of the public concerning anything contained in or omitted from it[14] and there was a further "provisional map" stage[15] before the "definite map," which was conclusive was prepared, public ignorance, apathy and inertia were widespread.

Thirdly, the surveying authorities were under a duty to consult with the councils of county districts and parishes when preparing the draft maps[16] and, very properly, owners or other persons interested in any land to which the draft map related would know of the survey. But it provided a signal for a conscious decision. Those who might otherwise have been prepared to acquiesce in a right of user realised that, unless they wished to authenticate it, they must object to keep it off the map. In the case of a bridlepath they might only concede a footpath. Again the surveying authority, faced with a mammoth task, were reluctant to add to it by contesting objections.[17]

However although the definitive rights of way maps are conclusive as to the existence of a right of passage the converse does not apply. The maxim "once a highway always a highway" still applies, *inter alia*, to bridleways and even to the meanest footpath; but if the path is not shown on the official map it will be necessary to prove that a right of way exists.

II—The Creation of Rights of Way

Highways can be created in three main ways:

1. *By statute*

Most statutory footpaths were created by Inclosure Acts and awards, and these should be consulted if the path is disputed. Similarly highways may originate under general statutory authority. The Highways Act 1959, s. 27 empowers a local authority to make "public path creation agreements" with landowners dedicating footpaths or bridleways with or without "limitations or conditions affecting the public right of way thereover"; and by the following section (28) compulsory powers are conferred upon these authorities for this purpose.

2. *By dedication and acceptance*

Dedication means that the owner or owners have shown an intention to confer upon the public at large the right of passage over their land and the public must tangibly accept the rights conferred upon them by using the way. A declaration, however unambiguous, is ineffective unless followed by user; but no deed or other formality is necessary to create a public right of passage in perpetuity or until it is closed by statutory authority. Immemorial antiquity, or existence prior to the accession of Richard I in 1189, the commencement of legal memory, also establishes a right of way but this is theoretical as in such circumstances it will be easier to imply dedication.

First, however, as a matter of law the alleged public rights of enjoyment must be capable of constituting user as a highway.[18] A definite track is not essential. A footpath or bridleway may go along an ill-defined mountain track,[19] or cross common land; but it must go from a given point or place to a given definite destination, and if it does so the public must pass and repass from the one to the other by a reasonably direct route. This has been judicially expressed as follows[20]: "If from one terminus to another . . . persons have found their way from time immemorial across a common, although sometimes going by one track and sometimes by another, I am not prepared to say that a right of road across the common from one terminus to the other may not be validly claimed, and may not be as good as a right over any formed road." But the public at large cannot acquire through user, but only by statute, a right to wander over commons and forests.[21] As Abbott C.J. said in *Blundell* v. *Catterall*[22]: "Many of those persons who reside in the vicinity of wastes and commons, walk or ride on horseback, in all directions, over them for their health and recreation . . . yet no one ever thought that any right existed in favour of this enjoyment, or that any justification could be pleaded to an action at the suit of the owner of the soil." In *Chapman* v. *Cripps*[23] the fact that there was a wood with a path or track through it, like many others leading in different directions, and people wandered wherever they pleased in the wood did not establish the existence of a highway.

Secondly, where this is legally possible, it is necessary to prove that in fact, there is a public right of passage.

An express *animus dedicandi* is rare and it is therefore usually necessary to rely on an implied dedication through user. In *R. v. Petrie*[24] Coleridge J. said: "It must frequently happen that a [person] is in entire ignorance of the state of the title to lands over which a right of way exists. All that he knows, and all that he can reasonably be asked to prove, is that the right has been enjoyed by the public"; and Erle J. stated briefly "Now I take it to be clear law that open user, as of right of a way by the public raises a presumption of a public right to use that way. . . ."

This presumption is based upon the simple thesis that if an owner sees the general public passing and repassing over his land and does nothing to stop them he concedes that they have a legal right to do so because he, or more usually his predecessors in title, whomsoever they may have been, had granted a right of user over the path in perpetuity, or dedicated it to the public at large. This attitude on the part of the owner is deemed to be a question of fact and will depend upon the circumstances. Common sense is an important factor and at common law no fixed time is laid down to raise this presumption; the period of user required to establish such an intent will depend upon the relative position and nature of the path, the type of land over which it passes, the nature of the user and even the characteristics of the ownership; but it may be quite short. Eight years was held by the court to be sufficient in *Petrie's* case, but the alleged highway had been laid out as a projected street. Conversely the court was reluctant to imply dedication where the alleged path went through a stable yard.[25] Similarly it may be inferred that the owner of the soil would be more reluctant to dedicate a right of passage over good farm land than over rough and unproductive terrain.[26]

The user must be open and as of right. Hilbery J., in the context of the dedication of a highway, said: "The essential quality of the acts—that is, as acts done as of right—has from early days in our law been established by showing that the acts were done openly, not secretly, not by force and not by permission from time to time given . . . Coke expresses the requirements thus: '*Longus usus nec per vim, nec clam, nec precario.*'[27] There is a long line of cases which supports this view. . . ."[28] As is the case with so much of the law relating to rights of way the user requirement, when employed as a practical tool to preserve such rights, is vague and uncertain. This is exemplified by the following passage from Lord Kinnear's speech in *Folkestone Corporation* v. *Brockman*.[29] "The nature of user, and consequently the weight to be given to it, varies indefinitely in different cases, and whether it will import a presumption of grant or dedication must depend upon the circumstances of the particular case." In practice the usual problem is to prove that user is of right and not by permission. This is considered below.

Finally circumstances relating to the owner or ownership of the soil may be relevant. User by the public over land belonging to a non-resident owner is less cogent evidence of dedication than where the user is necessarily brought to his personal notice.[30] This follows logically from the presumption of dedication; and so does the requirement that there must be a person, or persons acting together, who can legally dedicate. Thus it may be difficult to establish, on this ground, a right of way over a tenant farmer's field or other leasehold land. "Of course there can be no dedication by the lessee to bind the freehold" said Patteson J.[31] Conversely "a reversioner cannot maintain an action on the case against a stranger for merely entering upon his land held by a tenant on lease, though the entry be made in exercise of an alleged right of way."[32] The same reasoning applies to settled land; although under the Settled Land Act 1925, s. 56(1)(i) a tenant for life may dedicate, *inter alia*, streets, roads and paths for the use of the public but only "for the general benefit of the residents on the settled land." In this context trustees for sale have all the powers of a tenant for life.[33] If, however, there is clear evidence of public user the courts will readily infer dedication before the date of the lease or settlement or otherwise when the land was, even for a brief period, in absolute ownership.

Although there are dicta to the contrary the cases generally establish that where "declaration and acceptance" is alleged the onus of proof is throughout on those who assert that a right of way exists. "The jury must say, in all the circumstances of the case, whether there has been a dedication" said Littledale J.[34]

3. *By prescription for twenty years*

The Rights of Way Act 1932, s. 1(1) as amended is re-enacted in the Highways Act 1959, s. 34(1) which states:

> "Where a way over any land, not being a way of such a character that user thereof by the public could not give rise at common law to any presumption of dedication, has been actually enjoyed by the public as of right and without interruption for a full period of twenty years, the way shall be deemed to have been dedicated as a highway unless there is sufficient evidence that there was no intention during that period to dedicate it."

The section gives a new method, in addition to dedication and acceptance, whereby a right of way can originate. The former is still available where the user is for less than twenty years.[35]

The Act creates "a new statutory right to a highway by prescription in addition to the old right by dedication," said Denning L.J. in *Fairey* v. *Southampton County Council*.[36] It makes it easier to establish a public right of passage by creating a *presumptio juris*. Whereas previously the legal burden of proving what was usually a legally fictitious dedication was throughout on the public who asserted the right, now after twenty years' user the legal burden is on the landowner to refute it. Furthermore under subsection (5) of the said section 34 reversioners can contest the issue and the public can acquire a right of way if they neglect to do so. The case decided and the legislature has now enacted[37] that the period of twenty years is calculated retrospectively from the date when the right of the public to use the way is challenged irrespective of whether it terminated before the 1932 Act became operative. Any "uninterrupted" period of twenty years, however long ago it may have been will suffice.

Also user by a particular group *as of right* will be deemed to be user by the public. In *R* v. *Broke*[38] Pollock C.B. said that if a landowner allows "seafaring men and pilots to make use of the footpath for purposes connected with their calling" this was a user by the public. Similarly in *Fairey's* case no attempt was made to prevent local residents from using the path and this was held to preclude denial of the right of way to others.

As all these methods of proving that a right of passage exists are cumulative it might be thought that bridleways and public paths are adequately protected; but, in fact, preserving these rights is extremely difficult. In few fields is there a greater divergence between law and practice.

III—Challenges to the Right of Passage

Landowners dispute the right in many ways; usually by putting up a "notice inconsistent with the dedication of the way as a highway,"[39] informing members of the public that they have no right to be there or forcibly ejecting them as alleged trespassers, erecting barbed-wire and other barriers and padlocking gates.

It may not be true to say that landowners are less public spirited than in the past, although the splitting up of large estates into smaller holdings may result in a more aggressive attitude to the rights of ownership.

It is rather that the purpose of public paths is changing. A century ago in a small closely integrated community they were used by labourers to avoid a detour in getting to their work and to facilitate the mobility of villagers when travel was restricted to foot and horse. Now they are becoming recreational amenities. Urban dwellers on family outings and associations of ramblers in motor coaches descend upon them while the villager goes to work by car. The landowner sees a functional purpose being replaced by a "fun" activity for those unfamiliar with the ways of the countryside and the public easement over his property being thereby enlarged to his detriment. The landowner's objection usually takes the form either of a denial that persons are using the alleged right of way or, if they are, a contention that they are so doing only with his permission.

Whether "dedication and acceptance" or a prescriptive right is alleged user is the key requirement; and where the former is invoked the dice are somewhat loaded against the public. "A single act of interruption by the owner" said Parke B., "is of much more weight, upon a question of intention [to dedicate] than many acts of enjoyment."[40]

IV—Proof of User

The best proof of user is a well-worn track and the evidence of "old inhabitants" who will testify that for many years they have walked or ridden the disputed path; but it is difficult to persuade such persons to appear in court. When they do often their good nature is exploited by cross-examination to obtain an admission that, had they met the owner they would have asked his leave.

Although the oral evidence of good witnesses who subject themselves to cross-examination is the best available personal attendance is not necessary. The Civil Evidence Act 1968, s. 2(1) states that: "In any civil proceedings a statement made, whether orally or in a document or otherwise, by any person, whether called as a witness . . . or not, shall . . . be admissible as evidence of any fact stated therein of which direct oral evidence by him would be admissible." Documentary evidence is usually more satisfactory than indirect oral evidence. It is excluded from subsection (3) of the said section 2 whereby the latter is limited to that of "any person who heard or otherwise perceived it being made." Documentary evidence has the merits of permanence, which is particularly important after the deaths of the declarant and his hearers, and of precision. Conversely the documentary evidence of a witness may be useful even when he is personally called.

The precedent at the end of this essay has been drafted to provide such evidence. The emphasis is on simplicity. It recognises that it is easier to persuade persons to sign a short intelligible statement, and for the same reason, no provision for a witness has been made. Usually the person who, either in an individual capacity or as representing an association of ramblers or riders, is acting to establish that a disputed path is a right of way will himself have approached the user and can testify as to the signature; but if the signer is willing to have the statement witnessed this should be done.

Maps are particularly useful in this context. This is recognised by the Highways Act 1959, s. 35[41] which clarifies and consolidates the law of evidence relating thereto. It states:

> "A court or other tribunal, before determining whether a way has or has not been dedicated as a highway, or the date on which such dedication, if any, took place, shall take into consideration any map, plan or history of the locality or other relevant document which is tendered in evidence, and shall give such weight thereto as the court or tribunal considers justified by the circumstances, including the antiquity of the tendered document, the status of the person by whom and the purpose for which it was made or compiled, and the custody in which it has been kept and from which it is produced."

Ordnance Survey maps are the most generally available. Their relevance was considered by Farwell J. in *Attorney-General* v. *Antrobus*[42] who said:

> "Such maps are not evidence on questions of title, or questions whether a road is public or private, but they are prepared by officers appointed under the provisions of the Ordnance Survey Acts, and set

out every track visible on the face of the ground, and are in my opinion admissible on the question whether or not there was in fact a visible track at the time of the survey."

The position has probably been unaffected by the said section 35. Tithe maps can sometimes be produced, and ancient maps may be held by a local resident, museum or library.

Photographs serve a similar purpose and it is often advisable to take a picture of a track or path. There should be stated, preferably on the reverse of a print, the date on which and where the photograph was taken, the name, address and signature of the photographer and the name of anybody present at the time. The picture, if taken under suitable conditions, may not only show the track but also shoe or hoof marks indicating that it has been extensively walked or ridden.

For the purposes of the Civil Evidence Act 1968[43] "document" includes, *inter alia*, any map, plan, graph or drawing and any photograph.

V—Remedies for Obstruction

Evidence of user which is sufficient to establish the existence of a public right may be hard to obtain. An equally difficult decision may have to be taken when user is challenged. Before anything is done the alleged transgressor should normally, when circumstances permit, be approached and asked to desist from the conduct in question.

1. Self help

The most natural remedy is self help. The idea of citizens, guardians of freedom and all the nobler virtues, confronting proprietary exclusion has an emotive effect which has been reinforced by judges. "The landowner can challenge their right," said Denning L.J., "for instance, by putting a barrier across the path or putting up a notice forbidding the public to use the path. When he does so, the public may meet the challenge. Some village Hampden may push down the barrier or tear down the notice. . . ."[44]

Nevertheless such conduct is perilous and is not advised, especially if there is any doubt about a disputed way. Those using it will be trespassers. A trespasser, after first being asked to leave and failing to do so, may be forcibly expelled, no more force being used than is necessary to remove him. If the trespassing user opposes force by force he may be prosecuted before a magistrates' court or the Crown Court for committing a common assault or, where this results from the scuffle, occasioning actual bodily harm. Also it may lead to a breach of the peace. Although trespass, in spite of the familiar notice, is not *per se* criminal a prosecution may be brought if it is accompanied by even slight damage. Thus in *Gayford* v. *Chouler*[45] a trespasser who walked across a field in which "the grass was deep" was convicted "for that he did unlawfully wilfully and maliciously damage certain grass." However the Criminal Damage Act 1971[46] gives a new defence of an honest belief, whether justified or not, in the existence of a legal right. Conversely the criminal court, which will almost invariably be the magistrates' court, can order the defendant to pay compensation to the owner. The occupier of land may also, in these circumstances, take civil proceedings, usually in the county court, and claim damages for trespass to his person, land, or, referring back to Denning L.J.'s judgment, "barrier" or "notice." Those who assert that a right of way exists will usually make it clear that they will continue to use the path and the occupier may contest the claim, usually in the county court, by applying for an injunction to restrain the repetition or continuance of the alleged wrongful act. Where land is let to or in the occupation of another the reversioner or owner may also sue as a right of way, being permanent, will injure the reversion.

The better course for those who wish to assert the existence of a right of way is usually to counter obstruction by statutory and legal means; and through statutes and the courts to obtain positive affirmation of the right of passage.

2. *The local authority*

The first step is, where possible, to persuade others, the local authority or the police, to take up the cause; for this requires the minimum of effort and no expense on the part of the citizen.

At common law the highway authority are under a duty to prevent and remove obstructions. Under the Highways Act 1959, which retains the common law obligation,[47] it is the duty of a borough, urban district or rural district council "to assert and protect the rights of the public to the use and enjoyment of all highways" (which of course includes footpaths and bridleways) in their district and to prevent, as far as possible, the stopping up or obstruction of those highways. . . ."[48] It is an obstruction to erect a gate, stile, hedge, fence or to put wire across a public path where none has existed before without the consent of the highway authority; which may only be given to enable land to be efficiently used for agriculture and having regard to the convenience of the public using the way. It is also an obstruction to lock gates which are already on the path and it is no answer to the complainant to say that keys for the gates will be supplied.[49] "Asserting and protecting the rights of the public" would include preventing owners or occupiers from warning off those who seek to use the way; and obtaining the removal of "private," "no entry," "private road" and similar notices or signs which would lead the public to believe that no right of way exists. A letter, indicating the point of obstruction by a map reference or otherwise and supported by photographs and any other evidence, should be sent to the clerk, surveyor or footpaths officer (if one has been appointed) of the council in whose area the right of way in question lies.

3. *The police*

The Highways Act 1959, s.121 imposes a general penalty for wilful obstruction. It states that "if a person, without lawful authority or excuse, in any way wilfully obstructs the free passage along a highway he shall be guilty of an offence." The maximum fine is £50 and a constable may arrest without a warrant any person whom he sees committing such an offence. It is also an offence for any person to place or maintain on or near any way shown on the local authority's "rights of way maps" a notice containing any false or misleading statement likely to deter the public from using the right of way.[50] A complaint can be made to the police authority of the area but the police have a discretion as to whether or not to pursue the matter. If the police are unwilling to take proceedings a private prosecution may be instituted by the complainant. Generally such prosecutions are not viewed with favour and it has been suggested in some authoritative quarters that they should be abolished. The magistrates, before whom the case would normally be brought, can order the prosecutor to pay the costs of a successful defendant.

Civil remedies are not generally directly available to the ordinary citizen.

It is a public nuisance to obstruct or hinder the free passage of the public along a highway. A private individual, however, has a right of action in respect thereof only if he can prove that he has sustained particular damage, which is direct and not merely consequential, over and above that which is suffered by the public at large. In an Irish case[51] a farmer successfully sued when, because of an obstruction, he had to take, once a week, a longer route to the market town; but in Canada a plaintiff failed and was non-suited where he could only show that, in common with every one else, he had to pursue his journey by a less direct route.[52] The English courts would take a similar view. An ordinary user of a right of way cannot, as an individual, bring an action for damages or for an injunction if the way is obstructed. Neither can be maintain an action for a declaration that a particular *locus in quo* is a highway.[53]

4. *The Attorney-General as guardian of public rights*

Denning L.J. in *Fairey* v. *Southampton County Council*, having eulogised self-help, continued ". . . the local council may bring an action in the name of the Attorney-General against the landowner in the courts claiming that there is a public right of way." The Attorney-General is the custodian of the rights of the public. He does not only act to protect such rights at the instigation of a local authority but can do so on behalf of any aggrieved person or body. In this context the action is usually for a declaration affirming the existence of a right of passage coupled with an injunction to retrain the occupier from continuing to interfere with its lawful user. This is a relator action,[54] that is one in which a person or body claiming to be entitled to restrain interference with a public right or to abate a public nuisance or to compel the performance of a public duty is bound to bring such action in the name of the Attorney-General as a necessary party. The Attorney-General has an absolute discretion to decide in what cases it is proper for him to sue on behalf of relators. Such actions take place in the High Court, are time-consuming and costly, and are not recommended for the ordinary rambler or rider. If, nevertheless, such a High Court action is contemplated to test the existence of a public right of way the advantages of selecting a potential user who is entitled to full legal aid should be borne in mind. It is, perhaps, not unreasonable that public funds should be used to establish public rights.

When the existence of a right of way has been placed beyond dispute steps should be taken to get it appropriately designated on the surveying authority's definitive map as soon as possible, which will usually be at the next review.

Under the National Parks and Access to the Countryside Act 1949 [55] the authority by whom a definitive right of way map has been prepared are under a duty from time to time to review the particulars shown thereon in the light of events which have occurred since the date of the last review, and having regard to "the discovery by the authority of new evidence such that, if the authority were then preparing a draft map . . . they would be required . . . to show on the map, as a highway of a particular description, a way not so shown on the definitive map, or on the revised map. . . ." Such reviews must "in any case" be carried out at intervals not exceeding five years.

Again in theory this is excellent, but often the practical implementation of these provisions is all too limited. Many local authorities will not state, because they do not know, when they intend to carry out the next review, and on their attention being called to it, plead that they have neither the staff nor the time, and one suspects although this is never admitted, that they lack the inclination to meet the five-year deadline. The prerogative order of mandamus, a discretionary high court procedure whereby, in the spirit of Magna Carta, the citizen can ask the court to ensure that justice is not delayed nor denied to anybody, cannot be used to compel a local authority to perform their statutory duties to protect rights of way by those who are merely denied by such failure the right to roam. [56]

I, ———,[1] of ———[2] in the County of ———[3] hereby state that at various times [and approximately ——— times a ———][4] between the ——— day of ———[5] and the ——— day of ———[6] I have ———[7] [in the company of other persons][8] along the ———[9] coloured red on the map hereto annexed between the points "X" and "Y" on the said map openly and as of right [and in the knowledge that the said public way has been continuously used as of right for over 20 years by the public as a ———][10]

Signature ———
Date ———

Notes to Precedent

1. Insert full Christian name(s) and surname.
2. Insert postal address.
3. Insert the county.
4. Delete the words in square brackets if the user is too irregular for them to apply. Otherwise insert the approximate number of times per week or month or year as the case may be.
5. Insert the earliest date on which the road or bridle path or footpath

as the case may be was thus used. If the exact date cannot be specified insert the month, if known, and year, or if the month is not known, the year.

6. Insert the latest date of such user, or if the right of passage has been disputed by the owner or occupier of the land the latest date prior to such challenge to the right of passage.

7. Insert "driven a car or carriage or travelled therein," "ridden a horse" or "walked" as the case may be.

8. Delete the words in square brackets if they do not apply.

9. Insert "road" "bridle path" or "footpath" as the case may be.

10. Delete the words in square brackets if they do not apply. If they do apply except for the reference to 20 years delete "for over 20 years" only. In this case and where all the words in the square brackets are relevant insert "highway for all purposes," "bridle path" or "footpath" as the case may be.

NOTES

1. National Parks and Access to the Countryside Act, 1949 (hereafter in the notes referred to as "the Countryside Act 1949"), s. 32.
2. National Parks and Access to the Countryside Regulations, 1950, S.I. 1950 No. 1066, para. 5.
3. *Ibid.* and Countryside Act 1968, Sched. 3, para. 9(1).
4. S.I. 1950 No. 1066, para. 4.
5. Countryside Act 1949 was passed on December 16, 1949.
6. Countryside Act 1949, s. 4(a), (b) and (c).
7. Countryside Act 1968, s. 30.
8. *Halsbury's Laws of England* (3rd edn, Vol. 19, p. 12).
9. Per Byles J. in *Dawes* v. *Hawkins* (1860) 8 C.B. (N.S.) 848.
10. Highways Act 1959, Sched. 7, paras. 1 and 2(2).
11. Countryside Act 1949, s. 38.
12. *Ibid.*, s. 27(1).
13. *Ibid.*, s. 29(1).
14. *Ibid.*, s. 29(2) and (3).
15. *Ibid.*, s. 30.
16. *Ibid.*, s. 28(1).
17. *Ibid.*, s. 29(5).
18. *Eyre* v. *New Forest Highway Board* (1892) 56 J.P. 517.
19. *Macpherson* v. *Scottish Rights of Way and Recreation Society* (1888) 13 App. Cas. 744, H.L.
20. Per James L.J. in *Wimbledon and Putney Commons Conservators* v. *Dixon* (1875–76) 1 Ch. at p. 362.
21. A *jus spatiandi*.
22. (1821) 5 B. & Ald. 315.
23. (1862) 2 F. & F. 864.
24. (1855) 4 El. & Bl. 737.
25. *Thornhill* v. *Weeks* [1913] 1 Ch. 438.
26. *Chinnock* v. *Hartley Wintney R.D.C.* (1899) 63 J.P. 327.
27. *Coke on Littleton* (19th edn, p. 114(a)).
28. *Merstham Manor Ltd.* v. *Coulsdon and Purley U.D.C.* [1937] 2 K.B. 77 at p. 83.
29. [1914] A.C. 338 at p. 352.
30. *Chinnock* v. *Hartley Wintney R.D.C.*, *loc. cit.* in note 26, *supra*.
31. *R.* v. *East Mark (Inhabitants)* (1848) 11 Q.B. 877 at p. 833.
32. *Baxter* v. *Taylor* (1832) 4 B. & Ad. 72—headnote.
33. Law of Property Act 1925, s. 28(1).
34. *Barraclough and Others* v. *Johnson and Others* (1838) 7 L.J. Q.B. 172 at p. 173.
35. *Jones* v. *Bates* [1938] 2 All E.R. 237 at p. 251 *per* Farwell J.; Highways Act 1959, s. 34(9).
36. [1956] 2 Q.B. 439 at p. 458.

37. Highways Act 1959, s. 34(2).
38. (1859) 1 F. & F. 514.
39. Highways Act 1959, s. 34(3)(*a*).
40. *Poole* v. *Huskinson* (1843) 11 M. & W. 828.
41. Which reenacts the provisions of the Rights of Way Act 1932, s. 3.
42. [1905] 2 Ch. 188 at p. 203.
43. s. 10(1).
44. *Fairey* v. *Southampton County Council, loc cit.* in note 36 *supra*, at p. 456.
45. [1898] 1 Q.B. 316.
46. ss. 1 and 5(3).
47. s. 299.
48. s. 116(3).
49. *Guest's Estates Ltd.* v. *Milner's Safes Ltd.* (1921) 28 T.L.R. 59.
50. Countryside Act 1949, s. 57.
51. *Smith* v. *Wilson* [1903] 2 I.R. 45.
52. *Baird* v. *Wilson* (1872) 22 C.P. 491.
53. *Whitehouse* v. *Hugh* [1906] 2 Ch. 283.
54. R.S.C. Ord. 15, r. 11.
55. s. 33(1) and (2)(*e*).
56. "It is a summary offence punishable by a fine to drive a motor vehicle on to
    or upon any common land, moorland or other land of whatsoever descrip-
    tion, not being land forming part of a road, or on any road being a footpath
    or bridleway; and it is also an offence to drive a motor vehicle on any land
    within fifteen yards of a road, being a road on which a motor vehicle may
    lawfully be driven, for the purpose of parking the vehicle on that land."
    Road Traffic Act 1960, s. 18; amended by Road Traffic Act 1962, 1st Sched.

10. THE RIGHT TO INFORMATION ABOUT THE ACTIVITIES OF THE GOVERNMENT

BARBARA L. DE SMITH

DICEY was able to demonstrate that the so-called liberty of the Press in England was "a mere application of the general principle, that no man is punishable except for a distinct breach of the law."[1] "Hence . . . no such thing is known with us as a licence to print, or a censorship either of the press or of political newspapers."[2] However, he admitted that a breach of the law committed by publication can result in the penalties imposed by the law of libel, for "no one can maintain that the law of England recognises anything like that natural right to the free communication of thoughts and opinions which was proclaimed in France a little over a hundred years ago to be one of the most valuable rights of man."[3]

Dicey might well have approved the demonstration of repugnance to any "prior restraint" on the freedom of the press manifested by the majority of the Supreme Court (and in particular, as usual, by M. Justice Black) in *New York Times Co* v. *U.S.*[4], although any gratification on his part would probably have been qualified by the reflection that French influence was making itself felt through the strict application of the First Amendment to the United States Constitution: "The people shall not be deprived or abridged of their great right to speak, to write, or to publish their sentiments; and the freedom of the press, as one of the great bulwarks of liberty shall be inviolable."[5] The Supreme Court upheld this bulwark of liberty in unusual circumstances: a series of papers on high level policy discussions and decisions relating to the conduct of the war in Vietnam had been abstracted without authority from the Pentagon. The *New York Times*, the *Washington Post* and other newspapers had published part of and proposed to continue publishing an edited version of these papers. The Government of the United States sought to restrain the publication on the ground that such publication would endanger the national security. The Court was not asked to question the legislative validity of any Act of Congress: it was asked to take upon itself and exercise, as part of its equitable jurisdiction, a power which, it was argued, was essential in order to uphold in turn the Presidential power to protect the security of the United States.

In a six to three decision the Court refused to exercise any such power and was divided on whether such a power existed and its extent if it did. The Court left open any question of the criminal liability of the newspapers should a prosecution be brought against them under the Espionage Acts.[6]

This case has led to a reappraisal in the United States of the security

137

measures taken and needed with regard to information in the hands of the Government.[7] This has come at roughly the same time as a similar reappreciation in the United Kingdom.[8]

In September 1972 a report was issued by a committee set up by the Home Office, under the chairmanship of Lord Franks to "review the operation of section 2 of the Official Secrets Act 1911 and to make recommendations."[9] The Franks Committee examined the laws of Sweden, Canada and France as well as the laws of the United States pertaining to what had to be, despite the narrow wording of their terms of reference, an investigation of the need for the criminal sanction against improper revelation of information in the hands of the government and a consequent assessment of the needs of government for secrecy and of the public for information.

In this short essay it is impossible to do more than give a superficial account of the problem and its solution as seen by the Franks Committee and to make some comparisons with the position in the United States. It must be emphasised that the committee felt "[O]ur examination of the situation in this country suggested strongly that openness in government depended on political and constitutional factors rather than on legal provisions."[10] Thus the Committee refused to consider legislation based on the lines of the Swedish and United States laws on public access to official documents "because such a suggestion raised important constitutional questions going beyond our terms of reference."[11]

It is in the light of these limitations that one must consider their analysis of the problems raised by section 2 of the Official Secrets Act 1911 (as amended):

Wrongful communication etc. of information

"(1) If any person having in his possession or control any secret official code word, or pass word, or any sketch, plan, model, article, note, document, or information which relates to or is used in a prohibited place or anything in such a place or which has been made or obtained in contravention of this Act, or which has been entrusted in confidence to him by any person holding office under Her Majesty or which he has obtained or to which he had access owing to his position as a person who holds or has held office under Her Majesty, or a person who holds or has held office under Her Majesty, or a person who holds or has held a contract made on behalf of Her Majesty or as a person who is or has been employed under a person who holds or has held such an office or contract—

(*a*) communicates the code word, pass word, sketch, plan, model, note, document or information to any person, other than a person to whom he is authorised to communicate it, or a person to whom it is in the interest of the State his interest to communicate it; or
(*aa*) uses the information in his possession for the benefit of any foreign power or in any other manner prejudicial to the safety or interests of the State;
(*b*) retains the sketch, plan, model, article, note, or document in his possession or control when he has no right to retain it or when it is contrary to his duty to retain it, or fails to comply with all directions

issued by lawful authority with regard to the return or disposal thereof; or

   (c) fails to take reasonable care of, or so conducts himself as to endanger the safety of any sketch, plan, model, article, note, document, secret official code or pass word or information;

that person shall be guilty of a misdemeanour.

"(1A) If any person having in his possession or control any sketch, plan, model, article, note document or information which relates to munitions of war, communicates it directly or indirectly to any foreign power, or in any other manner prejudicial to the safety or interests of the State that person shall be guilty of a misdemeanour. "(2) If any person receives any secret official code word, or pass word, or sketch, plan, model, article, note, document, or information, knowing or having reasonable ground to believe at the time when he receives it, that the code word, pass word, sketch, plan, model, article, note, document, or information is communicated to him in contravention of this Act, he shall be guilty of a misdemeanour, unless he proves that the communication to him of the code word, pass word, sketch, plan, model, article, note, document or information was contrary to his desire."[12]

This wide "catch-all" section creates many offences. It is criticised in particular on the ground of the vagueness of the mental element required for the crimes.[13] In section 2(2) the onus is placed upon the accused to prove that the communication was "contrary to his desire" although the prosecution would need to show that he knew "or had reasonable grounds to believe" that the communication to him was in contravention of the Act. In the multitude of offences created under subsection (1) it would be possible to argue that certain absolute offences are created in the sense that all the prosecution is required to show is that there has been "possession" or "control" of any information or anything "made or obtained" in contravention of the Act which is then communicated to an unauthorised person without having to show that the accused knew or even had grounds for suspicion that his information had been "made or obtained" in contravention of the Act.[14] The memorandum submitted to the committee by Caulfield J. (who presided over the court in the *Sunday Telegraph* case) emphasises this point. "The Crown in the *Sunday Telegraph* case said, rather than conceded 'The Crown will not ask for verdicts of guilty against any accused unless mens rea is proved.' The Crown I think should not have to be so condescending on so important a principle."[15]

The *Sunday Telegraph* prosecution was the most recent of the twenty-three prosecutions under section 2 which have taken place since the war.[16] The case was not the cause for the appointment of the committee[17] which was occasioned by a suggestion of the Fulton Committee on the Civil Service.[18] The case, being a prosecution of a journalist, an editor and a newspaper,[19] who published a report on the "Biafra" situation after having obtained from the secretary of the "D" notices committee[20] an assurance that the report did not contain any matter which affected the national security, occasioned considerable public debate.[21] In his summing up

Caulfield J. was strongly critical of section 2 and sympathetic to the situation in which the Press found itself when it came into possession of information emanating indirectly only from a government source and was unable to obtain guidance on whether its publication would or would not result in a prosecution.[22]

The prosecution and subsequent acquittal of these accused also raised a discussion of the invidious position in which the Attorney-General can be placed in relation to such prosecutions, in that his consent is necessary before a prosecution can be instituted[23] but he is a member of the government, and as such not obviously free from political pressure.[24]

The parallel with the situation of the *New York Times* and *Washington Post* cases is obvious. In England there was no attempt made to impose a "prior restraint" but the fact that the accused were exposed to such a real risk of prosecution will operate as a strong inhibitory factor for the future unless some change is made in the law.

The fact that even eminent legal minds found the section obscure can be demonstrated by the letter to *The Times* by Sir Dingle Foot published on February 9th, 1971 in which he said "if a civil servant or even a minister informs someone outside the department of the colour of his wallpaper, then that would constitute an offence under this section."

The Franks Committee found that the situation was not quite as bad as that because the section only limits "unauthorised" disclosure. They found that there is an administrative concept of implied authority to disclose information. Thus Ministers are largely "self authorising" and apparently even the most lowly civil servant would have "implied authority" to reveal the colour of his wallpaper.[25] Sir Dingle Foot is not the only person who was apparently not quite clear on this limitation on the Act less than a year ago: see, for example, the evidence of Roy Jenkins.[26] This vague doctrine is merely a rationalisation of the revelations about government which do in fact take place.[27]

In the face of these obvious deficiences in the Act the Franks Committee made proposals which differentiated the varying degree of importance to be attached to the confidentiality of differing types of information in the hands of the government. Consequent upon this analysis were proposals for a redefinition of the criminal sanction and of those on whom it should fall. Various proposals were made for changes in administrative procedure but one would search the pages of the report in vain for an answer to the question of whether an injunction would issue against a newspaper in possession of "leaked" information, of the type involved in the "Pentagon Papers" trial, which it proposed to publish. It is possible that an injunction could issue to the Government to restrain a breach of copyright[28] or possibly even to restrain the revelation of information under the vague "law of confidentiality."[29] However, the Younger Committee on Privacy[30] was restricted by its terms of reference from considering information in the hands of the government.[31] It did propose that the law of breach of confidence should be referred to the Law Commission.[32] When such a reference is made the Commission will presumably not be inhibited by being asked to refrain from considering the impact of this area of law on information in the hands of the Government.

The main proposals for reform made by the Franks Committee are contained in their proposed "Official Information Act." Section 2 ought to be repealed (it was felt to be out of place anyway in an Act which deals mainly with espionage) and replaced with this Act.

First, the Act would utilise the classification system at present used by the Government as an administrative convenience, whereby documents are classified as "Top Secret," "Secret," "Defence Confidential," "Confidential," etc. The Act would give statutory authority to and, of necessity, formalise this system which, at the moment, because it is merely a matter of internal administration, varies in practice from department to department.

Information, to be subject to classification, would have to fall within certain broad categories.[33] These would be (a) "matters which concern the defence or security of the realm" and this would include similar information relating to the defence or security of allied powers, (b) "information relating to any matters which concern or affect foreign relations or the conduct of foreign relations and (c) official information relating to any proposals, negotiations or decisions connected with alterations in the value of sterling, or relating to the reserves, including their extent or any movement in or threat to them."

Within these broad categories, the identification of particular information "the disclosure of which is likely to cause serious injury to the nation"[34] was to be a matter for the Crown and not for the courts. The criminal sanction would apply only if the particular item of information had been properly classified, *i.e.* in accordance with regulations made by the Secretary of State[35] and was, if a document, marked "Secret" or words which included the word "Secret" or in relation to defence matters as "Defence Confidential."[36] There would be provision for the extension of the criminal sanction to information not contained in a document if "the information relates to the contents of a document which is classified" in accordance with the above provisions, or "is information which, if it had been contained in a document ought to have been so classified."[37]

The regulations to be made by the Secretary of State for the implementation of these classification provisions "should include provisions on levels of authority at which decisions on classification may be taken and on arrangements for review and declassification."[38]

As an added precaution against a prosecution being brought in respect of a document or information which had been overclassified or in respect of which the need for classification no longer existed, provision would be made for a certificate to be issued by the Minister himself which was to be accepted as conclusive by the courts in any prosecution, to the effect that at the time of the alleged disclosure the information was properly classified as "Secret" or above or "Defence Confidential" in the sense that its unauthorised disclosure would cause serious injury to the interests of the nation.[39]

This aspect of the Franks proposals can be compared with the Presidential executive order[40] which became effective on June 1, 1972. The executive order makes certain changes in the classification system for government information which exists in the United States. There is no direct statutory authority for this system although a bill has been brought before Congress in an attempt to implement such a statutory authorisation.[41] A classification system for documents began with the American Expeditionary Force during the First World War and provided for the use of the markings "Secret," "Confidential," etc. This was not extended to civilian departments until 1951 when by executive order[42] President Truman provided for classification under the headings "Top Secret," "Secret," "Confidential" and "Restricted." President Eisenhower in 1950,[43] by a further executive order, removed some of the defects of the Truman scheme *e.g.* by eliminating the "restricted" category and defining the other three categories, so that they only covered possible injury to national defence interests. The latest executive order[44] still further restricts the classification of Government documents. "Top Secret" is to be used "with the utmost restraint" and "Secret," "sparingly." Only twelve departments have authority to classify material as "top secret" and in addition thirteen others have power to classify as "secret." Powers to classify material as being in these categories are exercisable at only the highest practicable level, usually the department head, or his principal deputies and assistants. An Interagency Classification Review Committee is to be established to consider complaints with respect to the administration of the order. Provision is made for automatic downgrading and declassification, for example, "Top Secret" material is automatically downgraded to "Secret" after two years, "Confidential" after four years and declassified after ten years. There is provision for high level exemptions to be made to this scheme for automatic downgrading and declassification. A member of the public may request a classification review if the request describes the record with sufficient particularity to enable it to be found "with only a reasonable amount of effort."[45]

The Executive Order makes only very exceptional provision for the imposing of such a long period of secrecy on Government files as that imposed in the United Kingdom by the Public Records Act 1967[46] under which records are not made available to the public for search until they are thirty years old and, in some cases, 100 years old. However, the comparable United States legislation only requires that identifiable documents be made available to the public for inspection and copying.[47] This Act, the Public Information Act, has nine exceptions to the rules of availability, of which the first concerns matters covered by the Executive Order specified above.[48] Apart from this the executive order has administrative effect in that an individual must have the necessary security clearance for access to that level of material before he can get "Top Secret," "Secret" or "Confidential" information. If a civil servant wrongfully reveals classified information there are administrative sanctions which can be imposed upon him which include loss of his security clearance or even his dismissal.[49]

Under the Espionage Acts[50] the classification system, as such, has no relevance. Thus when criminal penalties are sought to be imposed under the Acts on revelation and in some cases receipt of documents "relating to the national defence" the question whether the documents involved are classified or not is inconclusive and the court can decide if any information falls within the ambit of the Act.[51] In cases arising under the Public Information Act there is provision for judicial review of a decision to withhold information but in respect of a decision to withhold "classified" information there is authority for the proposition that the review is limited to the question whether the classification was arbitrary or capricious: *Epstein* v. *Resor*.[52]

The Franks Report suggestions, as has been noted, take evaluation of a classification decision out of the hands of the courts (which, it can be argued, are not qualified to judge the policy implications of the matter) and place it directly on the responsible Minister in respect of any particular document involved in any particular prosecution. However, the Committee recognises that this system gives little help to the man who comes by a piece of information and wishes to publish it and wishes to know whether he will be subject to a criminal penalty if he does publish it. The Committee specifically provides that "*mens rea*" would be required where its proposed Act is made applicable to private individuals, for example journalists in the position of Jonathan Aitken in the *Sunday Telegraph* case.[53] The mere receipt of official information by a private individual would not be an offence as it is under section 2 of the Official Secrets Act 1911.[54] But[55] where an individual "knows or has reasonable ground to believe that information in his possession has been communicated (whether or not directly to him) in contravention of the Official Information Act . . . it should be an offence for him to communicate that information otherwise than in accordance with an authorisation given on behalf of the Crown. . . ."[56]

The Report suggests that it will be necessary for a non-statutory committee to be set up able to advise an inquirer whether the information which he has received is classified and to give him a chance to query the classification.[57] The Committee, which would include representatives of the Government and of the news media, would be "appointed by and report to the Prime Minister as the Minister with overall responsibility for matters of National Security."[58] Apparently this Committee would replace the "D" notices committee although the report does not make this point explicitly. It would have extra responsibilities in that it would be consulted about the classification regulations to be made by the Secretary of State as indicated above.[59] As with the "D" notices committee its advice would apparently give no protection against prosecution and indeed the mere fact of having consulted the Committee might be taken as showing that the inquirer had "reasonable cause to believe" that the information was classified.

The Committee is apparently not intended to give advice on the other types of information in the hands of the Government which the Committee considers should be covered by the criminal sanction. Thus it is proposed that all Cabinet documents (including papers of committees of the Cabinet the members of which are Ministers),[60] information given to the Government by private individuals or concerns "whether given by reason of compulsory powers or otherwise and whether or not given on an express or implied basis of confidence"[61] or information in the hands of the government (including police, post office and prison authorities) which (a) is likely to be helpful in the commission of offences (b) is likely to be helpful in facilitating an escape from prison custody or other acts prejudicial to prison security, or (c) its disclosure would be likely to impede the prevention or detection of offences or the apprehension or prosecution of offenders,[62] should be protected against improper disclosure by a criminal sanction being imposed on the persons covered by the act if they act in breach of it.

The persons to be liable to prosecution under the Official Information Act are to be first, all persons thought to be covered by the term "holding office under Her Majesty" at present used in section 2 of the Official Secrets Act.[63] These persons include all ministers of the Crown, civil servants, members of the armed forces, police officers[64] and former holders of such offices. At present also certain groups of persons are, by statute to be treated as "holding office under Her Majesty" for the purposes of section 2. These groups, officers of the Atomic Energy Authority and of the Post Office, by the nature of their work regularly deal with classified material. They should continue to be treated in the same way as servants of the central government by the Official Information Act.[65] At present certain employees of these groups (*e.g.* the civilian employees of the Police) would only be covered by section 2 of the 1911 Act if information were entrusted to them by "a person holding office under Her Majesty," but it is possible to argue that information directly obtained by reason of their employment, for example, information directly imparted to a civilian employee of the police by a member of the public would not be within the scope of the Act. So as to cover this possible loophole such persons would be treated as persons in one of the categories given above.[66] Classified official information, Cabinet documents and matters pertaining to the maintenance of law and order (*i.e.* all the categories to which the Official Information Act criminal sanction would apply with the exception of the confidences of citizens in the hands of the government) if entrusted to a government contractor or other person entrusted with the information in confidence by a Crown servant[67] was not to be improperly disclosed and any such improper disclosure would constitute an offence. As has been noted above a private individual could also be made liable for an offence under the Act.[68] A retired contractor or person entrusted with Government information in confidence would continue to be covered by the Act even after retirement.[69]

The Committee also proposed that a section should be added to the existing Official Secrets Acts to cover the communication by any person of any information which he knows, or has reasonable grounds to believe, has been obtained or communicated in consideration of section 1 of the Official Secrets Acts—except by telling a Crown servant that he has it or handing it to a Crown servant.[70]

The Report also proposes that the use of "official information' (by which they apparently mean only information described in the various categories above) for "private gain" or the communication of such information, to enable another person to make a "private gain," by a Crown servant or a government contractor or a person entrusted with the information in confidence should be an offence, and "in effect form an extension of the existing law on corruption."[71] The Committee similarly envisaged that the recipient of information disclosed in the above circumstances would be committing an offence if he used that information for the purpose of obtaining "private gain" (defined as the making of a gain or the avoidance of a loss, in money or money's worth). The Franks Report never deals explicitly with the impact of its proposals on the Press. In the way in which specific proposal 13(c) is expressed [72] a journalist who used information which he knew or had reasonable grounds to believe had been disclosed by a Crown servant contrary to "his official duty" would be guilty of an offence under this section if he wrote an article using the material to make money for himself from a newspaper. The newspaper itself would also presumably be guilty. One wonders if this is what the Committee really had in mind.

To turn again to the United States position for comparison one must note that the Espionage Act [73] relates only to "defence information." However, even though a wide reading of the Act (in particular s. 793(e)) could impose criminal liability on any person who revealed documents relating to the national defence to any person not entitled to receive them, the district court in the *New York Times* case [74] concluded that section 793(e) applied only to the clandestine communication of secret information and did not apply to publication by a newspaper. The point did not fall for decision by the Supreme Court although Douglas J. expressly agreed with the district court's conclusion.[75] Daniel Ellsberg has been indicted under section 793(d) of the Espionage Act in respect of the "Pentagon Papers" which forbids any person having lawful possession or access to information or documents relating to national defence to disclose any such material to anyone not entitled to receive it.[76] But Ellsberg removed these documents from the Pentagon apparently believing in good faith that by removing papers relating to high-level policy decisions about Vietnam and revealing them to the Press he would be helping the nation by providing essential information for public debate. The ultimate decision in his case is by no means a foregone conclusion.[77] There has been little litigation under the Espionage Acts and apparently only one attempt to use the Acts to punish a person for revelation to persons other than foreign agents.[78] Official information is in fact frequently "leaked" by senior government officers [79] and there has never been a prosecution based on memoirs of former government officials.

The United States does, of course, have other penal statutes concerning government information. Thus 18 U.S.C. § 1905 generally prohibits disclosure by public servants of confidential information concerning private business affairs by which is meant the unlawful disclosure of trade secrets and other business information. There are also a number of provisions in the law which prohibit the disclosure by persons other than public officials of certain narrowly defined types of information *e.g.* 18 U.S.C. § 1906–1908 which prohibits the disclosure of information by bank examiners without authority from the bank or Federal reserve officials.

However, the whole tenor of the United States laws is coloured by the political and constitutional situation. There is a tradition of disclosure of confidential information to Congress [80] and apparently rarely has there resulted a case of unauthorised disclosure. In a claim of executive privilege to withhold documents or information in a case arising out of private litigation the court is the proper body to decide if executive privilege is properly invoked. [81] But Congress is in a weaker position when it disputes a claim of executive privilege to withhold information from it. Short of cutting off supplies or bringing contempt proceedings against an executive officer there is little it can do and although by the procedure laid down by President Nixon a decision for this type of executive privilege to be claimed could be made only by the President himself, in fact the formal procedure is often not used. [82]

Where the formal procedures are used an agency head who wishes to claim executive privilege must confer with the Attorney-General. If after such discussion either of these persons consider that executive privilege should be claimed then the matter is referred to the President and Congress notified. [83] The Attorney-General has some similarities in role in the two countries but in the United States it is not he who must give his permission before there can be a prosecution under the Espionage Acts, as his fiat is required here before there can be a prosecution under the Official Secrets Acts.

The Franks Report keeps the requirement that his permission should be necessary before a prosecution can be instituted under the Official Information Act except for the offences relating to law and order and private gain where they feel that the appropriate officer is the Director of Public Prosecutions. [84] This is the type of point on which the Franks Report and its companion volumes of evidence are most useful. In deciding who is the appropriate officer it is useful to use the words of the Home Office written memorandum. "The practical difference between a control over prosecutions exercised by the Attorney General and one exercised by the Director of Public Prosecutions is that, in the latter case, the Director decides straightforward cases himself without reference to the Attorney-General." [85] However, knowing the facts does not make one's evaluation of the rights and wrongs of a situation any easier. Thus in his oral evidence Sir Elwyn Jones said of the *Biafra* case: "I think the position with regard to that was in this case—and this was the only case in my experience in six years, very nearly, of office, where I ever consulted a Minister about a case—the consultation I had was with the Foreign Secretary, and I was anxious to discover from him what the consequence would be on our foreign relations." [86] However, the Foreign Secretary was Mr. Michael Stewart and Jonathan Aitken alleged that it was possibly because of the fact, *inter alia,* that the Scott report revealed an inconsistency in the statements made by Mr. Stewart to the House that he had been prosecuted.[87] The Franks Committee found that there was no evidence of any political pressure having been placed on the Attorney-General[88]; Mr. Stewart did not approach him. Although the *possibility* of political influence still exists, the Franks proposals retain the requirement of the Attorney-General's fiat in the proposed Act.

In conclusion it must be emphasised that the Franks Committee makes proposals about an Act that it would like to see replace the present section 2 of the Official Secrets Act 1911. Their proposals are backed up by reasons and these reasons by the three volumes of evidence. However, they do not draft the Act. Many points may be made about the formulation of the proposals, for they raise formidable drafting problems. Coupled with the limitations on considerations of major constitutional and political issues imposed on the Committee one may wonder if it might not have been wiser for the Committee to suggest that the problems and the solutions as it saw them be referred to the Law Commission for the type of detailed consideration of legal niceties to which this body is so admirably suited. The Law Commission could perhaps give statutory form to this mysterious doctrine of "implied authorisation." It is because of this strange constitutional phenomenon, a sort of administrative convention, that the Franks Committee is able to conclude that the Official Secrets Act is not broken daily by ministers and others. The proposed "Official Information Act" presupposes the continued existence of this doctrine.

NOTES

1. Dicey, *Introduction to the Study of the Law of the Constitution* (10th edn, 1964), p. 248.
2. *Ibid.*, p. 249.
3. *Ibid.*, p. 246.
4. 403 U.S. 713, 29 L. Ed. 2d 822 (1971).
5. 1 Annals of Cong. 434.
6. Espionage Act 1917, Ch. 30, 40 Stat. 217, as amended, 18 U.S.C. §§ 793–794 (1970), see Douglas J. in 403 U.S. 713 (above) at p. 722.
7. See QU.S. Government Information Policies and Practices—The Pentagon Papers, Hearings before a Subcomm. of the House Comm. on Government Operations, 92nd Cong., 1st Sess., pt. 1 (1971) (Moorhead Hearings), Executive Privilege: The Withholding of Information by the Executive, Hearings on S. 112S Before the Subcomm. on Separation of Powers of the Senate Comm. on the Judiciary, 92nd Cong., 1st Sess. (1971) (The Ervin Hearings).
8. See Departmental Committee on Section 2 of the Official Secrets Act 1911, Cmnd. 5104 (1972); (the Franks Report); The *Sunday Telegraph* case (1971) (unreported): see *The Times*, February 4, 1971; *Conway* v. *Rimmer* [1968] A.C. 910; the Fulton Committee, Cmnd. 3638 (1968); and *Information and the Public Interest* (1969) Cmnd. 4809.
9. Franks Report, Vol. 1, p. 1.
10. *Ibid.*, vol. 1, para. 70.
11. *Ibid.*, para. 85.
12. Official Secrets Act 1911, s. 2 (as amended).
13. *e.g.* Franks Report, Vol. 1, Appendix I(B), para. 20.
14. *Ibid.*
15. Franks Report, Vol. 2, p. 350.

16. Franks Report, Vol. 1, Appendix II, pp. 117–118.
17. Franks Report, Vol. 1, para. 7.
18. Cmnd. 3638 (1968).
19. Jonathan Aitken, *The Sunday Telegraph*, its editor Brian Roberts, and Colonel Cairns, former Senior British Member of the International team of Military Observers in Nigeria during the Biafran conflict.
20. See Franks Report, Vol. 1, para. 65. "D" or Defence notices "may be issued only on the authority of the Defence, Press and Broadcasting Committee, which is composed of officials from Government Departments concerned with defence and national security and representatives of the press and broadcasting organisations. The notices are addressed to editors. Their purpose is to advise editors that the Government regards certain categories of information, which the notices usually but not always define in general terms, as being secret for reasons of national security, and to ask editors to refrain from publishing such information." The Secretary of the Committee will advise editors but the system, in effect one of voluntary censorship, is one which operates completely independently of the Official Secrets Acts.
21. *e.g.* letters to *The Times* on February 9, 1971 (Sir Dingle Foot), February 11, 1971 (Lord Shawcross), Jonathan Aitken's book *Officially Secret* (1971).
22. Franks Report, Vol. I, para. 8.
23. Official Secrets Act 1911, s. 8.
24. That the Attorney-General was free from political pressure in fact seemed clear to the committee: see Vol. I, paras. 37–39, Chap. 16.
25. Vol. I, para. 18.
26. Franks Report, Vol. 4, at p. 374.
27. See Jeremy Tunstall, *The Westminster Lobby Correspondents* (1970).
28. Copyright Act 1956.
29. *Prince Albert* v. *Strange* (1849) 1 H. & T. 1; *Argyll* v. *Argyll* [1967] Ch. 302; Jones, "Restitution of benefits obtained in breach of another's confidence" (1970), 86 L.Q.R. 463, at p. 482 and North, "Breach of Confidence: Is there a New Tort?" [1972] J.S.P.T.L. 149.
30. Cmnd. 5012 (1972).
31. It was appointed "To consider whether legislation is needed to give further protection to the individual citizen and to commercial and industrial interests against intrusion into privacy by private persons and organisations, or by companies, and to make recommendations."
32. Younger Report, para. 633.
33. Franks Report, paras, 124, 134, 139 and 149.
34. *Ibid.*, para. 149
35. *Ibid.*, para. 157.
36. NATO marking.
37. Franks Report, para. 157, a.ii. One can foresee certain problems arising on this point.
38. *Ibid.*, para. 157 b.
39. *Ibid.*, para. 161.
40. Executive Order 11, 652.
41. S. 2965, 92nd Cong., 1st Sess. (1971).
42. Executive Order 10, 290.
43. Executive Order 10, 501.
44. Made by President Nixon, see note 40 *supra*.
45. Executive Order 11, 652, § 5 (B) at 5213.
46. Franks Report, para. 66. All information classified under Order 11, 652 is declassified in 30 years.
47. Public Information Act 1967, 5 U.S.C. § 552 (a)(3) 1970.
48. The nine exceptions are for: (1) defence and foreign policy secrets specified by Executive Order; (2) internal personnel rules; (3) matters expressly excepted by statute; (4) privileged or confidential trade secrets or commercial information; (5) privileged intra-governmental documents and correspondence; (6) disclosures of personal and other files which would constitute an unwarranted invasion of privacy; (7) law enforcement regulations; (8) reports relating to supervision of financial institutions; (9) geological etc. data concerning wells. See Franks Report, Vol. I, Appendix IV, para. 22.
49. For the United Kingdom position see report of the Radcliffe Committee,

Cmnd. 1681 (1962), set up "in the light of recent convictions under the Official Secrets Acts to review the security procedure and practices currently followed in the public service and to consider what, if any changes are required."

50. 18 U.S.C. § 793 and 794.
51. *United States* v. *New York Times Co.*, 328 F. Supp. 324 (S.D.N.Y.).
52. 421 F. 20 930 (9th Cir. 1970), cert. denied, 398 U.S. 965 (1970).
53. Franks Report, para. 236, 237.
54. *Ibid.*, para. 233.
55. *Ibid.*, para. 236.
56. *Ibid.*, para. 278, Specific Proposals 20 and 21.
57. *Ibid.*, paras. 165, 166.
58. *Ibid.*, para. 166.
59. *Ibid.*, para. 165 and para. 157.
60. *Ibid.*, para. 190.
61. *Ibid.*, para. 200.
62. *Ibid.*, para. 175.
63. See Franks Report, para. 215.
64. *Lewis* v. *Cattle* [1938] 2 K.B. 454.
65. Franks Report, para. 211, 212, 215.
66. *Ibid.*, para. 215 (f).
67. "Crown servant" is to be taken to refer to any person specified in para. 215.
68. Franks Report, para. 236.
69. *Ibid.*, para. 239.
70. *Ibid.*, para. 238.
71. *Ibid.*, paras 201–205.
72. *Ibid.*, para. 278.
73. Note 50, *supra*.
74. Note 51, *supra*.
75. 403 U.S. 113 at p. 122.
76. *United States* v. *Russo*, Criminal No. 9373 C.D. (C.D. Cat., December 29, 1971).
77. See for the attitude of United Kingdom courts on a case under s. 1 of the Official Secrets Act 1911 involving the construction of the term "safety or interests of the State" *Chandler* v. *D.P.P.* [1964] A.C. 763. For a general discussion of the U.S. law in this area see "Developments in the Law—the National Security Interest and Civil Liberties" (1972) 85 Harv. L. Rev. 1130.
78. *U.S.* v. *Sawyer*, 213 F. Suppl. 38 (E.D. Pa., 1963).
79. See (1972) 85 Harv. L. Rev. 1130 at pp. 1206–1207.
80. *Ibid.*, p. 1208.
81. *U.S.* v. *Reynolds*, 345 U.S. 1 (1953); *Committee for Nuclear Responsibility Inc.* v. *Seaborg*, 40 U.S.L.W. 2249. For United Kingdom position see *Conway* v. *Rimmer* [1968] A.C. 910.
82. See *e.g.* Ervin Hearings 37–38—Letter from Secretary of Defence Laird to Senator Fulbright, December 20, 1969 refusing to release Pentagon Papers to Senate Foreign Relations Committee.
83. Memorandum from President Nixon for Heads of Executive Departments and Agencies, March 24, 1969, cited in Ervin Hearings 36–37.
84. See Franks Report, Vol. I, paras 240–256.
85. Franks Report, Vol. 2, p. 125.
86. Franks Report, Vol. 4, p. 398
87. Aitken, *Officially Secret* (1971), p. 135.
88. See note 24 *supra*.

11. CIVIL RIGHTS, A MORE CIVIL REMEDY
or
LITIGATION NOT DEMONSTRATION

C. P. GORDON

I—Introduction

MANY of us believe that the existence of a wide, developing and well-protected body of fundamental civil rights is a good thing and that the courts have an important role to play in fostering these rights. Certainly that is a premise of this volume. This essay will suggest that one of the most ingrained principles of civil procedure, that costs follow the event, that the loser pays most of the winner's costs in litigation, puts too severe a limitation on the legal system's function in defining and protecting civil rights. A minority group, the disadvantaged or ordinary citizen will be prevented by the principle from litigating upon the existence of a novel or somewhat doubtful but important civil rights claim, or other matter which it would be in the public interest to have considered by a court. The citizen will be discouraged from making his claim because the possibility of losing exists and if he loses he will be liable for the other side's substantial legal costs.

Secondly, the principle that costs follow the event also prevents the man of moderate means from initiating litigation that is less than certain. Although he can limit his own costs to an amount he can afford, he can not limit those of his opponent. Fear that if he is unsuccessful these will be more than he can pay deter the man of moderate income from bringing suit. Thus his fundamental right of making use of the law in adjudicating a claim is seriously restricted. Also economic theory suggests that having costs follow the event is inconsistent with an efficient allocation of legal resources.

II—Costs Follow the Event

The principle that costs normally follow the event has a seven hundred year history. It was first mentioned in 1275 and a brief history of its development is given in Holdsworth's *A History of English Law*.[1] The most important current statement of this principle is in Order 62, rule 3(2) of the Rules of the Supreme Court which provides,

> "If the Court in the exercise of its discretion sees fit to make any order as to the costs of or incidental to any proceedings, the Court shall, subject to [Order 62], order *the costs to follow the event* except when it

appears to the Court that in the circumstances of the case some other order should be made as to the whole or any part of the costs." (emphasis added)

Although this statement of the rule seems less than firm, as a practical matter the loser of a law suit almost invariably not only pays his own legal costs but most of the costs of the successful party in the litigation.

There is the occasional rare exception to this principle usually when the winning plaintiff has suffered only nominal damages or either party has been guilty of some misconduct such as causing unnecessary delay. A good discussion of the exceptions as well as costs generally can be found in Langan, *Civil Procedure and Evidence*.[2]

Costs are very broadly defined to include solicitor's and barrister's fees, court charges, expert witness fees and most other costs of the law suit. An expert on civil procedure will always point out that the loser of litigation only has to pay the winner's "taxed" costs. That is, some costs are fixed by scale and the winner always has to justify that all his costs are not excessive to a court official, the taxing master. But as the Final Report of the Committee on Supreme Court Practice and Procedure, 1953 (referred to as the Evershed Report), the most extensive consideration of the subject in the last several decades, pointed out, it is difficult for a taxing master to disallow an expenditure which a solicitor thinks is necessary.[3] Taxing masters of the Supreme Court on average allow the successful party about 80 to 85 per cent. of the costs he claims.[4]

III—Public Interest Litigation Should be Encouraged

The following are typical hypothetical examples of civil rights law suits which probably are discouraged by the rule that costs follow the event. A government department uses wire tapping or the Official Secrets Act apparently to stifle freedom of the Press. A local authority uses its planning powers to prevent minority group families from living in an area. Prison officials severely treat prisoners. The Department of Health and Social Security discriminates against unmarried mothers. Many other public interest law suits of the type illustrated by the following hypothetical examples also are discouraged. The government negligently supervises insurance companies or other regulated enterprises resulting in losses to users. Utilities charge rates which discriminate against the poor. Corporations create injury through negligent design or pollution.

It might very well be in the public interest to have these matters litigated. Many of them involve areas where the government considers that it has a right to complete discretion and secrecy. Yet both complete discretion and secrecy are anathema to civil rights. The possibility of litigation will cause the relevant government officials to think before they act and make sure that they can justify their actions with good reasons. The existence of the litigation will reveal the facts before a neutral and independent tribunal. The adversary system means that all possible interpretations of the facts will come out. Such litigation will let the public know whether a problem

or injustice does or does not exist. All these results are valuable in themselves whether or not the plaintiff is ultimately granted a remedy.[5]

Encouraging such litigation might have an adverse effect on the efficiency
of the government and enterprises. If the volume of such litigation became
exceedingly great, of course, values would have to be balanced.

There is another, perhaps more philosophical, reason why such litigation
should be encouraged. The plaintiffs in such cases frequently will be
members of minority or disadvantaged groups. They often do not have
effective access to the party political process because they are small in
numbers or their cause is unpopular with the majority. No M.P.s or local
councillors rush to their aid and they may not have peaceful ways of
getting press coverage. The courts can give these people a forum where
they can present their claim on their own initiative, where its justice can
be tested by the presentation of facts and reasoned argument, and where
if their claim proves just, an effective remedy can be granted to them. In
this way they will have an opening into the political system.

Democracy by its very premises should provide some method of effective
representation for all groups no matter how small or unpopular. This will
make it much less necessary for such groups to engage in demonstrations or
violence to get attention, forms of political access which are much less
convenient to the general citizenry. The government can act with a clearer
conscience and perhaps with greater public support when it does suppress
any violence by such groups. It can argue that they do have a useful
peaceful means of making their point.

A country with a political process run under law is a much more com-
fortable place for all to live in. One of the best ways of inducing all groups
to obey the law is by permitting and encouraging them to make use of it
for their own benefit. The government now is facing the problem of
attempting to introduce some regulative aspects into industrial relations.
The courts at the turn of the century appeared not to be giving the unions
fair treatment. The unions became politically strong enough to have
industrial relations taken outside the legal process. Now the unions and
shop stewards have become unused to, opposed to and unco-operative
with legal constraints being introduced into industrial relations. Had the
unions originally been given fairer access to the courts for their own purposes, perhaps they would be more accommodating to an attempt to
introduce some regulation into labour relations.

In many of these cases the plaintiff claiming that his civil rights had been
violated would be unsuccessful. The court might decide that the minister
did have complete discretion under the statute, or there was some reason or
statute to justify his decision. In other areas of public interest litigation the
court might find that the plaintiff could not prove on the balance of
probabilities that a company had negligently designed a product or an
insurance association had been guilty of misrepresentation. If the civil
rights or public interest claimant lost he would be liable to pay the legal
costs of the defendant government department or corporation. (The
Crown is in a somewhat more favourable position to recover its costs from

the opposing party than a private litigant as provided by section 7 of the Administration of Justice Act 1933.) These would quite justifiably be large. Since the behaviour of the organisation was being questioned it would be entitled to hire the best and most expensive counsel and put the maximum of time and effort into its defence. The possibility of having to pay such large costs would discourage most persons from bringing this valuable litigation.

If the possible civil rights or public interest plaintiff was not liable for the defendant's costs he would be much more likely to litigate. The maximum he would be out of pocket would be his own legal expenses. These are predictable, controllable and can be moderate. The plaintiff can be represented by younger counsel, can limit the amount of time spent on the case, and put limits on the amount of investigation done. In this way litigation can be carried on with a maximum possible outlay in the hundreds of pounds rather than the thousands of pounds at risk if the plaintiff had to pay defendant's costs. It is interesting to note in this regard that High Court litigation can be carried on at moderate expense if desired. The average spent in solicitors' and barristers' fees in High Court civil litigation financed by legal aid in 1970 was £155 per case.[6] Possibly the skill of representation would not be quite as high at these more moderate prices. But in view of the novelty of the typical action contemplated, the experience of more distinguished counsel may not be crucial.

Obviously in a scheme where each party bears his own legal costs, the civil rights plaintiff will also pay his own costs if he wins. Since these probably can be afforded by parties with moderate means they should not too greatly discourage such litigation from being brought. Indeed the civil rights plaintiff should believe his claim sufficiently important to be willing to commit some of his own funds in support of it. This is a good way of insuring that there is some merit or importance to the claim. If the claimant has a strong claim and is impecunious he should be entitled to legal aid. If the claim is important but more doubtful, a poor man hopefully should be able to find a civil rights, religious, ethnic or other organisation willing to finance the moderate cost of the litigation.

Legal aid is not the ideal method to finance this kind of law suit. The aid limits are quite low. There is a requirement that the claim have a moderately good chance of succeeding in law, which is probably fair since the state is paying for it. Most importantly much of this public interest litigation will be brought against the government in one guise or another. It is unwise for the government to be in a position of financing legal action against itself. The Legal Aid Certifying Committee could quite easily decide that litigation such as this should not be brought. Professor Gerald Dworkin seems to believe that a comment by the Master of the Rolls that legal aid was financing too many unsuccessful appeals, even though qualified by the proviso that it should not become too cautious either, resulted in a lower percentage of appeals being authorised.[7] However, the actual percentage of requests for appeal granted actually declined only from 63 per cent. to 58 per cent. which perhaps is too small a difference to generalise from. In admittedly quite a different governmental context there has been continuous political pressure by Governor Reagan of California to prevent lawyers provided to poor neighbourhoods by the war-on-poverty programme of the national government from suing the state.

The question may be asked, is it just to require a governmental body or corporation to pay its own costs in litigation brought against it which it has won? The financial burden will not be great for such institutions. More importantly all powerful organisations should have the burden of showing that they are not exercising that power unwisely or unjustly. This is one of the requirements that a polity can require of such organisations to permit their continued existence in a form far more potent than the ordinary citizen.

There have been a few recent examples where litigation was probably brought to focus public attention on an issue. The contempt of court action against *The Sunday Times*[8] for publishing an article about thalidomide children seemed to have been instigated by *The Sunday Times* which in advance brought copies of the article to the attention of all the parties. Though the newspaper's loss of the case in the Divisional Court, a decision later upheld by the House of Lords, prevented publication of the article the litigation seemed to have succeeded in creating more public attention and interest in the issue than the publication of the original article would have done.

Mr. Blackburn's case to get the police to increase activity against pornography failed.[9] However, it was useful in bringing out the enforcement procedures and criteria of the police. Obviously all sides of the political spectrum, left, right and centre could attempt such litigation in what they feel is the public interest.

There have been several recent situations where litigation was not brought but where it would have served a useful public function whether the plaintiff won or lost. Thus, it would be important for the protection of civil rights to know what the Home Secretary thinks is subversive political activity when he orders the deportation of an alien such as Rudi Dutschke. Indeed the knowledge that he might have to give real reasons for his actions might put certain constraints on his behaviour. Similarly a hearing before a court by adversary process might prove salutary in regard to the demise of the Vehicle and General Insurance Co. This may well have been a governmental mistake involving both political parties and where one might suspect that the parliamentary questioning would be restrained. The likelihood of litigation also might induce the relevant civil servants to inform the public about the state of the companies they are regulating.

IV—Litigation Should be Easier for Moderate Income Persons

The abolition of the principle that costs follow the event and its replacement with a general rule that each party shall pay its own costs in litigation might also serve a useful purpose in ordinary law suits where matters of special public concern are not at issue. However the weight of opinion seems to be contrary to this assertion.

A major argument in favour of the change is that people with plausible claims ought to be able to litigate them. Indeed it is one of the most fundamental aspects of the legal system. The present system of having costs follow the event discourages the man of moderate means from litigating because of the fear that if he loses (and even if the claim is quite strong there is always a possibility of losing) he will be seriously hurt financially. There is no way he can predict the opponent's costs in advance and they could be very large. A man of average income would not be unduly discouraged from litigating if he knows that his maximum outlay even if unsuccessful will be his own costs, a sum which he can probably keep to an affordable amount. (The less well-off person will have the protection of legal aid.) This argument was made earlier in the context of public interest litigation and has some support in the literature. A practitioner has made the point[10] and there is an interesting note in the *Solicitor's Journal*.[11] The Evershed Report considered the argument without ever specifically accepting or rejecting it.[12] But the Report did not recommend any changes which would imply acceptance of it. Professor Gower has also argued that parties of moderate means are unduly prevented from litigating by the cost of law suits.[13] He suggests that the costs of litigation could be substantially reduced by moving virtually all civil litigation to the county court.

The chief contenders for the rule that costs should follow the event are Professor Goodhart,[14] Professor Ehrenzweig,[15] and the Law Society in its presentation to the Evershed Committee.[16] It is also probably fair to say that a large majority of the legal profession, practising and academic, believe this as well.

Several arguments are advanced. The only way a man of moderate means can bring litigation is if he knows he is going to get his costs reimbursed at the end, especially if the claim is for a small amount. This is the only way he could ever afford to get the best counsel. The man who wins a law suit is much more likely to have the just claim and it is only right that he should receive both the money due to him and his legal costs. Many people would bring claims or make defences of no merit if they knew they would not be liable for the winner's costs.

These arguments have also been stated in another context in the United States law journals. A number of articles advocate that the United States adopt the English system that costs including legal fees follow the event in order primarily to reduce litigation and court congestion.[17] Generally each party bears his own litigation expenses in the United States. Although technically the successful party is awarded costs, costs do not normally include legal fees there and tend to be of a rather nominal amount.

Implicit in all the above arguments is that in most litigation there is a right and meritorious party and a wrong and malicious party. This premise can be questioned. In most disputes there might very well be some justice on both sides. Each feels his claim is sound. Negligence is an inherently nebulous concept. Clauses in statutes and contracts are unclear. The goods were not in first-class condition but the purchaser got them at an exceptionally low price. Frequently to complete a business transaction the lawyer must paper over disagreement with ambiguity. (It is far more important that a business transaction be made than that it falter over a disagreement upon a minor provision which most probably will never be significant.)

If these matters ultimately reach a decision in the court, the system generally requires that the court decide for one party or another. But the hope should be that in the large majority of situations the parties will be able to compromise the dispute sometime before it reaches judgment at an amount fairly reflecting the merits of each party's claim.

However, in most situations the first party has the money and the second party has the defective refrigerator, or the first party has the untouched lorry and the second party has the damaged wing. Frequently there is justice on both sides but the status quo is in favour of the first party. He has got the money. There is no effective way the second party can put pressure on the first party to settle at an amount fairly representing the relative merits. The threat to bring suit will not move the first party. Both know that the second party, especially if he is a man of moderate means, is unlikely to carry it through. Even if the chances are three to one that he will win, the fear of losing and having to pay the expenses of the other side will deter him. This is more likely to be the case where the first party is a large corporation, insurance company or governmental body. A policy on its part which the second party knows about, to fight expensively all claims will put off most second parties unless their case is iron-clad.

If each side paid its own costs in litigation, a second party would not be deterred from suing by the possibility of having to pay the other side's large costs. Both sides would know this and so the second party's bargaining strength would be greatly increased. There would be a much better chance to work out a compromise settlement based on the relative merits of each side's case.

It is true that in this conception a second party whose claim had some legitimacy but was weaker than the first party's would still have some bargaining power and could probably settle for some percentage of his claim. The first party would know that even if he won he would be out the legal costs of his defence. If you believed that there is more likely to be right and wrong in a dispute rather than relative merits you would probably think that this is an unjust result. But with the opposite belief it would be fair enough.

The above conception of disputes would also lead one not to be disturbed that a successful party in litigation which reached judgment would not receive his costs. The fact that a better result was reached in the large majority of disputes which were ultimately settled by the parties would outweigh the small number of cases which were decided by the courts and where the winner was not made whole. Indeed if there is not complete justice on the winner's side it would seem proper that the amount of his recovery would be reduced by his costs.

If the above model of a legal dispute is correct and there is some validity in its premise that there is usually merit on both sides, then a system where each side paid its own costs in a legal dispute would seem to help the man of moderate means by increasing his bargaining power. The result would be the same if the man of moderate means was the defendant though the examples were based on his being a plaintiff. This model would conflict with Professor Goodhart's belief that it is a good thing that parties are discouraged from bringing law suits which they do not intend to try.[18]

The argument that there usually is some merit to both sides in a legal dispute has some authority on its side as well as conviction. The point was made with considerable elegance in a *Solicitor's Journal* note[19] and the proposition seemed to be seriously considered by the Evershed Committee.[20] Conclusive empiric data is unlikely ever to be available since assessment of the relative merits of cases is so much a matter of opinion. Also the vast majority of claims will never reach the trial stage where they will be accessible to the public. It is interesting to note that an informal assessment of the justice of criminal jury decisions has just been completed in which the observers sat through the trial and compared their own views with that of the jury.[21]

We do have empiric evidence contradicting the argument that people of moderate means can bring medium-sized claims if costs follow the event. This argument is made strongest by Professor Ehrenzweig particulary as regards of consumer claims.[22] When the Consumer Council looked through the files of many county court cases and consulted a large number of solicitors they could find virtually no consumer claims which were even brought to the point of filing suit.[23] Such cases seem to be so rare that one which was actually litigated about a defective car made the national press for a week.[24] The plaintiff also happened to be a barrister.

It is interesting to note that somebody in the civil service seems to believe in the proposition that the person of moderate means is in a much better position to litigate a claim if each side bears its own costs. The Industrial Tribunal regulations for redundancy payments claims, unfair dismissals and actions under the Contracts of Employment Act 1972 provide that each party will normally pay his own costs.[25] In these situations there is usually an employee of average income suing a wealthier employer. But in cases which involve selective employment payments and what are registered dock premises the rules provide that costs can be taxed against the loser.[26] In these situations usually the more prosperous employer will be litigating against the government.

Fears that having each party bear his own costs will lead to many unmeritorious claims are probably based on the confusion of that concept with the contingent fee. It is probably true that in the United States the combination of each party paying his own costs with the contingent fee has led to the making of nuisance claims of little validity in personal injury litigation. A plaintiff risks nothing with such a scheme as he does not have to pay his own or the other side's legal costs if he loses. But if there is no contingent fee, a party will be out his own legal costs if he brings an unmeritorious suit and this will be a strong deterrent. The justification for the contingent fee in the United States that it provides legal services for the poor, has no relevance in England with its well-developed civil legal aid scheme.

V—Legal Resources Should be Used More Efficiently

The present system of costs also has very complex rules providing that a party who delays things unnecessarily, or carries forward unnecessary types of proceedings, will be penalised by having to pay the other party's costs of these delayed or unnecessary proceedings no matter what the ultimate outcome of the litigation.[27] Professor Goodhart believes that parties will engage in all sorts of underhanded tactics unless this sanction exists.[28] Both these arguments are based on, among other things, anxiety about the unnecessary or wrongful use of legal resources. Yet the principle that costs follow the event is itself the most inconsistent with the rational and efficient use of legal services in economic theory.

Most people with even a slight faith in the value of the market in rationally allocating resources will accept that normally resources are most efficiently used if the people who use resources pay the costs of them. If people pay for the electricity they use they will turn off the light when they leave the room. If they do not pay for it, they will not turn it off. If people pay for the water they use they will hire a plumber to fix a leak. If they do not pay, they will let the cold water tap drip.

Under the present system of costs if you win you pay nothing for the legal services you have hired and used. If you lose you pay not only your own costs but somebody else's as well. Hence there is little incentive to make use of younger, less experienced counsel or fewer expert witnesses. If you win, the saving of costs is meaningless since you do not save but the other party saves. With costs following the event the incentive is for each side to hire the most expensive counsel and maximise the number of witnesses put on the stand. Though the strength they add to the case may be slight in relation to their cost, the hope is they will turn the balance and the party will not have to pay for them at all. Indeed each party will probably believe that maximising costs will serve as "deserved punishment" to the other party who will hopefully pay them. The Evershed Report put forward a somewhat similar argument again without specifically accepting or rejecting it.[29]

A rule whereby each party pays his own costs is likely to be more consistent with a rational and efficient use of legal resources. A party will be disinclined to build up extra legal costs which will not add very much to the strength of his claim or defence when that party will have to pay those costs win, lose, or settle. It is unlikely that a party who knows he will have to pay the costs will hire the best Q.C. and five expert witnesses when the dispute is over the quality of £5,000 of wheat, and a young barrister and one expert witness will make the point almost as well.[30]

The present system of having costs follow the event is what makes it necessary to have complex special rules about taxing costs against parties who delay. Otherwise the party who delayed or commenced unnecessary procedures and won would not have to pay any of the costs of the delay or unnecessary proceedings. If each party paid its own costs, then a party would be deterred from causing delay or utilising vexatious procedures because he would have to pay his own substantial costs entailed by those tactics, win or lose.

VI—Conclusion

Shifting from a system where the loser pays the winner's costs to a system where each party bears his own costs in litigation will not create any dramatic new results. It will make it somewhat easier to bring before the courts matters involving fundamental rights so that those rights can grow and be clarified. It will encourage the civil rights or public interest claimant to litigate matters which it would probably be in the country's benefit to have brought before the courts. It may make it somewhat easier for the man of moderate means to exercise his fundamental right of having a court decide his dispute, and will put him in a fairer bargaining position. Possibly there might be the need for an occasional exception to a rule that each party bears his own costs in the probably rare case of the completely spurious claim or defence. Finally, and not in complete seriousness, may I be permitted the classic lawyer's stratagem of attempting to shift the burden of proof onto the other side. Most judges, barristers and solicitors believe that a market system is the most efficient way of allocating non-legal resources. Should they not have to show why it is not the best way of allocating legal services?

NOTES

1. (1924), Vol. 4, pp. 536–538.
2. (1970), Chap. 12. For a more detailed discussion of the exceptions see Samuels, "Costs Follow the Event: The Exceptions" (1964) 108 S. J. 470, 492.
3. Evershed Report (1953) Cmd. 8878, p. 233.
4. Civil Judicial Statistics for the Year 1971 (1972) Cmnd. 4982, p. 10.
5. For another discussion on the public interest in having certain types of law suits brought see Hornstein, "Legal Therapeutics: The Salvage Factor in Counsel Fee Awards" (1956) 69 Harv. L. Rev. 658.
6. Legal Aid and Advice, 21st Report of the Law Society to Parliament 1970–71: 1971–1972 [1973] H.C. 283, p. 24.
7. Dworkin, "The Progress and Future of Legal Aid in Civil Litigation" (1965) 28 M. L. R. 432, 436.
8. *Att.-Gen.* v. *Times Newspapers*, 3 All E.R. 54.
9. *Blackburn* v. *Metropolitan Police Commissioner*, *The Times*, November 28, 1972.
10. Harper, "What Price Justice!" (1960) 57 L. S. Gaz. 385.
11. E.A.W., "Punishing the Loser" (1959) 103 S. J. 866.
12. Evershed Report, p. 234.
13. Gower, "The Cost of Litigation" (1954) 17 M.L.R. 1.
14. Goodhart, "Costs" (1929) 38 Yale L. J. 849.
15. Ehrenzweig, "Reimbursement of Counsel Fees and the Great Society" (1966) 54 Calif. L. Rev. 792.
16. Evershed Report, pp. 234–235.
17. Stoebuck, "Counsel Fees Included in Costs: A Logical Development"

(1965–66) 38 U. Colo. L. Rev. 202; Greenberger, "The Cost of Justice: An American Problem, An English Solution" (1964) 9 Vill. L. Rev. 400; Cheek, "Attorneys' Fees: Where shall the Ultimate Burden Lie" (1966–67) 20 Vand. L. Rev. 1216; Kuenzel, "The Attorney's Fee: Why not a Cost of Litigation" (1963) 49 Ia. L. Rev. 75.
18. Goodhart, *op. cit.*, p. 870.
19. E.A.W., *op. cit.*, p. 867.
20. Evershed Report, p. 235.
21. McCabe and Purves, *The Jury at Work* (1972) reviewed in Berlin, "Survey Puts a Spanner in the Work of Law Reform," *The Times*, July 21, 1972.
22. Ehrenzweig, *op. cit.*, p. 792.
23. The Consumer Council, *Justice Out of Reach* (H.M.S.O. 1970).
24. "Rogue Car Man to Get his Money Back," *The Times*, December 19, 1972, p. 5.
25. Industrial Tribunal (Redundancy Payment) Regulations 1967, S.I. 1967 No. 359, reg. 10; Industrial Tribunal (Employment and Compensation) Regulations 1967, S.I. 1967 No. 361, reg. 10; Industrial Tribunal (Industrial Relations, etc.) Regulations 1972, S.I. 1972 No. 38, reg. 13(1).
26. Industrial Tribunal (Selective Employment Payments) Regulations 1966, S.I. 1966 No. 1231, reg. 9; Industrial Tribunal (Dock Work) Regulations 1967, S.I. 1967 No. 313, reg. 9; Industrial Tribunal (Industrial Relations, etc.) Regulations 1972, S.I. 1972 No. 38, reg. 13(3).
27. See the discussion in Langan, *op. cit.*, pp. 318–320.
28. Goodhart, *op. cit.*, p. 872.
29. Evershed Report, pp. 233–234.
30. For an attempt at a more detailed economic analysis of legal costs see Schwartz and Mitcher, "An Economic Analysis of the Contingent Fee in Personal Injury Litigation" (1969–70) 22 Stan. L. Rev. 1125.

12. A CONSTABLE'S DUTY AND FREEDOMS OF PERSON AND PROPERTY

J. G. CARTRIDGE

I—Introduction

THIS essay deals with police powers to detain for interrogation and to seize property for use as evidence. The essay is therefore concerned with two fundamental rights, rights of person and property.

Two ways in which the law secures these rights are as follows. First unsolicited interference from a third party with person or property may raise the justification of self-defence. Secondly such interference may be made either chargeable or actionable. The right is therefore the right to resist or take legal proceedings of the appropriate nature. In this sense it follows that if such interference may not be justifiably resisted or otherwise made the subject of legal proceedings, the right ceases to exist.

In the context under discussion unsolicited interference from a third party may often be neither justifiably resisted nor made the subject of legal proceedings, if that third party is the police. This may be put another way. Where the law affords the police power to detain the individual for interrogation or to seize his property for use as evidence, the individual's fundamental rights of person and property cease to exist.

The aim of this essay will be to consider these police powers to detain the individual for interrogation and to seize his property for use as evidence, but with this limitation. In the first instance only where the facts do not activate powers of arrest. If this aim is achieved, the area in which these police powers operate will be mapped out. So too will the area in which the rights affected may be said to cease existence.

One final word before the essay embarks upon its aim. The emphasis will not be upon the extent of the relevant police powers. It will be upon their nature.

II—The Nature of Police Powers

In the succeeding analysis police powers will be described as either "specific" or "general" in nature. The underlying theme will be as follows. That specific powers restrict the area in which the police may lawfully act against the individual's fundamental rights and therefore the area in which these rights may be said to cease existence. Conversely that general powers in the police expand both areas. The extra protection afforded by specific powers becomes more apparent if it is noted that the epithet "specific" may bear one of three meanings—

161

1. Specific in the sense that the power, by the requirement of reasonable belief in stated conditions, lays down two separate specifications. A specific state of mind and the independent existence of specific facts. Therefore a condition that AB must have reasonable cause to believe X before he is entitled to do Y calls for the following. First a belief by AB in X. Secondly the independent existence of facts sufficient to support a reasonable cause for AB's belief in X; it will not be enough if AB honestly thinks there is reasonable cause to believe X. To give these propositions substance, section 2(4) of the Criminal Law Act 1967 may be cited as an example of a specific power in the sense under discussion, "Where a constable, with reasonable cause, suspects that an arrestable offence has been committed, he may arrest without warrant anyone whom he, with reasonable cause, suspects to be guilty of the offence." The subsection therefore lays down two specifications. A suspicion that the arrestee has committed an arrestable offence. And the independent existence of the type of facts capable of supporting a reasonable cause for such suspicion. This will not be the case with a general power which in this sense will be characterised by the absence of any requirement of reasonable belief in stated conditions. An example of such a general power may be stated thus. In order to preserve the peace, constable AB is entitled to take the steps he feels are necessary to achieve that objective. The consequences for the individual whose rights are affected by a general power of this nature will be more fully developed in sections III and IV.

2. Specific in the sense that the power has already been specified in precedent or statute and is therefore limited to such specifications. The point here is that the form and substance of the power will have been crystallised by prior authority and will not be capable of application to novel fact situations unless on all four squares with those of the prior authorities.

3. Specific in the sense that the exercise of the power only authorises the police to act against a specific person or against specific property, and not against persons or property generally. By way of illustration, the power of search and seizure afforded the police by Palles C.B. in *Dillon* v. *O'Brien* may be given, ". . . constables . . . are entitled, upon a lawful arrest by them of one charged with treason or felony, to take and detain property found in his possession which will form material evidence in his prosecution for that crime."[1]

The power is specific in the sense that upon the arrest of X, it specifies that only property in the possession of X, which is evidence of the crime for which he was arrested, may be detained. Accordingly once seized with exercise of the power, the police are not entitled to proceed generally against other property of X or another third party *unless* the condition of that power's exercise are satisfied *de novo*.

The significance of the meanings attached to "specific" in 2 and 3 above will be more fully developed in section IV.

III—Power to Detain for Interrogation before Arrest

Four modern authorities will be considered.[2] Each one involves a charge under section 51 of the Police Act 1964, the material parts of which read,—

> "(1) Any person who assaults a constable in the execution of his duty . . . shall be guilty of an offence. . . .
> (3) Any person who . . . wilfully obstructs a constable in the execution of his duty . . . shall be guilty of an offence. . . ."

The key issue is of course what is meant by a constable "in the execution of his duty." In all four cases the constable in question wished to detain the defendant for interrogation but not to arrest him. In no case did the defendant contend that the constable was not seeking to achieve an objective of his duty recognised by law. Each time the objective was to detect or prevent crime. Resolution of this key issue therefore depended on whether the conduct of the constable, in seeking to achieve this objective, fell within the exercise of a power to detain and interrogate then available to him. And as stated in the introduction, it is with the nature and extent of such powers that this essay is concerned.

In the first case to be considered, *Rice* v. *Connolly*, Rice appealed to the Divisional Court against his conviction for wilful obstruction under section 51(3) of the 1964 Act. Briefly the facts were as follows. At 1 a.m. two constables were on the look-out for suspects following a number of breaking-in offences. They saw Rice walking around the streets of Grimsby in a suspicious fashion and approached him in order to ask for his particulars. Rice refused to respond fully and the constables directed him to accompany them to a police box so that his identity could be checked, but Rice refused to move. At no stage beforehand was arrest contemplated but for this alleged obstruction, Rice was arrested and later charged. In the Divisional Court Lord Parker held that Rice had obstructed the constables in the execution of their duty. However he quashed the conviction on the ground that the obstruction had not been wilful. To act wilfully the person obstructing must act without lawful excuse and this Rice did not do as there was no duty to answer the constables' question or accompany them to the police box.[3]

What does this decision tell us of police powers to detain and interrogate before arrest? In part of his judgment[4] Lord Parker said that Rice had the right to refuse to answer police questions and to accompany them to a police box, short of arrest. This dicta is important for it suggests that the police power to detain and interrogate is merely an adjunct to the power of arrest with no separate existence of its own. Following on from section II, this means that the individual whose right is affected knows his freedom of person from police interference only ceases if the police suspect he has committed an arrestable offence and are able to point to independent facts giving reasonable cause for such suspicion.

Unfortunately when dealing with the key issue of whether the constables were in the execution of their duty, Lord Parker let fall the following dicta which suggests the police are not restricted to the exercise of specific powers:

> "It is also in my judgment clear that it is part of the obligations and duties of a police constable to take all steps which appear to him necessary for keeping the peace, for preventing crime or from protecting property from criminal injury. There is no exhaustive definition of the powers and obligations of the police, but they are at least those, and they would further include the duty to detect crime and to bring an offender to justice."

This passage suggests that provided a constable is seeking to achieve a valid objective of his duty, he may take all the steps he feels are necessary for the purpose. This presents no problems if it applies to a constable who is merely interrogating a suspect in order to detect crime. Although incidentally it does deny the proposition that a constable who acts within the law to perform objectives of his duty acknowledged as valid by Lord Parker himself will not *per se* be in the execution of that duty; his conduct must first be felt necessary.[5] However it does present problems if it applies to a constable who is interrogating a suspect in order to detect crime and who uses force to detain him.

This sort of situation involves commission of a prima facie unlawful act and there are really two separate exercises for the court if it is to resolve the key issue of whether the constable is then in the execution of his duty. First it must determine the general objectives of a constable's duty, as Lord Parker did in the passage quoted from *Rice* v. *Connolly*. Secondly it must clearly articulate how the constable may achieve those objectives. Or to put it another way, it must clearly articulate the nature of the powers, if any, available to the constable for the achievement of those objectives. On this latter point it is suggested that the court has one of the following options:

1. To assume that a constable who commits an assault or other unlawful act *ipso facto* takes himself outside the execution of his duties. To keep the constable in the execution of his duty any prima facie unlawful act will therefore have to be purged of its unlawful element by falling within the exercise of either—

   (a) a specific power, such as arrest which justifies the use of force provided the specific conditions of its exercise are observed, or
   (b) a general power which justifies the use of force provided (i) the court feels the force was necessary or reasonable to achieve the objectives of the constable's duty or (ii) the constable himself feels the force was necessary or reasonable to achieve the objectives of his duty.

2. To assume that a constable who commits an assault or other unlawful act for the performance of the objectives of his duty does not necessarily take himself outside the execution of his duty.

The importance of the various options to the individual's freedom of person may be summarised thus:

A. If the option in 1(a) above is pursued, the court determines both the objectives of a constable's duty and regulates the means the constable may adopt for their achievement by requiring such means to fall within the exercise of a specific power possessed by the constable at the relevant moment of time. As a result in the context under discussion the individual knows the sanctity of his person from justifiable police interference depends on the existence of a specific state of mind in the constable together with sufficient facts in support.

B. If the option in 1(b)(i) above is pursued, the court will continue to determine the objectives of a constable's duty and to control the means adopted for their achievement, but now the individual's freedom of person will not depend upon the existence of a specific state of mind in the constable together with sufficient facts in support. Instead it will depend upon the value judgments of individual judges on what is reasonable; this in turn will depend upon whether they wish to give effect to the public interest of society in law or order represented here by the police or to the private interest of the individual.

C. If the option in 1(b)(ii) above is pursued, the court will still continue to set the objectives of a constable's duty but will now no longer control the means the constable adopts for their achievement. This latter part of the role will be abdicated in favour of the constable and will depend on his determination of what is necessary or reasonable for the achievement of the objectives of his duty. As a result the individual's freedom of person from police interference will no longer depend on the court but rather on the act of will of a particular constable.

D. If the option in 2 above is pursued, the court will be absolved from the necessity of finding any power, be it specific or general in nature, to justify the assault or otherwise and the individual's freedom of person will be at risk to police interference recognised by the law to constitute an unlawful act.

What the analysis of the remaining three cases hopes to show is that for the most part the court has not overtly reached its decisions by the means outlined above. That in particular it has failed to articulate the nature of the powers afforded the police for the execution of their duties. That as a result it is difficult to state with precision how a constable is entitled to execute his duty. That as a corollary the individual's freedom of person from lawful police interference (that is, from the police in the execution of their duty) is often uncertain.

In *Kenlin and Another* v. *Gardiner* two detective constables in plain clothes wished to interview the appellants after they had excited the constable's suspicions by approaching the front door of several houses. In fact the intention of the appellants was quite innocent; they were reminding friends of an impending rugger match. The constables went up to the appellants who mistook them for thugs and made as if to run away. At this point one detective caught hold of the first appellant to put further questions but the boy struggled and in the ensuing mêlée both detectives were assaulted. The appellants were convicted for assaulting the detectives in the execution of their duty under section 51(1) of the 1964 Act and appealed to the Divisional Court. Winn L.J. delivered the main judgment and quashed both convictions on the ground that the justification of self-defence was available to the appellants in the case of a charge of assault under section 51(1) if the prior police assault (catching hold of one appellant's arm to put further questions) was itself unjustified. Moreover that in this case it was unjustified as it did not constitute an integral step in the process of arresting and thus fall within the exercise of any power which the detectives as police constables then possessed in the prevailing circumstances of the case.

The principal point to note on this decision is that at no stage did Winn L.J. address his mind to the key issue of whether or not the officers were in the execution of their duty. Throughout the decision he concentrated on the wrong issue, namely whether the justification of self-defence was available to the appellants under a section 51(1) charge. Its effect as a general authority in this field must therefore be gauged with care. Certainly the decision holds that in determining whether or not police interference with the person constitutes a lawful or unlawful act, it must be justified by a power of the specific type rather than of the general type noted in 1(b) above[6] and this suggests adoption of the option set out in 1(a) above. But unfortunately Winn L.J.'s concern with the presence of an unlawful act (both he and Lord Parker held the action of the police constituted technical assault) was not on the basis that its commission would *ipso facto* take the constables outside the execution of their duty in the absence of a specific power to provide justification. His concern with the presence of an unlawful act was that it enabled the appellants to plead self-defence to the charge of assaulting a constable in the execution of his duty, an approach which presupposes that a constable who commits an assault to stop and interrogate a citizen remains within the execution of his duty.[7]

It may be argued that in any event the decision confirmed that police detention for interrogation short of arrest was unlawful. That it is therefore irrelevant if the suspect who resists will not be liable under section 51(1) on the basis that the prior police assault enables him to plead self-defence to the section 51(1) charge, rather than on the basis that the unlawful act of assault takes the constable outside the execution of his duty and prevents the charge from arising altogether. On the other hand there is nothing in Winn L.J.'s decision to prevent a person who uses unreasonable force in self-defence from being liable for conviction under section 51(1). In addition his failure to address himself to the objectives of a constable's duty and how they may be executed has led to a decision suggesting such execution may involve commission of an unlawful act. The position of the individual's freedom of person *vis-à-vis* interference from police in the execution of their duty is therefore fraught with ambiguities which the subsequent decision in *Donnelly* v. *Jackman* perpetuated for much the same reason.

This case also involved an appeal to the Divisional Court against conviction under section 51(1) for assaulting a constable in the execution of his duty. The constable in question wished to interrogate Donnelly and approached him in the street. At no stage did the constable contemplate arrest and Donnelly exercised his common law rights affirmed in *Rice* v. *Connolly* by walking away. The constable put himself in pursuit, repeatedly asked Donnelly to stop, and at one stage tapped him on the shoulder, only to receive one back on the chest. Eventually the constable realised Donnelly did not intend to stop and touched his shoulder with the intention of stopping him, not for the purpose of making any formal charge or arrest but for the purpose of interrogating him. At this point Donnelly struck the constable with some force and was arrested for assaulting the constable in the execution of his duty. Talbot J. delivered the main judgment of the Divisional Court and dismissed the appellant's appeal from conviction on the ground that it is not every trivial interference with a citizen's liberty that amounts to a course of conduct sufficient to take an officer outside the course of his duties, and that the facts of the case did not justify the view that this particular interference had.

The judgment creates uncertainties. On the assumption that Talbot J. recognises the constable had committed prima facie unlawful interference with the suspect[8] the following interpretations are possible:

1. That commission of an unlawful act would *ipso facto* take the constable outside the execution of his duty but that in this particular case powers available to the constable at the relevant time justified the use of force and negatived the unlawful element. In this event the judgment does not require the nature of the power to be specific for there is no finding that the constable in the case was or needed to be exercising powers of arrest or other statutory powers at the time he interfered with the suspect. This leaves powers of a general nature for which some support is found in Talbot J.'s reference to that passage in *Rice* v. *Connolly*, already cited, in which Lord Parker says a constable is obliged to take all steps which appear to him necessary for the performance of his duty.

2. In the alternative that commission of an unlawful act would not necessarily take the constable outside the execution of his duty provided it was no more than a trivial interference with the citizen's liberty nor a course of conduct sufficient to take the constable outside the course of his duties. Apparently these two qualities would be satisfied, paradoxically enough, by trespass to the citizen's property or assault of his person if done with intent to detain and actually successful.[9]

At this stage two problems remain unsolved. May a constable in the execution of his duty commit an unlawful act? If not, what is the nature of the power required as justification? Happily the decision in *Ludlow* v. *Burgess* answers the first explicitly and the second implicitly. In this case a constable boarding a bus was kicked in the shin by a youth. The constable thought the kick had been intentional but the youth attempted to disabuse him of the notion in strong language. The constable told the youth he was a police officer and then, as the youth began to walk away, put a hand on his shoulder in order to detain him for further questions. There was no intent to arrest the youth and he resisted forcibly with the aid of two companions. All three were charged with assaulting a constable in the execution of his duty under section 51(1) and convicted before the justices. On appeal to the Divisional Court the convictions were quashed. Detention of a man against his will without arresting him was held to be a serious interference with the citizen's liberty. Moreover as an unlawful act it could not constitute an act done in the execution of the constable's duty. The implicit element in the decision is that when faced with the commission of a prima facie unlawful act by the constable, the court required the unlawful element to be justified by a specific power as it found the constable was not exercising the power of arrest. This appears to be in line with the option noted in 1(a) above. The only possible red herring is the finding that the act of detention was also a serious interference with the citizen's liberty. But presumably, this does not qualify the type of unlawful act that will take a constable outside the execution of his duty. The explicit element that an unlawful act is not an act done in the execution of a constable's duty prohibits such deviation.

A permissible conclusion at this juncture would be that despite the brevity of the report in *Ludlow* v. *Burgess* and the omission to deal expressly with the ambiguities in the preceding authorities, the individual's freedom of person is adequately protected. However section IV of this essay will look at another aspect of police duties, the duty to preserve for use in court evidence of crime. Its purpose will be to suggest that the protection of personal rights discussed in section III may be shallowly founded; in particular that the present tendency for the judiciary is to shy away from specific powers and, in a society where crime rates are on the rise, to embrace the freedom of movement and adaptability afforded by general powers when determining the extent of police powers on the one hand and the fundamental personal or proprietary rights of the individual on the other.

IV—Power to Seize Property of Evidential Use

Performance of the duty to preserve for use in court evidence of a crime involves initial seizure and subsequent detention of property pending trial and *a fortiori* potentially unlawful interference with such property if the consent of the owner or other person lawfully in possession is lacking. There has always been authority for the proposition that the powers available to the police to justify such interference were specific in the senses noted in section II.[10] However, a trend is now in motion suggesting that in this context the police are entitled to act reasonably. In other words that powers of search and seizure no longer require a specific state of mind, nor specific facts in support, as a prerequisite to their exercise. Further that the power can be adapted to new situations and be used to proceed against persons and property generally. The aim of the section will be to plot the path of this trend and to state its consequences for the fundamental rights affected.

A good starting point is the case of *R.* v. *Waterfield and Lynn*[11] as it emphasises the protection afforded fundamental rights if the police are restricted to specific powers. In this case two constables attempted to prevent removal of the appellants' car without making any charge or arrest, but with reasonable grounds for believing it to be material evidence of an offence. Lynn thwarted the attempt by driving at the constable positioned in front of the car and was charged with assaulting the constable in the due execution of his duty, contrary to section 38 of the Offences against the Person Act 1861. Counsel for the appellants argued that the police have no power to detain the property of any person against his will unless a warrant has been issued or he is charged or arrested. Counsel for the Crown shied away from such a specific approach. He argued that the police have an undoubted duty and right to collect evidence and the test should be whether they are acting reasonably. Ashworth J. delivered the judgment of the Court of Criminal Appeal and held that the constable was not in the execution of his duty at the relevant time. He pointed out that the powers of a constable are not unlimited when execution of his general duties involves a prima facie unlawful interference[12] with person and property and in this case that neither of the appellants had been charged or was under arrest. The judgment may therefore be analysed as determining that the absence of any specific power (to arrest or prefer charges) meant the prima facie unlawful interference with the appellants' car by the constable had finally to be adjudged unlawful and as such sufficient to take the constable outside the execution of his duty.

Acceptance by Ashworth J. of the approach urged by counsel for the Crown would have had the following effect on the individual. Where the police interfere with his property, it would be more difficult for him to determine whether the constable was acting reasonably as opposed to determining whether the constable had reasonable cause to suspect him of having committed an offence. The constable might be held to be acting reasonably if he honestly thought the property was evidence of a crime committed by a third party about which the individual in possession knew nothing. The individual would therefore be unsure whether the constable's interference entitled him to resist and in this sense the existence of his rights of property would be uncertain.

The move towards affording the police general powers became apparent in *Chic Fashions (West Wales) Ltd.* v. *Jones* where the Court of Appeal had to consider whether police entering private premises pursuant to a search warrant under section 42 of the Larceny Act 1916, were entitled to seize property not mentioned in the warrant, but which they believed on reasonable grounds to have been stolen. Argument between counsel followed the pattern in *Waterfield's case*. Counsel for the plaintiff sought to restrict the police to specific powers[13] while counsel for the police contended that:

> "It is clear on the authorities that there is some additional power in the police which enables them to go outside the search warrant. There is nothing inconsistent with the authorities in saying that they can act reasonably in support of their duty to protect the public."[14]

What is interesting in this case is that unlike *Waterfield's* case, the contention on behalf of the police appeared to meet with judicial approval. In the process of giving judgment, Diplock L.J. (as he then was) said:

> ". . . the development of the common law in the last thirty years has tended towards equating civil liability with conduct which right-minded men in contemporary society would regard as blameworthy . . . and towards protecting those who act reasonably in intended performance of what rightminded men would deem a duty to their fellow men. . . ."[15]

Whatever was meant by Diplock L.J., it looked like a lurch in favour of the general power advocated by the defendant's counsel and as such it was given further momentum in *Ghani* v. *Jones*.[16] The issue before the Court of Appeal in this case was relatively narrow, but this did not restrict Lord Denning M.R. who delivered the only substantive judgment. It is enough for the purposes of this essay to note that for the first time the police were given general powers of search and seizure and in two different sets of circumstances.

First where police officers enter a man's house by virtue of a warrant or arrest a man lawfully, with or without a warrant, they are entitled to take any goods which they find in his possession or in his house which they reasonably believe to be material evidence in relation to the crime for which he is arrested or for which they enter. At this stage it may be noted that the power afforded is specific in the sense first noted in section II. Its exercise requires a specific state of mind in the police plus the existence of facts capable of supporting arrest or application for a warrant. Moreover it only entitles the police to proceed against specific property. Namely property which is evidence of the offence for which the police arrest or enter. However Lord Denning did not stop there. He said that if in the course of their search for goods that are material evidence of the crime for which they enter or arrest, the police: ". . . come upon any other goods which show him [the occupier or arrestee] to be implicated in some other crime, they may take them provided they act reasonably and detain them no longer than is necessary."[17]

Two points may be noted here:

> (1) Either "act reasonably" means there must be facts sufficient to support a reasonable cause for suspicion that the occupier or

arrestee has committed another offence, in which case it refers to reasonableness of belief and is a specific power in the sense noted above. Or "act reasonably" may refer to reasonableness of conduct, in which case the power afforded is general in nature.

(2) The power is general in the sense that it has not been previously specified in statute or precedent.

Lord Denning did not stop there either. Apparently if in the course of their search for such goods the police also find goods of any other person which implicate him in the occupier's or arrestee's crime, they may seize them too.

Three further points may be noted here.

(1) At this stage the judgment omits entirely to state whether this last power is specific or general in nature in the sense first noted above.

(2) The power is general in the sense that once more it has not been previously specified in statute or precedent.

(3) The power is general in the sense that it may relate to any person and not just the original arrestee or occupier. In other words when the police first enter, by authority of arrest or search warrant, they may initially proceed only against the property of the occupier or of the arrestee. But once seized with the exercise of that power, and provided they act reasonably, they seem to have a wandering brief to proceed generally against any property of any person which relates to the occupier's or arrestee's crime. The safeguards which hedge the operation of the initial power no longer apply.

Secondly Lord Denning afforded the police powers of a general nature in the following set of circumstances. Where the police are aware that a person is in possession of property but have no search warrant or powers of arrest, they may seize the property from that person where they have reasonable grounds for belief that:

(1) a serious offence has been committed,
(2) the property is the fruit thereof or instrumental in or material evidence of its commission, and
(3) either the person in possession committed the crime, is implicated therein or accessory thereto, or his refusal must be quite unreasonable.

There are two inherent dangers in this determination. First of all, in the process Lord Denning let slip the comment that in the type of situation occurring in Waterfield's case: ". . . nevertheless the police should be able to do whatever is necessary and reasonable to preserve the evidence of the crime, ..."[18] So the power to act reasonably appears to be extended to situations in which the police have no search warrant or powers of arrest. Secondly police powers of search or at least seizure are extended against persons who are not in any way implicated with a crime but are merely in possession of property which may constitute evidence of its commission. This is at variance with the earlier authorities which specified the person arrested or charged as the only person subject to police powers of seizure. It further creates difficulties in other areas of police duties where their powers of interference are limited to conditions activating the specific power of arrest or preferment of charges. The cases considered in section III of this essay establish that the police are not entitled to detain the suspect for interrogation short of arrest. But the position is now unclear where police interrogation establishes an individual is in possession of property which may constitute evidence of a crime with which the person in possession is unconnected. Will the police be in the execution of their duty if they use force to search for or seize the property where they believe its retention is unreasonable? Similarly will the individual be liable under section 51(1) of the Police Act 1964, if he forcibly resists? The answer of course depends on whether search and seizure is incidental to specific powers of arrest or to a general power to act reasonably for the achievement of the objectives of police duties. Moreover if the constable does not use force but merely requests delivery up and the citizen refuses, will the citizen then be liable for obstruction within section 51(3)? Following *Rice* v. *Connelly* it would be taken for granted that the constable was obstructed in the execution of his duty and the issue would therefore turn on whether there was lawful excuse for the citizen's refusal. On this the effect of *Ghani* v. *Jones* may be to make unreasonable refusal without such excuse. Of course if the citizen takes steps to remove the property by throwing it away, or, as in *R.* v. *Waterfield and Lynn*, by driving a car off but without assaulting the constable in the process, it may be that such action will in any event constitute sufficiently positive acts to amount to wilful obstruction in accordance with the decision in *Ingleton* v. *Dibble*.

As a result of this recent judicial activity the individual no longer knows in what circumstances police interference with his person or property may be pegged to certain fact situations or simply geared to what is reasonable or necessary for the performance of police duties. Nor does he know whether the powers already affirmed are static or yet to grow in number. Nor is it easy for him to gauge the permutations of persons and/or property against which these powers may lie.

V—Conclusion

To conclude, the theme of this essay has been the nature of police powers. The first part suggested that the citizen's fundamental rights were best protected by confining police activities which involved interference with the person within the exercise of specific powers as this precluded discretion from playing a dominant role in the execution of police duties. The second part expanded this theme and suggested that specific powers had other qualities which if denied would permit the judicial expansion of established powers or the creation of new ones. Taken together, the authorities prior to *Ludlow* v. *Burgess* and the recent judicial attitude towards the nature of police powers of search and seizure show that the individual's freedom from police interference short of arrest may still be at risk and also indicate the fashion in which that risk may be realised by the judiciary.

NOTES

1. (1887) 16 Cox C.C. 245 at p. 249.
2. *Rice* v. *Connolly* [1966] 2 Q.B. 414, *Kenlin* v. *Gardiner* [1967] 2 Q.B. 510, *Donnelly* v. *Jackman* [1970] 1 W.L.R. 562; and *Ludlow* v. *Burgess* [1971] Crim. L.R. 238.
3. At p. 419 Lord Parker said the police were acting throughout in accordance with their duty which implicitly confirms police powers of arrest for a suspected s. 51(3) offence. To have held that Rice on these facts was wilfully obstructing would therefore have given the police the power to pull in any person who simply refused to answer police questions. The subsequent decision in *Dibble* v. *Ingleton* [1972] 1 Q.B. 480 may have partially achieved this state of affairs with this proviso. Provided that Bridge J.'s distinction at p. 488 between a refusal to act and a positive act is authority for the proposition that while a refusal to act will be lawfully excused in the absence of a legal obligation to respond to police directions, a positive act will not. For in such a case the s. 51(3) offence will be made up by a positive act which is done with intent and which makes it more difficult for the constable to execute his duty, and a person who refuses to answer police questions and who then compounds his sin by making an active attempt to evade the police would be liable should his conduct be judicially classified as a positive act. This would limit *Rice* v. *Connolly* to feats of passive resistance until the police tire of the exercise of interrogation.
4. At p. 419.
5. *Piddington* v. *Bates* [1961] 1 W.L.R. 162 raises the same problem. Here Lord Parker upheld a conviction for wilful obstruction when a picket refused to comply with a constable's direction to move on. Like *Rice* v. *Connolly*, neither the conduct of the constable nor of the citizen (leaving aside obstruction) was unlawful; that is to say, neither actionable nor capable of forming the subject-matter of a prosecution. Unlike *Rice* v. *Connolly* the only relevant issue for Lord Parker was whether or not the constable was in the execution of his duty and not in addition whether or not the picket's conduct was with lawful excuse. Lord Parker held the constable was in the execution of his duty when he issued the direction to move on as he had reasonable grounds for anticipating that a breach of the peace was a real possibility. From this it follows that the absence of reasonable grounds would have led to the converse result without any unlawful conduct from the constable.
6. If the decision were otherwise, it is difficult to see why at p. 519 the police conduct was found to be technical assault on the ground that it ". . . was not done as an integral step in the process of arresting. . . ."
7. This is not a mistake it is likely Lord Parker would have made. During argument beforehand by counsel, he said (at p. 515) with regard to the constable's act of detaining by force, "The whole point is whether the men were acting in the execution of their duty? If not, was the assault by the boys justified on the grounds of self defence." This suggests that once it is established a constable has committed assault, *ipso facto* he takes himself outside the execution of his duty. He may then be liable for assault *simpliciter* but on no account will the suspect who resists forcibly be liable under s. 51(1). At worse use of excessive force will render him liable too for assault *simpliciter*.
8. This assumption is based on the fact that in considering the issue of whether the constable had gone outside the ambit of his duties, Talbot J. referred to a solution to the issue propounded by Ashworth J. in *R.* v. *Waterfield and Lynn* [1964] 1 Q.B. 164 which was applicable in circumstances where the police had committed prima facie unlawful interference with person or property.
9. This conclusion is drawn from Talbot J.'s distinction of *Davis* v. *Lisle* [1936] 2 K.B. 434 and *Kenlin* v. *Gardiner*, *supra* from the present case on the ground that the police, to take themselves outside the execution of their duty, had respectively committed trespass and assault which effectively secured detention.

10. See Leigh "Recent Developments in the Law of Search and Seizure" (1970) 33 M.L.R. 268.
11. [1964] 1 Q.B. 164.
12. A detailed analysis by Fitzgerald, "The Arrest of a Motor-Car" [1965] Crim. L.R. 23 suggests that on the facts of the case no unlawful act was committed by the constables; this does not affect the analysis in the text as it is clear that Ashworth J. proceeded on the basis that the constable's conduct was in fact flawed by an unlawful element.
13. [1968] 2 Q.B. at p. 303.
14. At p. 302.
15. At p. 315.
16. [1970] 1 Q.B. 693.
17. At p. 706.
18. At p. 708.

13. PUBLICITY FOR CRIMINAL TRIALS

M. E. BENNUN

I—Introduction

IT has become part of the shared ethic of civilised men that the social response to crime must not go beyond certain defined boundaries without itself becoming improper. Present and past experience supply irrefutable evidence of a need to ensure certain minimum standards in criminal procedure: the criminal and suspect are to be persons entitled to humane treatment. In this paper it is proposed to consider just one of the characteristics a criminal trial is now generally required to display: that is, one aspect of the principle that justice must be done and be seen to be done.

The discussion is confined essentially to proceedings in superior courts before a jury and generally little distinction will be drawn between Press and public gallery.

The keynote is set by the Universal Declaration of Human Rights (1948). Article 10 states that "Everyone is entitled in full equality to fair and public hearing by an independent and impartial tribunal, in the determination of his rights and obligations and of any criminal charge against him." Article 14 of the International Covenant on Civil and Political Rights (1966) uses much the same terms, but goes on to define a little more clearly the content of the words "public hearing" by setting out the circumstances in which the Press and public may be excluded from all or part of a trial:

> "for reasons of morals, public order or national security in a democratic society, or when the interest of the private lives of the parties so requires, or to the extent strictly necessary in the opinion of the court in special circumstances where publicity would prejudice the interests of justice; but any judgment rendered in a criminal case or in a suit of law shall be made public except where the interest of juvenile persons otherwise requires or the proceedings concern matrimonial disputes of the guardianship of children."

Article 14(3) sets out more fully other requirements of a criminal trial; in particular, Article 14(3)(d) requires the presence of the accused and defines his right to legal assistance.

Similar words appear in the European Convention on Human Rights (1966). Article 6(1) stipulates that "In the determination of . . . any criminal charge against him, everyone is entitled to a fair and public hearing . . .," and then goes on to limit the circumstance in which the Press and public may be excluded in much the same terms as the International Covenant. The American Convention on Human Rights (1969), at Article 8(5), says simply: "Criminal procedure shall be public, except in so far as may be necessary to protect the interests of justice."

There is no requirement that the Press and public *must* be present,[1] and the circumstances in which they may be excluded are fairly wide-ranging. The International Covenant seems to suggest that such exclusion is generally a matter of policy except where "publicity would prejudice the interests of justice"; presumably the court would always have a residual power of exclusion. Whether the decision is taken politically or judicially, however, it would seem that provided the power is exercised in terms of the Article a trial is not to be regarded as a "secret" and thus in breach of the Covenant. The exclusion of the Press and public does not necessarily mean that a trial flouts the fundamental civil right of the subject to a public hearing.

It is one of the oldest traditions of the criminal law in this country that a trial should be public.[2] It is not easy to state when the tradition became settled, but it is clear that it is of some antiquity and one to which great importance is rightly attached. Indeed it may well be that the very definition of a criminal trial requires as an element recognition that the public is actively and directly concerned in the proceedings. A civil court seems a little—and only a little—more willing and able to consider whether its doors may not be properly closed; there is, for example, no statute applicable primarily to criminal trials comparable with section 2 of the Domestic and Appellate Proceedings (Restriction of Publicity) Act 1968, whose short title indicates its narrow scope.

The characteristics of the criminal trial as we know it in Britain have emerged over a long period and the process of change and development continues, for the law changes with society. It is important that today we should not forget that even in very recent times important changes have been made or advocated: for example the verdict of the jury, the admissibility of confessions, and the right to silence have been touched on, affecting matters of fundamental principle. Such changes as have been made are not arbitrary. They have been put forward as necessary as a result of a better understanding of the operation of society and its institutions; of changes in technology; of changes in moral and ethical attitudes; in brief, as a result of changes in society itself.

Two topics will be mentioned briefly. They illustrate the ongoing evolution of the law, and it seems that they bear significantly on the operation of the principle that trials must be public in nature. First, it seems that the public first entered the criminal court in the form of the jury. Professor Jackson notes that it was simply not possible for a trial to be anything but public in the earliest stages of the criminal law for the jury were the prisoner's neighbours and were there precisely because they knew the facts. "Open court," he writes, "was not derived from liberal thought but was an almost inevitable consequence of our system of courts and use of juries."[3] The actors, as it were, remain the same but the plot changes: the circumstance today that a man knows something about the prisoner before the trial starts may serve to exclude him from the jurybox altogether. In such a case a challenge for cause may lie.[4] The jury today, starting by knowing nothing about the case, ensures justice is done by standing between the prisoner and those who seek to condemn him. In the final analysis, if it is dissatisfied with the prosecution it has in its hands a weapon which admits of no defence and which can never be taken from it: it may acquit, and that is the end of the matter. It is significant that the only verdict it may be ordered to return is an acquittal. The readiness of juries to reflect prevailing social attitudes and acquit is a frequent source of complaint from prosecuting authorities, and indeed has led to important changes in the law.[5] In theory at least the decision to convict or to acquit is taken by twelve individuals chosen almost at random from the prisoner's fellow citizens, and their decision in his favour cannot be impeached. So powerful is the role of the jury that the words Lord Devlin used in concluding his Hamlyn Lectures are surely not one word too dramatic:

> "The first object of any tyrant in Whitehall would be to make Parliament utterly subservient to his will; and the next to overthrow or diminish trial by jury, for no tyrant could afford to leave a subject's freedom in the hands of twelve of his countrymen. So that trial by jury is more than an instrument of justice and more than one wheel of the constitution: it is the lamp that shows that freedom lives."[6]

The Morris Committee linked citizenship with jury service[7] and recommended the abolition of the property qualification, and this is now law.[8] Perhaps we should go beyond regarding jury service as merely a duty flowing from citizenship; and see it instead as a right pertaining thereto no less fundamental than the franchise.

The second matter to be touched on is the development of the right to be defended by a lawyer. This is taken for granted today but it took two attempts before the Prisoners' Counsel Act 1837 became law. There was bitter opposition to the proposal that a defendant should be entitled to a legal representative. Without doubt the objections were advanced in all sincerity by men who genuinely feared for the quality of justice flowing from the courts, but in retrospect we can safely say that the stream runs only purer and sweeter for the change. Lawyers in both Houses spoke of cost,[9] delay, a slur on the presiding judge and an increase in his workload to such a degree that "no judge in the country possessed physical or mental power equal to the task."[10] It was suggested that there were dangers to the prisoner from the adverse statements that the judge would have to make. Lord Wharncliffe said that the judge would have to listen to defending counsel, and would then have to strip the speech in defence of the prisoner of counsel's highly coloured effects and "state the naked facts to the jury in order that their judgment ought not to be led astray by the meretricious arguments used by counsel."[11] We have gone a long way since those days.

There have been other developments also, cumulatively of tremendous importance. At about the same time as he was allowed counsel, the prisoner was given the right to see the depositions against him,[12] and later became a competent witness on his own behalf.[13] Public hangings and ultimately the death penalty itself were abolished—and it is merely a matter of impression if one suggests that the latter was the more bitterly opposed.[14] Sentencing has been clearly influenced by sociological thought and experience—*vide* the development of probation, extended and suspended sentences, and aftercare. The very institutions in which custodial sentences are served are changing, and now differ from each other to such an extent that they in fact form the essence of totally different sentences. The pressure is against removing the offender from the community. The sentencing phase itself takes more and more of the court's time, and indeed if there is a guilty plea it may be almost all that the court is concerned with.

One final matter of crucial importance must be mentioned, though this is not the context in which to probe its effects in detail; this is the development of the communications industry. Today it is vast and technologically highly developed, with tremendous commercial ramifications. It plays an important role in shaping the views of the criminal process held by various sections of the community, and its spokesmen speak of a duty it owes in regard to court proceedings towards the community.[15] It must surely affect the principle of open court.

II—The Law

There are comparatively few cases dealing with the right of access to the public gallery, and many of them relate to civil rather than criminal matters. In *Scott* v. *Scott*, Lord Halsbury stated simply, "I am of the opinion that every court of justice is opened to every subject of the King."[16] Viscount Haldane said that unless it was strictly necessary for the attainment of justice "there can be no power in the court to hear *in camera* either a matrimonial cause or any other where there is contest between parties."[17] In the same case the question of when the public may be excluded was considered. There is some uncertainty whether the various views reflected in the speeches are necessarily compatible with one another; but there was overall agreement that it is a serious matter to exclude the public although strictly limited grounds on which this might be done did exist. Lord Loreburn noted two: if the administration of justice would be rendered impracticable by the presence of the public because the case could not then be effectively tried, or because the parties entitled to justice would be deterred from seeking it at the hands of the court. In such circumstances the matter might be heard *in camera*.

The first situation is illustrated by *R.* v. *Governor of Lewes Prison, ex parte Doyle*.[18] This was a case arising out of the Irish "Troubles" of an earlier period, and in fact is a rare example of the consideration of the "open court" doctrine in the context of a criminal trial. Doyle had been convicted of treason and sentenced to be shot by a field general court-martial. Claiming that the prevailing conditions of disorder had made it inexpedient that he should be tried publicly, the Press and public had been excluded by the commander-in-chief. Viscount Reading found at the appeal that it was possible to conceive members of the public terrorising and possibly even shooting witnesses; he held that the closed nature of the trial did not invalidate it, and brought it within the scope of *Scott* v. *Scott*.

Further applications of the principle in the case of criminal trials are not readily found. In *R.* v. *Kray and Others*[19] the decision to take together two counts of murder was upheld because *inter alia* the interest taken by the Press in the affair—the Kray-Richardson gang on trial—was so great that if they were tried separately the publicity at the first trial would have made a fair trial of the remaining charges impossible. Where the Press has featured, the cases seem generally to concern contempt proceedings against particular newspapers arising out of their mishandling of criminal trials. Thus, in *R.* v. *Evening Standard*[20] the court condemned the publication of the work of "amateur detectives" as catering for the public appetite for sensational matter rather than for the purpose of performing what was represented as a duty. In *R.* v. *Bolam and Others, ex parte Haigh*[21] Lord Goddard described the publication of material in the *Daily Mirror* about the accused in a murder trial as a disgrace to English journalism and as violating every principle of justice and fair play which it had been the pride of this country to extend to the worst of criminals. He described the material briefly, and went on to state that in the long history of the present class of case there had never, in the opinion of the court, been one of such gravity as this, or one of such a scandalous and wicked character; it had not been done as a result of an error in judgment but as a matter of policy in pandering to sensationalism for the purpose of increasing the circulation of the newspaper. He committed the editor to prison for three months and fined the proprietors £10,000. In this case, there does seem to have been a real danger of prejudice to the accused. It is not proposed to explore this topic in this context for the cases in this aspect do not deal specifically with the principle of Press reporting.

However, in *R.* v. *Clement*[22] the court was concerned with a series of trials which were in effect all part of the same proceedings. Till the last defendant had been disposed of, it could not be said that any one trial had been completed. The court held that an order could be made restricting publication "in order to preserve the purity of the administration of justice"; the witnesses would otherwise have the opportunity to see their own evidence or that of other witnesses, and so if their evidence had to be repeated they could ensure that they told the same stories.

These seem to be cases where the feelings of the parties involved are not necessarily relevant. The second of the grounds noted by Lord Loreburn appears to be based largely on the interests of the parties as they themselves interpret them but the few reported cases are not easy to reconcile or to interpret. Thus, in *Moosbrugger* v. *Moosbrugger*[23] the witness on her own behalf in divorce proceedings was inaudible, and was rendered so by the people present in court; the gallery and court were then cleared. In *B.* (*Otherwise P.*) v. *Attorney-General*[24] Wrangham J. refused to clear the court in legitimacy proceedings despite a suggestion that the parties might be

deterred if the proceedings went ahead in public on the ground that proceedings affecting status should be the subject-matter of open and public
trial. In *Cleland* v. *Cleland*[25] counsel was of the view that real justice was
not possible if the case went ahead in open court; his application to clear
the court was upheld, but it is not clear on what grounds counsel made his
submission.

An additional ground for restricting publicity appears to exist; *i.e.*
where the presence of the public would defeat the object of the proceedings
and render them useless, then an application to exclude it may succeed.[26]

Archbold adds an interesting rider to the rule that on indictment a trial
must be held in public court with open doors; the point is made that "not
infrequently" the presiding judge may request women and young persons
to leave the court. No authority is given nor is it indicated what the consequences of a refusal to leave might be. Doubtless the presiding judge would
hope that the authority of his office would secure compliance with what is
not put at higher than a request. There is no doubt however that "No child
(other than an infant in arms) shall be permitted to be present in court
during the trial of any other person . . . except during such time as his presence is required as a witness or otherwise for the purposes of justice."[27]

Since *Scott* v. *Scott* there does appear to have been a clear change in
the exceptions. In 1966 the Law Commission observed that the extensions
to the rule in that case seemed all to be based either on the protection of
public decency or the need to protect infants or mental patients.[28] This
development seems contrary to the express comments in *Scott's* case to
the effect that this was not a sufficient reason for hearing a case in private.
The Report noted also that there was an anomalous situation in that a
young offender may have greater privacy in court than a young victim of
sexual assault. The Commission at that point seemed more concerned
with the publicity surrounding divorce and similar cases. An illustration
of the situation which might arise is afforded by *B.* (*Otherwise P.*) v.
Attorney-General[29] where during the course of legitimacy proceedings it
was suggested by counsel that harm to the infant petitioner might follow
if the proceedings were heard in public, and it was suggested that the
parties might moreover be deterred from seeking justice. The court refused
to continue behind closed doors, but Wrangham J. went on to invite
those of the public who were present "to consider whether they might not
in decency withdraw"; and invited the Press to restrain itself in its reports
of the case so that the parties could not be identified. He felt that this was
the limit of his jurisdiction, and following this case the Law Commission
was seised of the matter. Its proposals were subsequently embodied in the
Domestic and Appellate Proceedings (Restriction of Publicity) Act 1968.
This Act is of limited significance as far as criminal proceedings are
concerned; section 1(3) refers to appeals against conviction, sentence, or
other order made on conviction, and provides that it shall state in open
court the order made by it. It seems to envisage that the prior trial might
fall within the scope of an exception in *Scott* v. *Scott*.

Finally, it should also be mentioned that the common law rule has been modified more directly by statutes. Hearings may be private in a number of specific circumstances; apart from the Official Secrets Act all appear to be instances involving intimate family matters such as divorce, legitimation, and adoption.[30]

III Justification of the Doctrine

There seems to be surprisingly little study in depth of the reasons for maintaining the doctrine of open court, and the term itself is not altogether of clear meaning. Is it enough that facilities for the public and Press to be present are provided? Does the Press represent the public? There is evidence that the Press considers that it has a duty of some sort[31]; but this seems to be one frequently subject to commercial considerations, and one suspects that at times editors have been more preoccupied with circulation figures and shareholders than larger questions of principle. It is not always easy to see another reason for some of the news items whose publication has been stoutly defended by the editors responsible.[32]

The Tucker Committee on Proceedings before Examining Justices described as "weighty" and "formidable" the following objections to proceedings being held *in camera* before examining justices, in addition to a "general distaste for the idea": that where a charge is dismissed, there might be a suspicion of favouritism, or that the conduct of the proceedings did not come up to the normal high standards of magistrates' courts.[33] Today, of course, there are generally restrictions on Press reports of such proceedings[34] although the public are admitted unless there is an enactment to the contrary or the ends of justice would not be served by sitting in open court.[35] The Tucker Committee's observations could as well be extended to trials in higher courts. The Committee, incidentally, was of the opinion that the reporter represented the wider society. It is respectfully submitted that the point is not quite so simple or straight-forward, but the present context is not suitable for an examination in depth.

The role of the Press has been referred to several times in American courts. Probably the best example of the sort of situation which most needed comment is the trial described in *Sheppard* v. *Maxwell*,[36] a murder case which for some reason attracted the Press on a scale surely excessive even by American standards. The conviction was set aside simply as a result of the energy with which the Press, radio, and television sought it. The Ohio Supreme Court described the atmosphere surrounding the trial as a "Roman holiday"; and the Federal Supreme Court, after describing the proceedings in detail, said bluntly that "bedlam reigned." In the latter judgment, Clark J. referred to the Anglo-American distrust for secret trials and the principle that "justice cannot survive behind walls of silence." He went on:

"A responsible Press has always been regarded as the hand maiden of effective judicial administration, especially in the criminal field. Its

function in this regard is documented by an impressive record of
service over several centuries. The Press does not simply publish
information about trials but guards against the miscarriage of justice
by subjecting the policy, prosecution, and judicial process to extensive
public scrutiny and criticism."

Paradoxically, in this case it might be argued the exercise of that very
same extensive scrutiny and criticism was the basis of the conclusion that
there had been no fair trial. Had the journalists restrained themselves till
the proceedings were completed, they might have argued that they were
hampered in their task of drawing public attention to alleged failings of
the prosecution; might they not have been guilty of contempt if in addition
they linked an unpopular verdict to those failings? The problem in this
case seems to have been to decide when scrutiny and criticism go beyond
"extensive" and become unacceptable.

An illustration of concern for the principle of open court came after
the proceedings in *R.* v. *Sokol*.[37] Following committal proceedings affected
by section 3 of the Criminal Justice Act 1967 (*i.e.* without restrictions on
reporting having been lifted) the defendant pleaded guilty to murder and
the mandatory sentence of life imprisonment was imposed. The whole
hearing at the Leeds Assizes lasted for one minute. Under the circumstances, the facts were not dealt with by the prosecution for there was no
problem about the sentence. A Practice Direction followed in a matter of
days; Lord Parker C.J. introduced it by observing that "it would be
regrettable if, as a result of the Criminal Justice Act 1967 the press and the
public were deprived of the right inherent in our system of criminal justice
to know the circumstances of the crime for which an accused is convicted
and sentenced"; and went on to announce that following a plea of "guilty"
to a murder charge the prosecution should as in the case of other offences
state the facts in open court before sentence is passed.[38]

The Evershed Committee on Supreme Court Practice and Procedure[39]
concluded that one reason for public appeals was in order to ensure that
important points which were decided would be properly reported for the
future guidance of practitioners. This very point, however, was subsequently discounted by the Law Commission in its report on the powers
of appeal courts.[40]

Two of the most important comments on the admission of Press and
public to the courts are a decision of the Privy Council in a matrimonial
matter and a paper in a symposium on criminal procedure, separated widely
in time.

McPherson v. *McPherson*,[41] an appeal from Canada, concerned an
unopposed divorce on the grounds of misconduct on the part of the
husband, then a Minister of the Crown in Alberta. The case was heard in
the Judges' Library of the Court House at Edmonton—there appears to
have been a custom of using this venue, but the point was not explored.
The Privy Council was, however, concerned deeply with other aspects of
this hearing. Access to the library was through a double swinging door,
one wing of which bore the word "PRIVATE" while the other was left

unfastened and free to swing closed. The library door was opposite. The swinging door was on a public corridor, which led incidentally to the public entrances to the courtrooms. Familiars of the building such as practitioners were not deterred by the "PRIVATE" sign. During the hearing the library door was by order of the judge secured open but the other door was overlooked; robes of office were not worn, and the hearing itself took place in the lunch-hour for the convenience of the parties. The Privy Council accepted, it seems, that had the case been heard in a court-room no greater degree of publicity would have attended the proceedings. The trial judge made it clear that it was his desire to avoid publicity not out of deference to the position of the husband who was the plaintiff any-way but simply to restrict "unhealthy notoriety." In fact, no member of the public sought to attend the hearing. The circumstances did not find favour with the Privy Council. First, it was of the view that publicity is the "authentic hall-mark of judicial as distinct from administrative pro-cedure." Secondly, so long as divorce was not a matter of consent the public had an interest in the proceedings because not only was the status of individuals affected but also the "entire social structure and the preser-vation of a wholesome family life through the community." Thirdly, publicity would prevent the trial from becoming "stereotyped and stand-ardised." Finally, commenting sharply on the failure of Bench and Bar to robe, it was of the view that the potential presence of the public would invest the proceedings with some degree of formality, and would give some guarantee that they would be conducted with decorum. In this case it seems clear that the trial judge did not intend to deny access by the public; he simply did not wish to draw its attention to the proceedings. Neverthe-less, the circumstances were sharply criticised by the Privy Council. In passing, it is worth mentioning that there seems to be a slight element of confusion in precisely what was objected to. At one point Lord Blaneburgh seemed to attach importance to the "potential presence" of the public; while on the same page he notes the serious view taken of its "absence." [42]

In the context of a criminal trial, however, a most careful examination of the "open court" principle is by H. H. Marshall in a paper on criminal procedure in the former Commonwealth Dependencies. The key passage is worth quoting in full:

"What is the purpose of the provision for public trials? It is probably:—

(a) to ensure in the interests of the state that justice is not only done but is seen to be done, so that

(i) the public may have confidence in the courts of the country;
(ii) there can be no doubt as to what takes place at the hearing;
(iii) it cannot afterwards be said that a person who was fairly con-victed was unfairly convicted, that a person who has been properly acquitted has been acquitted through favour or influence, or generally, that a person who was fairly tried did not receive a fair trial;

(b) to ensure in the interests of the accused that:—

    (i) he receives a fair trial;
   (ii) that trial is conducted according to recognised procedure and
       both sides are heard;
  (iii) no irregular process such as torture is applied for the purpose of
       obtaining evidence;
  (iv) the behaviour of the prosecutor and of the judge is fair and
       above board—

in brief to enlist the assistance of the public in reducing the opportunities for the maladministration of justice, but not to provide the public with a means of entertainment." [43]

In the same paper Marshall considers why judicial proceedings ought not to be televised. This is an important point; for clearly he is of the opinion that not all techniques of publicity are today acceptable.

The principle of open court was established before the techniques of communication and the commercial interests linked with them became so immensely powerful and complex. Concepts of privacy and increasing knowledge about criminality and the appropriate social reactions thereto must surely also have an impact on the operation of the principle. At all times, however, the importance of the objectives mentioned by Marshall can scarcely be over emphasised. Through experience—sometimes bitter—we have learned that in a democratic society it is fundamental that there should be full public confidence in the courts and judiciary. It is partly for this reason that little attempt has been made in the foregoing to distinguish between civil and criminal courts. However the latter do involve some special aspects; and in conclusion it is proposed to refer briefly to some of them.

IV—Discussion and a Suggestion for Reform

There is little evidence that publicity on present lines has a significant deterrent effect on offenders. Probably the most recent and useful survey, by Willcock and Stokes in 1968, [44] is at best equivocal. For example, they found that out of eight deterrents listed only 12 per cent. of the youths they interviewed regarded the publicity or shame of having to appear in court as the most worrying thing about being found out by the police. Moreover this deterrent itself is not precisely what we are here considering for even proceedings *in camera* might be the publicity referred to. When other findings by these researchers are considered the matter becomes even more doubtful: for example, 79 per cent. thought that the impact on their families—a quite different deterrent—was more important than the shame of having to appear in court.

Bearing in mind the view that there is a need to individualise in sentencing [45] as a general rule and that the publicity attendant on a particular trial might have the most important consequences for the defendant both at the time and in his later career [46] ought the court not to have more power over that publicity? If, for example, some form of deterrence is sought in a particular case (operating generally perhaps by setting an example for all to see and to avoid, or by alerting the community to a *modus operandi*; or specifically, by alerting the community to a particular individual or by invoking some process of public shaming[47]) ought the court not to be in a position to control the publicity it deems suitable for the purpose? On the other hand the court may feel that in a particular case the privacy of an acutely distressed offender involved in what is experienced as a major and squalid tragedy ought to be preserved behind its doors. The controls and restrictions which do operate suggest a fear that the presence of the Press and public may actually cause harm.[48] Little is known about this aspect; it may well be that age has little bearing on the matter, and that adults need some protection also.

Referring to the considerations advanced by Marshall one must query the competence of the lay public to assess the quality of the proceedings taking place before it, and moreover the offence of contempt of court bears on its freedom to comment thereon. This applies particularly, it is suggested, with regard to findings on the facts and the views taken on the credibility of witnesses or the value of their evidence. An outsider who correctly concludes that such matters have been dealt with in a biased fashion on the basis of his own knowledge ought in all probability to have been a witness or otherwise directly involved in the proceedings.

Such a great defect in a trial might not be visible to the casual spectator or reader. Moreover, there is no effective provision for a member of the public who is dissatisfied, no matter how justifiably, with what he has read or seen of particular proceedings to have the matter investigated and if necessary set right. A convicted person himself who has exhausted the appellate procedures and who still feels aggrieved has an almost but not completely impossible problem on his hands, for against considerable handicaps he has to prove his innocence.[49] The most effective safeguards against improper conduct by the Bench or prosecution seem to be a jury properly representative of the community of the defendant and a lawyer for the defence supported by the tradition of independence characteristic of the British legal profession.

One is at all times faced with the problem that the presence of the Press or the public in a court is frequently a matter of luck and curiosity complicated in the case of the former by editorial and commercial considerations. A by-product of the power and authority of the Press may well be that information about crime may be concealed or distorted unintentionally simply by a failure to report particular offences at all or by paying special attention to them.

On the one hand, there is a need to secure public understanding of the extent of the problem of crime as well as the objectives set out *inter alia* by Marshall and by the Privy Council in *McPherson* v. *McPherson*; on the other hand, there is a need to respect the privacy and sentencing needs of the offender. It is suggested that the time for a new look at the law has come. The fundamental right to a public trial does not, it is suggested, require unrestricted access by the Press and any person who cares to attend. Perhaps under modern conditions this right may be more satisfactorily secured by ensuring that proper legal aid is present at interrogation,[50] committal proceedings, bail applications, and trial; by ensuring so far as possible that complainants, immediate families, and third parties with a direct interest in a case are present, and leaving the right to attend to be exercised by those such as friends, employers, practitioners, and students in the administration of justice; by giving the court the power to order the publication of material which in its view is necessary for specific purposes such as the tracing of witnesses, to constitute a just sentence, or to inform the public as to specific matters arising out of the case before it; and by ensuring that a full and accurate record of the proceedings is kept and that those with a proper interest in it have access thereto. Finally, it is suggested that the operation of the jury system must continue as a subject for close study and review in view of its role in securing that the justice dispensed by the criminal courts is of the highest quality. Its proper functioning requires a deep consciousness within the community of the collective and individual responsibility of its members for the administration of justice.[51] The encouragement of this consciousness for its own survival is simply one hall-mark of a democratic society.

NOTES

1. Cf. *McPherson* v. *McPherson* [1936] A.C. 177 (P.C.).
2. "In other countries the courts of justice are held in secret; with us publicly and in open view"; Emlyn, *State Trials* (2nd edn), Preface; quoted by Lord Halsbury in *Scott* v. *Scott* [1913] A.C. 417 at p. 441. Emlyn gives Coke for his authority but the earliest reported case seems to be *Daubney* v. *Cooper* (1829) 10 B. & C. 237 (an appeal from a magistrates' court).
3. *The Machinery of Justice in England* (5th edn), p. 20; the point is mentioned as settled law in respect of coroners' courts in a judgment by Blackstone J. in *Scott* v. *Shearman and Others* (1775) 2 Black. W. 977.
4. *R.* v. *Gash* [1967] 1 All E.R. 811; 51 Cr. App. R. 37; *R.* v. *Hood* [1968] 1 W.L.R. 773, 52 Cr. App. R. 265; *R.* v. *Box* [1964] 1 Q.B. 430.
5. See for example the history of the offence of dangerous driving; Elliott and Street, *Road Accidents* (1968), p. 20. The matter was considered in the Eleventh Report of the Criminal Law Revision Committee. See also McCabe and Purves, *The Jury at Work* (1972). The independent habits of juries formed the theme of much of the controversial address of Sir Robert Mark, Commissioner of the Metropolitan Police to the Royal Society of Medicine: *The Guardian*, Wednesday July 21, 1972.
6. Devlin, *Trial by Jury* (1966), p. 164.
7. Report of the Departmental Committee on Jury Service, Cmnd. 2627 (1965).
8. *Ibid.*, para. 62. See Criminal Justice Act 1972, s. 25.
9. Echoing Lord Tenterden in *Collier* v. *Hicks* (1836) 2 B. & Ad. 663. He referred to the "heavy and grievous expense" which would follow if the informer and hence the accused were allowed the aid of a professional advocate in summary proceedings.
10. Per Sir Eardley Wilmot, *Hansard* (1835), vol. xcv, col. 356.
11. *Hansard* (1836), vol. xxxvi, col. 174. Cf. *Collier* v. *Hicks* (1831) 2 B. & Ad. 663, where Lord Tenterden considered that in summary proceedings justice could be sufficiently well attained by hearing the parties alone "without that nicety of discussion, and subtlety of argument, which are likely to be introduced by persons accustomed to legal questions."
12. By the Prisoner's Counsel Act 1836; for a slightly confused consideration of the purpose of this Act see *R.* v. *Ward* (1848) 2 C. & K. 759.
13. Over a period of time, culminating in the Criminal Evidence Act 1898; but

the implications of this development were complex; see Stephen, *History of the Criminal Law* (1883), Vol. 1, pp. 439–460 for the background.
14. On the former, see Radzinowicz, *A History of English Criminal Law* (1948), Vol. 1. On the latter, *The Hanging Question* (ed. Blom Cooper, 1969) with its bibliography indicates the weight of authority drawn into the dispute which, sadly, refuses to lie down and die. Abroad, it continues with astonishing bitterness, see *e.g.* Van Niekerk, ". . . Hanged by the Neck Until you are Dead" [1970] S. A. L.J. 457, and the remarkable prosecution which followed this study: *S.* v. *Van Niekerk* [1970] 3 S.A.L.R. 655.
15. For a recent account and examination thereof, see the transcript of the conference on "The Law and the Press" under the auspices of JUSTICE, February 5, 1972. See also (1972) 122 New L.J. 200.
16. [1913] A.C. 417 at p. 440.
17. *Ibid.* at p. 438. And see *Cleland* v. *Cleland* (1913) 109 L.T. 744.
18. [1917] 2 K.B. 254. *Cf. Re Sherriff of Surrey* (1860) 2 F. & F. 236 (power of the judge to clear court to preserve quiet), and *Norman* v. *Mathews* (1916) 85 L.J.K.B. 857, affd. 32 T.L.R. 361 (power of judge to rule that proceedings involving seized political books and documents should be held *in camera* to prevent their being discussed in open court).
19. [1970] 1 Q.B. 125; *cf. R.* v. *Clement* (1821) 4 B. & Ald. 218.
20. (1924) 40 T.L.R. 833.
21. (1949) 93 S. J. 220; and see also *R.* v. *Malik* [1968] 1. W.L.R. 353.
22. (1821) 4 B. & Ald. 218. Examples of applications to exclude the public in civil matters are *Cleland* v. *Cleland* (1913) 109 L.T. 744 (argued as necessary to preserve public morality and as otherwise the court could not hope to do real justice); and *Re Agricultural Industries Ltd.* [1952] 1 All E.R. 1188 (argued as necessary to prevent third party knowing of possible proceedings and thus have an opportunity to frustrate justice).
23. (1913) 29 T.L.R. 658.
24. [1965] 3 All E.R. 253.
25. (1913) 109 L.T. 744.
26. *Re Agricultural Industries Ltd.* [1952] 1 All E.R. 1188, citing *Mellor* v. *Thompson* (1885) 31 Ch.D. 55; and *Norman* v. *Mathews* (1916) 85 L.J.K.B. 857, affd. 32 T.L.R. 369.
27. Children and Young Persons Act 1933, s. 36.
28. Report of Powers of Appeal Courts etc., Cmnd. 3149, para. 17.
29. [1967] P. 119.
30. *Halsbury's Laws of England* (6th edn), Vol. 9, p. 345.
31. See *e.g.* the addresses at the JUSTICE conference, *supra*: note 15, and Levy, *The Press Council* (1967). One speaker at the conference referred to the "very real danger of some crime not being publicised at all" (Mr. R. M. Taylor, President of the Guild of British Newspaper Editors).
32. Levy, *op. cit.*, Chaps. 15, 18.
33. Cmnd. 479 (1958); see para. 29.
34. Criminal Justice Act 1967, ss. 3, 4, 5.
35. *Ibid.*, s. 6.
36. 384 U.S. 333, 16 L. ed. 600. In *People* v. *Jelke*, 48 A.L.R. 2d. the New York Court of Appeals had occasion to look into the history of the principle. The conclusions it reached do not take account of the consideration that in fact at one time it was simply not possible to conduct a trial without the public.
37. *The Times*, March 29, 1968; Bradford *Telegraph and Argus*, March 28, 1968.
38. [1968] 2 All E.R. 144.
39. Supreme Court Practice and Procedure, Cmnd. 8878 (1953). Lord Evershed himself was consistent in his views on the point: see *Re Agricultural Industries Ltd.* [1952] 1 All E.R. 1188.
40. Cmnd. 3149 (1966). See now the Domestic and Appellate Proceedings (Restriction of Publicity) Act 1968.
41. [1936] A.C. 177 (P.C.).
42. At p. 202; but see p. 200.
43. *The Accused—A Comparative Study* (ed. Coutts, 1966), pp. 163 *et seq.*
44. Government Social Survey, 1968; H.M.S.O.
45. See *e.g.* Thomas, *Principles of Sentencing* (1970), Chap. 1; Cross, *The*

English Sentencing System (1971), esp. Chap. 11; Walker, *Sentencing in a Rational Society* (1972) esp. Chap. 9.

46. See the joint report by JUSTICE, the Howard League, and NACRO *Living it Down: the Problem of Old Convictions* (1972).

47. See Nigel Walker, *Sentencing in a Rational Society* (1972), p. 17; for an illustration of what the report seems to have in mind see *The Guardian*, Tuesday July 18, 1972 ("Probyn's Mother appeals to Parole Board").

48. For a list of those statutes regulating publicity, see Halsbury, *op. cit.*, n. 25.

49. See the Report by JUSTICE, Home Office Reviews of Criminal Convictions (1968).

50. The eleventh Report of the Criminal Law Revision Committee, on Evidence, is to be deplored in so far as it appears to ignore the role of the lawyer at this stage—not so much in securing the liberty of his client, but in ensuring that justice is done.

51. The Morris Report, *op. cit.*, was of the view that "jury service should be regarded as a duty which is the counterpart of being a citizen. From this view it follows that citizenship should be the basis from which the duty to serve arises." It went on to recommend that inclusion in the register of voters at Parliamentary and local government elections should be the basic qualification for jury service. See now Criminal Justice Act 1972, s. 25.

14. A RIGHT TO KNOW THE REASONS FOR A DECISION OF A MAGISTRATES' COURT?

C. F. PARKER

THE opportunity is taken in this short essay to "think aloud" on a problem which has troubled me during the past few years since I began sitting as a lay magistrate. Briefly the question is this: Should magistrates—and in this context I shall use this term with reference exclusively to lay magistrates—give reasons for their decisions? Or, to reword the question within the framework of this volume, has the citizen a fundamental right to know the reasons for a decision made by a magistrates' court?

The whole matter has been ventilated again within the last year or so in the Memorandum on The Law and Practice on Appeals from the Criminal Jurisdiction of Magistrates' Courts prepared by the Law Society's Standing Committee on Criminal Law under the chairmanship of Mr. David Napley, endorsed by the Council of the Law Society and published in October 1971. The Memorandum was commented on by Mr. A. J. Brayshaw, the Secretary of the Magistrates' Association,[1] and these comments in turn evoked a reply from Mr. Napley.[2]

To state the pith of the divergence of views on this particular issue, the Law Society is emphatically in favour of magistrates stating their reasons. "If the system of trial which affects so many coming before the criminal courts is based on reason and common sense, then those who are adjudicating must be assumed to be capable of reaching a reasoned decision and ought to be sufficiently articulate in legal matters to make the basis of their decision known, taking the advice of their clerk where necessary."[3]

However, the law as it stands does not require magistrates to state their reasons for conviction, nor in practice do they normally do so. To quote Mr. Brayshaw, "when the Association has considered these points it has always been tacitly against magistrates giving reasons for conviction." Even more important than the additional time and work involved, is, according to Mr. Brayshaw, the consideration that, since the reason for conviction is often simply that the court has believed one witness and disbelieved another, to voice this in open court would exacerbate the dispute and "would cause one party to crow and the other to smart."

It is precisely this divergence of views which has troubled me since sitting as a magistrate. On the one hand, I feel considerable agreement with the view of the Law Society, not in this instance as a solicitor myself, but rather as an academic lawyer concerned with that evasive quality "natural justice," which prompts me to say, "Of course a person should know why he has been convicted, not only to enable him or his legal

189

advisers to determine whether he has good grounds for appeal, but also, perhaps indeed mainly, to assure the public and the convicted person himself, in so far as he is open to such assurance in the circumstances, that he has had a 'fair trial'."

One may quote the paragraph in the Report of the Committee on Administrative Tribunals and Enquiries[4] on "Reasoned Decisions."

> "We are convinced that if tribunal proceedings are to be fair to the citizen reasons should be given to the fullest practicable extent. A decision is apt to be better if the reasons for it have to be set out in writing because the reasons are then more likely to have been properly thought out. Further, a reasoned decision is essential in order that, where there is a right of appeal, the applicant can assess whether he has good grounds of appeal and know the case he will have to meet if he decides to appeal."

These then are the arguments which weigh upon me on the one hand. Yet, when sitting as a magistrate, I usually have no qualms in participating in decisions of my bench, knowing that we, through the chairman, will in most cases make no attempt to state the reasons for our decisions. Am I then betraying the principles of "fair play" or "natural justice"?

I—Natural Justice

As far as natural justice in its technical sense is concerned, it appears that it does not require that reasons for decisions should be stated. "In the absence of any requirements by the law that reasons should be given, the mere failure to give reasons could not establish a decision as being contrary to natural justice."[5] Or one can cite Professor de Smith[6]: "There is no general rule of English law that reasons must be given for administrative (or indeed judicial) decisions." And he then devotes two chapters to Natural Justice, the first being sub-titled "The Right to a Hearing," the second "Interest and Bias."

However, the Report of the Committee on Ministers' Powers[7] went so far as to say: "It may well be argued that there is a third principle of natural justice, namely that a party is entitled to know the reason for the decision."

Be that as it may, the fact that natural justice in its technical sense may or may not demand the giving of reasons for a decision does not conclude the issue of whether reasons *should* be given.

II—Reasons for Decision

So far, I have spoken simply of "reasons for decisions," but any development of the topic calls for a distinction between reasons for sentence and reasons for conviction (or dismissal of the charge). This distinction, Mr. Brayshaw points out, is not apparent in the Law Society's Memorandum, although, as he also points out, as far as the giving of reasons for sentence is concerned, the Council of the Magistrates' Association resolved in 1968 that this was a matter for the discretion of the bench which might wish to consider explaining briefly an exceptionally light or heavy sentence. From my own limited experience and without attempting to generalise, I can say that our practice is certainly to state quite succinctly the reasons for any particular sentence which is decidedly out of line with the "norm" or the "tariff" for that particular offence. One might almost say that this is part of our defence mechanism which operates automatically to forestall criticisms in or by the local press. As for cases when one gives the normal or tariff sentence, what reasons could one indeed give, other than that it is the norm, unless one embarked on a discussion of criminological and penological aims and theories?

There is in some circumstances a statutory requirement to give reasons for deciding upon a particular form of punishment. Thus, section 107(3) of the Magistrates' Courts Act 1952 imposes a mandatory duty on magistrates to state the reason why they consider that no sentence other than imprisonment is appropriate when sentencing a person under the age of twenty-one. Even so, failure to state any reasons does not affect the validity of the sentence passed. This was stated by the present Lord Chief Justice, Lord Widgery, in a Divisional Court case, *R.* v. *Chesterfield Justices, ex parte Hewitt.*[8] Presumably the position is the same under section 14 of the Criminal Justice Act 1972, which imposes a similar duty to state reasons in passing a sentence of imprisonment on a person over the age of twenty-one who has not previously been sentenced to imprisonment.

The main debate however centres on the giving of reasons for conviction, and, since one of the main arguments in favour is that the convicted person or his legal advisers should know if there are good grounds for an appeal, we must now distinguish between the two channels of appeal open from decisions to convict by magistrates' courts, *viz.* (i) by an appeal to the Crown Court[9] and (ii) by asking the magistrates' court to state a case for the opinion of a Divisional Court of the Queen's Bench Division on the ground that the decision is wrong in law or is in excess of jurisdiction.[10] (It is not thought necessary in this context to include the procedure by way of prerogative order, *e.g.* certiorari, in view of its very restricted purview.)

III—Some Statistics on Appeals

The Criminal Statistics for England and Wales for 1971[11] show that 1,714,667 persons were dealt with summarily in magistrates' courts; of these, 1,648,204 either pleaded guilty or were found guilty. There were 7,950 appeals against conviction to quarter sessions (the predecessor for this purpose of the Crown Court). The number who appealed by way of case stated to the Divisional Court was much smaller still, only 125.

It will be seen from these figures that about 96 per cent. of persons who are dealt with summarily by magistrates' courts, *i.e.* who are not committed for trial to the Crown Court, are convicted. The statistics do not enable one to ascertain how many of these actually plead guilty, but my own experience is in line with the result obtained by Mr. Michael Zander from a limited investigation reported in *The New Law Journal*[12] where, in a sample of 840 cases, the defendant pleaded guilty in 729 (*i.e.* 87 per cent.). Thus, out of a list of, say, 40 cases, it would be unusual to have more than four or five contested. Of course, however small a proportion such contested cases may constitute, overall they probably take up as much time in court as all the vastly more numerous guilty pleas put together. But the point is that in something like 85 to 90 per cent. of cases dealt with summarily by magistrates no appeal will be possible to the Crown Court, because a person who has pleaded guilty has no such right of appeal.[13] (I leave aside in this context the rare cases where the defendant may be allowed to change his plea or where there is ambiguity as to what his plea really is.)

IV—Appeals to the Crown Court

Where there is an appeal to the Crown Court, it may seem strange that there is no statutory authority that such an appeal should be by way of a re-hearing of the case, but this is the established procedure. The prosecution opens, and witnesses are called to give evidence afresh, the case being tried by a circuit judge or recorder, with lay magistrates but without a jury. Since such an appeal is by way of a re-hearing, there would seem to be no reason for there to be available to the appeal bench either a note of the evidence given in the magistrates' court or a note of the reasons for the magistrates' decision. On the contrary, if such information were known to the appeal bench, it might be thought that the re-hearing could hardly be unprejudiced. Indeed, if one is to have a completely unprejudiced re-hearing, one might deprecate the practice of cross-examining witnesses on what they had said in evidence in the magistrates' court; and one can hardly see any good purpose served by the appeal bench knowing that the reason for the conviction by the magistrates was that they had completely disbelieved witness X when this is the sort of issue on which the appeal bench should make its own decision *de novo* at the re-hearing.

Consequently, it would seem that for the purpose of the appeal proceedings themselves in the Crown Court, no case can be made out for the taking of a note of evidence in the magistrates' court or for the giving of reasons by the magistrates for conviction. Indeed, even if, for other reasons, it were decided that a record of the evidence should be made and that reasons should be given, it might be better that these should not be communicated to the Crown Court, however anomalous this might seem. At present it is understood to be the practice to submit to the Crown Court with the notice of appeal any note which may have been made of the evidence given in the magistrates' court, but some clerks make sure that there is no such note, and this may well be the better course if any such note would be superfluous and possibly prejudicial to the re-hearing.

V—Appeals by Way of Case Stated

On the other hand, when the appeal is by way of a case stated, a statutory duty is laid upon magistrates to include in the case stated the facts found by them,[14] but not the evidence on which those findings are based, unless one of the arguments put forward is that there was no evidence at all on which the magistrates could arrive at their findings. As to the mechanics of drawing up a case, reference is often made to the guidance offered by Lord Goddard C.J.:[15]

> "We also desire to say that as a rule it is better practice, though it cannot be insisted on, that where justices agree to state a case, if they state it themselves or cause their clerk to draft it, it should be submitted to both parties, and in case of any complication it should be left to the parties themselves to draft the case and submit it to the justices for their consideration. . . ."

In a previous case, *Spicer* v. *Warbey*,[16] Lord Goddard had already expressed the view that there was no "obligation on the clerk to the justices to submit the draft of the case to the respondent for revision, although it is done in many cases." But he went on to say: "If, however, a respondent is of opinion that some of the facts as found by the justices . . . have been omitted from the case as stated by them, it is open to him to make an application to a Divisional Court, supported by an affidavit setting out the findings of fact which in his opinion have been omitted, for a restatement of the case."

To some extent this is a safeguard against the danger of the case "being stated out of court," *i.e.* the facts being manipulated in the case stated so as to make untenable the argument being raised on the point of law, an occurrence which is said by the Law Society's Memorandum[17] to be the "all too frequent experience of practitioners in these courts." But unless the magistrates have stated the facts as found when they declare their decision, how can the respondent know which facts, if any, have been omitted from the case stated?

One may think that in most cases when an appeal is eventually brought by case stated on a point of law, this would have become apparent during the course of the hearing before the magistrates, either because it was raised in argument, especially if there was legal representation, or because it had been raised by the clerk. In those circumstances, one could expect the parties, the magistrates and their clerk to be alerted to the possibility of an appeal, so that a note of the findings would be a wise precaution. Not only would this constitute a valuable record for the purpose of stating the case, but also, if it were read out in court at the time of the decision, it would prevent the parties from assuming that the magistrates' decision had been based on the question of law which had been keenly contested before them, only to find when they asked for a case to be stated, that actually the magistrates had decided on a pure question of fact which made the point of law irrelevant.

It is however the opposite case which is more likely to arise, that the point of law does not emerge during the hearing in the magistrates' court; and it may well be true that its emergence would be facilitated by a brief statement of the facts found by the magistrates in reaching their decision. Of course, one may be tempted to take the view that a party cannot complain, especially if he is legally represented, although in one sense it is then above all that he may feel that he has a right to complain, if he is denied the right to raise on appeal a point of law which he failed to argue before the magistrates. However, to cite once again the words of Lord Goddard, who contributed so much to the jurisprudence of the Divisional Court in its appellate function, this time in *Whitehead* v. *Haines*[18]:

> "In my judgment, it would not be right for this court to decline to entertain and determine, on appeal raised by a Case Stated, a point of pure law open, on the facts found in that Case, to an appellant convicted on a criminal charge, which, if sound, might afford him a defence, merely because that legal objection to the charge has been first appreciated after his conviction. In particular it appears to be essential to the due performance of justice that the court should not uphold a conviction for an offence non-existent in law."

It must be noted however that it is only a statement of the facts found by the magistrates that should be included in the Case Stated, not a record of the evidence itself, except in the case where it is alleged that there was no evidence at all before the magistrates on which they could base their findings. But how can a prospective appellant assess his chances of succeeding on this ground unless he knows what the facts found were and has a record of the evidence, such as it was? Even in the more likely case that he may want to challenge whether the evidence given before the magistrates really justifies their findings, when the appeal should be to the Crown Court on a question of fact, or at most on a question of mixed law and fact, how can he assess his chances unless he knows what those findings were?

VI—*Questions of Law in Magistrates' Courts*

Perhaps at this point some reference can be made to the extent to which points of law do arise in magistrates' courts. The difficulties, indeed the impossibility, of any clean distinction between questions of law and questions of fact are notorious.[19] Even so, the statement of Mr. Brayshaw that "real points of law arise only rarely in magistrates' courts" and the statement of the late Lord Parker C.J. that "there is hardly a decision which falls to be made which is not mixed law and fact" are not so contradictory as Mr. Napley would seem to imagine. Of course, relevant questions which fall to be decided in a court of law involve law, in the same way that relevant questions which fall to be decided by doctors in hospital wards involve "medicine." Unless a fact produced some consequence *in law*, it would not need to be determined; to this extent and in this sense *all* questions which fall to be decided in magistrates' courts, as in any other court, are at least mixed questions of law and fact. But the number of

cases which arise in magistrates' courts where the *only* question in issue
is the law itself, as to what the law is which applies to a given situation
once the facts have been definitively established, is surely very small. One
recalls the well-known statement of Megarry J.:

> "Put as a proposition, law as taught is mainly law, whereas law as
> practised is mainly facts. . . . In a reported case, the report reveals
> all the relevant facts as found by the judge, as concisely as possible,
> and then turns to the delicious problem of law with which the court
> had to wrestle. In daily practice, the position is usually the reverse.
> So often the law is perfectly clear; the only question is what happened.
> . . . Once find the facts, and the law gives little enough trouble; but
> the facts are the devil." [20]

He has also been heard to add, provocatively, "that is why academic law
is so useful in practice."

One last point in connection with appeals by way of case stated: if
appeals were to be facilitated because of the giving of reasons by the
magistrates, they would be facilitated for the unsuccessful prosecutor just
as much as for the convicted defendant, since either party can ask the
magistrates' court to state a case to the Divisional Court. On the other
hand, there is no appeal by an unsuccessful prosecutor to the Crown
Court, although, if a successful appeal has already been brought in the
Crown Court by a person convicted in the magistrates' court, the prosecutor, who *ex hypothesi* has lost in the Crown Court, can ask for a case to
be stated, on a point of law to the Divisional Court. [21] Since 1960, there is
also the possibility of a further appeal from the Divisional Court to the
House of Lords, but this is hardly relevant to this discussion. [22]

VII—A Prima Facie Case Established? But What Objections?

So far then it would seem that at least a prima facie case has been made
out in favour of more information being available about the proceedings
in the magistrates' court, either by way of the giving of reasons by the
magistrates for their decision to convict or by way of a note of the evidence
given before them, or both. What then are the main arguments against
such change or changes?

As for the giving of reasons, this would certainly involve more time and
more work, both for the magistrates and for their clerk, and more time at
least for all persons having business in the court. The hearing of cases
would take longer as the reasons would presumably have to be composed
at the time so that the chairman could announce them with the decision.
For reasons to be composed and not then announced would miss the
point of the exercise in so far as it is intended to assure the public, and the
defendant, that the magistrates have conducted themselves properly, by
addressing themselves to the right issues, considering only relevant and
admissible evidence, and reaching a reasoned decision.

Proceedings would be slowed down even more if a complete record
were made of the proceedings, although this is suggested by the Law

Society as being the most important single improvement in the present system. However, for the immediate future it would be content if the clerk were able to dictate a contemporaneous note of the evidence on to tape, as is done in matrimonial cases heard by magistrates. This particular proposal occurs in that part of the Law Society's Memorandum which deals with appeals by way of case stated to the Divisional Court, not with appeals to the Crown Court, presumably because these latter appeals are by way of re-hearing as already discussed. But it has already been pointed out that even the Divisional Court does not want a record of the evidence which has been given before the magistrates, only their findings of fact, except where it is alleged that there was no evidence at all on which the magistrates could reach those findings. No statistics are easily available as to how many of these latter cases arise each year; the number is probably very small indeed, and yet it would seem that ideally a record of the evidence should be kept in every case in order to provide against the possibility that it might become one of these rarities.

Another objection raised to the giving of reasons by magistrates is that a bench might find it exceedingly difficult to draft a statement of their reasons, but such an objection is no justification for a conclusion that their decisions must therefore be unreasoned. After all, whatever may be the criteria these days for the appointment of magistrates, the ability to write reasoned judgments can hardly be one of them, and one knows very well that the gift of clear and lucid exposition, either in speech or writing, does not necessarily accompany other valued qualities such as common sense, intelligence, impartiality, and human understanding. Nor is the drafting of reasons by magistrates always assisted by the advocacy which they hear before them and which all too often fails to present in an orderly manner the precise issues to which they should be addressing themselves. Even so, one might hope that constant practice in the art of reducing one's reasons to paper, under the guidance of the clerk, would in most cases lead to a fair degree of proficiency.

But what if a bench could not agree among themselves on the constituent components in their collective or majority decision? They might all be agreed that the defendant was guilty of careless driving, but one might emphasise the excessive speed, another the misjudgment of distance, the third the failure to see the other vehicle. How, in such a case, can one state the facts on which the decision was based, beyond saying that, in the light of all the evidence, the bench was satisfied that the defendant had been driving carelessly? Before examining further the ambiguity inherent in this very expression "the findings of fact," let us briefly consider the further argument against the giving of reasons raised by Mr. Brayshaw, which has already been mentioned, namely that the reason is often quite simply that the court believes witness A and disbelieves witness B.

> "Since the social purpose of the courts is to resolve the matter justly and close the issue in a way that will as far as possible reconcile the contestants—often it is looked upon as a contest between the defendant

and the chief prosecution witness—and certainly in a way that will avoid exacerbating their dispute, to oblige the court to stigmatise some witnesses as liars would in many cases make things far worse by causing one side to crow and the other to smart."

One may feel, with respect, that this objection is being taken too far and that magistrates could easily find a formula which would be less provocative in its effect on the parties, for example, "After careful consideration, we prefer the evidence of witness A." Indeed, this is the formula suggested by the Law Society in its first suggestion for a new "appeals procedure": [23] "(a) the court should state the facts which it has found and give the reasons for its decision. (In many cases this would merely involve a statement that the evidence of one party has been preferred.)"

However, there is in this apparently simple suggestion an ambiguity which bedevils much of the discussion of this issue when conducted at a general level, and so let us turn in conclusion to a few specific examples of cases which may arise in magistrates' courts.

VIII—Some Specific Examples

For our first, let us consider a charge of careless driving arising out of an incident, all too familiar, when the defendant is driving his car out from a side road on to a main road and collides with a car travelling along the main road. Often there is no actual eye-witness other than the occupants of the two cars. These give evidence on the usual lines. The prosecution witness, the driver of the car on the main road, will say that he was driving along at a moderate speed, that he saw this other car coming down the side road, that, although it was travelling fast, he assumed that it would stop or at least slow down at the junction with the main road, that, instead of so doing, it continued out at speed and put itself in his path so that it was impossible for him to avoid the collision.

Against this, the defendant will say that he was coming down the side road at a very moderate speed, that he was exercising a proper look-out as he approached the main road junction, that he saw no other vehicle and so commenced to pull out, only then to see, for the first time, the other car bearing down on him so rapidly that he could not possibly avoid the collision. Now let us assume that the magistrates convict. This is their decision, and the immediate reason for it is that they are satisfied, beyond reasonable doubt, that the defendant was guilty of careless driving. But how much further, if at all, should they be required to go in their statement of their reasons? If they avail themselves of the formula suggested by the Law Society, they will merely say: "We have preferred the evidence of the prosecution witness and we find you guilty of careless driving." But on analysis it will be realised that the preferring of that evidence is the reason for the *finding of the facts* on which the decision was based, rather than the reason for the decision itself. Are then the facts found also to be stated? "We find you guilty of careless driving because we are satisfied that you were driving at an excessive speed when you emerged from the side road on to the main road/that you were not keeping a proper look-out/that you misjudged the speed of the other car, and we are satisfied as to these facts because we prefer the evidence of the prosecution witness." Even then, the point may be made that these are not indeed the facts found; they are already conclusions drawn from the primary facts as established by the evidence, *i.e.* that he was driving at approximately x miles per hour, that he did not turn his head sufficiently often to left and right; and this line of reasoning leads in turn to doubt whether the evidence actually given was indeed fact or rather opinion.

Be that as it may, unless such facts or conclusions, whatever they may be called, are included in the reasoned decision of the magistrates, it would seem that a mere statement that the evidence of the other side is preferred would really add nothing to the decision itself, because it must be obvious, if the defendant is convicted, that it was the other side's evidence that was believed, and the simple expression of this fact hardly takes the matter any further. Certainly it can hardly make it easier to ascertain whether there are good grounds for appeal. On the other hand, if all the facts are stated which have been found, they may not all have been found or relied on by all the magistrates. Thus, even though the Crown Court, on an appeal, may be persuaded otherwise on any one of these facts, it may still find the appellant guilty on the remainder, always remembering that these issues will arise before the Crown Court afresh through the submissions of the parties and the evidence there brought, not because of any record of these reasons of the magistrates.

As our second example, let us take a charge under section 8 of the Road Traffic Act 1972, failing, without reasonable excuse, to provide a specimen of breath for a breath test, where the issue turns on whether the policeman who makes the request has reasonable cause to suspect that the defendant has alcohol in his body. Let us assume that the prosecution evidence consists essentially of that of the policeman who testifies that he saw a very large and cumbersome motor tractor being driven in the early hours of the morning in a town centre in a very erratic and jerky manner; that it disappeared down a side street only to reappear a few minutes later and turn back in the direction from which it had originally come. He then decided to stop the vehicle and administer a breathalyser test.

The defendant, for his part, asserts that the tractor is a difficult machine to drive at any time, with a tendency to wander, that he had been working late on a nearby building site and had afterwards stopped to have a meal, that he had lost his way in a strange town and had been advised to turn into the side road in order to turn the vehicle round, since he had been travelling in the wrong direction. In these circumstances, he argues, the policeman had no reasonable cause to suspect that he had alcohol in his body and so was not entitled to require a specimen of his breath, so that no offence had been committed in refusing. Let us once again assume that the magistrates find him guilty.

Their decision is that the offence has been committed under section 8, that the defendant did refuse, without reasonable excuse, to provide a specimen of breath for a breath test. The reason for that decision is that they were satisfied beyond reasonable doubt that the specimen was being properly required because they were satisfied, beyond reasonable doubt, that the policeman did have reasonable cause to suspect that the defendant had alcohol in his body. Once again, once may ask: Would this be a sufficient statement of the reasons for the decisions? Should the statement go further and specify the facts on which the magistrates based their conclusion that the policeman had reasonable cause, namely the erratic progress of the vehicle, its disappearance and immediate reappearance? In fact, in such a case as this, it would not be a case of the magistrates preferring the evidence of the policeman, since the facts were not disputed by the defendant; it was just that he offered an innocent explanation for them.

It may well be that the magistrates in such a case could advantageously include in their decision a succinct statement that, on the facts of the case as undisputed, they were satisfied that at the time in question the policeman had reasonable cause to suspect that the driver of the vehicle had alcohol in his body. This would help to pinpoint the legal issue involved and to explain the decision to the defendant, the Press and to the public, although it would not add much to the information of the legal advisers of the defendant as to whether to bring an appeal or not because, even if it were not expressed, the same reason would be implicit in the decision.

IX—Conclusion

In conclusion, I am persuaded that there are some cases where the administration of justice in the magistrates' courts would benefit by a brief, carefully framed statement of the reasons of the magistrates for the conviction, which could satisfy the public, the Press and the defendant himself, to the extent that he is in a mood to be satisfied, that the magistrates knew what they were about and had addressed themselves to the proper issues. Whether this could be done without creating opportunities for frivolous and unmeritorious appeals may be doubted, but financial considerations might take care of this danger.

But how are the cases to be selected? Even Mr. Napley concedes that "no one is suggesting that this should be done in relatively trivial cases." Who is to decide what is "relatively trivial," and at what stage is this decision to be made? And what of the "relatively trivial" traffic offence which would lead to the third indorsement and disqualification under the "totting-up" procedure?

Indeed, one might think that if the giving of reasons were to be made mandatory, there would be little alternative to requiring them to be given in all contested cases for the possible benefit of a few. There would then arise the question whether such a change in practice could be accommodated within the present structure of lay magistrates or whether it would require the presence of a legally qualified chairman, for example, reminiscent of the legally qualified chairman of county quarter sessions, as indeed was suggested in an earlier Memorandum of the Law Society.[24] Another side effect of such a change would be to emphasise more than ever the anomaly presented by the system of jury trial where, even though the offences on the whole are much more serious than those tried in magistrates' courts, the simple verdict of Guilty or Not Guilty is returned, with no reasons whatsoever. Are magistrates to be less trusted than jurors to have applied their minds to the proper issues and to have taken into account only proper evidence?

However, even if one rules out a universal mandatory requirement for the giving of reasons by magistrates, there is nothing to prevent benches voluntarily adding to the bald statement of their decision, in cases which appear to them and their clerk to permit this and to be appropriate, a brief statement of their reasons, in whatever depth and detail the circumstances appear to warrant, perhaps with the encouragement of the Lord Chancellor or of the Magistrates' Association, and the experience gained from such a limited experiment might show whether any further development was possible or desirable, without a radical overhaul of the administration of summary justice.

NOTES

1. *The Magistrate*, February 1972 (Vol. 28, No. 2, p. 19).
2. *The Magistrate*, April, 1972 (Vol. 28, No. 4, p. 52).
3. Para. 13 of the Memorandum.
4. The Franks Committee, 1957, Cmnd. 218, para. 98.
5. *Per* Megarry J. in *Fountaine* v. *Chesterton and Others*, *The Times*, August 20, 1968.
6. *Judicial Review of Administrative Action* (2nd edn, p. 133).
7. The Donoughmore Committee, 1932, Cmnd. 4060, p. 80.
8. *The Times*, December 13, 1972.
9. Magistrates' Courts Act 1952, s. 83, as amended by the Courts Act 1971, s. 18 and First Sched.
10. Magistrates' Courts Act 1952, s. 87.
11. 1972, Cmnd. 5020.
12. November 23, 1972, p. 1041.
13. Magistrates' Courts Act 1952, s. 83(1).
14. Magistrates' Courts Rules 1968, r. 68; Magistrates' Courts (Forms) Rules 1968, Form 148.
15. *Cowlishaw* v. *Chalkley* [1955] 1 W.L.R. 101.
16. [1953] 1. W.L.R. 334.
17. p. 11.
18. [1965] 1 Q.B. 200. *Per* Winn J. at p. 209.
19. *Cf.* de Smith, *op. cit.*, pp. 113 *et seq.*; Wilson, "A Note on Law and Fact" (1963) 26 M.L.R. 609; *Solle* v. *Butcher* [1950] 1 K.B. 671.
20. (1967) 9 J.S.P.T.L. 176, 177.
21. Criminal Justice Act 1925, s. 20.
22. Administration of Justice Act 1960, s. 1.
23. Para. 43.
24. Practice and Procedure in Magistrates' Courts (May 1967).

15. PRISONERS' RIGHTS:
QUIS CUSTODIET IPSOS CUSTODES?

P. ENGLISH

I—Rights or Privileges?

"A prisoner has no absolute rights, he has only privileges." This stark
and somewhat startling statement was recently made by the National
Council For Civil Liberties.[1] If one accepts it, he may well wonder what
the organisation PROP (Preservation of the Rights of Prisoners) can seek
to achieve, for there would seem to be nothing to be preserved. Of course,
PROP may be concerned not so much to preserve a prisoner's rights qua
prisoner, as to preserve rights he had as an ordinary free citizen, before
he became a prisoner. Indeed a study of PROP's stated aims and its
"Prisoners' Charter of Rights" makes it plain that such really is PROP's
principle aim.[2] Inasmuch as the status of prisoner inevitably involves the
loss of many of the rights one had as a free citizen, there is obviously much
campaigning territory for PROP to traverse. Even PROP, one would
assume, will accept that the citizen must lose some rights on being imprisoned. The questions are *which* rights should be lost and whether the
present situation in this country is such that too many rights are forfeited
by the prisoner. But can it really be, as the opening quotation suggests,
that *all* rights are forfeited and that the prisoner has no rights, even qua
prisoner? If that were the case then our society must long ago have ceased
to heed the words of one of its greatest modern heroes. In 1910 Winston
Churchill said this:

> "The mood and temper of the public in regard to the treatment of
> crime and criminal is one of the most unfailing tests of the civilisation
> of any country. A calm, dispassionate recognition of the rights of the
> accused, *and even of the convicted criminal*, against the State—a
> constant heart searching by all charged with the duty of punishment—
> . . ., unfailing faith that there is a treasure, if you can only find it, in
> the heart of every man. These are the symbols which mark and
> measure the stored-up strength of a nation, and are a sign and proof
> of the living virtue in it." (Italics supplied)[3]

One would hope that the message of those words has not been entirely
neglected. In fact, there is evidence to be found in the less eloquent language of the Prison Rules, that a prisoner does have rights.[4] Rule 7 provides
that prisoners shall be given written information about the Prison Rules.
A prisoner who cannot read or has difficulty in understanding is to have
the information explained to him so that "he can understand his rights
and duties." It may be said, however, that though there is this mention

of "rights" there is no list of "rights" set out in the rules, certainly nothing akin to PROP's charter, and so there are no "absolute" rights, to recall again the words quoted at the beginning. Yet English law is not in the habit of laying down "lists" and "charters" of rights. Such rights as the ordinary, unimprisoned citizen has are not to be discovered by the perusal of some "list" set out by the law, rather one has to study the whole of the law to see what it is forbidden to do and then deduce that the citizen is free to, has the right to, do what is not forbidden. In some areas, for example the franchise, the law does go further and state positively that citizens possessing certain qualifications have the right to engage in the activity concerned, *i.e.* voting. So, with the prisoner's situation it should be possible to survey the relevant statutes and rules to see the extent to which his life is managed and controlled in prison.[5] If it appears that he is in certain respects to be controlled in certain ways then it may be said to be his right to be so controlled. If it appears that there are areas of his life which are not stated to be subject to any control then it may be inferred that in respect of those areas of activity he has a right to act as he wills. Further, if the statutes and rules state, or appear to state, that he is entitled to do certain things then may it not be said that he has the "right" to do those things?

Here one meets a difficulty. The wording of the rules may appear, at one place, to be such as to grant rights, but at another place the wording appears to treat the matter in question not as one of "right" but as one of "privilege." It has already been noted that the 1964 Rules speak of a prisoner's "rights." The earlier, 1949, versions of the Rules had contained a similar provision.[6] Under rule 74(1) of the 1949 Rules a prisoner was allowed to write and receive a letter on reception and then once every four weeks. This seemed to give the prisoner a clear right. The next part of rule 74 went on to state that "the letters and visits to which a prisoner is entitled" (under rule 74(1)) "shall not be liable to forfeiture under rules 43 and 44." Those rules empowered the Governor or Visiting Committee to order "forfeiture or postponement of privileges" where a prisoner had been found guilty of a disciplinary offence.[7] So, at one instant, rule 74 seems to treat the sending and receipt of a letter as a right, while at the next treating it as a "privilege" albeit one not liable to forfeiture. The 1964 Rules avoid the problem (whether consciously or not, one does not know) by providing that punishment by way of loss of privileges shall be loss of any "privileges under rule 4" and that rule does not relate to letters or visits,[8] so letters and visits do not now seem to be ranked as privileges. Indeed, rule 34(5) speaks of the "right of a prisoner to a visit" when it provides that the Governor may defer that right in the case of any prisoner under-going cellular confinement. So it may not be unrealistic to consider these matters as matters of "right" rather than of privilege, although the fact that there can be postponement of the right to a visit may be sufficient reason for withholding the epithet "absolute" from the word "right" in this context.

There may be a further reason for so doing; again, the example of letters and visits may be taken. If the ordinary person were told that he had the right to receive and send letters, say, when he was in hospital he would (after expostulating that of course he had such a right and he did not need anyone to tell him so) assume that he could write to whomsoever he pleased and receive letters back from them. He might, let us imagine, choose to write to a marriage bureau and nobody would think anything of it even assuming they knew about it. In November 1967 a prisoner wrote to a marriage bureau; the prison authorities discovered that he had done so. Here is the first major difference between the position of our hypothetical patient in hospital and our real prisoner. Prison mail is censored; under rule 33(3), the Governor may "at his discretion, stop any letter or communication on the grounds that its contents are objectionable or that it is of inordinate length." The prison authorities stopped this letter and sought Home Office advice. This, it will be recalled, was in November 1967. "The Home Office did not reply immediately," related the Parliamentary Commissioner for Administration, in his account of the episode (for ultimately the prisoner complained to him).[9] Indeed they did not, for nothing happened until March 1968 when the prisoner raised the matter again with the prison officials. The Home Office's advice was again sought and it was ruled that the man could write to the bureau "subject to certain conditions." He did not "take advantage of this offer," as the Parliamentary Commissioner put it, and later the Home Office ruled that prisoners should not write to marriage bureaux, a ruling the merits of which the Parliamentary Commissioner did not question. The justifications, real or supposed, for censorship of prisoners' mail will not be explored here though it is only fair, in passing, to record that experiments in the relaxation of censorship are being carried out.[10] What is in issue for present purposes is whether, in the light of these restrictions, it is meaningful to speak of the "right" to send and receive letters. Likewise, is it meaningful for the rules to speak, as rule 34(5) does, of the "right of a prisoner to a visit," when under rule 33(1), the Home Secretary may "impose restrictions, either generally or in a particular case, upon the communications to be permitted between a prisoner and other persons"? When does a "right" that may be so qualified, so subject to restriction and postponement, cease to be a "right"? It would be possible to pursue such questions but the following discussion will not take up that challenge. It will, for good or ill, be accepted that one can usefully speak of a prisoner's rights. It has earlier been suggested that such rights may be taken to arise in certain ways, and certain instances may be examined. It is not possible, here, to do more than take a few examples. A full review of prisoners' rights, together with a comparison between English rules, those in other countries and the standards required under the United Nations "Standard Minimum Rule for the Treatment of Prisoners," and the European Convention on Human Rights, is being undertaken by the Cobden Trust.[11]

Prison Acts and Rules have, over the years, laid down that prisons shall be run in certain ways and that prisoners shall be treated in certain ways. One may cite, as a current example of this, rule 1 of the 1964 Rules:

"The purpose of the training and treatment of convicted prisoners shall be to encourage and assist them to lead a good and useful life." Rule 2 provides that order and discipline shall be maintained firmly "but with no more restriction than is required for safe custody and well ordered community life." The treatment of prisoners is to be such "as to encourage their self-respect and a sense of personal responsibility." These rules indicate to the prison staff the manner in which they are to carry out their tasks but it is not fanciful to suggest that they also confer rights, nebulous ones perhaps, upon the prisoners. It may be said that it follows from these particular rules that a convicted prisoner has a right to be treated in such a way that he *shall* be encouraged to lead a good and useful life, that such discipline and order that is imposed upon him shall *only* be that which is necessary to ensure his safe custody and the good ordering of the community life of the prison. The Rules could go further and forbid the prison staff to do anything that was not necessary for those purposes. It is noteworthy that the 1933 Rules contained this particular rule: "No officer shall by word, gesture or demeanour do any thing which may tend to irritate any prisoner."[12] The corresponding 1949 rule forbade the officer to "deliberately act in a manner calculated to provoke a prisoner," and such is the wording of the current rule.[13] While it is not suggested that this change was designed to permit staff to irritate prisoners, so long as they did not actually provoke them, it seems that there is in theory a diminution in the prisoner's right, as measured against the yardstick of what an officer is not, according to prohibitions within the Rules, to do to him.

It has been an important feature of the administration of English prisons that prisoners have been classified and separated according to this classification. In 1782 a statute provided for forms of separation in local Houses of Correction.[14] The 1823 Act enjoined Visiting Justices to have "strict regard" to the classification of prisoners.[15] One important feature of classification and separation is that unconvicted prisoners have been treated differently from convicted ones. The present rule 3(2) provides: "Unconvicted prisoners shall be kept out of contact with convicted prisoners as far as this can reasonably be done." The rule, sensibly, goes on to state that its adherence should not be such that a prisoner is to be "deprived unduly of the society of other persons." It scarcely requires to be stated why an unconvicted prisoner should be entitled to be treated more liberally than his convicted fellow prisoner but one does find the reason clearly articulated in the Prison Act 1877. Section 39 instructed the Secretary of State to make special rules for the treatment of unconvicted prisoners because "it is expedient that a clear difference shall be made between the treatment of persons unconvicted of crime and in law presumably innocent during the period of their detention for safe custody only, and the treatment of prisoners who have been convicted of crime during the period of their detention in prison for the purpose of punishment."

Subsequent consolidation of the law has swept those words from the statute book.[16] Again, one does not imagine that some perversity was at work when the removal was effected but one may ask whether it might not have been better if the clear principle involved could not have been allowed to remain stated in "black letter law." In fact one famous prison official, Fox, writing in 1934 when the requirements of the 1877 Act were still part of the law, displayed a certain amount of equivocation about section 39.[17] Having recited the presumption of innocence to which the section refers he added:

> "There is, however, today the further presumption that in all proper cases the courts will release an untried offender on bail, so that when such a person is received into prison it must as a rule be supposed that the court considers detention necessary either to ensure his appearance for trial . . . or to prevent him from interfering with the course of justice."

So, Fox continued, the treatment of such prisoners must provide not only for their safe custody but also for their adequate supervision "and will be compatible with the discipline and general regime of an establishment populated mainly by convicted prisoners." Fox then added that it followed, "from our second presumption" that many of these untried prisoners "are not, as may often be supposed, respectable and probably innocent people, but 'old hands' with, in all probability, quite a string of previous convictions—whatever may be their fate on the charges pending."[18] He may well have been right on that score but it hardly matters. The objectionable nature of his comments need no underlining but perhaps it does bear comment that these remarks were addressed to the general public at a time when section 39 of the 1877 Act was still on the statute book. If this was what the Secretary of the Prison Commission thought of the presumption of innocence one may well wonder how an ordinary prison officer dealing with the "presumably innocent" prisoner would have reacted to the mention of it.

Existing rules provide that the unconvicted prisoner is to be treated differently from the convicted prisoner, in particular with regard to clothes, work, letters and visits.[19] His rights clearly are greater. That is how one would normally put it, yet the Parliamentary Commissioner has written of "certain privileges to which untried prisoners are entitled." His Annual Report for 1968 mentioned the case of a prisoner who had, on reception into prison, been treated as a convicted prisoner when in fact he had been remanded to prison for a medical report as to his fitness to plead.[20] He spent eight days in prison under this wrong classification and for this "injustice" the Home Office made him an "*ex-gratia* payment of £100 as compensation." The Home Office is not renowned for profligacy in the handling of funds used for *ex-gratia* payments and so, notwithstanding that the Parliamentary Commissioner spoke of "deprivation of privileges to which untried prisoners are entitled" rather that "rights of untried prisoners," it is submitted that in the eyes of the Home Office this man deserved compensation for loss of a right.

II—The Enforcement of Rights

If the general statements in the rules may be said to give rise to rights adhering to prisoners it must be asked how those rights are to be enforced. How, in the last analysis, are the authorities to be compelled to adhere to the rules and treat their prisoners in the prescribed manner? It is obvious that such a rule as rule 44 (1)—no officer is to use unnecessary force on a prisoner—may be enforced by ordinary process of civil or criminal action. Such action would not rely on the rule itself but on the common law or the Offences against the Person Act.[21] But could rule 44(2)—no officer shall act deliberately in a manner calculated to provoke a prisoner—be so easily enforced in a court of law? If the provocation caused the prisoner to suffer nervous shock then there might be a cause of action in tort.[22] Could any legal remedy be invoked to compel obedience to rule 1? It would be difficult to imagine it. The prison authorities face the problem of overcrowding as best they can with the resources at their disposal. It would be difficult to imagine that they could be shown to be intentionally or negligently bringing about a situation in which conditions make it difficult or impossible to realise the aims set out in rule 1.

Even if a breach of rule 1 could be shown it seems that no legal action could be brought as a result. The courts will not entertain any action based solely upon an allegation of breach of the Prison Rules. Though there are two nineteenth-century cases which might tend to give support to the view that such breaches could be actionable, the twentieth century authorities are against such a view.[23] The position may be summed up in the words of Winn J.: "it is manifest that the control of prisons and prisoners by the prison commissioners and the visiting justices should not be interfered with by the courts unless, in any particular case, there has been some departure from law and good administration amounting to an offence in law."[24]

To those who would urge that any interference with the individual's liberty is unlawful unless sanctioned by a particular rule of law—and they might well argue that this applied to the details of the prison régime—the point might not seem so obvious. Yet it would be idle to deny that the English courts have displayed, in matters of prison administration, "an invincible reluctance to interfere."[25]

One way in which enforcement of rule 1 might be achieved has recently been suggested by Lord Kilbrandon. He suggested that judges might take the view that they were only authorised by law to send convicted persons to establishments where the aims of imprisonment, as for example stated in rule 1, were actually being carried out. Thus they would not be entitled to send anyone to an existing prison where those aims could not be realised. Judges might say, his lordship was reported as remarking, that unless places were supplied to which they could send people without moral, mental and physical degradation being endured then they would not imprison people.[26] It is a brave suggestion but one cannot see it happening, somehow. In the final analysis, at present, the observation of the letter and the spirit of the Prison Rules is up to the prison authorities themselves. Though some of the rules may be susceptible of enforcement through normal legal procedures many are not and in practice society must rely on its prison custodians to treat the prisoners according to the rules—rules which, it may be added, the custodians have made themselves. So duties imposed on the custodians are to that extent self-imposed. Ever since 1898 it has been left to the Secretary of State to make prison rules, subject to some limited statutory control.[27] So the imposition of standards of behaviour regarding the treatment of prisoners has, in the main, been a self-imposed burden for the executive. Prior to 1898 the source of this burden was statutory in that the various Prison Acts contained detailed rules concerning the management of the prisons and the treatment of the inmates.[28] However, Parliament was not content simply to state that such and such was to be done. It was further stated that senior prison officials should regularly inspect the premises to ensure that such and such were indeed being done.[29] Further provision was made for some outside body of persons to visit and inspect the prisons. This imposition of particular duties on senior prison staff and this granting of visiting rights—and duties—to an outside body has long been a feature of English prison law and it continues to be so. It is reasonable to infer that Parliament has seen these methods as the means of ensuring that prisons should be managed properly and prisoners treated as befitted them—which would of course vary from age to age.

Serious parliamentary concern for the state of prisons is not really to be found before the mid-eighteenth century. Then legislation required local justices to make rules for the management of their prisons.[30] Later Acts laid down particular provisions which were to be enforced. The first code of rules for prisons is to be found in the Gaols Act of 1823. Here we find duties of the keeper set out. He was to live at the prison and inspect the premises daily. He was to keep proper records—for example of punishments inflicted—and he was to report to quarter sessions, at regular intervals, on the state of the prison.[31] The Prison Act 1865 replaced these provisions with a more detailed code of rules under which, for example, the gaoler was to visit the whole of the prison and see every prisoner once in every twenty-four hours so far as was practicable. He was "at least once during the week," to "go through the prison at an uncertain hour of the night" and record the nocturnal journey in his journal.[32] One also finds particular duties imposed by this code on the prison surgeon and upon the chaplain.[33] Many details of the duties to be carried out by various officials were repeated in the Prison Rules and survived in the 1933 and 1949 versions.[34] The current Rules are much less detailed and no doubt take account of the fact that, from the Home Office viewpoint at any rate, the increasing professionalism in the prison service that has taken place in the twentieth century has made it unnecessary for the rules to spell out in detail the duties of the Governor and other key staff members.

To every prison there is appointed a Board of Visitors, which has the duty, in the words the Prison Rules, to "satisfy themselves as to the state of the prison premises, the administration of the prison and the treatment of the prisoners."[35] Boards of Visitors are probably better known as Visiting Committees of Magistrates. Though there were differences between the two bodies, that title conveys, as it were, the historical tradition of this institution.[36] Local prisons were originally administered by the local justices. Legislation came to require that the justices should appoint some of their number to act as visiting justices to inspect the local prison as the 1791 statute stated: "for better preventing all abuses."[37] Under the 1823 Act two visitors were to be nominated by the justices "in sessions assembled" for each prison. One was to "visit and inspect" the prison at least three times a quarter and investigate the state of the premises, the régime and the behaviour of the officers, and abuses were to be reported.[38] In addition, any Justice of the Peace, acting in the locality, was entitled "at his own free will and pleasure" to visit the prison and report any matter back to his assembled colleagues.[39] It was provided that these powers of visitation were not to be taken to authorise a justice to "converse or hold any intercourse or communication" with any prisoner committed to the prison for close confinement except in so far as was necessary in order to receive representations from that prisoner about his treatment "and to enquire and examine into the same."[40] Similar provisions existed in the 1865 Act with the odd addition that a justice who was not a Visiting Justice was not to be entitled to visit any prisoner who was under sentence of death[41]—one does not know whether there had been a spate of death cell visits by morbidly curious justices. In 1877 the management of local prisons was transferred from justices to central government and the "Prison Commissioners" were instituted.[42] They were to be assisted in their task by inspectors of prisons. Inspectors had, in fact, existed since 1835.[43] The local justices still had a role to play; by what Fox has called "one of our characteristic English compromises" local supervision was retained despite the transfer of management of the local prison to central government.[44] Section 13 of the 1877 Act prescribed that a "Visiting Committee" of justices was to be appointed to each prison by the local quarter sessions court or local bench(es) of magistrates. A member of the Committee was to be able to visit the prison at any time and was to have "free access to every part of the prison and to every prisoner therein" at all times. Members were to visit "at frequent intervals and hear any complaints which may be made to them by the prisoners and, if asked privately." The right of any justice to visit was preserved with the same reservations as those laid down in 1865.[45]

The legislation, thus far mentioned, dealt with local prisons. There did also exist prisons that had been erected to receive those prisoners who in earlier times would have been disposed of by way of transportation or the rope. In 1779 a statute had been passed authorising the construction of "two plain, strong and substantial edifices which shall be called Penitentiary House." It was intended that courts should be able to sentence prisoners to hard labour in those places in lieu of transportation. The régime was to be of the grimmest kind. Prisoners were to be kept "to labour of the hardest and most servile kind in which drudgery is chiefly required." Prison clothes were to be "a course and uniform apparel with certain obvious marks or badges affixed to the same, as well to humiliate the wearers as to facilitate discovery in case of escapes."[46]

Yet into this awful place any local justice was entitled to enter, to visit, inspect and report any abuses or mismanagement.[47] In 1850 the "Directors of Convict Prisons" were appointed to manage the "national" prisons and in 1898 that management was transferred to the Prison Commissioners.[48] The Home Secretary was to appoint, for each convict prison, a Board of Visitors "of whom not less than two shall be Justices of the Peace," who would in effect be the "Visiting Committee" for the prison.[49]

It is probably reasonable to surmise that the Visiting Justices were expected to pay as much—if not more—attention to the rigours of the punishment nineteenth-century prisoners were expected to endure, as to complaints those prisoners might have.[50] In this century, however, the role they play in receiving complaints has become much more important. Fox described the function as a "most valuable" one, the Committee acting "as an impartial, judicial and non-official body," and he mentions the power of the Committee to report abuses to the Home Secretary.[51] They have the power in emergencies to suspend a prison officer.[52] During this century the Prison Rules, in their various versions, have laid down that any prisoner's request to see a member of the committee, on one of the regular visits or at the monthly meeting, should be promptly relayed to the visiting member or the whole committee.[53] It is one thing to provide a system whereby an outside body receives complaints from the prisoners and acts on them by way of raising the matter with the Governor or reporting it to the Home Secretary. It is quite another thing to ensure that the prisoner feels that he thereby has access to an "impartial, judicial and non-official body," which will, in appropriate cases, take his side "against" authority when he has a grievance. Writing in 1957, Winifred Elkin, said that "prisoners did not always accept the view that the co-operation of unofficial persons provides a safeguard against harshness or oppression by authority."[54] It is difficult to assess how valid that comment would be if made today but there must be doubts about the matter. One may say that however much this body strives to be impartial it will only be effective in performing its function of providing an adequate means of having a prisoner's complaints aired if the prisoner himself has confidence in the group as an impartial, non-official body. This could be a difficulty in any setting, but is more of a difficulty in the prison setting where mistrust and resentment of any group of people who have a formal role to play may easily flourish. This particular difficulty faces the Visiting Committee.

III—Prisoners' Dicipline

The "Complaints Function" they perform—and have performed for so long—is not the only task whose performance has brought them into contact with the prisoner. They have always had a disciplinary function to perform—one, indeed, which Fox described as their "principal" function.[55] Keepers, gaolers and governors have, under the various Acts, been empowered to impose punishments on prisoners guilty of offences against prison discipline but the more serious cases, the "enormous offenders," as a side note in the 1779 Act described them, were to be reserved for the Visiting Committee.[56] Such has remained the position and it is difficult to imagine that a prisoner would consider that a group of individuals having disciplinary powers over him was a "non-official body." It is a situation in which the fact that the body has these disciplinary functions may well lead to prisoners having the reservations Elkins wrote of when they meet the visitors carrying their other function.

In exercising their disciplinary function the Committee have for long been subject to some minimum procedures laid down by the legislation.[57] Initially this governed the extent of their powers of punishment and also empowered them to conduct the adjudication under oath. In 1877 it was made clear that there was to be no corporal punishment inflicted unless the inquiry had been held under oath and when, in 1898, Boards of Visitors were introduced for convict prisons a general requirement was laid down that awards of corporal punishment could only be made if three members of the Board or Committee had been present, including two justices.[58] The inquiry had to have been under oath and the order had, before it was carried out, to have been confirmed by the Home Secretary. The Act also restricted the use of corporal punishment to prisoners guilty of serious specified offences of mutiny, incitement to mutiny or gross personal violence to a prison officer. Little was laid down in the way of procedural matters and that remained so under Rules made in the twentieth century. The Criminal Justice Act of 1948, however, required the Home Secretary to make rules "for ensuring that a person who is charged with any offence under the rules shall be given a proper opportunity of presenting his case."[59] The 1949 Rules provided that a prisoner should be informed of the offence charged "and shall be given a proper opportunity of hearing the facts alleged against him and of presenting his case."[60] The Governor had power—as he had had under earlier Rules—to segregate an accused prisoner pending adjudication.[61] One can imagine reasons why this might be necessary in many cases but one consequence of course is that the prisoner looses the chance to contact fellow prisoners—or officers—who might be potential witnesses in his defence. The 1964 Rules, which also preserve this power to segregate the accused prisoner, require that the prisoner be informed of the offence charged "as soon as possible and in any case before the time when it is inquired into by the Governor." The rule goes on to say: "At any inquiry into a charge against a prisoner he shall be given a full opportunity of hearing what is alleged against him and of presenting his own case."[62]

There is no provision for the prisoner to be represented either by a lawyer or by a "friend" and to date, the Home Office have opposed such suggestions. In the debate on the 1964 Rules, in the House of Commons, Mr. Brooke, the then Home Secretary, was asked to consider the suggestion that a prisoner should have the right to have a friend present to help him present his case in disciplinary hearings. This was Mr. Brooke's reply:

> "One cannot go more than a certain distance in these cases. A man who has got himself into prison cannot hope to have all the advantages that a free man would have outside if he was having his case presented by a lawyer or a trade union official or someone like that. My experience is that in such cases the visiting committee or the board of visitors is very anxious to get to the bottom of what is troubling or biting the man who has complained to it, but I do not think that a right way of doing that would be to insert in the rules a provision that a prisoner who came up before the visiting committee or the board of visitors could have as of right a friend by his side."[63]

As well as confusing the two functions of the Visiting Committee, this answer ignores the fact that many who have "got themselves into prison" are there as unconvicted prisoners. Whatever rights one thinks ought to be held by a convicted prisoner in peril before an adjudicating committee the rights of the unconvicted prisoner should not necessarily be as limited. In any case this answer does not really begin to examine the issues involved in the case of either sort of prisoner. In 1970 the Home Secretary said, in a written answer, that he did not think it was "necessary or practicable" to take steps to provide legal aid for prisoners in proceedings before visiting magistrates where these were liable to result in a loss of more than one month's remission.[64] Thus the concern to provide representation for accused persons in courts of law has not been extended to accused prisoners before the Visiting Committee.

The expression "prisoner in peril before an adjudicating committee" was not lightly used for the punishment powers of the committees are extensive. They were in fact increased in 1964 and the explanatory note to the 1964 Rules is perhaps too modest when it states that the powers "are increased in certain respects". Stoppage of earnings, for example, can be for up to 56 days (it was 28 days under the 1949 rules) and cellular confinement can be for up to 56 days (only 14 days under the 1949 Rules).[65] These increased powers were probably designed to encourage visiting magistrates to resort to these methods of punishment rather than corporal punishment and restricted diet. In 1967 the power to impose corporal punishment was abolished.[66] This humane change however brought about a consequence which might not be considered in the interests of prisoners' rights. Whereas, formerly, the Visiting Committee could only impose the most serious penalty after investigation under oath there is now no such requirement. Long periods of loss of remission and cellular confinement may be ordered without a word having been heard on oath.[67] The nature of the composition of the committee is likely to guarantee a searching inquiry and perhaps the absence of the oath is of no great consequence— perhaps the incidence of perjury is thereby kept down. But the prisoner could be forgiven for asking whether, looking at disciplinary proceedings as a whole, the situation is entirely satisfactory. He could surely be forgiven if he wondered whether it was really what one would normally expect to find in proceedings which could lead to the imposition of serious punishments.

IV—Conclusion

To consider the work of Boards of Visitors—and their predecessors—is to encounter the sort of issues that can be found in other areas related to the question of prisoners' rights. One asks whether the rules are clear enough, whether they give rights that ought to be given. One asks whether the system designed to ensure adherence to the rules is one that inspires confidence as being likely to ensure such adherence. And one asks whether there are ways in which over the years the rights of a prisoner have been diminished, not deliberately perhaps, but as a result of some revision, some "tidying-up" of the rules and statutes. No one could deny the great improvement that has taken place this century in prison conditions, and it may well be that many rules imposing particular duties on staff or forbidding staff to do this or that are simply unnecessary in the modern prison system. Yet the importance of the "book of rules" in a closed institution, its significance to staff and inmates alike, may well be considered such that the loss of a right once clearly—or perhaps only inferentially—guaranteed may be seen as unfortunate. One example may be cited. As long ago as 1865 a statute enjoined the gaoler to ensure that an abstract of the regulations should be posted in each cell and read to illiterate prisoners on reception.[68] In this way it was to be ensured that prisoners were made aware of the rules governing their treatment and conduct. Much later, the 1949 Rules spoke of "full information [being given] about the rules governing the treatment of prisoners of his class and about any other regulations of which he should have knowledge, including those relating to earnings and privileges, to the proper method of submitting petitions to the Secretary of State, and of making complaints, to food, clothing, bedding and other necessaries, and to the disciplinary requirements of the prison."[69] The present rule is less detailed: "Every prisoner shall be provided . . . with information in writing about those provisions of these Rules and other matters which it is necessary that he should know, including earnings and privileges and the proper method of making complaints and of petitioning the Home Secretary."[70]

In the Commons debate on the 1964 Rules it was asked who was to decide "what is necessary for the prisoner to know." Mr. Brooke assured the House that "what prisoners are allowed to do is set out in the information booklet which is available to every prisoner."[71] Of course the current rule, if fully complied with, goes as far as the 1949 rule, yet there is room for the view that the loss of particularity is such that the 1964 grant of rights is not as ample as the 1949 one had been. One curious contrast may be made between the 1949 Rules and the current ones, by comparing rule 82 (1949) and rule 36 (1964). They both cover the case of someone committed to prison in default of finding some required sum of money. Both rules declare that such a prisoner may write to or receive a visit from a friend or relative for the purpose of arranging payment of the sum and so getting out of prison. The 1949 rule went on to state "and every such prisoner shall on his reception be informed of this Rule." There are no such words in the 1964 rule. One would imagine that this is one of the rules considered necessary for such a prisoner to know but one wonders why it is not specifically mentioned as it had been in 1949.

The ordinary ways in which a free citizen may turn to friends or a lawyer in order to ventilate a grievance and perhaps secure redress are obviously not open to a prisoner. In their place he has the right to complain to senior staff within the prison, to complain to the Board of Visitors or to petition the Home Secretary. He may also write to a Member of Parliament about his treatment though he is expected first to have raised the complaint through the "official channels." [72] If he has a complaint about "maladministration" he may—and examples have already been cited—complain to the Parliamentary Commissioner. He may, these days, complain to the European Commission of Human Rights where, unlike the case of a complaint to the Parliamentary Commissioner, he will find himself dealing with a body that will be willing to question the merits of given rules and not simply confine itself to the question of "maladministration." In one recent case the rules governing contact with lawyers for the purpose of bringing proceedings against the prison authorities came under consideration and in the event the Home Office has made changes in the rules. [73] This new right to apply to the Commission may prove, in the long run, to be of considerable significance for the administration of this country's prisons but it would be unfortunate if future changes were to be seen to have been introduced only after the present Rules had been found deficient—in some matter relating to prisoners' rights—by the Commission.

It is to be hoped that Parliament and the Home Office will not need to be so prodded into making changes when it is right to do so. It is always timely to consider questions of human rights but the events of 1972 when, perhaps for the first time, members of the public came to hear of the "Preservation of the Rights of Prisoners" made it particularly timely that the question of prisoners' rights should be seriously considered. In its "Prisoners' Charter of Rights," PROP calls for the right to trade union membership, the right to confidential communications with lawyers, the right to legal representation in disciplinary hearings, the right to marry as well as other rights. [74] One of the claimed rights is the right to vote. It is noteworthy that this right did exist until 1969 though it was a somewhat illusory right in that a prisoner could not seek habeas corpus to be released in order to vote. [75] If a legislature was concerned to preserve that right—and to make it effective—it could take steps to enjoin officials to facilitate voting by prisoners. Parliament however took the simpler step of disenfranchising convicted prisoners with scarcely any debate on the matter. It was hardly a step calculated to give any encouragement to supporters of PROP!

In an age when all manner and condition of men seek a clear statement of their rights and clear means of enforcing them it must be asked what rights a prisoner should have and it must be asked whether the present Rules are satisfactory both in terms of stating those rights and of ensuring their observance. "One cannot go more than a certain distance in these cases," Mr. Brooke said in 1964 when speaking of the absence of the right for a prisoner to have a friend present at disciplinary hearings. The comment could well have been made with regard to all aspects of prisoners' rights. How far one should go has, by and large, been left to the executive to determine in this century. It is now clear that increasing awareness of the need for and value of clear statements of rights and the obligation which the United Kingdom has to adhere to international standards make it no longer possible for the executive to be so certain that they have gone far enough.

NOTES

1. *Civil Liberty—The NCCL Guide*, Coote and Grant (eds) (1971) at p. 37.
2. *PROP*, No. 1 (1972) p. 6 [mimeographed].
3. Churchill, speaking as Home Secretary, in the House of Commons July 25, 1910: quoted in Cross, *Punishment, Prison and the Public* (1971), p. 40.
4. The Prison Rules 1964, S.I. 1964 No. 388.
5. The 1964 Rules cover a wide variety of matters affecting the prison régime *e.g.* religion (rr. 10–16), education (rr. 29–32) and remission (r. 5). The current relevant statute is the Prison Act 1952. However, this statute and the 1964 Rules do not, by any means, provide the whole picture. Many of the Rules empower the Home Secretary to make directions and impose particular conditions—see *e.g.* rr. 3, 33 and 34. It needs a full working knowledge of these Prison Standing Orders for one to be fully aware of the restrictions imposed on prisoners. A copy of these Standing Orders is available, in the Library of the House of Commons, to M.P.s [see H.C. Deb., Oral Answers, Vol. 811, col. 2095 (February 18, 1971)]. The Standing Orders are not available for general public inspection. In 1919 the Executive of the Labour Research Department instituted an inquiry into the prison system and requested from the Prison Commission a copy of the Standing Orders. This request was refused. The authors of the report of the inquiry did somehow manage to get a copy of the 1911 edition of the Standing Orders for Local Prisons and they quoted extensively from it in their report: Hobhouse and Fenner-Brockway, *English Prisons Today* (1922), pp. vi *et seq.*
6. The Prison Rules 1949, S.I. 1949 No. 1073.
7. r. 42 of the 1949 Rules set out the list of punishable offences against discipline.
8. r. 4 provides for the establishment within each prison of "systems of privileges . . . which shall include arrangements under which money earned by prisoners in prison may be spent by them within the prison."
9. Second Report of the Parliamentary Commissioner for Administration—Session 1968–69. Annual Report for 1968, p. 47.
10. In 1971 an experiment was begun in the relaxation of censorship at an open prison and in 1972 it was announced that it would be extended to another, and possibly a third open prison. See Report on the work of the Prison Department 1971, Cmnd. 5037 (1972).
11. The Cobden Trust produced a mimeographed draft outline of their projected study late in 1972. The subject of prisoners' rights was discussed at the inaugural conference of the British Institute of Human Rights, November 24–26, 1972. See (1972) 116 S.J. 918.
12. The Prison Rules 1933, S.I. 1933 No. 809, r. 73(2).
13. r. 34(2) of the 1949 Rules and r. 44(2) of the 1964 Rules.
14. 22 Geo. 3, c. 64, s. I.
15. 4 Geo. 4, c. 64, s. XVI.

16. The Prison Act 1952 consolidated earlier legislation but the Criminal Justice Act 1948 had already repealed s. 39 of the 1877 Act, as s. 52 of the 1948 Act empowered the Home Secretary to make rules for the management of prisons and the classification of prisoners. The 1952 Act is the current one. Prison Rules are made under s. 47.

17. Fox, *The Modern English Prison System* (1934), p. 147. At the time Fox was an Assistant Commissioner and Secretary to the Prison Commission. He became Chairman of the Prison Commissioners in 1942.

18. *Ibid.*, p. 148.

19. Prison Rules 1964, r. 20(1) (clothing); r. 28(5) (work); r. 34(1) (letters and visits). By r. 62(1) the rules applicable to appellants (rr. 58–60) were applied to prisoners awaiting sentence or trial, and these rules made special provision for visits, medical examination letters and legal facilities for appellants. R. 61 provided that successful appellants should be entitled to pay at a special rate for any work they had done while in prison as appellants. In November 1972 rr. 57–62 were revoked—Prison (Amendment) Rules, S.I. 1972 No. 1860.

20. *Op. cit.* at p. 46.

21. Criminal assaults would be punishable under the various provisions of the 1861 Act. Civil actions could be brought for assault and this could be done where it was alleged that unreasonable force had been used. In *R.* v. *Morton Brown, ex p. Ainsworth* (1910) 74 J.P. 53 the Divisional Court held that a summons for alleged assault could not issue against the Home Secretary but it could against the prison governor and medical officer. The rule nisi for mandamus to the magistrate to issue summonses was not made absolute at that stage and the applicant later withdrew the application in view of the decision in *Leigh* v. *Gladstone* (1909) 26 T.L.R. 139. Such actions are brought under general rules of law quite apart from *e.g.* r. 44 of the 1964 Prison Rules, which forbids an officer to use unnecessary force upon a prisoner. In Hobhouse and Fenner Brockway, *English Prisons Today* (1922) it is reported, at footnote 7, p. 392, that the Visiting Committee of Justices for Manchester Prison were held liable for damages at Manchester County Court in 1909. A prisoner had refused to leave his cell and the Committee ordered a hose-pipe to be used to dislodge him.

22. *Cf. Wilkinson* v. *Downton* [1897] 2 Q.B. 57 and *Janvier* v. *Sweeney* [1919] 2 K.B. 316.

23. See *Morriss* v. *Winter* [1930] 1 K.B. 243, *Arbon* v. *Anderson* [1943] 1 K.B. 252, *R.* v. *Governor of Leeds Prison, ex p. Stafford* [1964] 2 Q.B. 625. The two nineteenth-century cases which Goddard J. distinguished in *Arbon* v. *Anderson*, as relating to the nature of the imprisonment and not as to the conditions of the imprisonment, are *Cobbett* v. *Grey* (1849) 4 Ex. 729 and *Osborne* v. *Milman* (1886) 17 Q.B.D. 514. It may be thought, in view of these cases, that the Home Office were being "generous" in making the *ex gratia* payment in the case mentioned by the Parliamentary Commissioner, *supra*.

24. *Hancock* v. *Prison Commissioners* [1960] 1 Q.B. 117 at p. 128.

25. The phrase is that of Lord Hewart C.J. in *R.* v. *Graham-Campbell, ex p. Herbert* [1935] 1 K.B. 594 at p. 602. His Lordship was speaking of the reluctance of the courts to interfere in matters relating to the internal affairs of the House of Commons.

26. Lord Kilbrandon was speaking at the inaugural conference of the British Institute of Human Rights on November 26, 1972. See *The Times*, November 27, 1972, p. 4.

27. Prison Act 1898, s. 2 enabled the Home Secretary to make Prison Rules. S. 4 provided that Rules made as to the mode in which sentences should be carried out should pay regard to the sex, age, health, industry and conduct of prisoners. S. 5 restricted the authorisation, under Rules, of the imposition of corporal punishment.

28. The 1823 Act, included a code of rules to be applied—see s. 10. The Prison Act 1865, which amalgamated Gaols and Houses of Correction as Local Prisons, had a Schedule containing 104 regulations. Ss. 38 and 39 of the Prison Act 1877, which vested local prisons in the Home Secretary, empowered him to make certain alterations or additions to the 1865 Regulations.

29. For example, under s. 10 of the 1823 Act, r. 3, the prison keeper was to visit each ward, see each prisoner and inspect each cell daily.
30. See, for example, 32 Geo. 2, c. 28 (1758). A table of the major legislation regarding prisons is set out in Appendix A of Fox, *op. cit.* For a general history of local prisons see S. and B. Webb, *English Prisons under Local Government* (1922).
31. 4 Geo. 4, c. 64, s. 10, rr. 4 and s. 14.
32. Prison Act 1865, Sched. 1, reg. 71.
33. *Ibid.*, regs. 45–52 (chaplains) and 86–92 (surgeons).
34. Prison Rules 1933, rr. 39–43 and 96–104 (chaplains) and rr. 105–114 (medical officers). Prison Rules 1949, rr. 59–66 (chaplains) and rr. 85–95, 97 and 99. Further particular duties can be found in these sets of rules.
35. Prison Rules 1964, r. 94(1).
36. Courts Act 1971, s. 53(3), provided that Visiting Committees should be replaced by Boards of Visitors. Consequential changes in the Prison Rules were made by the Prison (Amendment) Rules 1971, S.I. 1971 No. 2019.
37. 31 Geo. 3, c. 46, s. 5.
38. 4 Geo. 4, c. 64, s. 16.
39. *Ibid.*, s. 17.
40. *Ibid.*, s. 18. The 1791 statute had authorised any local justice to visit and inspect a local prison but it was held in *R.* v. *Eaststaff* (1818) Gow 138; 171 E.R. 864 that notwithstanding this power the Secretary of State could forbid a justice, who was not a Visitor, to visit a prisoner who was committed to custody awaiting trial for treason.
41. Prison Act 1865, s. 55.
42. Prison Act 1877, s. 6. The Prison Commission remained in being until 1963 when it was abolished by S.I. 1963 No. 597 made under s. 24 of the Criminal Justice Act 1961. Its functions are now carried out by the Prison Department of the Home Office.
43. By virtue of 5 & 6 Will. 4, c. 38, the Secretary of State was empowered to appoint persons to inspect prisons.
44. *Op. cit.* at p. 57. It seems that for many years the compromise did not work well—see S. and B. Webb, *op. cit.* at pp. 215 *et seq.*, and Hobhouse and Fenner Brockway, *op. cit.*, at pp. 389–391.
45. Prison Act 1877, s. 15. Currently, the right is preserved by Prison Act 1952, s. 19.
46. 19 Geo. 3, c. 74, ss. 32 and 35.
47. *Ibid.*, s. 41. No such penitentiary was built but prisons were erected at Millbank, Pentonville and Parkhurst. See Fox, *op. cit.*, Chap 1.
48. 13 & 14 Vict. c. 39 (1850) and the Prison Act 1898.
49. Prison Act 1898, s. 3. Only the Board of Visitors in a convict prison could impose corporal punishment under s. 5 of the Act. Formerly such a punishment could be imposed on the order of a Director.
50. For example, s. 16 of the 1823 Act enjoined Visiting Justices to pay strict regard to "employment or hard labour." Industrious prisoners could be recommended to the Crown for mercy.
51. Fox, *op. cit.*, at pp. 57 and 58.
52. Prison Rules 1964, r. 94(4).
53. Prison Rules 1933, r. 67; Prison Rules 1949, r. 51; Prison Rules 1964, r. 8.
54. Elkin, *The English Penal System* (1957), at p. 188.
55. Fox, *op. cit.*, at p. 57.
56. 19 Geo. 3, c. 74, s. 47.
57. See Prison Act 1865, Sched. I, reg. 58. The power of punishment could be exercised by one member of the Committee. S. 14 of the Prison Act 1877 required the presence of two members at the inquiry before corporal punishment could be ordered. The power to deal with offences, except those carrying liability to corporal punishment, could be exercised by one member of the Committee or Board. Equally the prisoner could find himself facing the whole assembled body. This situation was criticised by the Franklin Committee in 1951: Report of the Committee to Review Punishments in Prisons, etc., Parts I and II (1951) Cmd. 8256, paras. 112–115. The Prison Rules were amended so as to provide that the disciplinary functions should be exercised

by not less than two nor more than five of the members of the Committee or Board. Prison Rules 1952, S.I. 1952 No. 1405, r. 6(5).
58. Prison Act 1877, s. 14 and Prison Act 1898, s. 5.
59. S. 52(2) re-enacted in s. 47(2) of the Prison Act 1952.
60. Prison Rules 1949, r. 40; r. 45 provided that hearings of the gravest charges should be held before at least three but not more than five of the Board or Committee.
61. *Ibid.*, r. 39.
62. Prison Rules 1964, r. 48(2) (segregation) and r. 49 (rights of prisoners charged).
63. H.C. Deb., Vol. 687, col. 1413 (January 23, 1964). In 1951 the Franklin Committee had reported on punishments in penal establishments. The committee reported that the balance of evidence and argument was against allowing legal representation (or representation by a "prisoner's friend") at disciplinary hearings even when corporal punishment might ensue. At para. 127 the committee made the following remarks: "The character of some recidivist prisoners is such that they would be prepared to risk a flogging by striking an officer in order to have the opportunity afforded by legal representation of maligning the character of individual officers or of discrediting the prison authorities. If prisoners of this type were allowed to be legally represented the effect on prison discipline would, we believe, be disastrous." Report of the Committee to Review Punishments in Prisons etc., Parts I and II (1951), Cmd. 8256. The present writer has never encountered such a startling justification for not providing representation to accused prisoners.
64. H.C. Deb., Written Answers, Vol. 807, col. *237* (November 27, 1970).
65. Prison Rules 1964, r. 51(4); Prison Rules 1949, r. 44(2).
66. Criminal Justice Act 1967, s. 65.
67. In the twelve months ending May 31, 1971, 149 awards of 15–28 days cellular confinement were made and 30 awards of 29–56 days made. H.C. Deb., Written Answers, Vol. 820, col. *363* (July 6, 1971). In 1967 it was stated that a certain prisoner had been found guilty of offences against discipline on fourteen separate occasions, in the preceding two years. In all he was punished with 346 days loss of remission, 68 days cellular confinement, 52 days restricted diet and 299 days loss of privileges. H.C. Deb., Written Answers, Vol. 745, col. *272* (April 25, 1967). R. 44 of the 1949 Rules which dealt with the referring to the Committee or Board of serious cases (but not those involving the possibility of corporal punishment) stated that the Committee should "inquire into the report (such inquiry if they or he [i.e. one member of the Committee exercising the power] think it desirable being on oath)." The 1952 Rules substituted a new r. 44 which omits the words in brackets. (*Cf.* r. 51 of the 1964 Rules.) This change of wording in 1952 did not, it is submitted, abolish the right to hold inquiry under oath but it could be interpreted as an attempt to discourage the practice. If it was such one may ask whether the attempt should have been made so quietly.
68. Prison Act 1865, Sched. 1, reg. 72.
69. Prison Rules 1949, r. 21.
70. Prison Rules 1964, r. 7.
71. H.C. Deb., Vol. 687, col. 1402 (January 23, 1964).
72. See Mr. Brooke's remarks *ibid.* at col. 1403.
73. The application to the European Commission was made by one Mr. Knechtl (Application No. 4115/69). He complained that he had not been allowed to write to lawyers in order to seek their advice about a claim he wished to make alleging negligent medical treatment by the prison authorities. Under rule 34(8) a prisoner requires the permission of the Home Office in order to write letters in connection with any legal business. In December 1970 the Commission declared the application admissible (Collection of Decisions of the European Commission on Human Rights, vol. 36, p. 43) and on March 24, 1972 it announced that a settlement had been reached. A sum of £750 was paid to Mr. Knechtl by the U.K. Government as settlement of his claim. His claim had involved the assertion that the Home Office decision had been in violation of Art. 6(1) of the European Convention on Human Rights which guarantees a right to a fair hearing before an independent tribunal.

It would have been argued that the right of access to a court embraced the right of access to a lawyer in the first place. The Prison (Amendment) Rules 1972, S.I. 1972 No. 1860 added to the existing r. 37 provisions that a "prisoner who is a party to any legal proceedings" may correspond with his legal adviser and the correspondence is not to be read or stopped unless it is believed that it relates to matters other than the proceedings in question.

74. *Op. cit.*, note 2 *supra*. In November 1972 the Home Secretary stated that he would continue to refuse to negotiate with PROP: H.C. Deb., Oral Answers, Vol. 845, col. 1171 (November 9, 1972).

75. Representation of the People Act 1969, s. 4, makes convicted persons legally incapable of voting during their detention. Formerly only felons and traitors were disqualified during sentence though misdemeanants were effectively unable to vote as they could not secure temporary release to go out and vote—*Re Jones* (1835) 2 Ad. & E. 436. The Criminal Law Act 1967 by abolishing felony had the effect, in theory at least, of enfranchising a large number of prisoners. The enjoyment of the right was, however, to be short-lived. It is noteworthy that the Criminal Law Revision Committee in their Seventh Report which made the proposals enacted in the 1967 Act (Cmnd. 2659 (1965)) said "It seems to us unnecessary to preserve any of these consequences [of disqualification] in relation to any offences especially as no similar consequences follow from conviction in Scotland" (para. 79).

Addendum

On June 12, 1973 the Home Secretary, Mr. Robert Carr, in his address to the Annual Conference of Boards of Visitors, announced that he intended to introduce various changes in the Prison Rules. Among the changes he outlined were these: the abolition of dietary punishment; improved arrangements for visits and communications for prisoners; giving Governors and Boards of Visitors power to suspend any disciplinary award; giving Governors and Boards of Visitors power to restore remission that a prisoner had earlier forfeited as a result of disciplinary award; giving Governors increased powers to order loss of remission or earnings.

Many of the changes will involve amendments to the existing Prison Rules and these would be laid before Parliament in due course. Mr. Carr also announced the setting up of a working party to review the procedures for the hearing of disciplinary charges against prisoners.

16. INTERNMENT AND DETENTION WITHOUT TRIAL IN THE LIGHT OF THE EUROPEAN CONVENTION ON HUMAN RIGHTS

E. T. McGOVERN

I—Introduction

THE subject of emergency powers in general and internment in particular has been largely neglected by academic writers in the United Kingdom. This essay seeks to compensate for this neglect by examining the law and practice relating to internment in the United Kingdom and the Irish Republic in the light of the standards imposed on both of those countries by the European Convention on Human Rights.

There are considerable advantages in adopting this approach. In the first place the Convention provides a measure of objectivity in a subject which all too easily suffers from emotion. Secondly, this objectivity incorporates ideas and concepts of justice worked out with considerable thought by persons with the benefit of practical experience. Thirdly, although some of the standards of this Convention are very broadly worded the problems which emerge in its application are in many cases ones to which the techniques of legal analysis can usefully be applied.

II—Internment in the United Kingdom and Irish Republic

By the word "internment" is meant detention without trial of persons believed to be a danger to the State, but the terminology is not of great significance. The present legislation in both Northern Ireland and the Irish Republic merely speaks of "detention," the same idea is referred to elsewhere as "preventive detention" or "administrative detention."[1]

For practical purposes, and those of this essay, such powers of detention are in the British Isles to be found in legislation. This is not to deny the existence of a prerogative power to detain enemy aliens but the negligible relevance of this power at the present day is unlikely to increase. In the Irish Republic the relevant legislation is the Offences against the State (Amendment) Act 1940; in Northern Ireland until November 7, 1972 internment was practised under regulations 11 and 12 of the Civil Authorities (Special Powers) Act (N.I.) 1922 as amended (henceforward referred to as the Special Powers Act); on that date a more sophisticated system was introduced under the Detention of Terrorists (Northern Ireland) Order 1972[2] itself made under powers granted to Her Majesty in Council by section 1(3) of the Northern Ireland (Temporary Provisions) Act 1972. In Great Britain powers of internment disappeared at the end of the war with the demise of the constitutionally famous Regulation 18B, equivalents for which existed in the Irish Republic under the Emergency Powers Act 1939 and the Emergency Powers (Amendment) Act 1940.

For reasons of space it is not possible here to include the appropriate provisions nor to examine on their own merits the judicial decisions to which they gave rise, although some of these decisions will be relevant to the investigation of the application of the European Convention.

III—*The European Convention*

The United Kingdom and the Irish Republic have been parties to the Convention since 1953, the year of its inception. The United Kingdom however did not allow a right of petition by individuals, nor submit to the jurisdiction of the European Court of Human Rights (under Articles 25 and 43 respectively) until 1966 (a delay which hardly accorded with the traditional common law concern for the procedural aspects of the protection of human rights).

The Court has decided only one case concerning internment, that of *Lawless* v. *Republic of Ireland*.[3] The European Commission of Human Rights, which technically acts in a judicial capacity only on issues of admissibility, but which behaves in a judicial manner in drawing up all its reports, has considered internment on three occasions: (1) the petition brought by Greece against the United Kingdom in 1956 concerning emergency legislation in Cyprus, (2) The *Lawless* case,[4] and (3) the case of *Denmark, Norway, Sweden and the Netherlands* v. *Greece*[5] commenced in 1967. Unfortunately the report on the first of these cases has never been published,[6] and in the third the Commission found it unnecessary to consider the matter in any detail having come to the conclusion that there was no emergency under Article 15. Consequently the *Lawless* case remains virtually the sole source of authoritative opinion on the legality of internment under the Convention.[7]

IV—*Article 5*

Article 5 provides a logical starting point for an analysis of internment because if its requirements are satisfied there is no need to consider the possibility of derogation under Article 15, and, it can be argued, no need to discuss the attributes of a fair trial laid down in Article 6. The relevant provisions are as follows:

> "(1) Everyone has the right to liberty and security of person. No one shall be deprived of his liberty save in the following cases and in accordance with a procedure prescribed by law: . . .
> (c) the lawful arrest or detention of a person effected for the purpose of bringing him before the competent legal authority on reasonable suspicion of having committed an offence or when it is reasonably

considered necessary to prevent his committing an offence or fleeing after having done so, . . .

"(3) Everyone arrested or detained in accordance with the provisions of paragraph (1)(c) of this article shall be brought promptly before a judge or other officer authorised by law to exercise judicial power and shall be entitled to trial within a reasonable time or to release pending-trial. Release may be conditioned by guarantees to appear for trial."

The Irish Government in the *Lawless* case sought to justify internment under Article 5(1)(c) as effected ". . . when it is reasonably considered necessary to prevent [the internee] committing an offence . . .", they were faced, however, with the problem of explaining the requirement of Article 5(3) that persons so arrested should be brought promptly before a judge, and tried within a reasonable time. The explanation they adopted [8] involved citing the *travaux préparatoires* to show that the Parties to the Treaty did not intend that this requirement should apply to arrests of a preventive type. It is doubtful whether the document cited is capable of bearing this interpretation, but in any case the attitude of the Court was to reject reference to the *travaux préparatoires* as unnecessary since the meaning of the Article was already clear. In fact it has been demonstrated [9] that the steps leading up to the Treaty tend to support the Court's interpretation. For example an early draft of Article 5(3) read "*Toute personne arrêtée ou détenue* sur l'accusation d'une infraction *dans les conditions prévues au paragraphe 1(c) doit être immédiatement traduite* . . .,*" there is, apparently, no recorded explanation of the later deletion of the words emphasised. The question can well be asked what relevance does the latter part of Article 5 (1)(c) have to a trial, for how can a person be tried when he is not suspected of committing any offence? The Court's answer was to say that the judge would examine the question of deprivation of liberty or decide on the merits [10] (the authentic French version is no more illuminating, speaking of "*l'examen du problème de la privation de liberté*" and "*jugement sur le fond*") a view which contemplates a procedure of preventive detention unknown to the common law.

It is worth noting here some points of English law. First, a constable has the power under section 2(5) of the Criminal Law Act 1967 to arrest a person whom he reasonably suspects to be about to commit an arrestable offence. Now, this cannot simply mean a person doing something which constitutes an attempt, as defined in English law, because such an attempt would itself fall within the definition of arrestable offence for which summary power of arrest would already exist under section 2(2) thereby leaving section 2(5) redundant. Presuming therefore that section 2(5) includes a power to arrest persons who have not committed any offence, inchoate or otherwise, paragraphs (1)(c) and (3) of Article 5 of the Convention appear to require the authorities in such cases to justify the arrest before a court. The same obligation also arises when for some reason a person arrested for an offence is not prosecuted. In English law it lies upon the person arrested to raise the question of legality by, normally, an action for false imprisonment. There is no procedure which, by throwing the onus on the authorities, appears to satisfy the requirements of the Convention as interpreted by the Court.

Secondly, under the Justices of the Peace Act 1361 magistrates have a power to "take of all of them that be not of good fame, where they shall be found, sufficient surety and mainprize of their good behaviour towards the King and his people. . . ." This is quite clearly a preventive power[11] exercisable when it is apparent that "there might be a breach of the peace in the future."[12] A person who refuses to be bound over may be imprisoned and such refusals have been common in cases involving political protest from the time of the Boer War to the present day.

Thirdly, the phrase preventive detention was used to describe the sentence which since the Criminal Justice Act 1967 has been more prosaically known as an extended term of imprisonment. Under section 37 of the Act certain recidivists may be sentenced to long terms of imprisonment if, *inter alia*, there is a likelihood of their committing further offences and the public will thereby be protected. From the point of view of Article 5 however, the most important limitation to note is that such sentences may only be imposed following conviction, and it would appear[13] that in the Commission's opinion this is clearly within the Convention.

Whatever the position of these aspects of English law under the Convention, the Court[14] and the Commission[15] were both of the opinion that the internment procedure applied to Lawless was in breach of Article 5.

V—Article 6

This Article, which specifies the requirements of a fair trial, received little attention in the *Lawless* case. The Commission seems to have regarded it as completely dependant on Article 5(3) and therefore irrelevant because the Irish Government was purporting to derogate entirely from its obligations under that provision. The Court, after pointing out,[16] with perhaps a hint of criticism, the Commission's failure to express a view on Article 6, reached[17] the same conclusion on the grounds that no criminal charge had been laid against Lawless. The adequacy of these approaches will be discussed in the context of Article 15.

VI—Article 15

The Articles establishing substantive rights in the Convention may be divided into three categories, those from which no derogation is permitted, those which themselves contain some provision for derogation, and those from which derogation is permitted under Article 15. The rights incorporated into Articles 5 and 6 fall within the final category and consequently the interpretation of Article 15 has been an issue on all the occasions on which the Commission and the Court have been concerned with internment. There are those who, seeing rights as absolute, are not prepared to admit any deviation no matter what circumstances may arise. The Convention expresses a more pragmatic view by recognising that some derogation may be justified in an extreme situation to prevent a greater evil. The danger of this relativist approach, like any other, is that standards will be gradually whittled away by States perhaps quite genuinely intending to deal with threats to their very existence. It is a danger which has certainly been recognised by the Commission and the Court; whether it has been adequately catered for may to some extent be judged from their handling of the issue of internment.

The Convention itself lays down the limitations, direct and indirect, on the right of derogation. Thus under Article 15(3) the Secretary-General must be notified of the details of derogation. This serves as an indirect check on Governments by forcing them to publicise their activities in an area where they would usually prefer to remain silent.[18] Article 15 (3) has been the source of argument before the Commission and Court on questions such as the nature of the notification;[19] it is however proposed in this essay to concentrate on the limitations having a more direct effect.

It is in Article 15 (1) that such direct limitations are to be found, they relate to the existence of an emergency justifying derogation and the extent of derogation permissible.

The Court in the *Lawless* case[20] said "the natural and customary meaning of the words 'other public emergency threatening the life of the nation' is sufficiently clear . . . they refer to an exceptional situation of crisis or emergency which affects the whole population and constitutes a threat to the organised community of which the State is composed." The (authentic) French version speaks significantly of *"une situation de crise ou de danger exceptionnel et imminent."* Such a situation was, it said, reasonably deduced by the Irish Government

> "from a combination of several factors, namely: in the first place, the existence in the Republic of Ireland of a secret army engaged in unconstitutional activities and using violence to attain its purposes; secondly the fact that this army was also acting outside the territory of the State, thus seriously jeopardising the relations of the Republic of Ireland with the neighbour; thirdly, the steady and alarming increase in terrorist activities. . . ."

It is noteworthy that the Court unlike the majority of the Commission[21] did not use the concept of a State's "margin of appreciation" in determining the existence of an emergency.

It is possible to criticise the Court's interpretation of this part of Article 15 for introducing the concept of emergencies which are only imminent, and its application of this interpretation to the facts of the *Lawless* case is also doubtful.[22] The element of Article 15 most relevant to internment is not however the existence of an emergency (although of course this is necessary), but the limiting of any derogation "to the extent strictly required by the exigencies of the situation."

Once again the *Lawless* case constitutes the principal source of the views of the Commission and Court. There are, Fawcett suggests,[23] two questions to be asked if derogation from Article 5 is to be permitted to the extent of no longer requiring an arrested person to be brought before a court. Are the courts inadequate to contain the emergency and is the procedure which is substituted accompanied by satisfactory safeguards? The Irish Government when it introduced detention without trial had available to it a number of other alternatives to the ordinary courts. In the first place there were the Special Criminal Courts created under Part V of the Offences Against the State Act 1939. The special character of these courts is evident from the following provisions of the Act:

> s. 39 "(2) Each member of a Special Criminal Court shall be appointed, and be removable at will, by the Government.
> "(3) No person shall be appointed to be a member of a Special Court unless he is a judge of the High Court or the Circuit Court, or a justice of the District Court, or a barrister of not less than seven years standing, or a solicitor of not less than seven years standing, *or an officer of the defence forces not below the rank of commandant.*"
> s. 40 "(1) The determination of every question before a Special Criminal Court shall be according to the opinion of the majority of the members of such Special Criminal Court. . . ."

In other respects however these courts were no different from the ordinary criminal courts; the ordinary rules of evidence applied (s. 41(4)), appeal lay to the Court of Criminal Appeal (s. 44) and they had no special powers of punishment.[23a]

The power to create such courts existed (and continues to exist) under Article 38(3) of the Irish Constitution "where the ordinary courts are inadequate to secure the effective administration of justice and the preservation of public peace and order." For more extreme circumstances Article 38(4) permitted military tribunals to be established "to deal with a state of war or armed rebellion," and this provision together with Article 28(3)[24] was used to justify the setting up of military tribunals during the Second World War under the Emergency Powers Act 1939. In one prosecution for murder before such a tribunal the ordinary rules were set aside by Order in order to permit the conviction of three members of the IRA on evidence contained in written statements. One of those convicted was executed.

The European Court held[25] that not only were the ordinary courts inadequate to deal with the situation but that "even the special courts or military courts could not suffice to restore peace and order." The reasons given for this inadequacy were that "the amassing of the necessary evidence to convict persons involved in activities of the IRA and its splinter groups was meeting with great difficulties caused by the military, secret and terrorist character of those Groups and the fear they created among the population" and, the Court added, "the fact that these groups operated mainly in Northern Ireland, their activities in the Republic of Ireland being virtually limited to the preparation of armed raids across the border was an additional impediment to the gathering of sufficient evidence."

It would seem to follow from this assessment of the problem that any derogation under Article 15 would have had to contribute to one of the following objectives: (1) the collection of adequate evidence to secure convictions and (2) the prevention of criminal acts pending the achievement of these convictions. Whether the Court would have been prepared to accept so broad a statement of the situation does not emerge from the judgment, which proceeds rather hurriedly from the observation quoted above as to the inadequacy of special and military courts to the conclusion that administrative detention (subject to safeguards) was justified, pausing only to consider and reject the possibility of sealing the border. Nor are the opinions expressed by the Commission much more helpful in this respect. It is submitted that the question of effectiveness must be clearly distinguished from that of justification.[26] The Court's view seems to have been that only sealing the border or internment would have been effective, and that only the latter was justifiable. In the Commission Sir Humphrey Waldock[27] came to a more limited conclusion; he was doubtful as to the inadequacy of even the ordinary courts but was prepared to accept the Irish Republic's view as, in the circumstances, within their "margin of appreciation." As for Special Courts, he thought they "might have been effective," but, since he was prepared to accept the Irish Government's case, he presumably felt that the margin of appreciation justified its being unwilling to take the risk that they might prove insufficient. Because he regarded military courts as more objectionable than internment the question of their effectiveness did not arise. A majority of the Commission agreed with him in this but were more convinced about the inadequacy of Special Courts making the point that they did nothing to meet the principal problem facing the courts, that of protecting witnesses.[28] Thus while the Court was concerned with assessing the relative acceptability of internment and sealing the border, for the majority of the Commission the choice lay between internment and military courts.

Except for the question of safeguards, discussed below, remarkably little written consideration was given by either body to the decision that internment was preferable, or at least not less preferable, to the alternative. One might have expected from the Commission some explanation of why the derogations from Article 6 resulting from the use of military courts were worse than those from Article 5 consequent on internment. Furthermore, it is not clear that sealing the border would have involved derogation from any provision of the Convention[29] despite the view of the Court[30] that it "would have had extremely serious repercussions on the population as a whole, beyond the extent required by the exigencies of the emergency." The Irish Government had argued[31] before the Commission that even Special Courts were more objectionable to internment because they were so regarded by the Irish population; only Mr. Süsterhenn in a dissenting opinion took up the point[32] saying it was incorrect, and that the Government should have educated people to realise this. Here again the distinction needs to be made between the effectiveness and the justification of the measures adopted, the attitude of the population being best regarded as a factor in the former only.

It is interesting to note here the views of the Diplock Commission[33] on the similar choice open at the time of writing to the Government in Northern Ireland when faced with the problem of securing witnesses, between radically altering their judicial procedures or continuing to use internment. In order to preserve the reputation of the judiciary in a divided community such as Northern Ireland their Report advised that no ordinary court, or body consisting of judges who also sat in the regular courts, should derogate from the minimum standards of Article 6. Whether the European Court of Human Rights would necessarily agree that all the Diplock proposals were above this minimum is open to question.[34] The Report's silence on military tribunals implies a view that they would be more objectionable than internment.

VII—Safeguards

The existence of safeguards in the internment procedure was regarded as critical to its acceptability by both the Court and the Commission, but, surprisingly, the concept was developed without reference to any provision of the Convention other than that of Article 15 limiting derogation to that strictly required by the exigencies of the situation. In other words, why the measures of the Irish Government which were associated with internment actually constituted safeguards seems to be regarded as self evident. There are however a number of lessons to be learnt from examining these measures with a view to determining their distinctive characteristics.

The Court saw[35] three types of safeguard: the first provided by Parliament, the second by the Detention Commission and the third by the Government's promise to release persons who gave an undertaking.

The role of the Irish Parliament as a safeguard lay, according to the Court and the Commission, first in its power to annul by resolution of either House the Government's Proclamation bringing into operation Part II of the Offences Against the State (Amendment) Act 1940 which contained the internment power, and secondly in the Government's statutory obligation under the same Act to provide it with details of the exercise of this power. The control envisaged by these measures is not that of a judicial body determining the limits of legislative and executive powers according to the law, but that of a politically representative body supervising a Government with wide discretionary powers. Rather than attempt to find some residual aspects of the Convention remaining despite derogation under Article 15, a different kind of protection of human rights has been substituted albeit one which is presumed by the Convention and made explicit in its parent, the Statute of the Council of Europe. It is interesting to compare the specific provisions for parliamentary control to be found in the Irish statute with those of the Special Powers Act and the Northern Ireland (Temporary Provisions) Act 1972.[35a] Neither of the latter Acts makes provision for information to be given to Parliament (Northern Ireland and Westminster respectively) concerning the operation of internment, nor is the power of internment made subject to the constant control of each House of Parliament.[36] This is not to deny that adequate opportunity for control might not already exist in the ordinary rules of Parliamentary procedure.

The Detention Commission provided for in the Offences Against the

State (Amendment) Act 1940 consisted of an officer and two judges or experienced lawyers. The Court regarded it as a safeguard because the detainee had a right to insist that it considered whether there were any "reasonable grounds" for his detention and because if it found that there were no such grounds the Government were obliged to release him.[37] In the European Commission the power of the Detention Commission to order the production of documents was also emphasised.[38]

It is difficult to escape the conclusion that the elements in the Detention Commission procedure which caused the Court and the Commission[39] to regard it as a safeguard were the very ones which as elements of Article 6 they had held to be irrelevant. In other words the Detention Commission was being regarded as a substitute for a trial and the more closely it resembled a trial the more of a safeguard it would constitute. This being so it is of interest to examine in the light of Article 6 the formal aspect of the Detention Commission, and its equivalent in Northern Ireland. It is perhaps a consequence of the *Lawless* case that, whereas the Offences Against the State (Amendment) Act 1940 and the Special Powers Act devote only a few sentences to procedural matters, the details of the system introduced in the North in 1972 cover seven pages.

The requirements of Article 6 may be stated generally as follows: (1) *Independence and impartiality*. None of the members of the various review bodies are guaranteed security of tenure but against this should be set requirements of varying stringency that at least some of their members should be legally qualified and experienced. In the latter respect the system established under the Detention of Terrorists (N.I.) Order 1972[39a] is the most exacting and also the only one to provide an appeal system (from a "commissioner" to a Detention Appeal Tribunal). This system shares with that of the Republic two further characteristics tending to greater independence, first the power to obtain documents[40] and secondly the fact that their decisions are binding on the Government.

(2) *Publicity*. All the hearings are either explicitly or impliedly required to be in private.

(3) *Presumption of innocence*. Little or no guarantee is offered to the review bodies by the instruments creating them whether they should require proof on the balance of probabilities or beyond reasonable doubt. The Diplock Commission seems to presume the latter in respect of the present Northern Ireland procedures.[41]

(4) *Adequate information of the accusation to be given to person charged*. The inadequacy of the information given to persons appearing before the Advisory Committee set up under the Special Powers Act was the subject of a successful action in the Northern Ireland High Court in *Re Mackey*,[42] where Gibson J. held that the internee should be given a written summary of the information giving rise to suspicions against him but excluding all matters which in the opinion of the Minister would if disclosed by contrary to public safety. Whether this decision resulted in any substantial improvement remains doubtful in view of the concern of the security forces to protect their sources of information. The present procedure in the North

requires that the detainee "be served with a statement in writing as to the nature of the terrorist activities which are the subject of the inquiry" three days before the hearing.[43]

(5) *Access to legal assistance.* No mention is made of legal assistance in the Offences Against the State (Amendment) Act (although in fact Lawless was represented by counsel when his case was reviewed) or the Special Powers Act but in *Mackey's* case the applicant sought the right to representation before the Advisory Committee by solicitor and counsel. Gibson J. held that at common law the job of speaking before the Committee could be delegated to an agent, whose position was to be distinguished from that normally performed by a solicitor (but he did not explain how). It appears that in practice solicitors were allowed to act as agents. The present Order makes specific provision for representation "by counsel or a solicitor."[44]

(6) *Cross-examination of witnesses.* Since a principal objective of internment is to avoid exposing witnesses to the defendant or his representatives one hardly expects to see very much respect for this aspect of Article 6. Of the three procedures only that under the Detention of Terrorists (N.I.) Order makes any sort of explicit provision. It envisages that except "where it would be contrary to the interests of public security or might endanger the safety of any person" the detainee should be present[45] and may make representations to the Commissioner (or Appeal Tribunal). In practice it appears that detainees are invited to ask questions of witnesses called by the review body but that the only witnesses called are police officers.[46] Similarly, despite the lack of statutory provision, when Lawless appeared before the Irish "Detention Commission" his counsel was allowed to cross-examine a police witness. Inevitably, many questions the prisoner would like to ask will be barred, the implication being that the review body will ask them itself in his absence.

The resulting confusion of investigatory and adjudicatory functions is probably prejudicial to public confidence, and there is an argument for inserting another party into the proceedings in a role akin to that of counsel to the tribunal in investigations under the Tribunals of Inquiry (Evidence) Act 1921.

(7) *Adequate definition of the accusation.* The Detention of Terrorists Order requires the review body to satisfy itself, *inter alia*, that the detainee has actually done some act, *i.e.* that he "has been concerned in the commission or attempted commission of any act of terrorism or the direction organisation or training of persons for the purpose of terrorism."[47] Such a provision is analogous to the Convention requirement (found in Article 7 rather than Article 6) that criminal offences be closely defined. It is also in sharp contrast to the vague language of the Irish statute ("engaged in activities . . . prejudicial to the preservation of public peace and order or to the security of the State")[48] and the even vaguer language of the Special Powers Act ("suspected of acting or having acted or being about to act in a manner prejudicial to the peace and the maintenance of order").[49] Such phrasing is not unknown to the ordinary law of the land, for example section 68 of the Army Act 1955 provides "Any person subject to military

law who is guilty of any act, conduct or neglect to the prejudice of good order and military discipline that, on conviction by court martial, be liable to imprisonment . . ." but it is certainly exceptional. The greater definition of the present law in Northern Ireland is quite clearly what the European Court would regard as a safeguard.

The final safeguard associated with the procedure under which Lawless was detained (and the one by which he secured his freedom) was the promise by the Government to release anyone who gave an undertaking to observe the law and refrain from activities contrary to the 1940 Act.[50] The Court's view that in a democratic country such a guarantee "constituted a legal obligation on the Government"[51] is difficult to uphold, but if, more acceptably, the obligation is characterised as political[52] or effective rather than legal the value of the safeguard is hardly reduced. It is interesting to note in passing the curious insight into the *mores* of the IRA which is provided by the evident confidence of the Irish Government in the effectiveness of such a procedure. As Sir Humphrey Waldock pointed out[53] there seems to be scope here for the use of binding over powers (as under the Justices of the Peace Act 1361), the only problem being that of providing the initial low level of evidence as to the suspect's likely future behaviour. If the evidence of police witnesses were to be accepted as sufficient then the Government would be in a strong position for either the suspect would refuse to be bound over in which case he would receive a fixed-term prison sentence or he would agree and, apparently, respect the obligation involved. Curiously Sir Humphrey left the point open and the remaining members of the Commission and the Court did not give it any consideration.

To some extent the safeguards mentioned in the *Lawless* case can be placed into separate categories. Thus Parliament and the Detention Commission can be regarded as providing political and judicial control respectively. Another distinction can be made between those emergency measures which involve the substitution of some other and less effective procedure for that which the Convention requires in normal times, and those which are merely the residue which remains after more expendable rights have been abandoned in the exigencies of the situation. Looked at in this way the word safeguard might seem more appropriate if its use was restricted to the former as for example where Parliamentary control is substituted for that provided by the courts, leaving procedures of the Detention Commission type to be regarded as simple derogations from the various requirements of Article 6. The misleading impressions created by the word safeguard in this context are confirmed when the question of the undertakings is considered. Regarded as a safeguard it appears as a factor limiting the rigours of internment, but a more coherent picture is obtained if it is looked upon not as a limitation but as an alternative. If this approach is accepted then the procedure involving undertakings must be examined on its own merits, in the same way as Special and Military Courts were examined, to see in the first place whether it is effective and in the second whether it is less objectionable than internment. In practice no doubt the issue would tend to be more complicated because, for example, a person might only be considered for release by the procedure involving an under-taking after he had been processed by a review body, nevertheless this approach does seem to give a clearer picture of the issues than those adopted by either the Commission or the Court. In particular it would have focused more attention on the relationship between this procedure and that, presumably compatible with the Convention, of binding over a suspected person, with the former being seen as itself a derogation from the latter under Article 15. Moreover it cannot be doubted that obtaining such undertakings is considerably less objectionable than keeping people interned.

VIII—Conclusion

Examination of the opinions and judgments in the *Lawless* case has shown that the concept of derogation contained in Article 15 of the European Convention is one of considerable complexity. Fortunately it has only required elucidation on a relatively small number of occasions, but this should not be a ground for lack of interest. From the point of view of human rights those occasions have been ones of critical and often dramatic importance; just as the power of arbitrary imprisonment is the cornerstone of tyranny, so the limitations on this power form a large part of the foundations of democracy. If the mechanism of the Convention is to operate effectively in this crucial area, the concepts which are adopted must be the subject of continuing analysis.

NOTES

1. The Diplock Commission (Report of the Commission to consider legal procedures to deal with terrorist activities in Northern Ireland, Cmnd. 5185, 1972) distinguished "detention" following an extra judicial process from "internment" at the arbitrary Diktat of the Executive Government "which to many people is the common connotation of the term 'internment'."
2. S.I. 1972 No. 1632 (N.I. 15).
3. 4 *Yearbook of the European Convention on Human Rights* (hereafter cited as *Yearbook*), p. 430.
4. Publications of the European Court of Human Rights Series B, 1960–61, *Lawless Case* p. 223—henceforth referred to as *Lawless* case. For an account of the whole Lawless affair see O'Higgins [1962] Camb. L.J. 234.
5. Applications No. 3321–4/67, published in four volumes by the Commission, 1970; also 12 *Yearbook*, Vol. ii.
6. These reports have however been quoted in later cases, particularly the *Greek* case, *ibid.*
7. Internment is also an element in the applications filed by the Irish Republic and a number of individuals against the United Kingdom in respect of events in Northern Ireland which are at present (February 1973) being considered by the Commission.
8. *Lawless* case, p. 223.
9. Pelloux, R. "L'arrêt de la cour européene des droits de l'homme dans l'affaire Lawless," 1961 Annu. franc. Dr. int. 251.
10. 4 *Yearbook*, p. 464.
11. *Sheldon* v. *Bromfield Justices* [1964] 2 Q.B. 573.
12. *Per* Lord Parker C.J. in *R.* v. *Aubrey Fletcher, ex. p. Thompson* [1969] 1 W.L.R. 872 at p. 874.
13. Case 99/55, 1 *Yearbook*, p. 160.
14. 4 *Yearbook*, p. 466.
15. *Lawless* case, p. 66.
16. 4 *Yearbook*, p. 456.

17. *Ibid.*, p. 464.
18. Committee of Ministers Resolution (56) 16 requires the Secretary-General to circulate notifications.
19. *Lawless* case, p. 70.
20. 4 *Yearbook*, p. 472.
21. *Lawless* case, p. 82.
22. See Morrison, *The Developing European Law of Human Rights* (1967), pp. 167 *et seq.*
23. Fawcett, *The Application of the European Convention on Human Rights* (1969), p. 248.
23a. Special rules of evidence were made in 1972
24. "Nothing in this Constitution shall be invoked to invalidate any law . . . which is expressed to be for the purpose of securing public safety and the preservation of the State in time of war or armed rebellion."
25. 4 *Yearbook*, p. 476.
26. Some confusion between the two is evident in the otherwise illuminating analysis contained in *Emergency Powers: A Fresh Start* (Fabian Tract, 1972) where (p. 12) internment is said to be justifiable to prevent disruption if it is (a) the only means of achieving security, (b) likely to achieve this (c) not likely to have disproportionate secondary effects (d) accompanied by adequate safeguards and (e) provided with effective remedies. In (a) the word "only" should surely be replaced by "least objectionable."
27. *Lawless* case, pp. 114 *et seq.*
28. *Ibid.*, pp. 130 *et seq.*
29. The Fourth Protocol would now be relevant.
30. 4 *Yearbook*, p. 477.
31. *Lawless* case, p. 108.
32. *Ibid.*, p. 150.
33. *Op. cit.*, Chap. 4.
34. For example on the issue of the burden of proof in prosecutions for possession of weapons *ibid.*, pp. 25 *et seq.*
35. 4 *Yearbook*, p. 478.
35a. Now the Northern Ireland (Emergency Provisions) Act 1973.
36. Regulations under the Special Powers Act providing for internment "shall be laid before both Houses of Parliament as soon as may be after they are made, and if an address is presented to the Lord Lieutenant by either House within the next fourteen days . . . praying the regulation may be annulled, the Lord Lieutenant *may* annul that regulation" (s. 1(4)). Para. 4 of the Schedule to the Northern Ireland (Temporary Provisions) Act 1972 requires that regulations be approved by each House of the (Westminster) Parliament either in draft or within 40 days of laying.
37. No express indication is given by the Act as to what the Detention Commission should regard as reasonable grounds; presumably it adopts the same test as the Minister in making his original detention order: has the person engaged in activities prejudicial to the preservation of public peace and order or to security of the state?
38. *Lawless* case, p. 121.
39. See *e.g. Lawless* case, pp. 122, 133, 134.
39a. See note 1 above.
40. The former also contains a power to obtain the attendance of witnesses.
41. *Op. cit.*, pp. 14, 15.
42. *Re the application of John Mackey 1972*, Case 1971 No. 126.
43. Detention of Terrorists (N.I.) Order 1971, paras. 11 and 22 of Sched. See note 1.
44. *Ibid.*, Sched., paras. 13 and 23.
45. *Ibid.*, Sched., para. 15.
46. *The Times*, January 14, 1973; *The Sunday Times*, January 15, 1973.
47. Art. 5(1)(a). See note 1.
48. Offences Against the State (Amendment) Act, s. 4(1).
49. Reg. 12 (1).
50. This replaced an earlier, more stringent formula.
51. 4 *Yearbook*, p. 478.
52. As Sir Humphrey Waldock did in the Commission: *Lawless* case, p. 123.
53. *Ibid.*, p. 128.

17. SOME ASPECTS OF FUNDAMENTAL RIGHTS IN THE ENGLISH CONFLICT OF LAWS

P. A. STONE

I—Introduction

THE concept of fundamental rights necessarily implies that some rights are more important than others. A right is considered to be fundamental if its denial is likely to result in what is regarded as serious injustice. Thus the ascertainment of fundamental rights must be a matter of individual opinion and value judgment, ultimately based on emotion rather than intellect. Though value judgments should be made with caution and consciousness of fallibility, they are the necessary basis of any rational system of law; a legal system which excluded all value judgments would be a technical structure with internal logic, but no necessary relationship to any human need other than order.

In the area of conflict of laws, it is submitted that, broadly, justice requires that a person's rights should be determined by a court which is reasonably convenient in all the circumstances; that the court should, so far as is reasonably practicable, give him a fair opportunity of presenting his evidence and arguments, and should endeavour to decide his case, in good faith, in accordance with a substantive law which is just, not only from a general standpoint but also in its operation in the particular case. The existence of a foreign element in the fact situation necessitates the court's having regard to additional considerations to those relevant in purely domestic cases, but the object of the conflict of laws is nonetheless to do justice.[1] The existing English system seems, however, to be based largely[2] on Savigny's theory that each legal relation has its seat in a particular local law which should be applied regardless, except in extreme cases, of the effect on the result of the particular case. In extreme cases, the public policy and natural justice exceptions provide an accepted escape device, but they are often narrowly construed,[3] and judges[4] who have refused to apply rigidly the existing conflict rules and instead adopted a wide view of the policy-based exceptions in order to avoid serious injustice have been subject to unjustified criticism.[5]

Since it would be impracticable to discuss here the whole of the English conflict system to ascertain the extent to which its rules have caused serious injustice, attention will be confined to three matters: (1) the adequacy of the policy-based exceptions to the jurisdiction-selective rules which govern the recognition of foreign decrees affecting marital status,

(2) in connection therewith, the inability of the English courts (subject to exceptions) to award financial provision in favour of an ex-wife against her ex-husband after a recognised foreign decree has terminated the marital status, and (3) the extent to which choice of law should be determined by policy considerations. But first some general observations will be made.

As in the past, most countries are today governed by totalitarian régimes. Their laws and judicial decisions give little cause for confidence. Liberal democracies, such as England and the United States, are exceptional. The more rigid and mechanical the English rules as to choice of law and recognition of foreign judgments, the greater will be the likelihood that oppression will be imported from foreign tyrannies into England, of the engrafting on free countries of the paralysing restrictions of despotisms.[6] But even in free countries some domestic rules may cause injustice, either because of their nature and hence even in purely domestic cases, or when applied to conflict cases to the surprise of one or both of the parties; and judicial proceedings may produce unfair results in consequence of judicial error, fraud of a party, or a party's inability to defend himself effectively in a distant forum. No claim can be made for the perfection of English domestic law or procedure, but that is no reason to tolerate unnecessary extension of injustice across borders. An English domestic rule may be established by statute or precedent, so that in a domestic case the judge feels unable to avoid applying it, however unsatisfactory the result. But in a conflict case the English court should be able to avoid applying an unjust substantive rule, whether of English or foreign law, whenever some other connected law supplies a rule which produces a more satisfactory result.[7] Few statutes obstruct the judicial development of the English conflict system, and a bold court should be able to distinguish outmoded precedent whenever justice so requires.

II—Foreign Status Decrees

In matters of marital status, uniformity regardless of forum is rightly regarded as a major policy objective, particularly in view of the hardship which may occur when one party to a marriage is regarded as a single in the country to which he or she belongs, while the other is regarded as married in his or her country, and, partly for this reason, the jurisdictional connecting factors sufficient for the recognition in England of foreign divorces[8] and nullity decrees[9] have undergone considerable expansion in the last twenty years. This development is entirely welcome. But uniformity is not the only objective in status cases, and the power of the English courts to refuse, on grounds of public policy or natural justice, to recognise decrees granted by courts regarded as jurisdictionally competent, is well-established,[10] and in the case of divorce is now statutory.[11] In some cases the foreign decree involves injustice sufficiently grave to outweigh the undesirability of creating a "limping marriage" by refusing recognition. Conflicting judicial views have, however, been expressed as to the scope of the exceptions,[12] and greater willingness to invoke them has been shown in respect of nullity decrees than divorces.[13]

It is submitted that a wide and flexible view of the scope of the exceptions should be adopted: the English court should exercise its power in this matter "to do whatever the justice of a particular case may require, if that is at all possible."[14] Though the court which granted the decree is regarded as jurisdictionally competent, its decree should be refused recognition if there was any substantial injustice, according to English ideas, in the circumstances in which, the manner in which, or the grounds on which, it was obtained, unless the party to the marriage who was unjustly treated has unequivocally waived his right to oppose its recognition (as by remarrying in reliance on it). Even then, if the decree involving substantial injustice is a nullity decree, recognition should be prospective only, with the same effects as are now produced by an English decree annulling a voidable marriage,[15] so as to avoid any possibility of its causing the children to be treated as illegitimate[16] or the wife as having been a mere mistress,[17] regardless of the effects of the decree in the country of rendition. The fact that, as the law now stands, recognition of a foreign divorce or nullity decree will normally deprive the wife of her right to apply to the English courts for an order for financial provision for herself against her husband,[18] is an additional reason for refusing to recognise a decree involving substantial injustice obtained by the husband, but, as will be submitted, this restriction on the court's power to award financial provision should be abolished by statute even where the foreign decree is not vitiated by any injustice. The reason for refusing to recognise decrees which involve substantial injustice is one of principle: a person should not be compelled to submit to having his marital status in England affected by a foreign decree which involved substantial injustice according to English ideas of justice.

A wide view should be taken as to what amounts to substantial injustice. It may result from the petitioner's being compelled to petition by duress;[19] from the application of a substantive law unjust in its nature, or unjust in its application to the particular case having regard to the foreign elements;[20] from the application of a reasonable substantive law in bad faith;[21] from a party's fraud in deceiving the court as to facts relevant to its jurisdiction or to the merits;[22] from the failure to take proper steps, with the full co-operation of the petitioner acting in good faith, to inform the respondent of the proceedings in time to enable him to defend;[23] from refusal to hear the respondent's arguments or evidence;[24] or from the fact that the divorce took place by unilateral declaration of one spouse without sufficient safeguards for the other.[25] But the mere fact that notice did not reach the respondent in time to enable him to defend should not, of itself and without more, be regarded as rendering the proceedings substantially unjust[26] (this can happen in England under the Matrimonial Causes Rules 1968, r. 14), nor should the mere fact that the decree was granted on grounds which would not be sufficient under English domestic law.[27]

If the foreign decree is vitiated by substantial injustice, the party unjustly treated should be taken to have waived his right to complain of the injustice if he has remarried in reliance on the decree, and it should then be recognised[28] (though, in the case of a nullity decree, with prospective effect only[29]), unless after the decree and before the remarriage the parties to the first marriage had cohabited and children had resulted.[30] Similarly if the party unjustly treated petitions the English court for a declaration that the decree is recognised,[31] unless he petitions in the alternative for the grant of divorce (or other matrimonial relief on the basis of the continued subsistence of the marriage).[32] A petition of the latter kind merely indicates that the petitioner wishes to have his status in England clarified in any event.[33]

When the authorities are examined, it is submitted that most of the actual decisions can be reconciled with the principles here suggested. In respect of divorces obtained outside the British Isles,[34] these issues are now governed by the Recognition of Divorces and Legal Separations Act 1971, s. 8(2), which provides that such a divorce, if otherwise entitled to recognition,[35] may be denied recognition if and only if (a) it was obtained by one spouse (i) without such steps having been taken for giving notice of the proceedings to the other spouse as, having regard to the nature of the proceedings and all the circumstances, should reasonably have been taken, or (ii) without the other spouse having been given (for any reason other than lack of notice) such opportunity to take part in the proceedings as, having regard to their nature and all the circumstances, he should reasonably have been given, or (b) its recognition would manifestly be contrary to public policy. It is to be noted that the refusal of recognition is expressed to be discretionary, which should make it easier for the courts to have regard to approbation on the part of the party unjustly treated (*e.g.* by his remarrying),[36] that public policy is not defined (and so, presumably, previous decisions will continue to throw light upon its requirements), and that natural justice is defined more widely than it was construed in some of the previous decisions.

Section 8(2)(*a*)(i) of the 1971 Act clearly confirms the view[37] that recognition is not to be refused merely because the respondent did not receive notice in time to defend. It also preserves the decision in *Macalpine* v. *Macalpine*,[38] where recognition of a Wyoming divorce was refused because the proceedings did not come to the respondent's knowledge until after the decree as a result of the petitioner's fraudulent evidence to the Wyoming court that he did not know her address. But it is submitted that the Nevada divorce recognised in *Wood* v. *Wood*[39] should now be refused recognition: the husband, having deserted the wife in England, went to Nevada, acquired a domicile there, and obtained the divorce there; the wife knew nothing of the proceedings until after the decree, as the husband intended, "service" being effected by advertisement in a Las Vegas newspaper in assumed[40] compliance with Nevada law. Since it seems that there would have been no difficulty in giving the wife effective notice by post, reasonable steps to notify her were not taken, and, as she did not remarry in reliance on the decree or otherwise approbate it,[41] the discretion should now be exercised by refusing recognition, notwithstanding that the husband had remarried.

As has been seen, public policy is not defined in the 1971 Act. It is well-established that recognition of a divorce is not contrary to public policy merely because the grounds on which the decree was granted are not sufficient grounds for divorce under English domestic law,[42] but it does not follow that any ground whatever would be immune from objections of public policy. It is submitted that, for example, a decree granted on overtly racial or religious grounds should be refused recognition,[43] subject to approbation by the respondent. Recognition has been accorded to divorces obtained by the husband's unilateral declaration (*talaq*),[44] even without the wife's consent,[45] and though there has usually[46] been some kind of official intervention, it is submitted that such decisions should be reconsidered and recognition denied where the wife has throughout maintained opposition to the divorce.[47] It is generally thought that fraud on the merits (as opposed to the jurisdiction) is no ground for withholding recognition of a divorce,[48] though it is difficult to suppose that it was the fraud on the jurisdiction alone which moved Cairns J. to refuse to recognise the Illinois divorce obtained by the husband in *Middleton* v. *Middleton*,[49] where the husband had fraudulently misled the Illinois court into the belief both that he had resided there for more than a year and that the wife had deserted him; and, in principle, material fraud, whether as to jurisdiction or to merits, could properly be regarded as rendering recognition contrary to public policy in the absence of approbation. It is undoubtedly contrary to public policy (in the absence of approbation) to recognise a divorce which the petitioner was compelled to obtain by duress;[50] indeed, if the duress did not emanate from the respondent, approbation would have to be by both spouses.

The recognition of foreign nullity decrees remains subject to the common law. The public policy exception was rightly invoked in *Gray* v. *Formosa*[51] and *Lepre* v. *Lepre*[52] to deny recognition to Maltese decrees annulling marriages celebrated at English register offices in accordance with English law between women domiciled in England and men of Maltese origin and Roman Catholic faith, domiciled at the time of the marriage in England (in *Gray* v. *Formosa*) or Malta (in *Lepre* v. *Lepre*); in each case the husband, having returned to Malta and deserted the wife, and being then domiciled in Malta, obtained the nullity decree from the Maltese court on the ground that under Maltese law he could not validly marry except in Roman Catholic form. The Maltese law on which the decrees were based, if not wholly unreasonable in respect of marriages celebrated in Malta, was monstrously oppressive when applied to marriages celebrated in England, *a fortiori* when at least one of the parties was domiciled here. Similarly, the refusal in *Ogden* v. *Ogden*[53] to recognise a French nullity decree obtained by the husband's father on the ground that under French law the husband, who was a French national and domiciliary aged nineteen, could not validly marry without the father's consent, although the marriage was celebrated in England where the wife was domiciled, would have been entirely justifiable if the wife had not remarried in reliance on the decree. The recognition, in *Corbett* v. *Corbett*,[54] of a decree annulling a marriage on the ground that a Jewess lacked capacity to marry a Christian, is defensible only because the contrary decision would have invalidated the wife respondent's remarriage.

It must be admitted, however, that in *Re Meyer*[55] Bagnall J. adopted a much narrower view of the public policy exception. He refused to recognise a German divorce obtained in 1939 by a non-Jewish wife against her Jewish husband because she had been compelled to petition for the divorce by duress resulting from the Nazi persecution of the Jews, her will having been overborne by genuine and reasonably held fears caused by serious and continuously existing dangers to her life, health and liberty, for which she was not responsible, and the couple had later cohabited (as far as the husband's health permitted) in England after the War. But he also held *obiter* that the fact that the stated grounds for divorce (the husband's desertion, refusal to have intercourse, and failure to maintain the wife and child), on which the decree was ostensibly granted, were untrue and a sham, and the real reason for the grant of the decree was that the husband, but not the wife, was Jewish, was not a ground on which recognition could be refused, for the English court could not consider the truth or falsity of the evidence of matrimonial offences on which a foreign decree was pronounced, nor substitute its own view as to the merits of the case for that of the foreign court, nor disregard the express grounds on which the foreign decree was based and decide that it was in reality based on some other ground. He adopted the view of Simon P. in *Szechter* v. *Szechter*[56] that the court, faced with a situation of hardship brought about by heroism in the teeth of cruelty and oppression, should resist the temptation to stretch the law, for it was no service to those who live under the rule of law to introduce uncertainty and capriciousness, even with the aim of meeting a hard case; if there was a substantial area of hardship which the existing law did not reach, the remedy lay in the hands of Parliament, and if even the most sagaciously framed general rule was still liable to throw up, exceptionally, some cases of hardship, Parliament could, if it thought desirable, establish a court of equity to deal with such cases on their merits; but a court of law could not deal out "palm-tree" justice. But Simon P. was in fact able to annul a marriage entered into solely in order to escape the gravest oppression by making somewhat dubious findings as to Polish law, which he held not to be different, in the relevant respect, from English law.[57]

It is submitted that, in respect of recognition of foreign decrees affecting marital status, there is sufficient authority[58] to justify the English court operating as a court of equity. Capriciousness must be avoided, but the courts can be trusted to understand what is substantially unjust according to English ideas of justice, and to apply the test with reasonable consistency.[59] The doctrine of waiver or approbation by the party unjustly treated has not always been clearly recognised,[60] but it is supported by sufficient authority,[61] and should assist in clarifying the law.

III—*Financial Provision after Foreign Divorce*

Oppression of wives seems to have been, at times, almost a deliberate policy of the English conflict system. "The last barbarous relic of a wife's servitude,"[62] the rule that during the marriage she invariably takes her domicile from her husband's,[63] though somewhat ameliorated in its effects by statutes[64] and decisions[65] permitting the use of other connecting factors for some purposes, remains a fertile source of injustice,[66] particularly in respect of the essential validity of wills of moveables[67] and of English adoption jurisdiction.[68] There is, however, reason to hope that this relic will soon be swept away by the Domicile and Matrimonial Proceedings Bill, now before Parliament.[69] Other conflict rules virtually aimed at causing hardship to wives will, however, remain: one of the most serious is the rule that after a recognised foreign divorce the English courts normally have no power to order the ex-husband to make financial provision[70] for the ex-wife.

This rule is a result of the limited scope of the English statutes empowering the courts to award financial provision in favour of one party to a marriage against the other. The powers under the Matrimonial Proceedings and Property Act 1970, ss. 2 and 4 are exercisable only when the English court itself grants a decree of divorce, judicial separation or nullity, and application can only be made under section 6 of the 1970 Act (on the ground of wilful neglect to maintain), or under the Matrimonial Proceedings (Magistrates' Courts) Act 1960, s. 1, while the marriage is subsisting.[71] If, before a recognised foreign divorce, the wife has obtained a maintenance order[72] from an English magistrates' court under the 1960 Act, the order does not cease automatically upon the divorce, but remains in force and can be varied by the magistrates under section 8 despite the divorce; and in a proper case it will be varied, after the divorce, by increasing the amount of maintenance payable.[73] Similarly, where, before the recognised foreign divorce, she has obtained an order from the High Court or a county court under section 6 of the 1970 Act, it remains in force and can be varied under section 9, including by increasing the amount of periodical payments, after the divorce.[74] Where, before the recognised foreign divorce, she has obtained an English decree of judicial separation, any order for financial provision made under sections 2 and 4 of the 1970 Act, the power to make such an order, and to vary such an order under section 9, continue to subsist despite the divorce.[75] And the court's power to vary a maintenance agreement under s. 14 of the 1970 Act subsists despite a recognised foreign divorce, provided that the agreement itself subsists. Despite these exceptions, the position remains that, in general, the English courts have no power to make an order for the first time after a recognised foreign divorce (or nullity decree) requiring the ex-husband to make financial provision for the ex-wife.[76] An ex-husband is similarly prejudiced where the court would otherwise have ordered the ex-wife to make financial provision for him.

The position of the children is rather more satisfactory. Under the Guardianship of Minors Act 1971, s. 9(2), a mother of a legitimate (or legitimated) child can obtain an order against the father for periodical payments for the child's maintenance, regardless of whether the parents' marriage has been dissolved.[77] If after a foreign divorce, the mother petitions the English court for a decree of divorce (or nullity or judicial separation), perhaps alternatively petitioning for a declaration that the foreign decree is recognised, and the court dismisses the divorce petition after the suit has been called on for trial because it recognises the foreign decree, then, at any rate if the petition was brought in good faith, the court may nonetheless make orders for periodical or lump-sum payments for the benefit of the children under section 3 of the Matrimonial Proceedings and Property Act 1970;[78] it seems also that such orders made before the dismissal of the petition remain in force despite its dismissal; that, once such an order is made in respect of a child after the dismissal of the petition, further such orders may be made in respect of him from time to time; and that such an order for periodical payments for the benefit of a child (whether made before or after the dismissal of the petition) may be varied after its dismissal.[79] And, where after the divorce, the mother applies to the magistrates under section 1 of the Matrimonial Proceedings (Magistrates' Courts) Act 1960, but, on hearing the complaint, they find that the divorce must be recognised, *semble*, they may, and must consider whether they should, make an order for periodical payments for the maintenance of the children.[80] But orders for the transfer of property, the making, and the variation, of settlements, for the benefit of the children, can only be made when the English court itself grants a decree of divorce, nullity or judicial separation, or there is a subsisting maintenance agreement.[81]

Thus, after a recognised foreign divorce, the ex-wife cannot obtain an order from the English courts requiring her ex-husband to make financial provision for herself, except where prior to the divorce she has obtained a matrimonial order from an English magistrates' court under the 1960 Act,[82] she has obtained an order from the High Court or a county court under section 6 of the 1970 Act, or she or her husband has obtained an English decree of judicial separation, or where there is a subsisting maintenance agreement; even then, in the first two of the four exceptions the only financial provision she can obtain for herself is by way of periodical payments. Despite the divorce, she can always[83] obtain an order requiring her ex-husband to make periodical payments for the maintenance of the children, and sometimes also lump-sum payments for their benefit. But the only cases in which she can obtain an order requiring him to transfer the matrimonial home in England to her or settle it on the children are where before the foreign divorce there was an English decree of judicial separation or where there is a subsisting maintenance agreement. These limitations should be removed.

A wife who has lived all her life in England may be deserted by her husband, who may obtain a divorce in the country where he is domiciled, habitually resident or a national. The divorce will often not be open to attack on grounds of public policy or natural justice: in view of the Divorce Reform Act 1969, s. 2(1)(*e*), a divorce granted on the ground of a year's separation, regardless of fault or consent, could not be regarded as substantially unjust according to English ideas, and the wife may have received actual notification of the proceedings by post. She may actually wish to be divorced. But she may not appear in the foreign suit, even to claim maintenance, because it is brought in a distant and inconvenient forum, because she has no immediate need of maintenance, or because the foreign law is so unfavourable that it is not worthwhile for her to pursue her claim there.

Even when there is no good reason why she did not appear in the foreign suit to pursue her claim for financial provision, or when she did so unsuccessfully, justice surely requires that a wife or ex-wife should be permitted to pursue her claim for financial provision from her husband or ex-husband in the country to which she belongs. If she has already obtained an English maintenance order before the foreign divorce, the order subsists and the court can increase the amount of maintenance after the divorce.[84] Why should she be prejudiced because her husband obtains the foreign divorce before she applies to the English court for maintenance? In the United States, the Supreme Court[85] has upheld the constitutionality of a New York statute empowering the New York courts to award maintenance for the first time to an ex-wife against her ex-husband after he had obtained a divorce in Nevada which New York was obliged to recognise under the "full faith and credit" clause of the United States Constitution,[86] the wife not having been served with process in Nevada nor appeared in the divorce suit.

It is submitted that what is needed is a short statute[87] providing that, where either party to a marriage is domiciled in England or has been habitually resident in England for a year, either party may petition the English court for a declaration that the marriage has been validly dissolved or annulled by a foreign decree[88] obtained by either party, and that on making such a declaration one court may exercise all the powers to order either party to the marriage to make financial provision for the other party and the children which it could have exercised if it had itself granted a divorce or nullity decree.[89]

The jurisdictional test of either party's domicile or one-year habitual residence is that proposed for English divorce and nullity jurisdiction by the Law Commission[90] and by Mr. MacArthur's Domicile and Matrimonial Proceedings Bill 1973.[91] It seems equally appropriate for the purpose of declarations that a foreign decree is recognised and relief ancillary thereto. It may be noted that the EEC Convention on Jurisdiction and the Enforcement of Civil and Commercial Judgments, 1968, now in force in the original Member States, confers jurisdiction over claims for maintenance if the defendant is domiciled, or the claimant is domiciled or usually resident, in the forum.[92]

Even under existing English law, after a valid divorce or annulment the former wife is independent as to domicile.[93] The petitioner's domicile or one-year habitual residence is well adapted to the primary purpose of the proposed jurisdiction in respect of declarations and ancillary relief. An ex-wife[94] who is domiciled in England or has habitually resided here for a year is appropriately connected with England to deserve the protection of the English courts in respect of the financial provision to be made for her (and the children) by her former husband. English law has a substantial interest in protecting such a petitioner. Where it is the respondent former husband who is domiciled here or has habitually resided here for a year, the exercise of such jurisdiction is justified by the considerations that an Englishman should not be able to escape making financial provision for his foreign ex-wife (and *a fortiori* the children) which the English courts would have compelled him to make for an English wife (and the children), that it would be undesirable for one of the former spouses, but not the other, to be able to invoke the jurisdiction, and that England is likely to be the place where any order against such a respondent can most readily be enforced.

The jurisdiction should be available at the suit of the party who obtained the foreign decree, as well as of the party who was respondent abroad. A foreign wife who, having obtained a divorce from her English husband in the courts of her own country, then petitions the English court for a declaration as to its validity and for ancillary financial provision, probably does so because of the difficulties of enforcing a foreign maintenance order in England[95] or because English law is more favourable to her financial claims than the law of her country. Against an English ex-husband the latter reason is entirely unobjectionable. There seems little reason why the English wife of a foreign husband should obtain a divorce in his country and then petition the English court for a declaration of its validity and ancillary financial relief, but, if she did so, there is no reason why the English court should not grant her financial relief in such a case. There may be cases, however, where a couple are divorced in a country to which both belong at a time when neither has any connection with England, but one of them later becomes domiciled or resident here and the ex-wife then seeks a declaration and financial provision. In such a case, in the absence of strong reasons to the contrary, the English court would properly exercise its powers by refusing to award greater financial provision for her (as opposed to the children) than she would be entitled to in the country to which both had belonged, on the ground that in the circumstances it would not be just, having regard to the parties' "conduct" (widely construed), to award her more,[96] the foreign law in effect operating as a datum.

The jurisdiction should be equally available after a foreign nullity decree as after a foreign divorce, for the same arguments apply in both cases.

It should be provided that, in exercising its proposed powers to grant ancillary relief after making declarations as to the validity in England of foreign divorces and nullity decrees, the court should apply English domestic law.[97] But, as against a party who had obtained the foreign decree, appeared in the foreign proceedings (otherwise than to contest the jurisdiction), or been habitually resident in the foreign country when the proceedings were commenced there, the court should be authorised to take into account, to such extent as may be just and equitable, any relevant findings made by the foreign court as to the conduct of the parties.[98] If a foreign order for financial provision had been, was being, or was likely to be, complied with or enforced, this would affect the relevant financial resources of the parties.[99]

IV—Policy and the Choice of Law Process

The current English choice of law system consists of a set of mechanical rules which purport to refer a category of issue (*e.g.* intestate succession to moveables) to the law of the country which has a given connection with the factual situation (*e.g.* the deceased's last domicile), regardless of the substantive content of the law referred to, except in extreme cases where the public policy exception operates to exclude the application of foreign law whose substantive content renders its application intolerably offensive to the conscience of the English court. The exception is designed only to obviate extreme injustice. It is necessary in almost any choice of law system,[1] for all the facts may be connected with a single country whose law, though gravely oppressive, could not be refused application on any other ground, but it is insufficient to enable the courts to reach the most satisfactory results in the majority of cases.

Its operation is well illustrated by the much criticised, but entirely sound, decision of the Court of Appeal in *Kaufman* v. *Gerson*,[2] where the court refused to enforce a contract which was valid by its proper law, French law, because the defendant had entered it under duress, in that the plaintiff had threatened to prosecute the defendant's husband for misappropriating the plaintiff's money unless she entered the contract to repay it herself. On the other hand, it is surprising that even in 1860 the English court was prepared to enforce a contract to sell slaves in Brazil,[3] though the decision seems to have turned as much on the construction of English statutes as on foreign law. Moreover, the willingness of the English courts to respect confiscatory legislation of the *situs* of property,[4] and exchange control legislation of the proper law of the contract,[5] merits reconsideration: better justice would be done by declining to recognise such foreign legislation except in favour of a purchaser without notice or when recognition is expressly required by English statute.[6] Abuse of the public policy exception has not been unknown: there is little to be said for the refusal[7] to enforce a Maltese judgment against the estate of the father of an illegitimate child for periodical payments for the child's maintenance on the ground that "the general recognition of the permanent rights of illegitimate children and their spinster mothers as recognised in Malta" was contrary to English public policy "especially having regard to the fact that the child's interest is not confined to minority." And the refusal to grant matrimonial relief as between the parties to a polygamous marriage[8] produced grievous injustice[9] until swept away by the Matrimonial Proceedings (Polygamous Marriages) Act 1972.

Apart from public policy, the existing choice of law rules can sometimes be manipulated to produce the desired result by suitable characterisation of the issue, ascertainment of the connecting factor, or use of *renvoi*. An employee's claim against his employer for damages for personal injuries caused by negligence can be regarded as contractual or tortious.[10] Transactions relating to land can be viewed as raising questions of property or of contract.[11] The procedure category can be widely construed.[12] Domicile can be ascribed to a suitable country by appropriate findings as to intention.[13] In the absence of express choice, the proper law of a contract can be inferred so as to reach the preferred result.[14] Thus the existing rules allow the court much flexibility to reach a just result, but give no guidance as to its exercise, and not surprisingly advantage has sometimes not been taken of this flexibility in cases where there was little difficulty in reaching a better result.[15] Sometimes, indeed, a mechanical rule has been adopted in order to enable the court to reach a just result in the instant case, although that rule would produce the opposite result in other cases.[16]

It is submitted that we would be better off without choice of law rules.[17] We should instead adopt an approach based on choice-influencing considerations which focus attention on the real policies involved in the choice of law process, drawn from the work of modern American academic writers[18] which has received substantial acceptance by the American courts[19] and has already received some judicial acceptance in England.[20] The choice-influencing considerations[21] may, it is submitted, be summarised as: (i) preference for the better substantive (or dispositive) rule; (ii) preference for the law of the country which has the greatest interest in the application of its substantive rule to the decision of the instant case; (iii) protection of the justified expectations of the parties; (iv) the basic policies underlying the particular field of law; (v) certainty, predictability and uniformity of results; and (vi) ease in the determination and application of the applicable law. The weight to be given to each factor will vary according to the kind of issue before the court, and the factors to some extent overlap, but it is submitted that the first, second and fourth will frequently have particular weight.

The substantive content of the connected laws should be of primary importance. A major consideration should be preference for the better substantive rule.[22] This has three aspects. First, it means the rule which is considered to be more just from a general standpoint: thus a rule whereby damages are apportioned in case of contributory negligence may be thought preferable to one whereby contributory negligence constitutes a complete defence; a rule permitting marriage despite affinity (*e.g.* marriage with deceased wife's sister) to one prohibiting such marriage; a rule enabling a married woman to contract to one which denies her capacity to do so. Secondly, it should include consideration of the effect of applying the conflicting rules in the instant case; thus, while a rule preventing a person under sixteen from marrying may be thought to be wiser, in general terms, than one enabling a seven-year-old to marry, yet, where a girl of fifteen has purported to marry and afterwards cohabited for years and borne children, but she or the man now petitions for nullity, better justice is achieved by application of the validating rule in the circumstances of the case, and it is not material that in a purely domestic case the English court would have to hold the marriage to be void. Thirdly, it should include considerations derived from the international character of the case—in particular, the undersirability of applying a law which would invalidate a transaction contrary to the expectations of the parties except for some strong reason, and, generally, the principle of equal justice, *e.g.* as preventing a defendant who has acted and caused injury in one country to a person resident there from escaping liability on the ground that he was a transient visitor domiciled elsewhere.[23] Preference for the better rule is not the only consideration, but its importance will often be very great, especially where more than one legal system has a significant interest in the application of its substantive rule. The better rule is not necessarily, or even probably, that of the *lex fori*, for the court has no duty to believe in the perfection of its own domestic law,[24] though a considered finding that the *lex fori* does indeed contain the better rule should not be dismissed as narrow-minded.

Another important consideration is preference for the law of the country which has the greatest interest in the application of its substantive rule to the decision of the particular issue in the instant case.[25] A substantive rule was presumably adopted in order to achieve some policy or purpose: if no such purpose can be discovered, that is a reason for not applying that rule, which would presumably also be the inferior rule. A legal system is to be regarded as interested in the application of its substantive rule in a particular case if the factual situation is so connected with its country that one or more of the purposes for the achievement of which its rule could reasonably have been adopted would be furthered by the application of that rule in the case. The forum should attempt, by examination of the foreign or domestic law as a whole, with the aid of its common sense, to infer what policies each connected legal system might reasonably have sought to further by adopting its substantive rule, and should attempt to ascertain whether and to what extent those policies would be furthered by the application of that rule in the instant case in view of the manner in which the factual situation is connected with that legal system. Attention should be paid to each law as a whole, to enable the function of the substantive rule to be inferred from the effect which it would be likely to have in its domestic context. Foreign judicial pronouncements as to the purpose of a rule, at the present stage of development, and legislative debates, are insufficiently likely to throw light on its function to justify their consideration. The forum should not speculate as to possible minor interests; only substantial interests are likely to be important.

Often only one legal system will have a substantial interest in the application of its rule in the case.[26] That rule should then be applied unless other considerations are very cogent. But frequently more than one law will have a significant interest, and then the conflicting interests should be weighed with reference to the strength of the policies, the strength of the connections with the factual situation, and the merits of the policies. Even so, no clear result may emerge, and then (as when no legal system has a significant interest) the decision will have to turn on other considerations. Preference for the law with the dominant interest is not, in any event, the only consideration: a disinterested law may properly be applied if other considerations warrant, *e.g.* to protect the parties' expectations and thereby further the basic policy underlying the particular field of law.

Whatever its difficulties, interest analysis can at least avoid some unnecessary unsatisfactory decisions. Thus a law which precludes a married woman from guaranteeing her husband's liabilities can have no substantial interest in its rules' application unless the woman is habitually resident or (in some reasonable sense) domiciled in its country, since the rule was presumably designed for the woman's protection.[27] A law which restricts damages for personal injuries by limiting the relevant heads of damage or imposing an arbitrary maximum on the amount recoverable would have little interest in its rules' application if the defendant were domiciled and resident elsewhere, for such rules are primarily designed to protect defendants from what is regarded as excessive liability, and only marginally to encourage persons to engage in risk-taking activities. Similarly a rule denying liability in case of contributory negligence is primarily designed to protect defendants from liability for claims considered to lack sufficient merit, and only marginally to induce plaintiffs to take care or to prevent the waste of the court's time; thus only if the defendant were a local domiciliary or resident would the country have a substantial interest in the application of such a rule.

Emphasis on interests is likely to lead to greater application of the personal laws of parties rather than the territorial law of the place where an event occurred. This will often be desirable, provided that the personal law is ascertained in a reasonable manner and not, *e.g.* under the existing English rules as to domicile.[28] Thus the *situs* of land, while strongly interested in invalidating unregistered transfers against purchasers in order to promote security of title, has little interest in preventing a foreign wife from disposing of it without her husband's consent or mortgaging it to secure his debts, or in compelling a foreigner to leave a share of the land to his foreign wife and children.

The considerations of protection of the reasonable expectations of the parties and furtherance of the basic policies underlying the particular field of law often lead to preference for a validating law in contracts,[29] marriages[30] and wills.[31] All laws permit contracts, marriages and wills, and in a case connected with several countries the general policy in favour of validity, and the probable expectations of the parties, argue strongly for application of a validating law in the absence of a strong and meritorious policy to the contrary of the law of dominant interest, unless the result would be intolerably offensive to the conscience of the forum.[32] In case of doubt, or arguable or dubious policy, the decision should be for validity.

The importance of the considerations of certainty, predictability and uniformity of results, though real, is easily exaggerated. They are most important where the transaction is planned (*e.g.* contracts, marriages and wills), but even here they may be outweighed. There is little to be said for the certain, predictable and uniform application of a gravely inferior rule, *e.g.* which invalidates a marriage on trivial grounds.[33] These considerations are most persuasive in conjunction with others, as when they support application of the law expected by the parties so as to validate a transaction in accordance with the basic policy underlying the area of the law, or when they support application of a law whose policy and interest is to promote security. This the *situs* of moveables could legitimately uphold the formal validity of a will as to such moveables by application of its own law against the invalidating rule of the testator's domicile, nationality and residence, despite the resulting severance of the devolution of the estate. Ease in the determination and application of the applicable law is seldom of major importance except to justify application of forum law to matters of procedure where application of foreign law would be unduly burdensome and not worthwhile,[34] or when it coincides with other considerations, such as the parties' expectations and predictability.

The operation of the choice influencing considerations can usefully be illustrated in relation to capacity to marry,[35] *i.e.* such questions as whether a person aged fifteen can validly marry or whether an uncle can validly marry his niece, it being assumed that a formally valid marriage ceremony has taken place and that recognition of the validity of the marriage would not so intolerably offend the conscience of the forum that public policy would require it to be treated as void even in a case wholly unconnected with the forum (as in the case of a marriage between brother and sister or parent and child). The considerations of the parties' expectations, the basic policy in favour of the validity of marriage, certainty, predictability and (it may be hoped) uniformity of results, lead to the conclusion that the marriage should be upheld if it is valid by any connected law (*e.g.* that of the place of the celebration or the antenuptial domicile of one of the parties), unless it is invalid under the law of the country which has the dominant interest in the issue, which would normally have to be, as a minimum, the antenuptial domicile of one party and the immediate postnuptial home of both. Even then, the forum of dominant interest should uphold the validity of the marriage unless satisfied that its rule embodied a sufficiently strong and meritorious policy to justify invalidation in the circumstances of the case despite the other considerations, and a forum elsewhere should not invalidate unless the forum of dominant interest would have done so and the forum elsewhere is itself satisfied that the rule does indeed embody a policy of sufficient strength and merit to justify that result in the circumstances. Where the parties have left the country of dominant interest and settled elsewhere before the litigation, the interest of that country will have greatly diminished and can scarcely ever justify invalidation. The circumstances in which annulment is sought, or the marriage is collaterally attacked, are highly material: if a person lacking sufficient age under the law of dominant interest petitions for nullity shortly after the celebration, the factors supporting validity are weaker, and the policy of the invalidating law need be less strong, than if the issue is raised after the parties have cohabited for years and children have been born.

The approach here proposed would have produced a better result in

Brook v. *Brook*,[36] where the House of Lords invalidated a marriage with deceased wife's sister by application of English law, which was the law of the forum, the domicile and nationality of both parties, and the intended matrimonial home, despite its validity under Danish law, the *lex loci celebrationis*. The English rule was the inferior rule, operated to basterdise the children, and hardly embodied a policy sufficiently strong to require its application to invalidate the marriage, even if it was celebrated in Denmark solely in order to evade English law. Similarly, in *Pugh* v. *Pugh*,[37] the English rule that a person under sixteen could not marry was not so clearly the better rule or the embodiment of so strong a policy as to justify the invalidation of a marriage celebrated in Austria between a domiciled Englishman and a girl aged fifteen domiciled in Hungary, although England was the intended matrimonial home, after the parties had cohabited for four years and had a child, when the marriage was valid by both Austrian and (in the circumstances) Hungarian law. In the light of the choice-influencing considerations, the decisions upholding the marriages in *Ogden* v. *Ogden*[38] and *Chetti* v. *Chetti*[39] were entirely justified, and that in *Radwan* v. *Radwan* (*No. 2*)[40] was plainly sound and would have been reached with less difficulty if the appropriate considerations had been brought to the attention of the court.

The choice of law process in England may be at or near the opening of a new stage of its development. The approach adopted by Lords Wilberforce and Hodson, and Lord Denning M.R., in *Chaplin* v. *Boys*[41] gives cause for hope that major advances are possible. The normal judicial techniques of distinguishing and, when the time is ripe, overruling earlier but outmoded precedents and of narrowly construing obstructive statutes, should enable the courts to adopt a more satisfactory approach once the direction of the advance is understood and accepted. Mechanical choice of law rules were originally a' great advance over invariable application of forum law or denial of jurisdiction over causes of action arising abroad, but the time for their demise has now arrived. Significant advances have been made in the United States, and the courts in England will not have to chart entirely unexplored seas. The fundamental search for the best justice in international cases, however, requires a creative approach and the acceptance of some uncertainty. Otherwise there will be needless injustice or disingenuous manipulation.

NOTES

1. As is asserted by both Cheshire, *Private International Law*, 8th ed., jointly with North (1970), at pp. 3–4 and Morris, *The Conflict of Laws*, 1971, at p. 6.
2. See, however, *Gray* v. *Formosa* [1963] P. 259, *Hornett* v. *Hornett* [1971] P. 255, *Middleton* v. *Middleton* [1967] P. 62 at pp. 69–70, 76, *Re Fuld* [1968] P. 675 at p. 698, *National Bank of Greece and Athens* v. *Metliss* [1958] A.C. 509 at p. 525, *Chaplin* v. *Boys* [1971] A.C. 356 at pp. 379–380, 391–393, 406.
3. *e.g. Re Meyer* [1971] P. 298 at pp. 307–310, *Qureshi* v. *Qureshi* [1972] Fam. 173 at p. 201.
4. *e.g.* C.A. consisting of Lord Denning M.R., Donovan and Pearson L.JJ. in *Gray* v. *Formosa* (*supra*).

5. *Gray* v. *Formosa* (*supra*) is criticised by Cheshire at pp. 151–152, 408–410 and Morris at pp. 171–172, 512–513, was followed "with some misgiving" by Simon P. in *Lepre* v. *Lepre* [1965] P. 52 at pp. 63–65, and was narrowly construed by Bagnall J. in *Re Meyer* (*supra*) at pp. 309–310.

6. A phrase used by Wharton, *A Treatise on the Conflict of Laws*, 3rd edn 1905, s. 104 in respect of penal incapacities, cited by Cheshire at p. 148.

7. See the approach of Lord Kenyon C.J. and Grose J. in *Inglis* v. *Usherwood* (1801) 1 East 515 at pp. 524–525, preferring the foreign rule, and of Lord Denning M.R. in *Boys* v. *Chaplin* [1968] 2 Q.B. 1 at p. 25, preferring the English rule. See also in the House of Lords, *sub nom. Chaplin* v. *Boys* [1971] A.C. 356, *per* Lord Hodson at pp. 378–380, Lord Wilberforce at pp. 391–393, and Lord Pearson at p. 406.

8. *Travers* v. *Holley* [1953] P. 246, *Robinson-Scott* v. *Robinson-Scott* [1958] P. 71, *Indyka* v. *Indyka* [1969] 1 A.C. 33, and now (replacing these decisions) the Recognition of Divorces and Legal Separations Act 1971, ss. 2–5.

9. *Corbett* v. *Corbett* [1957] 1 W.L.R. 486, *Abate* v. *Abate* [1961] P. 29, *Merker* v. *Merker* [1963] P. 283, *Lepre* v. *Lepre* (*supra*).

10. *e.g. Macalpine* v. *Macalpine* [1958] P. 35, *Gray* v. *Formosa* (*supra*), *Re Meyer* (*supra*).

11. Recognition of Divorces and Legal Separations Act 1971, s. 8(2). A divorce granted after 1971 by a court elsewhere in the British Isles (excluding Eire) cannot, however, be refused recognition on these grounds, see ss. 1 and 8.

12. Contrast the wide view of their scope expressed in *Gray* v. *Formosa* (*supra*), *Middleton* v. *Middleton* (*supra*), *Indyka* v. *Indyka* (*supra*) *per* Lords Morris, Pearce and Pearson at pp. 73–74, 88, 111 and *Hornett* v. *Hornett* (*supra*), with the narrow view in *Qureshi* v. *Qureshi* (*supra*), at p. 201 and *Re Meyer* (*supra*) at pp. 307–310.

13. Contrast *Gray* v. *Formosa* (*supra*) involving a nullity decree, with *Wood* v. *Wood* [1957] P. 254, *Qureshi* v. *Qureshi* (*supra*), and *Re Meyer* (*supra*), which involved divorces.

14. *Gray* v. *Formosa* at p. 271, *per* Donovan L.J.

15. Under the Nullity of Marriage Act 1971, s. 5.

16. It is arguable that children born of a marriage which is valid under English choice of law rules are legitimate in England under the rule in *Shaw* v. *Gould* (1868) L.R. 3 H.L. 55, notwithstanding that the marriage is later annulled by a (substantially just) foreign decree having retrospective effect in the country of rendition and recognised (for other purposes) as having such effect in England. While perhaps sound in principle, such a view seems inconsistent with *Salvesen* v. *Administrator of Austrian Property* [1927] A.C. 641 and dicta in *Gray* v. *Formosa*. *Pace* Morris at p. 171, the children in the latter case were not affected by the Legitimacy Act 1959, s. 2, since the marriage was not "a marriage, not being voidable only, in respect of which the High Court has or had jurisdiction to grant a decree of nullity, or would have had such jurisdiction if the parties were domiciled in England" (see s. 2(5)), for the marriage was not voidable nor void, but valid, under English choice of law rules.

17. Which could affect rights to property in England.

18. The rule, and the exceptions, are discussed below.

19. As in *Re Meyer* (*supra*).

20. As in *Gray* v. *Formosa* (*supra*); *Lepre* v. *Lepre* (*supra*); and *Ogden* v. *Ogden* [1908] P. 46.

21. As in *Re Meyer* (*supra*).

22. As in *Middleton* v. *Middleton* (*supra*).

23. As in *Macalpine* v. *Macalpine* (*supra*) and *Wood* v. *Wood* (*supra*).

24. *Cf. Mitford* v. *Mitford* [1923] P. 130.

25. As in *Qureshi* v. *Qureshi* (*supra*).

26. To this extent the approach in *Igra* v. *Igra* [1951] P. 404, *Wood* v. *Wood* (*supra*) and *Hornett* v. *Hornett* (*supra*) must be supported.

27. See *Harvey* v. *Farnie* (1882) 8 App. Cas. 43; *Bater* v. *Bater* [1906] P. 209; *Robinson-Scott* v. *Robinson-Scott* (*supra*); and *Indyka* v. *Indyka* (*supra*); as to nullity, *Merker* v. *Merker* [1963] P. 283.

28. As in *Igra* v. *Igra* (*supra*); a point disregarded in *Ogden* v. *Ogden* (*supra*).

29. See above.

30. *Cf. Hornett* v. *Hornett* (*supra*) at pp. 260–261.
31. As in *Munt* v. *Munt* [1970] 2 All E.R. 516 and *Hornett* v. *Hornett* (*supra*).
32. As in *Macalpine* v. *Macalpine* (*supra*), *Gray* v. *Formosa* (*supra*), and *Middleton* v. *Middleton* (*supra*).
33. Moreover, as the law stands, refusal of recognition and grant of an English decree will enable the court to grant ancillary financial relief.
34. *i.e.* England, Scotland, Northern Ireland, the Channel Islands and the Isle of Man: s. 10(2). A divorce granted by a court in Scotland etc. after 1971 cannot be attacked in England on grounds of public policy or natural justice: ss. 1 and 8. A divorce granted by a court in Scotland etc. before 1972, and non-judicial divorces taking place in the British Isles at any date, remain subject to the common law.
35. *i.e.* if a jurisdictional connecting factor sufficient under ss. 2–6 existed, and there was a subsisting marriage to be dissolved (see s. 8(1)).
36. *Cf. Wood* v. *Wood* (*supra*) at p. 296, where Hodson L.J. considered that if want of notice were a ground for refusing recognition, the defect could not be waived by the party who received no notice. It is difficult to see why not.
37. Established by *Igra* v. *Igra* (*supra*), *Wood* v. *Wood* (*supra*) and *Hornett* v. *Hornett* (*supra*).
38. [1958] P. 35.
39. [1957] P. 254. In fact, recognition of the divorce did not affect the outcome of the case.
40. *Per* Lord Evershed at p. 275. But it is thought that the divorce was void in Nevada (and throughout the United States) for denial of procedural due process as required by the U.S. Constitution Amendment XIV: see *Mullane* v. *Central Hanover Bank & Trust Co.*, 339 U.S. 306 (1950). For the same reason it is thought that the Wyoming decree in *Macalpine* v. *Macalpine* was void (and not, as Sachs J. found on the evidence, merely voidable) in Wyoming and elsewhere in the United States.
41. Unless her counsel's concession in the English maintenance proceedings that the divorce had to be recognised is to be considered as approbation. But it should not, since he was arguing that she was entitled to relief not because of, but notwithstanding, the recognition of the divorce.
42. See the authorities cited in note 27.
43. The point is left open in *Re Meyer* (*supra*) at p. 310.
44. *Russ* v. *Russ* [1964] P. 315 and *Qureshi* v. *Qureshi* (*supra*).
45. *Qureshi* v. *Qureshi* (*supra*).
46. Though not in *R.* v. *Hammersmith Superintendent Registrar of Marriages, ex p. Mir-Anwaruddin* [1917] 1 K.B. 634, where recognition was refused.
47. As in *Qureshi* v. *Qureshi* (*supra*). Non-recognition of non-judicial divorces obtained in the British Isles (excluding Eire) is proposed by Mr. MacArthur's Domicile and Matrimonial Proceedings Bill 1973, cl. 16.
48. In reliance on *Bater* v. *Bater* [1906] P. 209, *Crowe* v. *Crowe* [1937] 2 All E.R. 723, *Vardy* v. *Smith* (1932) 48 T.L.R. 661, affd. 49 T.L.R. 36, *Perin* v. *Perin*, 1950 S.L.T. 51, *Macalpine* v. *Macalpine* (*supra*) at p. 42 and *Middleton* v. *Middleton* (*supra*) at p. 69. *Cf. Indyka* v. *Indyka* (*supra*) at pp. 73, 88, 111, and, in respect of nullity decrees, *Salvesen* v. *Administrator of Austrian Property* [1927] A.C. 641 at pp. 652, 659, 663, 671–672, and *Syndica-Drummond* v. *Syndica-Drummond* [1966] C.L.Y. 1611, *The Times*, July 23, 1966.
49. [1967] P. 62. It may be that the divorce was void in Illinois (and throughout the United States) for want of due process, for, unless, as seems doubtful, the husband was domiciled, in the American sense, in Illinois, there was probably, in the circumstances, no constitutional basis for the assumption of jurisdiction: see *Williams* v. *North Carolina* (*No. 2*), 325 U.S. 226 (1945) and *Restatement* II, ss. 70 73.
50. *Re Meyer* (*supra*).
51. [1963] P. 259.
52. [1965] P. 52.
53. [1908] P. 46.
54. [1957] 1 W.L.R. 486.
55. [1971] P. 298.
56. [1971] P. 286 at p. 289.
57. Even if under Polish law the marriage was void for duress (as the evidence

indicated) it seems doubtful that the Polish courts would have been willing to give any assistance to the parties.

58. In respect of divorce, the Recognition of Divorces and Legal Separations Act 1971, s. 8(2), *Indyka* v. *Indyka* (*supra*) at pp. 73, 88, 111, *Middleton* v. *Middleton* (*supra*), *Hornett* v. *Hornett* (*supra*), and also *Russ* v. *Russ* [1964] P. 315 at pp. 327–328, 333–334, 335; and as to nullity, *Gray* v. *Formosa* (*supra*).
59. As in *Lepre* v. *Lepre* (*supra*).
60. *e.g. Wood* v. *Wood* (*supra*) at p. 296 (see note 36).
61. *Igra* v. *Igra* (*supra*) at p. 412; *Russ* v. *Russ* (*supra*) at pp. 325, 327, 332, 335; *Hornett* v. *Hornett* (*supra*) at pp. 260–261; *Re Meyer* (*supra*) at p. 313.
62. *Gray* v. *Formosa* (*supra*) at p. 267, *per* Lord Denning M.R.
63. *Lord Advocate* v. *Jaffrey* [1921] 1 A.C. 146; *Att.-Gen. for Alberta* v. *Cook* [1926] A.C. 444; *H.* v. *H.* [1928] P. 206; *Herd* v. *Herd* [1936] P. 205; *De Reneville* v. *De Reneville* [1948] P. 100.
64. Matrimonial Causes Act 1965, s. 40, Recognition of Divorces and Legal Separations Act 1971, Wills Act 1963.
65. *e.g. Ramsay-Fairfax* v. *Ramsay-Fairfax* [1956] P. 115.
66. *e.g. Garthwaite* v. *Garthwaite* [1964] P. 356, *Kern* v. *Kern* [1972] 3 All E.R. 207.
67. Governed by the law of the testator's domicile at death: *Re Annesley* [1926] Ch. 692.
68. Adoption Act 1958, s. 1(1). Even if the English court's jurisdiction is extended by the bringing into force of the Adoption Act 1968, ss. 1–3, apart from other limitations, the exclusion by s. 3(2) of cases where both the applicant and the child are United Kingdom nationals habitually resident in England will frequently prevent the extension from removing such hardship.
69. A Private Member's Bill introduced by Mr. Ian MacArthur, given a Second Reading by the House of Commons in February 1973, when it was welcomed by the Lord Advocate on behalf of the Government.
70. "Financial provision" is here used to mean such as may be ordered after an English divorce under the Matrimonial Proceedings and Property Act 1970, ss. 2 and 4, *i.e.* by way of unsecured periodical payments, secured periodical payments, lump-sum payments, the transfer of property, the making or variation of settlements.
71. *Wood* v. *Wood* [1957] P. 254 at p. 292. In *Turezat* v. *Turezat* [1970] P. 198, Lloyd-Jones J. held that he could not make an order under the predecessor of the 1970 Act, s. 6, although the marriage was subsisting when the application was made, because it had been dissolved by a recognised foreign divorce before the hearing of the application; *sed quaere.*
72. *Semble*, a matrimonial order under the 1960 Act which did not contain a provision for payments for the wife's maintenance (but only *e.g.* a non-cohabitation clause and an order for custody of the children) could be varied by adding such a provision after a foreign divorce: see s. 8(1).
73. *Wood* v. *Wood* (*supra*). Presumably the same applies where the Supplementary Benefits Commission have obtained an order for the maintenance of the wife under s. 23 of the Ministry of Social Security Act 1966.
74. *Wood* v. *Wood* (*supra*) at p. 295, criticising *Pastre* v. *Pastre* [1930] P. 80.
75. See ss. 13(2) and 14(1).
76. If the ex-wife were to petition the English court for a decree of divorce, nullity or judicial separation, or to apply under s. 6 of the 1970 Act, any interim maintenance order made under s. 1 or s. 6(5) would terminate when the petition or application was dismissed because the foreign divorce was recognised.
77. Or, indeed, even if it never existed (as when the child is legitimate under the Legitimacy Act 1959, s. 2). Similarly, the mother may obtain periodical maintenance for the child from the father under the Family Law Reform Act 1969, s. 6, by making the child a ward of court.
78. *P.* (*L.E.*) v. *P.* (*J.M.*) [1971] P. 318.
79. See ss. 3 and 9.
80. Matrimonial Proceedings (Magistrates' Courts) Act 1960, s. 4(1).
81. Matrimonial Proceedings and Property Act 1970, s. 4, 13 and 14.
82. Or her husband has obtained such an order on the ground that she is an habitual drunkard or a drug addict (1960 Act, ss. 2(2) and 8(1))! Or the Sup-

plementary Benefits Commission have obtained an order for the maintenance of the wife under the Ministry of Social Security Act 1966, s. 23.
83. Provided that the English court is otherwise jurisdictionally competent.
84. *Wood* v. *Wood* (*supra*).
85. In *Vanderbilt* v. *Vanderbilt,* 354 U.S. 416 (1957).
86. Art. IV(1).
87. Perhaps to be entitled the Matrimonial Proceedings (Declarations and Ancillary Relief) Act.
88. Including a non-judicial act effective as a divorce or annulment under foreign law.
89. *i.e.* the powers conferred by the Matrimonial Proceedings and Property Act 1970, ss. 2–4.
90. Report on Jurisdiction in Matrimonial Causes, Law Com. No. 48, 1972. They also recommend that the same test should apply to English jurisdiction in judicial separation and, with the addition of the respondent's residence, to applications under s. 6 of the Matrimonial Proceedings and Property Act 1970.
91. See note 69. The Bill gives effect to the Law Commission recommendations in respect of English jurisdiction in divorce, nullity, judicial separation, and (substituting "habitual residence" for "residence" of the respondent) applications under s. 6 of the 1970 Act.
92. Arts. 2 and 5(2). As to the law to be applied to determine a person's domicile for the purpose of the Convention, see Art. 52.
93. *Har-Shefi* v. *Har-Shefi* [1953] P. 161.
94. Or, where he is the petitioner, ex-husband. In the discussion it is assumed that it is the ex-wife who is seeking the declaration and ancillary relief, but the same arguments operate in the converse case.
95. Which admittedly will be reduced if the Maintenance Orders (Reciprocal Enforcement) Act 1972, Part I, is brought into effect in relation to the country in question.
96. *i.e.* in applying the Matrimonial Proceedings and Property Act 1970, s. 5(1). Such an approach would not, however, be applicable to the exercise of the court's powers for the benefit of the children, which is governed by s. 5(2).
97. *i.e.* the Matrimonial Proceedings and Property Act 1970, s. 5.
98. Their conduct being relevant, under s. 5(1), to the provision to be made by one party for the other (but not for the children, to whom s. 5(2) applies).
99. To be taken into account under s. 5(1) and (2). *Cf. Qureshi* v. *Qureshi* (*supra*) at pp. 200–201.
 1. Though not if the forum invariably applied its own domestic law, or whichever of the connected laws (including the *lex fori*) it considered to provide the better substantive rule.
 2. [1904] 1 K.B. 591.
 3. *Santos* v. *Illidge* (1860) 8 C.B. (N.S.) 861.
 4. *Luther* v. *Sagor* [1921] 3 K.B. 532; *Princess Paley Olba* v. *Weisz* [1929] 1 K.B. 718; *Frankfurther* v. *Exner* [1947] Ch. 629 at p. 644; *cf. Anglo-Iranian Oil Co.* v. *Jaffrate* [1953] 1 W.L.R. 246.
 5. *Kahler* v. *Midland Bank* [1950] A.C. 24; *Zivnostenska Bank* v. *Frankman* [1950] A.C. 57; *Re Helbert Wagg & Co's Claim* [1956] Ch. 323 (though see at pp. 351–352).
 6. *e.g.* Bretton Woods Agreement Act 1945.
 7. *Re Macartney* [1921] 1 Ch. 522.
 8. Stemming from *Hyde* v. *Hyde* (1866) 1 P. & D. 130.
 9. *e.g. Sowa* v. *Sowa* [1961] P. 70.
10. See *Matthews* v. *Kuwait Bechtel Corp.* [1959] 2 Q.B. 57 and *Sayers* v. *International Drilling Co. N.V.* [1971] 1 W.L.R. 1176.
11. Contrast *Norris* v. *Chambres* (1861) 29 Beav. 246, affd. 4 L.T. 345, and *Deschamps* v. *Miller* [1908] 1 Ch. 856, with *Re Courtney* (1840) Mont. & Ch. 239, *Re Smith* [1916] 2 Ch. 206 and *Re Anchor Line* [1937] Ch. 483.
12. *Leroux* v. *Brown* (1852) 12 C.B. 801, *Chaplin* v. *Boys* [1971] A.C. 356, *per* Lord Guest at pp. 381–383 and Lord Donovan at 383 (see also *per* Lord Upjohn [1968] 2 Q.B. at pp. 31–33).
13. Contrast the extremely dubious decision in *Ramsay* v. *Liverpool Royal Infirmary* [1930] A.C. 588 with *Doucet* v. *Geoghegan* (1878) 9 Ch. D. 441,

May v. *May* [1943] 2 All E.R. 146 and *Gulbenkian* v. *Gulbenkian* [1937] 4 All E.R. 618.

14. Often validation of the contract, as in *Re Missouri Steamship Co.* (1889) 42 Ch. D. 321, and *Coast Lines Ltd.* v. *Hudig & Veder Chartering N.V.* [1972] 2 Q.B. 341. *Quaere* whether the decision in *Sayers* v. *International Drilling Co. N.V.* (*supra*) is to be regarded as satisfactory.

15. In *Kahler* v. *Midland Bank* (*supra*), justice could easily have been done by finding that Kahler and the Bohemian Bank had no common intention as to the governing law and that the transaction was most closely connected with England, where the shares were situate: see Lord Reid's dissenting speech. And in *R.* v. *International Trustee* [1937] A.C. 500, the decision that the proper law was that of New York resulted in the application of American legislation retrospectively invalidating the gold value clause, thereby giving the British Government (and taxpayers) an uncovenanted benefit at the expense of Americans who had lent money to this country in 1917 probably in the expectation (justified by existing English authorities) that English law would govern.

16. Thus in *Udny* v. *Udny* (1869) 1 Sc. & D. 441, the House probably adopted the rule that a domicile of choice may be simply abandoned and the domicile of origin thereby revived, in order to apply the better rule of Scottish law, which permitted legitimation by subsequent marriage, rather than the inferior rule of the then English law, which did not. In view of the substantial contacts of the factual situation with Scotland, where the land was situate, the marriage was celebrated, and the father resided from the marriage until his death, the better rule of Scottish law should have been applied by a Scottish (or English) court without reference to technical questions of domicile.

17. As Currie has argued, see (1959) 8 Duke L.J. 171.

18. Especially Leflar, *American Conflicts Law* (2nd edn 1968); Reese, Reporter to A.L.I. *Restatement II* (1969); and Currie, *Selected Essays on Conflict of Laws* (1963).

19. *e.g. Babcock* v. *Jackson*, 191 N.E.2d 279 (1963) (New York), *Lee Reich* v. *Purcell*, 432 P.2d 727 (1967) (California), *Clark* v. *Clark*, 222 A.2d 205 (1966) (New Hampshire) and *Zelinger* v. *State Sand & Gravel Co.*, 156 N.W. 2d 466 (1968) (Wisconsin).

20. *Chaplin* v. *Boys* [1971] A.C. 356, *per* Lord Hodson at pp. 379–380, Lord Wilberforce at pp. 389–393, and Lord Pearson at pp. 403–406, and in C.A. *per* Lord Denning M.R. [1968] 2 Q.B. at pp. 24–26.

21. See Leflar, Chap. 11, and *Restatement II*, s. 6.

22. This is controversial in the United States. Preference for the better substantive rule is supported by Leflar (Chap. 11) and Yntema "The Objectives of Private International Law" (1957) 35 Can Bar Rev. 721—"comparative justice of the end result." It can be traced back to Aldricus (about 1200) "the better and more useful law." But it is rejected by *Restatement II* (s. 6) and by Currie (*Selected Essays*, Chap. 2, but see (1963) 28 L. & Contemp. Probs at pp. 775–780). It is expressly adopted in *Clark* v. *Clark* (*supra*) and *Zelinger* v. *State Sand & Gravel Co.* (*supra*). For its recognition in England, see *Chaplin* v. *Boys* [1971] A.C. at pp. 379–380, 389–393, 405–406 and [1968] 2 Q.B. at pp. 24–26, and *Inglis* v. *Usherwood* (1801) 1 East 515 at pp. 524–525.

23. See Cavers' first principle of preference in *The Choice-of-Law Process* (1965).

24. See *Inglis* v. *Usherwood* (*supra*).

25. See *Babcock* v. *Jackson* (*supra*), *Lee Reich* v. *Purcell* (*supra*), *Chaplin* v. *Boys* (*supra*) at pp. 379–380, 391–393. Interest analysis has long been advocated by Currie, who, however, takes a very limited view of the extent to which courts may properly weigh conflicting interests (see (1959) 8 Duke L.J. 171), but this seems an unduly narrow view of the judicial function.

26. As in *Babcock* v. *Jackson*, *Lee Reich* v. *Purcell*, and *Chaplin* v. *Boys*.

27. Thus *Bank of Africa* v. *Cohen* [1909] 2 Ch. 129 cannot be supported.

28. In *Chaplin* v. *Boys*, Lords Hodson and Wilberforce relied on the fact that the parties were British nationals habitually resident in England, and not on technical domicile.

29. As in *Re Missouri Steamship Co.* (*supra*), *Vita Food Products Inc.* v. *Unus Shipping Co.* [1939] A.C. 277, *Coast Lines* v. *Hudig & Veder Chartering N.V.* (*supra*).

30. *e.g. Taczanowska* v. *Taczanowski* [1957] P. 301.
31. *e.g.* Wills Act 1963.
32. As in *Kaufman* v. *Gerson* (*supra*).
33. *e.g. Brook* v. *Brook* (1861) 9 H.L.Cas. 193.
34. *e.g.* as to competence and compellability of witnesses, form of, and method of serving, pleadings.
35. See *Restatement II*, s. 283.
36. (1861) 9 H.L.Cas. 193.
37. [1951] P. 482.
38. [1908] P. 46. The refusal to give any recognition to the French nullity decree has been criticised above.
39. [1909] P. 67.
40. [1972] 3 W.L.R. 939.
41. *Supra*.

18. THE RIGHTS OF INDIVIDUAL SHAREHOLDERS IN COMPANIES

J. A. USHER

I—Introduction

THE rights of individual shareholders in companies may not at first sight seem the most obvious topic for inclusion in a collection of essays devoted to fundamental rights, which are often regarded as the province of the constitutional lawyer rather than the commercial lawyer. Indeed, whether or not one may even become a shareholder in a company depends on the system of economics applied in the state in which one happens to live, and in that sense the rights of a shareholder could hardly be regarded as fundamental. On the other hand, one can be a shareholder in this country, and if fundamental rights are regarded generally as applying to the relationship between the individual and the state, it is worth remembering that writers from Sir W. S. Gilbert in 1893, who based his libretto in "Utopia Ltd." on the idea of ruling a state on the principles of the 1862 Companies Act, to Dr. Tom Hadden in 1972, who states that "the company is in a sense a commercial statelet,"[1] have been struck by the analogies between company law and constitutional law. Furthermore, the position of minority shareholders in small companies has even been deemed worthy of a report by a sub-committee of JUSTICE.[2]

The aim of this essay is to deal in general terms with the position of the individual shareholder within the company, which, of course, will inevitably lead to the vexed question of minority protection. There could hardly be claimed to be any lack of legal literature on this point,[3] but, since we are now members of the European Economic Community, the intention is to approach the question from a European angle. This will entail mentioning French substantive law as well as English, and considering any proposed EEC directives relating to the topic and any relevant provisions in the EEC Commission's draft regulation governing "European Companies."[4]

The existence of directives in this field is the result of a specific provision of the EEC Treaty. Under Article 54(3)(g), the Council and the Commission are given the duty of issuing directives co-ordinating to the necessary extent and rendering of equal value the safeguards which Member States require of companies (as defined in Article 58—a nice point which fortunately is not directly relevant here) so as to protect the interests of both members and others. On the narrowest interpretation this gives authority to issue directives harmonising legislation governing the rights of individual shareholders in companies, though the Commission's own interpretation[5] appears to cover nearly the whole of company law.

As far as the proposals for a European Company are concerned, although they may in some quarters be regarded as a pious hope rather than practical reality, they are at the least useful as a repository of current Commission thinking which may emerge in the form of directives for the harmonisation of national legislation.

In a comparative study of this nature, it is unfortunately necessary to define what is meant by a company. Whilst an English lawyer may have a clear idea of the distinction between partnerships and companies, the *société* of French law is defined[6] as a contract under which two or more persons put something in common with a view to sharing the profit which may result. This definition is wide enough to include a partnership (indeed it bears a remarkable similarity to the English definition of a partnership[7]) yet because of its inclusion of the profit motive would exclude English charitable companies. However, despite the broad general definition, French law treats different types of *société* quite distinctively, and it is possible to choose two types which correspond fairly closely with type of company the English lawyer usually has in mind when dealing with minority protection, the public or private company limited by shares.

The private company of English law is one which by its articles[8] restricts the right to transfer its shares, limits the number of its members to fifty (though it need only have two as opposed to the usual seven) excluding employees and former employees, and prohibits any invitation to the public to subscribe for any shares or debentures. This definition is fairly similar to that of the French *société à responsabilité limitée* (hereinafter referred to as the S.a.r.l.), in which shares may not be transferred to a non-member without the consent of members holding three-quarters of the capital,[9] the maximum number of members is fifty,[10] and no freely transferable securities may be issued.[11]

The so-called "public" company of English law can only be defined as one which is not a private company. One of the criticisms made of English company law, particularly in this field, is that it tends to apply the same principles to all companies, whatever the economic realities behind them. It has been suggested for some time[12] that clearer legal distinctions should be drawn between different types of company; a textbook has recently been written treating companies on this basis,[13] and some writers have detected that in certain recent decisions the courts are beginning to make a distinction between the small private company and the large public one.[14] If the term "public" company is taken in its popular connotation of the larger trading corporation, then its French equivalent is the *société anonyme* (S.A.). This, *inter alia*, requires a minimum of seven members[15] as opposed to the usual two of French law and a minimum capital of 500,000F if it invites the public to invest in it, or 100,000F if it does not[16] (this compares with the figure of 20,000F for a S.a.r.l.).

Although the conceptual point as to the nature of the companies with which we are concerned may appear rather laboured, its interest lies in seeing whether the fact that French legislation does draw a clear distinction between the two types of company with which we are concerned affects the legal principles governing the individual shareholder in these companies.

II—The Relationship of Members

The rights of individual shareholders in companies must, initially, rest on their legal relationship with the other members of the company and the company itself. In both English and French law, this relationship is based on contract. Under section 20 of the 1948 Companies Act, the memorandum and articles of association of a company bind the company and its members as if sealed and signed by each member—curiously, no mention is made of their being sealed and signed by the company, presumably because the section is based on the practice of the deed-of-settlement companies which preceded the modern registered company, and did not have separate legal personality.

It has long been established that this means that each member is bound to the company in his capacity as member and that the company is bound to each member in his capacity as member. The distillation of a long line of cases can be found in *Hickman* v. *Kent and Romney Marsh Sheepbreeders' Association*[17] in which it was held that a member in dispute with the company was bound by an arbitration clause in the articles of association. However, the notion of a member acting in his capacity as a member has perhaps been too subtly interpreted, and whilst it may be clear that section 20 does not create a contract between a company and its solicitor[18] one might doubt the wisdom of saying that an arbitration clause contained in the articles does not apply to a dispute involving a member acting in his capacity as director rather than as member.[19]

Surprisingly, in view of the drafting of the section, it is only relatively recently that it has been affirmed that under section 20 the articles and memorandum may constitute a contract between the members themselves —at least in so far as they create individual rights. In the nineteenth century, it had in fact been suggested by Lord Herschell, in his dissenting judgment in *Welton* v. *Saffoy*[20] that individual rights could only be enforced through the company. However, in *Rayfield* v. *Hands*,[21] where a provision in the articles of a private company stated that a member wishing to transfer his shares must inform the directors, and that the directors "will take the said shares equally between them at a fair value," Vaisey J. delivered a judgment that was bold in two respects. He held that this provision bound the directors in their capacity as members (as a finding of fact), and that the obligation was enforceable by one member against another, so that the directors were bound to buy the plaintiff's shares. It is still, however, debatable how far this decision is of general application, since, whatever lack of legislative distinction there may be, Vaisey J. did point out that he was dealing with a small company like a partnership.

More recently, it could be argued from the first-instance decision in *Bamford* v. *Bamford*[22] that members have a general contractual right to have the company's affairs conducted in accordance with the memorandum and articles of association, but this point will be discussed later with reference to the remedies available to individual shareholders.

In France, there is no need for the constitutive documents of a *société* to be deemed to be a contract since, as we have already seen, a *société* is defined in terms of a contract between its members. Under Article 1843 of the Civil Code it is still the basic rule that a *société* begins to exist from the moment the contract is made—the separate legal personality derives from the contract, not the issue of a certificate of incorporation as in this country. However, the law of July 24, 1966 changed this for both the S.a.r.l. and the S.A., and indeed any other *société commerciale*, providing that a *société commerciale* enjoys legal personality only from the date of its registration in the register of commerce.[23]

It is now recognised by the French courts that although a *société* is in concept a contract, it cannot be doubted that it is more than a contract, an institution whose formation and functioning are governed by statutory provisions.[24] Nonetheless, as far as the individual rights of members are concerned, the contractual basis of a *société* is still important.

It does seem to be clear in French law that the *statuts* (*i.e.* memorandum and articles of association) of a *société* do create rights between the members themselves. So, a member of a S.a.r.l. can enforce a clause obliging the other members to buy his shares proportionately to the shares they already possess.[25] Arbitration clauses also appear to be enforceable between members, and in a case where one member brought an action to have a *société* wound up on the grounds of disagreement between him and the other two members, it was held that he must first go to arbitration under a clause of the *statuts* submitting all disputes between members or between members and the *société* to arbitration.[26]

Although both French and English law base the rights of individual shareholders in a company on contract, it is in one respect at least a most unusual contract. This is because it can be varied and indeed can be varied against the wishes of those affected by the variation. As many French writers have pointed out, if the basis of a *société* really were an ordinary contract, then it could only be varied by the unanimous consent of the members.[27] As we shall see, English case law usually manages to deem the victim to have consented to his fate, but the French approach is perhaps more honest.

Although in neither system is the unanimous consent of the members required, special procedures must be followed to alter the articles or the *statuts*. Under section 10 of the 1948 Companies Act, a company may, subject to the provisions of the Act and its memorandum of association, alter or add to its articles by special resolution, which requires twenty-one days' notice and a majority of three quarters of those voting.[28] For the S.a.r.l. in France, any modification in the *statuts* other than changing the nationality of the *société* may be decided upon by members representing three-quarters of the capital[29]—not just three quarters of those voting. For the S.A. any modification in the *statuts* must be carried out by an extraordinary general meeting.[30] On the first attempt to call such a meeting a quorum of one-half of the members with voting rights is required, and at the second attempt a quorum of one-quarter is sufficient. If this quorum cannot be obtained at the second attempt, then the meeting can be postponed for up to two months. When a valid meeting has been called, a majority of two-thirds of those voting is required. So the requirements of French law are somewhat stricter than those of English law.

On the other hand, it should be remembered that in English law the memorandum of association cannot be altered at all except for the objects clause, which by section 5 of the 1948 Companies Act may be altered for seven specified purposes, the widest being to carry on some business which under existing circumstances may conveniently or advantageously be combined with the business of the company. The section requires a special resolution, but also gives the holders of 15 per cent. of the issued shares or any class thereof, provided they did not consent to or vote for the resolution, the right to apply to the court. If this is done, the resolution will have no effect except in so far as it is confirmed by the court.

As far as the alteration of the articles and the *statuts* is concerned, the attitude of the courts is not always consistent, even within one jurisdiction. In England the dictum commonly cited is that of Lindley M.R. in *Allen* v. *Gold Reefs of West Africa Ltd.*[31] stating that an alteration in the articles must be bona fide for the benefit of the company as a whole. The Court of Appeal has usually taken the view that what is for the benefit of the company is a matter for the members of the company to decide.[32]

One of the fundamental problems affecting individual members of companies is the question of expropriation of shares. In *Sidebottom* v. *Kershaw, Leese & Co.*[33] a minority shareholder had an interest in a competing business, and a special resolution was passed altering the articles so as to enable the directors to compel any shareholders with competing interests to transfer their shares. The Court of Appeal upheld the alteration, saying that the benefit of the company was a point to be decided by business men who understand the business and understand the nature of competition; their bona fides were not affected by the fact that the alteration was aimed at the person who had caused the crisis. This decision might seem to make the position of the individual shareholder rather precarious. On the other hand, there are two first-instance decisions[34] in which the judges found on the facts that the alterations in question, which gave certain members the power to buy out the shares of others, were for the benefit of the majority of the members as then constituted but not for the benefit of the company as a whole. However, these judgments in tone imply that the view of the court is to prevail, and so hardly accord with *Sidebottom*. But it is worth noting that the legislature thought it necessary to enact in section 209 of the 1948 Companies Act a specific statutory provision enabling the transferee company in a take-over situation to acquire the outstanding shares in the transferor company, subject to certain safeguards, once it has obtained nine-tenths of those shares.

In France, in so far as there are reported cases on the subject, the attitude of the courts seems to vary, depending on whether the *société* involved is a S.a.r.l. or a S.A. The courts seem more willing to intervene in the case of the smaller S.a.r.l., using a legal test which, at least in phraseology, is similar to that employed by the English courts. The principle appears to be that an alteration will be annulled if it is not in the *intérêt social*,[35] *i.e.* not for the benefit of the company as a whole, and usually this is so where it favours the majority or harms the minority—often the same thing. An example is where the *statuts* were altered so as to increase the salaries payable to the majority shareholders, which meant that the profits available for dividend would be reduced by half, and if the business of the *société* declined might mean that no profits would be available for dividend.[36]

In relation to the S.A. the attitude of the courts appears to be somewhat stricter. The basic rule is that decisions of extra-ordinary general meetings, when they have been taken by the majority, in the forms, and subject to the conditions laid down by the law, and come within the powers of such meetings, are binding on the shareholders and may not be modified by the courts.[37] However, writers have suggested[38] that the general basis for the courts' intervention in the case of the S.a.r.l., the legal concepts of *abus du droit* and *détournement de pouvoir* (which in this context bear a great resemblance to the English doctrine of fraud on the minority) are available in the case of the S.A.

One problem in relation to both the S.a.r.l. and the S.A. is Article 360 of the Law of July 24, 1966, which states that the nullity of an act altering the *statuts* may only result from an express provision of that law or of the laws governing contracts. On a literal interpretation this could leave the individual member with no remedy against an alteration of the *status* except for (mostly) formal defects. However, although detailed discussion of this article is outside the scope of this essay, it seems to be though[38] that it is only meaningful if it is interpreted in a loose manner, allowing the courts to apply their jurisprudential concepts of *abus du droit* and *détournement du pouvoir*.

The only proposals that the EEC Commission has made in this field relate to the mechanism for altering the articles and memorandum of association or *statuts* rather than the protection of individuals affected by such alterations. It is suggested in Article 39 of the proposed Fifth Directive governing the structure of *sociétés anonymes* (and their equivalents) that the *statuts* should only be able to be altered by a two-thirds majority of those present. However, where national legislation requires a quorum of the holders of at least one-half of the issued capital to be present (which is a stricter requirement than that obtaining for the second attempt to call an extraordinary general meeting in France), then an absolute majority of those present would suffice.

In the case of the draft regulation governing European Companies, an alteration of the *statuts* can only be made by a majority of three-quarters of those voting at a general meeting.[39] The quorum for this meeting is the presence of the holders of one-half of the capital, but if this quorum could not be obtained, then a second meeting could be called without regard to quorum (though presumably there must be enough persons present to constitute a "meeting"). The draft regulation would allow the *statuts* to impose stricter rules.

III—Special Rights

So far we have only mentioned the basic position of the individual share-holder, but it is quite possible that the articles or *statuts* may grant an individual shareholder or a class of shareholders special privileges. Two of the commonest of these privileges in England relate to voting rights and to preferential rights to dividend and it is interesting to see how attitudes towards them differ in France and under proposed EEC legislation.

As far as special voting rights are concerned, it appears that in England they can even be used to achieve a *de facto* evasion of legislative provisions, as a result of the decision in *Bushell* v. *Faith*.[40] Under section 184 of the 1948 Companies Act a director may be removed at any time by an ordinary resolution notwithstanding anything in the articles. The articles of the company in question provided that in the event of a resolution being proposed at any general meeting of the company for the removal from office of any director, any shares held by that director shall on a poll in respect of such resolution carry the right to three votes per share. On the facts this would make it impossible to remove any director, but both the Court of Appeal and the House of Lords held that the provision was valid, largely on the basis that the directors could have been given weighted voting rights on any resolution, if that had been desired. Although in one respect this does give certain individual shareholders special rights, it in fact acts to the detriment of many other individual members.

French law on the whole refuses to countenance weighted voting. In relation to the S.a.r.l. it is laid down in Article 58 of the Law of July 24, 1966 that each member has a number of votes equal to the number of shares he possesses, and any clause to the contrary is deemed to be of no effect. For the S.A. Article 174 provides that, subject to legislative excep-tions, voting rights should be proportional to the capital held, and each share should confer at least one vote; again any clause to the contrary is deemed to be of no effect. The exceptions which are relevant here are that under Article 175 double voting rights may be granted by the *statuts* or by an extraordinary general meeting to the holders of nominative shares which have been registered in the name of the same member for at least two years (it is possible for this right to be reserved for French nationals and nationals of EEC countries), and under Article 177 the *statuts* may limit the maximum number of votes which any single member may exer-cise, provided this limitation applies to all classes of shares.

Hence, a *Bushell* v. *Faith* situation should be impossible in France. The proposed EEC legislation tends to follow the French pattern, and under Article 33 of the proposed Fifth Directive voting rights would be pro-portional to the amount of capital held, subject to limitations if the shares are given special advantages (*i.e.* the usual position with preference share-holders in England) and general limitations on the maximum number of votes an individual shareholder can exercise. The draft regulation on European Companies lays down in Article 91 that voting rights should be proportional to the capital held, but allows in Article 49(2) that, subject to certain safeguards, up to one half of the shares may be non-voting shares! Whether or not this rather surprising provision will ever take effect remains to be seen.

A special right which is more generally accepted is that of preferential payment of dividend. In England the precise rights of preference share-holders depend on the articles of the particular company, or even the terms of the particular issue. There is not much legislative interference except in relation to redeemable preference shares, which are governed by section 58 of the 1948 Companies Act. The rights most usually given are for payment of a particular percentage dividend before any payment is made to ordinary shareholders, and for prior repayment of capital on winding up. However, the English courts treat the statement of rights in the articles as exhaustive, so a right of priority to repayment of capital on winding-up means that there is no right to participate in any surplus assets, as was starkly revealed in *Scottish Insurance Corporation Ltd.* v. *Wilson's & Clyde Coal Co. Ltd.*[41]

In France, the general tenor of the legislation governing the S.a.r.l. might at first appear to be against the creation of preferential rights. However, the only positive statement is in Article 35 of the Law of July 24, 1966 which states that the capital must be divided into shares of equal value; it does not say that the shares must carry equal rights, and members may in fact be given preferential rights to dividend, for example.[42]

In the case of the S.A. there is a more specific legislative provision; under Article 269 *actions de priorité* may be issued which enjoy advantages in relation to the other shares. These advantages are most usually a prefer-ential right to dividend and preferential right to repayment of capital on winding-up.[43] It is interesting to note, however, that even in relation to the S.A.—from which the practice with regard to the S.a.r.l. was copied—specific legislation was required in 1903 before these preference shares could validly be issued, since they breached the principle of equality or rights between shareholders.

In so far as special rights are granted, English and French law and the proposed EEC legislation all make some attempt to protect their holders. Perhaps the least satisfactory situation is in England, where section 72 of the 1948 Companies Act states that where provision is made by the memoran-dum or articles for the variation of rights attached to any class of shares, then if such a variation is carried out dissentients holding at least 15 per cent. of the issued shares of that class may within twenty-one days apply to the court for the cancellation of the variation, which then has no effect until confirmed by the court. This, of course, creates difficulties if no provision is made for variation, though the standard provision in Table A, Article 4 provides that rights may be varied with the sanction of an extraordinary resolution (which requires a three-quarters majority) at a separate general meeting of holders of shares of that class, or with the written assent of the holders of three-quarters of the issued shares of the class.

In France no special provision is made in relation to the S.a.r.l. so presumably the usual rules for the modification of the *statuts* would apply. However, in the case of the S.A. Article 156 of the Law of July 24, 1966 requires a special class meeting of the holders of shares of a particular class to approve any modification in the rights relating to that class. This meeting requires a quorum of one-half of the members of the class on the first attempt to call it, and a quorum of one-quarter on the second attempt, and if this cannot be obtained, the meeting can be postponed for up to two months. A majority of two-thirds of those voting is required—in other words, it acts as a class version of an extraordinary general meeting under Article 153.

The EEC's proposed Fifth Directive also, in Article 40, requires a separate class vote at least where the decision in question would harm the members of the class, and the majority laid down as necessary in a general meeting to alter the *statuts* would be needed in the class meeting.

The draft regulation on the European Company would also require any decision to the detriment of one class of members to be approved by that class,[44] or would allow any members of the class with non-voting shares to vote on this particular issue.

Unfortunately, although the meaning of the word "modification" has not given the French courts any trouble, the English courts have construed "variation" so narrowly as almost to deprive the safeguards of effect. In relation to voting rights, in *Greenhalgh* v. *Ardenne Cinemas*[45] it was held that there was no variation where, in a company with 10s. shares and 2s. shares which were to rank *pari passu* for voting purposes, it was resolved to subdivide the 10s. shares into 2s. shares each carrying a vote, so as effectively to prevent the holder of the original 2s. shares from being able to block a special resolution—though it would have been a variation to give five votes to each 10s. share or to say that there should be only one vote for every five 2s. shares.

The problem is perhaps more serious in relation to preference shares. A fairly recent example is *Re Saltdean Estate Co.*[46] where besides preferential payment of dividend and prior repayment of capital, the preference shareholders were entitled to share the "balance of profits" equally with the ordinary shareholders. The Company had enough undistributed profits to have paid a dividend of 1625 per cent! It was resolved to reduce the company's capital by paying off the preference shareholders at a small premium and this reduction was confirmed by the court. According to Buckley J. the cancellation by prior repayment of the preference shareholders' shares was not a variation of their rights, but a liability forming an integral part of the definition or delimitation of the bundle of rights which make up a preferred share.

Apart from the protection of class rights, the substantive law governing reduction of capital in France would not allow such a procedure there. It is laid down both for the S.a.r.l. and the S.A.[47] that a reduction of capital must not harm the equality between members, which means that the *société* may not cancel or reduce the value some classes of shares and not others. Furthermore, as a general principle it is said that a basic right of a member of a *société* is to remain a member, and he cannot be deprived of this right without his consent unless, for example, he fails to pay any calls due on his shares.[48] Preference shareholders can usually only be removed if their shares were expressly stated to be redeemable when they were issued.[49]

In this matter the proposed EEC legislation is again more like the French solution than that prevailing in England. The proposed second Directive on the capital of *sociétés anonymes* suggests in Article 28 that where there are several classes of share, the validity of a reduction of capital should be subject to a separate vote by each class, at least where the operation would harm the holders of shares in that class. The draft regulation on European Companies would only permit, by its Article 44, reduction of capital by means of a reduction in the nominal value of the company's shares, not by means of a cancellation of certain shares.

IV—Meetings

Meetings can be important in relation to the position of the individual shareholder, because it is through meetings that, in so far as he is allowed to do so, the individual shareholder can put his point of view and try to persuade others to support him and in some circumstances defend himself. It has recently been demonstrated in relation to the Distillers' Co. Ltd. and the thalidomide affair what effect on other shareholders even the procedure of convening a meeting can have.

It is proposed to deal here briefly with the question of what rights a member has at meetings, and what right he has to call meetings. In English law this facility is not available to everyone, since, although notice of a meeting must, unless the articles otherwise provide, be sent to every member,[50] members who have no right to vote—and very often this means preference shareholders unless their dividend is in arrear—have no right to attend meetings.[51] Apart from the statutory requirement to hold annual general meetings, in principle, unless the articles otherwise provide, a meeting may be called by two members holding one-tenth of the share capital[52]—Table A, Article 49, however, provides that a meeting can be called by any two members, but only when a quorum of directors is not available.

Nevertheless, whatever the articles may say, section 132 of the 1948 Companies Act provides that the directors may be required to convene an extraordinary general meeting by the holders of at least one-tenth of the paid-up capital carrying voting rights, and if the directors do not proceed to convene the meeting within twenty-one days, half or more of the re-quisitionists may themselves convene a meeting and charge reasonable expenses to the company, which must deduct them from the directors' remuneration. Unfortunately, as the Jenkins Committee pointed out, although the directors are obliged to convene the meeting (*i.e.* send out notices), there is no obligation for it to be held within a particular time-limit, so it could be convened for a date several months in the future.[53]

In a last resort, however, if for any reason it is impracticable to call a meeting of a company in any manner in which meetings of that company may be called, any member may apply to the court under section 135 to order a meeting of the company to be held.

It is also possible for a group of members to require the company to circularise their resolutions in certain circumstances. Under section 140, members representing one-twentieth of the voting rights, or 100 members averaging £100 paid-up capital each, may require the company to give notice of their resolutions to be moved at an annual general meeting, or to circularise a statement of up to one thousand words with respect to any resolution or business proposed to be dealt with at any general meeting. The requisitionists must pay the expenses—which should be low if the information is circulated with the notices convening the meeting—and deposit their resolutions at the registered office not less than six weeks before the meeting and other requisitions at least a week before the meeting.

At the meeting, members should have a reasonable opportunity to speak,[54] and prima facie any member has the right to demand a poll. In any event the articles may not invalidate a demand for a poll made by more than five members, or by members holding one-tenth of the paid-up capital carrying voting rights.[55]

Most often, of course, and particularly in the case of larger public companies, members do not themselves attend meetings, but if they have a right to attend and vote, they may appoint a proxy, order section 136 of the 1948 Act. However, a proxy does suffer disadvantages compared with the member himself since, unless the articles otherwise provide, he is not allowed to speak except at a meeting of a private company, and he is only allowed to vote on a poll, not on a show of hands (though this might be difficult to enforce in a crowded hall). A general proxy may be given for use at any meeting, or a special proxy can be given for use in relation to a particular resolution—and there is here a temptation for directors to send out "two-way" proxy forms in their favour. However, public companies quoted on the Stock Exchange are now required to send out "two-way" proxy forms with notices calling meetings.[56]

French law is simpler in relation to the S.a.r.l. but not in relation to the S.A. A member of a S.a.r.l. has a statutory right to attend and speak at meetings and to have a number of votes proportionate to the number of shares he holds.[57] A meeting may be demanded by a quarter of the members if they hold a quarter of the capital, or by any number if they hold one half of the capital.[58] This is perhaps rather a high proportion of the members, but it is perhaps appropriate in the case of a smaller *société*. In any event, any member has the right to go to court and ask the court to appoint a person to convene a meeting and draw up an agenda, if necessary.

The position of a member of a S.a.r.l. in relation to a proxy is relatively limited by English standards. Unless the *statuts* provide otherwise, he may only appoint another member or his spouse as proxy,[58] and basically the appointment is only valid for one meeting.[59]

In relation to the S.A., as with the S.a.r.l., voting rights should be proportional to the capital held and each share should carry at least one vote, under Article 174 of the Law of July 24, 1966. However, given the sheer weight of numbers that could be involved, not every member has to be given the right to attend ordinary general meetings (in France, an "extra-ordinary" general meeting is the special meeting required to change the *statuts* which has already been mentioned). Under Article 165 the *statuts* may require members to hold a minimum of up to ten shares in order to participate in general meetings—the right to vote is not lost, however, since the small shareholders have the right to join together into groups holding the requisite minimum number of shares and appoint one of themselves or the spouse of one of them to act as proxy.

However, under Article 166 every member has the right to attend extraordinary meetings, and every member holding shares of a particular class has the right to attend class meetings.

As far as convening meetings is concerned, under Article 158, members holding a tenth of the capital may go to court to ask for a person to be appointed to convene a meeting, and in the case of an emergency any person interested may do so. There is also provision for resolutions to be proposed by members if they represent 5 per cent. of the capital by virtue of Article 160 (in fact this percentage is reduced where the capital is in excess of 5 million F by means of a complicated formula referring to slices of capital above 5 million F, with only 0·5 per cent. being required for the slice of capital above 100 million F).[60] The proportion of members required here is lower than in the case of the S.a.r.l. and in fact basically identical with the parallel legislation in England. These resolutions must be sent to the *société* within ten days of the agenda being published, in the case of an S.A. which invites public to invest in it, or in effect within ten days of the agenda being posted to a member where the S.A. does not invite the public to invest.[61]

As in the case of a S.a.r.l., a member of a S.A. may appoint another member or his or her spouse to act as proxy under Article 161, but again the proxy is only valid for one meeting.[62] Although there is no specific requirement to send out "two-way" forms, proxy forms must state clearly that if they are returned without naming a specific proxy they will be used to vote in favour of the resolution proposed by the *conseil d'administration* or the *directoire*, and that to vote against these resolutions, a proxy must be named who agrees to vote against.[63]

The proposed Fifth Directive contains provisions along similar lines. Under Article 23, a meeting should be able to be demanded by members holding 5 per cent. of the capital or shares worth 100,000 units of account (*i.e.* approximately $100,000). If it is not convened within a month, the court should be able to convene it. Article 25 would provide that the same proportion of members could demand that their resolutions should be included on the agenda and circularised in the same way as the notices calling the meeting. In format, these proposals are perhaps more like the English system than the French, though both are fairly similar.

Every member would be able to appoint a proxy, under Article 27, but it is proposed in Article 28 that if the company or any other body solicits the appointment of proxies, then all members must be circularised, the proxy would only be valid for one meeting, and must be revocable, *inter alia.*

The draft regulation on European Companies contains very similar proposals in relation to convening a meeting and for circulating resolutions, in this case provided they are deposited before the notices convening the meeting are sent.[64] It also provides that the same proportion of members can require their amendments to resolutions on the agenda to be circulated ten days before the meeting, in certain circumstances.[65] As for proxies, the regulation would give a general right to appoint a proxy, but would prohibit members of the *directoire* or of the *conseil de surveillance* or employees of the company or its subsidiaries from acting as proxy,[66] a provision which strikes against some old-established habits. The maximum duration of a proxy's appointment would be six months, it would always be revocable, and it would always have to be on a gratuitous basis. The intention of this would appear to be to stop the soliciting of proxies by the existing directors (and members of the supervisory council under the two-tier system of management) or by commercial institutions.

V—Action for Damages or Injunction

A logical corollary of the importance of meetings in company law is that companies are ruled by the majority—unfortunately a majority in voting power rather than a majority in number or even in capital of the members, though it should now be apparent that the distinction is more relevant to English law than to French. Much ink has been spilt in this country over the question of when an individual member of a company can sue, particularly on the matter of classification of the actions available. For the purposes of this essay, and so as to make comparison with French law easier, it is proposed to use a classification which is gaining acceptance in modern usage and deal separately with the case where it is alleged that the company has suffered harm and where it is alleged the individual member himself has suffered harm—though obviously there is some overlap.

Where the company itself has suffered harm, the basic English rule is contained in the notorious case of *Foss* v. *Harbottle*[67] where Wigram V.C. stated that a majority of the members has power to bind the whole body and every member becomes one on the terms of being so bound: the plaintiffs might be the only ones who disapprove, and if the courts declared the acts void, the governing body could defeat the decree by confirming the acts which are the subject of the action.

The case in effect lays down a procedural rule that, whatever the substantive merits of the case, where what is alleged is harm to the company, it is for the company (*i.e.* the voting majority) to decide what action to take

—provided (if the exceptions might be generalised) that it lies within the majority's power to approve or disapprove the acts in question. The exceptions will be dealt with later. Unfortunately the courts have taken a very wide view of what amounts to harm to the company; in *MacDougall* v. *Gardiner*,[68] where the articles provided for a poll to be held on the demand of five shareholders, and the chairman refused to hold one, it was said that it was for the company to sue, not an individual shareholder who had demanded a poll.

The basic rule in France is also that the *société's* action (the *action sociale*) is exercisable by the *société*, and it is for the general meeting, in so far as it has legal power to do so, to decide whether or not to invoke the action.[69] However, the statutory modifications are such as to make the position of the individual member considerably stronger than in England.

The modern position in relation to the S.a.r.l. is derived from the law governing the S.A. Under Article 52 of the Law of July 24, 1966 the *action sociale* may be invoked either by an individual member or by a group of members of a S.a.r.l. The group involved must hold at least one-tenth of the capital, and if so may appoint one or more of their number to represent them and agree to meet their costs; the later withdrawal of one or more members of the group is deemed to have no effect on the action.[70] Obviously it is cheaper for the individual members to act together rather than separately; but in any event the plaintiff is entitled to recover full damages on behalf of the *société*.

The argument of English law that it is pointless to allow individuals to sue against the wishes of the majority is dealt with in the most important respect by enacting that no decision of a general meeting can have the effect of extinguishing an action against the directors for a fault committed during the course of their functions, and that any clause in the *statuts* will be ineffective in so far as it requires notice to be given of the use of the *action sociale* or amounts to a renunciation of its use.

In the case of the S.A. Article 245 provides similarly that the *action sociale* may be invoked by an individual member or by a group of members, though in the case of the S.A. the group of members need only represent one-twentieth of the capital in order to appoint and finance a representative or representatives to bring the action and for it not to matter if one or more of their number withdraw.[71] Again the general meeting may not extinguish the action and the *statuts* may not require notice to be given or renounce its use, under Article 246.

Both in the case of the S.A. and the S.a.r.l. although the *action sociale* is being invoked by individual members, it is essential in order for the action to be heard that the *société* is joined as a party.[72] It is also specifically laid down that the *action sociale* which may be exercised by individual members or groups of members is that of the *société* against its directors,[73] and not any other action; but it is this action that in virtually every case a minority is likely to wish to invoke against the wishes of the majority.

The EEC's proposed Fifth Directive adopts a similar approach to that of French law. It would require national legislation to impose civil liability on the members of the two organs involved in the two-tier system of management it proposes, for any violation of the law or of the *statuts* and for any fault committed by them during the course of their activities.[74] Apart from the company, this liability would be able to be invoked by members holding five per cent. of the capital or who hold shares with a nominal value of 100,000 units of account.[75] There is no provision, however, for an individual member as such to invoke the company's action.

As far as renunciation of the action by the company is concerned, the directive would permit it provided all the facts were known and there was an express decision of the general meeting; but even such an express renunciation would not be allowed to prevent the prescribed minority from exercising the action provided they voted against the decision or minuted their opposition.[76]

The draft regulation on the European company contains a briefer version of the proposals in the directive, allowing the *action sociale* to be exercised against the members of the *directoire* or the *conseil de surveillance* by members holding five per cent. of the capital or shares with a nominal value of 100,000 units of account.[77]

Although English law does not give specified minorities the right to exercise the company's action—a deficiency which will have to be remedied if the Fifth Directive takes effect in its present form—there are certain generally recognised exceptions to the rule in *Foss* v. *Harbottle*. It could be submitted that some of these are not really exceptions but are examples of personal actions, but since the same act may often have both the company and the rights of an individual member, the dividing line is sometimes difficult to draw. Indeed, before the 1966 legislation, the right of the individual member in France to use the *action sociale* was a case-law development of his personal action.[78]

However, one situation which is fairly clearly an exception to the rule is where the acts of the controllers of the company are a fraud on the minority. This is a question of fact in each case; there may be fraud on the minority where directors who control the company use their power to obtain contracts for themselves which they should obtain for the company,[79] yet there is nothing in principle to stop controlling directors from voting on transactions in which they are interested.[80] It appears largely to depend on whether their conduct amounts to oppression of the minority.[81] Also, and here there may not necessarily be fraud on the minority, though the actions are often framed as if there were, the rule in *Foss* v. *Harbottle* does not apply where, particularly in the case of share issues, the question of who is the majority and who is the minority may depend on the validity of the act in question.[82]

The other cases which are usually categorised as exceptions to *Foss* v. *Harbottle* are where the act in question is *ultra vires* the company[83]—the right of the individual member to raise the point does not appear to be affected by section 9(1) of the European Communities Act—or if the act complained of could only be effective if resolved upon by more than a simple majority vote, which means in most cases that it would amount to a *de facto* alteration of the articles.[84]

It could, however, be argued that these are in fact personal actions relating to infringements of the rights of individual members. This confusion is not surprising, however, since the rationale of *Foss* v. *Harbottle* has often been thought to apply to any case where the act in question could be ratified by the majority irrespective of whether it harms the company or individual members,[85] and the personal action itself is sometimes defined as an exception to the rule.

It has long been settled that an individual member of a company can bring an action to protect his individual private rights in so far as they are recognised as such. So, in the leading case of *Pender* v. *Lushington*[86] a member was able to bring an action to have his vote counted. More recently, however, there has been some authority for a wider interpretation of private rights. We have already discussed the decision in *Rayfield* v. *Hands* to the effect that the contract created by section 20 of the 1948 Companies Act is enforceable by individual members against other individual members. In *Bamford* v. *Bamford*,[87] where it was alleged that an allotment of shares issued to defeat a takeover was in excess of the directors' powers, the plaintiffs sued in respect of their own individual contractual rights on the basis that the articles are a contract and that each member is entitled to require that the affairs of the company be conducted according to the articles in force. This basis appears to have been accepted at first instance, though in the Court of Appeal,[88] Russell L.J. suggested that the situation was analogous to *Foss* v. *Harbottle* and that it should really be for the company to bring the action, since the act in question could be (and was) ratified by the company. However, it might be submitted that if this is a personal action, then the question of ratification is irrelevant, even though it may be inconvenient for the controllers of a company to have actions brought against them.

If there is a personal right to have the articles and memorandum observed, this would be a useful general principle into which to put the "exceptions" to the rule in *Foss* v. *Harbottle* which we have suggested may be examples of personal actions, and its effect should be, in such cases, to shift the focus of discussion away from the procedural point of whether the action can be brought and into the substantive point of whether or not the act in question can be ratified, as in *Bamford* v. *Bamford* itself.

In France, certain rights are recognised as inherently personal, such as the right to vote,[89] and may be protected by the individual member as such. However, there is little need for a wide concept of private contractual rights, since the *action sociale* may be invoked by an individual member and disputes relating to the *contrat de société* seem to be regarded as coming within its scope.[90] What is usually meant by the *action individuelle* in France is the action by which an individual member can invoke the delictual (*i.e.* tortious) liability of the directors. This action is expressly mentioned both in relation to the S.A. and the S.a.r.l. by the Law of July 24, 1966.[91] Articles 52 and 244 lay down that the directors are civilly liable for breaches of the law or of the *statuts* or for faults committed during the course of their management. An individual member can invoke this liability under the general principle of Article 1382 of the French Civil Code which states that any act of a person which causes harm to another obliges the person by whose fault it happened to compensate for it. Without going into too much detail, it is only necessary to prove fault and a causal link with the harm suffered by the plaintiff. English notions of the duty of care are irrelevant. One important point, given the number of criminal offences created by the law of July 24, 1966, is that every criminal act constitutes a "fault" for civil law purposes, and so an individual member may join himself as a *partie civile* to criminal proceedings and recover damages.[92]

The most difficult problem in invoking this liability in fact lies in proving personal damage: a member who shows that the value of his shares has fallen, even if he can show it was the direct result of the fault of the directors, has been held not to be showing damages peculiar to himself, but to the *société* and the damage he suffers is only the corollary of that suffered by the *société*.[93]

However, although it is reckoned difficult to bring the *action individuelle* in France, it would at present be a virtual impossibility in England because of the theory that the directors owe their duties to the company—not to the individual members.[94] Nevertheless, in the recent case of *Gething* v. *Kilner*,[95] Brightman J. did say that in a take-over situation, the directors of a company have a duty towards their own shareholders which clearly includes a duty to be honest and a duty not to mislead. Also, purely accidentally, it may well be that individual members of companies may be able to benefit from the provisions of the Criminal Justice Act 1972 allowing compensation to be awarded to the victims of criminal acts—presumably only a causal link is required between the criminal act and the harm suffered.

In any event, application of the EEC's proposed Fifth Directive would bring charges in English law, since its Article 20 would require national legislation to ensure that the civil liability of the members of the two management bodies can be invoked when a member suffers personal harm as a result of breaches of the law or *statuts* or other faults committed by the members of these bodies.

However, an action for damages or an injunction is not the only remedy available to an individual shareholder and it proposed to deal with three other remedies categorised in a manner appropriate to English law. These are special remedies in the case of oppression, the possibility of external inspection of the company and the availability of winding-up.

VI—Other Remedies

(i) Oppression

Recognising the basic deficiencies of English law in relation to the individual member's ability to bring an action, the 1948 Companies Act introduced a statutory remedy in the case of oppression. It is provided by section 210 that the affairs of the company are being conducted in a manner oppressive to some part of the members (including the plaintiff) and the facts would justify a winding-up order on the grounds it was just and equitable to wind the company up, but to wind the company up would unfairly prejudice that part of the members, the court may make such order as it thinks fit.

"Oppressive" was defined as "burdensome, harsh and wrongful" in *Scottish C.W.S. Ltd.* v. *Meyer*[96] where the oppression in effect consisted of a holding company starving its subsidiary of raw materials to the detriment of the independent shareholders in the subsidiary. Oppression has been taken to include running a company as if it were the private business of the member holding the majority of the votes[97] but not the performance of a series of careless or incompetent acts by the managing director.[98]

Unfortunately the courts have interpreted the requirement that the facts would justify a winding-up literally, and since a member cannot get a winding-up order if there would be no assets available for him on a winding-up, neither can he get a section 210 order,[99] which might be suggested to be illogical, since the whole idea of section 210 is to remedy the oppression without having recourse to winding-up and so to permit the company to continue trading. In fact a reference to a winding-up is omitted in the equivalent section 205 of the Irish Companies Act 1963.

In France, there is no direct equivalent of section 210, though in the case of the S.a.r.l. under Article 55 of the Law of July 24, 1966, any member may ask the court to dismiss a director *pour cause légitime*, which can include what in England would be categorised as oppression.[1] However, there is no such provision in relation to the S.A. whose directors are dismissible only by the general meeting, under Article 90 or Article 121 depending on the system of management used.

However, the French courts have developed a remedy which can be used in cases of oppression, although its scope is wider than this.[2] This is the power to appoint an *administrateur provisoire*. The best known illustration of this in relation to oppression is the "arrêt Fruehauf."[3] Fruehauf-France S.A. was a subsidiary of the American Fruehauf Corporation, and received a large order in 1964 from Automobiles-Berliet S.A. for trailers to be exported to China. This was before the recent American-Chinese *rapprochement*, and the American company, as a result of government pressure, ordered its French subsidiary not to fulfil the contract. Berliet, who were Fruehauf S.A.'s most important customer, refused to accept repudiation of the contract. The French *président-directeur général* of Fruehauf S.A. resigned, and the minority of three French directors applied to the court, against the wishes of the five American directors representing the majority of the voting power, for the appointment of an *administateur provisoire* with power to fulfil the *société's* existing contracts. This appointment was confirmed by the Paris Court of Appeal, on the basis that whatever the wishes of the majority of the members, failure to perform the contract would mean that Fruehauf S.A. would be ruined financially—which would certainly amount to oppression of the minority (though the court also noted the fact that otherwise 600 workers would become unemployed, a factor not normally observed in English company law judgments).

(ii) *Inspection*

The provisions of the 1948 Companies Act permitting the inspection of a company by inspectors appointed by the Department of Trade and Industry (D.T.I.) may be useful to individual shareholders in the company. Under section 164, application may be made to the D.T.I. by either 200 members or members holding one-tenth of the issued shares, and there is a connection with the previous topic in that under section 165 the D.T.I. may appoint inspectors if it appears that the business is being conducted in a manner oppressive to some members, or that the persons concerned with its management have been guilty of fraud, misfeasance or other misconduct towards the company or its members, or that the members have not been given reasonable information about the company's affairs. Further, under section 35 of the 1967 Companies Act, the D.T.I. is given power to present a petition under section 210.

However, and almost inevitably unless a company police force is to be created, D.T.I. investigations are relatively rare, and usually concern cases of relatively major importance.

In France, no provision is made for inspection by a government agency —but since a D.T.I. inspection is usually carried out by a barrister and an accountant,[4] a similar effect can be achieved. French company law uses the institution of the *commissaire aux comptes* as a kind of financial watchdog over a *société*. Basically, a S.a.r.l. is not obliged to have a *commissaire aux comptes* unless its capital exceeds 300,000F,[5] but even below this figure, members representing one fifth of the capital may ask the court to appoint one, under Article 64 of the Law of July 24, 1966.

In the case of the S.A., there must always be at least one *commissaire aux comptes*,[6] but under Article 226 shareholders representing at least one-tenth of the capital may ask the court to appoint an *expert* to present a report on particular operations carried out by those managing the company. This provision has been interpreted as enabling minority groups to obtain information about operations likely to cause damage to them even if these operations have been approved by the majority.[7]

The draft regulation on European Companies would make provision for what is termed special control of the organs of the company. It provides in Article 97 that, *inter alia*, members holding 10 per cent. of the capital or shares to a value of 200,000 accounting units may ask the court to appoint one or more *commissaires spéciaux* where it appears that the management bodies or one of their members have committed a grave violation of their obligations or are unable to carry out their functions normally, and it is shown that serious harm could result for the company. These *commissaires spéciaux* would present a report back to the court which, under Article 99, would be able to suspend or dismiss members of the management bodies and provisionally appoint new members. Although its scope is very restricted, this could almost be said to be a combination of inspection and the appointment of an *administateur provisoire*.

Unfortunately, the proposed Fifth Directive contains no such proposals, although the original draft of Professor Houin did provide for *commissaires spéciaux*.[8]

(iii) *Winding up*

The most draconic remedy available to the individual shareholder is to have the company wound up—though obviously this is only useful very much as a last resort. In England, an individual member would most probably wish to petition under section 222 (*f*) of the 1948 Companies Act, on the ground that it is just and equitable that the company should be wound up. On occasion this can be very beneficial to a small number of members, as in *Re German Date Coffee*[9] where it was held just and equitable to wind up a company formed to use a German patent to manufacture coffee from dates which had in fact used a Swedish patent to do so, on the petition of just two members, the grounds being that the main substratum of the company had gone. This is one of the few cases in which the English courts do expressly take account of the real nature of the companies they are dealing with, and it is now well established that where a small company resembling a partnership is involved, it is just and equitable to wind the company up for reasons which would be grounds for dissolving a partnership *e.g.* deadlock between the (by definition few) members[10] or even removing a member from his position as director under the statutory power contained in section 184 of the 1948 Companies Act.[11] In any event, the individual shareholder should not leave things too late, since he can only petition if there will be assets available to distribute to him.[12]

For both the S.a.r.l. and the S.A. the Law of 24 July, 1966 provides in its Article 402 that the court may order the liquidation of a *société* at the request of members representing at least one-tenth of the capital—the same proportion in this case applies to both types. However, an individual member may demand the dissolution of the *société* under the general rules laid down in Article 1871 of the Civil Code. This allows individual action only for *justes motifs* such as the failure of a member to fulfil his obligations, or a recurring illness preventing him being of use in the business, or similar cases whose legitimacy and gravity is left to the discretion of the judges. The examples given obviously really only apply to the equivalents of partnerships, but they are not exclusive, and the general principle is taken to apply in all types of *société* including the S.A. and the S.a.r.l.[13]

One of the things most commonly held like a *juste motif* is disagreement (*mésintelligence*) between the members when this has a sufficiently paralytic effect on the *société*, and this is so whether it is a small *société* with two members who are both directors,[14] or a full-blown *société anonyme* racked by disputes between two major factions.[15]

However, it must be emphasised once more that winding-up is not really a very satisfactory remedy for the individual shareholder, since it involves the destruction of the very thing he probably wishes to profit from.

VII—Conclusion

Although the casual reader might be forgiven for thinking that the rights of an individual shareholder are hidden in mists of confusion, it should be tolerably clear that the individual is somewhat better protected in his voluntary association with the economic mini-state of the company than in his involuntary association with the political state. In principle, this should be the case, since, as Professor Roblot has pointed out, a company and its directors do not have sovereign power—at least in legal theory.[16]

As far as the comparison between French and English law is concerned, there is on the whole a remarkable similarity in the legal principles and concepts involved, except perhaps in relation to the French insistence on the right to vote and on the right of the individual member to exercise the company's action against its directors. On this latter point, although the rule in *Foss* v. *Harbottle* is recognised as causing hardships (subject to a possible wide interpretation of personal rights of members), it is frequently suggested that it would be equally undesirable from a practical point of view to give too much freedom to individual members to start actions involving the company. However, as far as one can tell from reported cases, the powers of the individual shareholder do not appear to have been abused in France.

In any event, if the Fifth Directive comes into force in its present form, then the right to exercise the company's action will have to be given, basically, to members holding 5 per cent. of the issued capital of a public company. This, incidentally, one would imagine to be one of the less controversial of the directive's proposals.

On the subject of French law, it is interesting to note that despite the legislative distinction between the S.A. and the S.a.r.l., the same general principles tend to be applied to both, and the only real distinction comes in the detailed application—usually in the form of requiring a larger percentage group to exercise a particular right in the small S.a.r.l. than in the bigger S.A.

Although great legislative care has been taken to produce complicated formulae to enable specified numbers of members to call meetings, propose resolutions and exercise other powers, one cannot help feeling that many of these powers are theoretical rather than practical, because of the difficulty an individual shareholder experiences in exercising any continuous check on the way the company is being run.

To revert to our original metaphor of the state, it might be suggested that the great defect of company government, particularly in relation to the larger public company, is that it does not allow for continual opposition—indeed this was the reason why, in W. S. Gilbert's *Utopia Ltd*, the Monarchy Ltd. was eventually turned into a limited monarchy with party government. Without wishing to impose that on companies, one might look towards the major proposal of the Fifth Directive. This is the proposed two-tier system of management for public companies derived from the German system, and accepted in France in the Law of July 24, 1966.

This envisages a *directoire* to manage the company, and a *conseil de surveillance* to supervise the *directoire*. It may well turn out to be no better than two boards of directors, but if the *conseil de surveillance* does, as intended,[17] truly represent the different sectional interests in the company, it may well in fact act as a continuous check on the way the company is being run, and so be a real protection for the individual member—though the member of the small private company will still have to look after his own interests.

NOTES

1. Hadden, Company Law and Capitalism, p. 75.
2. JUSTICE, *Minority Shareholders in Small Companies*, March 1969.
3. See recent articles by Barak (1971) 20 I.C.L.Q. 58, and Rajak (1972) 35 M.L.R. 156.
4. *Proposition d'un règlement du conseil portant statut des sociétés anonymes européennes* of June 24, 1970.
5. See *e.g.* Memorandum on the creation of a European commercial company of April 22, 1966, *Bulletin of the European Communities* (1966), nos 9–10, supp.
6. Code Civil, Article 1832.
7. Partnership Act 1890, s. 1.
8. Companies Act 1948, s. 28(1).
9. *Loi no. 66–537 dur 24 juillet 1966 sur les sociétés commerciales*, art. 45, (hereinafter referred to as the Law of July 24, 1966).
10. *Ibid.*, Art. 36.
11. *Ibid.*, Art. 42.
12. See Fogarty, "A Companies Act 1970?", P.E.P., Vol. XXXIII, No. 500, October 1967. In the light of events, the title has proved to be rather optimistic.
13. Hadden, *op. cit.*
14. See Schmitthof, "The Future of the European Company Law Scene," U.K.N. C.C.L. 1972 Leeds Collogium.
15. Law of July 24, 1966, Art. 73.
16. *Ibid.*, Art. 71.
17. [1915] 1 Ch. 881.
18. *Eley* v. *Positive Government Security Life Assurance Co. Ltd.* (1876) 1 Ex. D. 88.
19. See *e.g. Beattie* v. *E. & F. Beattie Ltd.* [1938] Ch. 708.
20. [1897] A.C. 299, at p. 315.
21. [1960] Ch. 1.
22. [1968] 3 W.L.R. 317 at p. 321.
23. Law of July 24, 1966, Art. 5.
24. Paris March 26, 1966. Gaz. Pal. 1966. 1. 400.
25. Paris November 18, 1969 D.70. 170, note Guyon.
26. Com. January 30, 1967, D. 68. 370.
27. See *e.g.* Ripert and Roblot, *Traité Élémentaire de Droit Commercial* (6th edn 1968), No. 676.
28. s. 141(2).
29. Law of July 24, 1966, Art. 60.
30. *Ibid.*, Art. 153.
31. [1900] 1 Ch. 656, at p. 671.
32. See *Shuttleworth* v. *Cox Bros.* [1927] 2 K.B. 9.
33. [1920] 1 Ch. 154.
34. *Brown* v. *British Abrasive Wheel Co.* [1919] 1 Ch. 290, *Dafen Tinplate Co.* v. *Llanelly Steel Co.* [1920] 2. Ch. 124.
35. Com. October 11, 1967 D. 68, 136: Pau December 24, 1935, Gaz. Pal. 1936. 1.399.
36. Pau. December 24, 1935. *supra.*
37. Req. June 22, 1926 D.P. 1927, 1. 117.
38. Ripert and Roblot, *op. cit.*, No. 1230.

39. Art. 243.
40. [1970] A.C. 1099.
41. [1949] A.C. 462.
42. Catenot, "Les catégories de parts sociales dans les sociétés à responsabilité limitée." Journ. not. 1952, 429.
43. Ripert and Roblot, *op. cit.*, No. 1184.
44. Art. 49, para. 5.
45. [1946] 1 All E.R. 512.
46. [1968] 1 W.L.R. 1844.
47. Arts. 63 and 215 of the Law of July 24, 1966.
48. Ripert and Roblot, *op. cit.*, Nos. 1235, 1236 and 1582.
49. Req. November 16, 1943, S. 1944. 1. 15.
50. Companies Act 1948, s. 134(9).
51. *Re Mackenzie & Co. Ltd.* [1916] 2 Ch. 450.
52. Companies Act 1948, s. 134(*b*).
53. Report of the Company Law Committee, June 1962, Cmnd. 1749, para. 458.
54. *Wall* v. *London & Northern Assets Corp.* [1898] 2 Ch. 469.
55. Companies Act 1948, s. 137 (1)(*b*).
56. Federation of Stock Exchanges in Great Britain and Ireland, *Requirements for Quotation*, Sch. VIII, Part A, para. 14.
57. Law of July 24, 1966, Art. 58.
58. *Ibid.*, Art. 57.
59. Décret no. 67–236, March 23, 1967 sur les sociétés commerciales, Art. 39. (hereinafter referred to as the decree of March 23, 1967).
60. *Ibid.*, Art. 128.
61. *Ibid.*, Art. 129, 130.
62. *Ibid.*, Art. 132.
63. *Ibid.*, Art. 134.
64. Art. 85.
65. Art. 86.
66. Art. 88.
67. (1843) 2 Hare 461.
68. (1875) 1 Ch. D. 13.
69. Ripert and Roblot, *op. cit.*, No. 1374.
70. Decree of March 23, 1967, Art. 45.
71. *Ibid.*, Art. 200.
72. *Ibid.*, Art. 46 and 201.
73. Law of July 24, 1966, Arts. 52 and 244.
74. Art. 14.
75. Art. 16.
76. Art. 18.
77. Art. 72 and 81.
78. Ripert and Roblot, *op. cit.*, No. 1375 note.
79. *Cook* v. *Deeks* [1916] 1 A.C. 554.
80. *North West Transportation Co.* v. *Beatty* (1887) 12 App. Cas. 589; and see *per* Lord Russell in *Regal* v. *Gulliver* [1942] 1 All E.R. 378.
81. *Menier* v. *Hooper's Telegraph* (1874) 9 Ch. App. 350.
82. See *Piercy* v. *Mills* [1920] 1. Ch. 77; *Hogg* v. *Cramphorn* [1967] Ch. 254 could be explained on this basis.
83. See *Parke* v. *Daily News* [1962] Ch. 927.
84. *Salmon* v. *Quin* [1909] A.C. 442.
85. See Gower, *Principles of Modern Company Law* 2nd edn (1957), p. 530; *cf.* 3rd edn (1969), p. 586.
86. (1877) 6 Ch. D. 70.
87. [1968] 3 W.L.R. 317 at p. 321.
88. [1970] Ch. 212 at p. 242.
89. Paris, December 6, 1954 D. 1955, 119.
90. See *e.g.* Crim. October 10, 1963 D. 64 Som. 62.
91. Arts. 52 and 245.
92. Crim. November 4, 1969, D. 1970 Som. 83.
93. Com. January 26, 1970 D. 70 643, note Guyénot.
94. The *locus classicus* is *Percival* v. *Wright* [1902] 2 Ch. 421; but *cf. City Code on Takeovers and Mergers*, rule 30. See also *Pavlides* v. *Jensen* [1956] Ch. 565.

95. [1972] 1 W.L.R. 337.
96. [1959] A.C. 324.
97. *Re Harmer Ltd.* [1959] 1 W.L.R. 62.
98. *Re Five Minute Car Wash* [1966] 1 All E.R. 242.
99. *Re Bellador Silk Ltd.* [1965] 1 All E.R. 667.
1. See Dijon, November 2, 1955, Gaz. Pal. 1956 1. 42, where *inter alia* the director refused to call meetings.
2. See the long list of cases in Dalloz, *Petit Code des Sociétés* (1971), p. 36, no. 6.
3. Paris, May 22, 1965, Gaz. Pal 1965 2, 86.
4. See *e.g. Re Pergamon Press* [1970] Ch. 388.
5. Decree of March 23, 1967, Art. 43.
6. Law of July 24, 1966, Art. 218.
7. Rouen, March 17, 1970, D. 1971, 177.
8. Avant-projet de directive sur l'administration et le contrôle de la société par actions, Art. 36.
9. (1882) 20 Ch.D. 169.
10. *Re Yenidje Tobacco Co.* [1916] 2. Ch. 426.
11. *Re Westbourne Galleries Ltd.* [1972] 2 W.L.R. 1289.
12. *Re Othery Construction Co.* [1966] 1 W.L.R. 69.
13. Req. March 1, 1903 D.P. 1904. 1. 89; Com. January 23, 1950 D. 1950, 300.
14. Com. February 20, 1957, Bull civ. III, p. 57.
15. Com. February 16, 1970, Bull civ. IV, p. 56.
16. Ripert and Roblot, *op. cit.*, No. 1232.
17. Art. 4.

19. THE EUROPEAN SOCIAL CHARTER

M. EVANS*

1—Introduction

THE European Social Charter,[1] which was signed in Turin on October 18, 1961 and which entered into force on February 26, 1965, was concluded on the basis that the signatory States thereto were "resolved to make every effort in common to improve the standard of living and to promote the social well-being of both their urban and rural populations by means of appropriate institutions and action."[2]

Yet, notwithstanding the loftiness of its aim and the fact that it represents one of the most significant realisations of the Council of Europe, the Charter has, to a large extent, failed to capture the attention either of the general public or of legal commentators. One has only to compare the "scattered and repetitive" literature concerning the Charter[3] with the enormous quantity of books, monographs and articles produced in connection with the European Convention on Human Rights listed in a Bibliography published in 1969, with its two supplements of 1970 and 1972, which contain more than 120 pages of entries.

The reason for the comparatively cool reception accorded to the Social Charter may well reside to a certain extent in a number of superficial similarities between it and the Human Rights Convention which raised hopes which have not been fulfilled. Indeed, did not the Committee of Ministers of the Council of Europe in a Special Message addressed to the Consultative Assembly in 1954[4] refer to the future Charter as being "complementary" to the Human Rights Convention? Furthermore, the Preamble of the Charter specifically refers to that Convention as an instrument designed to secure the protection of civil and political rights and freedoms and in the following paragraph insists on the requirement that "the enjoyment of social rights should be secured without discrimination on the grounds of race, colour, sex, religion, political opinion, national extraction or social origin" which likewise recalls the substantially similar wording of Article 14 of the Human Rights Convention.

Be this as it may, any objective analysis of the provisions of the Charter must avoid pressing too far the analogy between the treaties for this approach has given rise to a number of misconceived criticisms which this article will attempt to refute. Before examining them, however, the principal features of the Charter should be recalled.

II—*Principal Features of the Charter*

Part I of the Charter lists nineteen rights and principles which are, according to Article 20, para. 1 (a), to be regarded as "a declaration of the aims which each Contracting Party will pursue by all appropriate means." The rights and principles are the following:

1. Everyone shall have the opportunity to earn his living in an occupation freely entered upon.

2. All workers have the right to just conditions of work.

3. All workers have the right to safe and healthy working conditions.

4. All workers have the right to a fair renumeration sufficient for a decent standard of living for themselves and their families.

5. All workers and employers have the right to freedom of association in national or international organisations for the protection of their economic and social interests.

6. All workers and employers have the right to bargain collectively.

7. Children and young persons have the right to a special protection against the physical and moral hazards to which they are exposed.

8. Employed women, in case of maternity, and other employed women as appropriate, have the right to a special protection in their work.

9. Everyone has the right to appropriate facilities for vocational guidance with a view to helping him choose an occupation suited to his personal aptitude and interests.

10. Everyone has the right to appropriate facilities for vocational training.

11. Everyone has the right to benefit from any measures enabling him to enjoy the highest possible standard of health attainable.

12. All workers and their dependents have the right to social security.

13. Anyone without adequate resources has the right to social and medical assistance.

14. Everyone has the right to benefit from social welfare services.

15. Disabled persons have the right to vocational training, rehabilitation and resettlement, whatever the origin and nature of their disability.

16. The family as a fundamental unit of society has the right to appropriate social, legal and economic protection to ensure its full development.

17. Mothers and children, irrespective of marital status and family relations, have the right to appropriate social and economic protection.

18. The nationals of any one of the Contracting Parties have the right to engage in any gainful occupation in the territory of any one of the others on a footing of equality with the nationals of the latter, subject to restrictions based on cogent economic or social reasons.

19. Migrant workers who are nationals of a Contracting Party and their families have the right to protection and assistance in the territory of any other Contracting Party.

It is essential, then, to realise from the outset that Part I of the Charter creates no obligation to guarantee these rights and principles. Nor indeed does Part II, in which, however, are to be found the essential substantive provisions of the Charter (Articles 1–19). In fact, each of the nineteen articles corresponds to one of the rights or principles set out in Part I and states that with a view to the effective exercise of the right in question, the Contracting Parties undertake certain obligations which are then set out in numbered paragraphs.

While the substantive provisions of the Charter are to be found in Part II, the principal procedural provisions are to be found in Parts III and IV, the former dealing with the undertakings of States under the Charter and the latter with the supervisory machinery for its application.

Part III contains a single article, Article 20, para. 1 of which is drafted in the following terms:

"1. Each of the Contracting Parties undertakes:
   (a) to consider Part I of this Charter as a declaration of the aims which it will pursue by all appropriate means, as stated in the introductory paragraph of that Part;
   (b) to consider itself bound by at least five of the following Articles of Part II of this Charter: Articles 1, 5, 6, 12, 13, 16 and 19;
   (c) in addition to the Articles selected by it in accordance with the preceding sub-paragraph, to consider itself bound by such a number of Articles or numbered paragraphs of Part II of the Charter as it may select, provided that the total number of Articles or numbered paragraphs by which it is bound is not less than 10 Articles or 45 numbered paragraphs."

This provision was clearly inspired by the long and arduous negotiations leading to the conclusion of the Social Charter during which it became apparent that the member States of the Council of Europe did not consider themselves able to subscribe to all the undertakings contained in Articles 1 to 19.[5] However, the possibility of a State progressively accepting obligations contained in Part II which it had not accepted at the time of ratification is specifically provided for in paragraph 3 of Article 20 and constitutes one aspect of the dynamic character of the Charter.

As regards the supervisory machinery, for which provision is made in Articles 21 to 29 of the Charter, it is essentially based on the following elements:

(a) an obligation on the Contracting Parties to submit to the Secretary-General of the Council of Europe, at two-yearly intervals, a report concerning the application of such provisions of Part II of the Charter as they have accepted (Art. 21) and, in respect of the provisions of Part II which they have not accepted, a report at appropriate intervals (Art. 22);

(b) the examination of these reports by a Committee of Independent Experts who are appointed for a period of six years[6] (Arts. 24 and 25); this Committee is assisted by a representative of the International Labour Organisation who participates in their deliberations in a consultative capacity (Art. 26);

(c) a second examination of the reports submitted by the Contracting Parties together with the conclusions of the Committee of Independent Experts by a Sub-Committee of the Governmental Social Committee of the Council of Europe[7] (Art. 27, para. 1) composed of one representative of each of the Contracting Parties[8] (Art. 27, para. 2);

(d) the submission by this Sub-Committee to the Committee of Ministers of the Council of Europe of a report containing its conclusions to which is appended the report of the Committee of Independent Experts (Art. 27, para. 3);

(e) the association of the Consultative Assembly of the Council of Europe with the procedure to the extent that the conclusions of the Committee of Independent Experts shall be transmitted to it by the Secretary-General and that it shall communicate its views on these conclusions to the Committee of Ministers (Art. 28);

(f) the possibility for the Committee of Ministers, by a two-thirds majority of the members entitled to sit on it, on the basis of the report of the Sub-Committee, and after consultation with the Consultative Assembly, to make to each Contracting Party "any necessary recommendations" (Art. 29).

III—*Analysis of the Provisions of the Charter*

On the basis of this general account of the structure of the Social Charter, it is now possible to proceed to an examination of its strengths and weaknesses. With this end in view, it is perhaps useful to examine the principal criticisms which have been made of the Charter and which may be summarised as follows:

(i) the vagueness of the provisions of the Charter;
(ii) its essentially conservative character;
(iii) the weakness of the supervisory machinery.

Of these various charges, the first is certainly the least convincing although it has gained wide currency.[9] It must, of course, be admitted that the formulation of the rights and principles listed in Part I of the Charter is extremely general but, as is stressed in Article 20, para. 1 (a), this Part is to be regarded as a declaration of aims rather than as creating precise legal obligations. If the allegation of vagueness is to have any real meaning, it should then be directed to the undertakings contained in Articles 1–19 of the Charter and, here, as might be expected, in a convention dealing with social questions which raise important political issues, the degree of precision of the obligations for States varies considerably. While, for example, the practical effect of the undertaking in Article 2, para. 3 "to provide for a minimum of two weeks annual holiday with pay" would seem unlikely to cause serious difficulties of interpretation, the provision contained in Article 4, para. 4 whereby the Contracting Parties recognise "the right of all workers to a reasonable period of notice for termination of employment" is admittedly vague. However, as has been pointed out, the vagueness of this, and many other substantive provisions of the Charter, is intentional and indeed desirable. Even assuming that the Member States of the Council of Europe had been able, in 1961, to agree, for example, on a specific minimum period of notice, which it may confidently be assumed would have represented the lowest common denominator, it is highly likely that such a period would, in 1972, be considered unacceptable. This lack of precision in the Charter is indeed a fundamental aspect of its dynamic character.

Moreover, is not the European Convention on Human Rights itself open to the same charge of vagueness, for example Article 8 which guarantees the right to respect for private and family life, home and correspondence and Article 5, para. 3 which provides that arrested or detained persons shall "be entitled to trial within a reasonable time or to release pending trial"? It will, perhaps, be objected to this comparison between the two instruments that the Human Rights Convention, unlike the Social Charter, makes provision for judicial control and, in consequence, authoritative and binding interpretation of its provisions. This is true, but on the other hand it should be recalled that while in the case of the Human Rights Convention the case law concerning some articles is undeveloped, the fact that Italy has accepted the whole of Part II of the Social Charter led the Committee of Independent Experts during the first cycle of supervision to give some indications of its understanding of all the substantive provisions of the Charter which, in many cases, give a much clearer indication of the elements of the rights set out in Part I than does the Human Rights Convention.

In connection with the assertion that the Charter is essentially a conservative instrument, the charge is based on a number of different aspects of the Charter, both substantive and procedural which, for the sake of clarity, should be dealt with individually.

As regards the substance of the Charter, reference has been made to the high-sounding phrases contained in the Universal Declaration of Human Rights, the American Declaration of the Rights and Duties of Man and the Inter-American Charter of Social Guarantees, but, as has been observed, these texts are not of a binding character.[10] A more useful comparison would be with the International Covenant on Economic, Social and Cultural Rights[11] and with the standards laid down in the Conventions and Recommendations of the International Labour Organisation.[12] While in a number of cases, the standards set out in the Social Charter are substantially similar to those laid down within the framework of the International Labour Organisation, it must be admitted that there are, however, certain articles of the Social Charter which fall short of the ILO provisions, for example in connection with the right to organise, hours of work and labour inspection. In other cases the Charter goes further and here particular reference should be made to the protection of migrant workers and their families and the right to strike, it being useful to recall that the Social Charter is the first binding international instrument expressly to recognise this right.

In other words, it does not seem possible to draw up a balance-sheet allowing one to state categorically that the Social Charter is more, or less, progressive than the standards worked out in Geneva during the last fifty-four years. It may however be asked whether statements such as *"pour la plupart des pays membres du Conseil de l'Europe, les dispositions de la Charte n'entraînent guère de difficultés d'application"* [13] can really be taken seriously when only nine of the seventeen member States of the Council of Europe have so far ratified the Charter and of those only one has accepted all its substantive provisions. Nor does it seem likely that this reticence can be attributed to unwillingness to accept the supervisory machinery for applying the Charter since no fewer than four States (Belgium, Iceland, Luxembourg and the Netherlands) which have recognised the competence of the Commission to receive individual petitions and the compulsory jurisdiction of the Court under the Human Rights Convention, have not so far ratified the Charter.

A second ground of the allegation of conservatism is the restricted scope, *ratione personae*, of the Charter. It has been pointed out that although the Preamble refers to the improvement of the standard of living and the promotion of the social well-being of both the urban and rural populations of the Contracting Parties, in fact *"nombreuses sont les dispositions de la Partie II qui ne visent que les travailleurs salariés, à l'exclusion des travailleurs agricoles et des indépendants."* [14] Furthermore, Appendix I provides that:

> "Without prejudice to Article 12, paragraph 4 and Article 13, paragraph 4, the persons covered by Articles 1 to 17 include foreigners only insofar as they are nationals of other Contracting Parties lawfully resident or working regularly within the territory of the Contracting Party concerned, subject to the understanding that these Articles are to be interpreted in the light of the provisions of Articles 18 and 19.
> "This interpretation would not prejudice the extension of similar facilities to other persons by any of the Contracting Parties."

It must immediately be admitted that these criticisms are not without foundation. Nevertheless, certain considerations must be borne in mind. In the first place it is difficult to see how certain rights dealt with in the Charter can be accorded to self-employed persons, for example the right to a fair remuneration, as this concept automatically pre-supposes the relationship of employee and employer. The special position of the self-employed person also creates certain problems in relation to the application of some of the provisions of Article 2 of the Charter, for example the provision of public holidays with pay or a minimum of two weeks' annual holiday with pay. It is also in this context that the problem of agricultural workers is particularly acute since the large number of family concerns which often provide the only revenue for the family, especially in certain countries on the continent of Europe, *de facto* brings many farmers into the class of the self-employed and, as we know, a farm cannot be closed down for two weeks like a factory. Similarly, members of the family of the owner of the farm cannot really be equated with industrial workers so as to ensure the effective exercise of certain of the rights enumerated in the Charter, although there is no reason why an employed agricultural labourer should not be regarded as being on an entirely equal footing with industrial workers in respect of all these rights.[15]

The possibility for persons who are not nationals of the Contracting Parties to be placed at a disadvantage in comparison with nationals of the Contracting Parties is less easy to justify but here we must recall that the Charter was signed in 1961 and that serious preparation of it began as long ago as 1954. Attitudes to the social problems of migrant workers have changed radically during the last decade and although much has still to be done, the basic principle of equality of treatment with nationals is gaining wider acceptance.[16]

Nevertheless, if comparison is made with the Human Rights Convention, it will be recalled that the rights and freedoms guaranteed thereunder are secured to everyone within the jurisdiction of the Contracting Parties. It can, of course, be argued that whereas that Convention is primarily concerned with preventing unjustified invasion of rights and freedoms, the Social Charter is concerned more with active intervention to ensure the effective exercise of social rights and that this might justify certain discriminatory measures. Even so, and without overlooking the important economic questions involved, one cannot escape the conclusion that the possibility of discrimination specifically contemplated by the Social Charter must lead to serious hesitations as to how far the rights enumerated therein may be considered fundamental, and virtually deprives of all meaning the description of the Charter as being "complementary to the Human Rights Convention."[17]

The third element of the charge of "conservatism" in the Charter is related to the possibility for a State to take measures under Article 30, para. 1 "derogating from its obligations under this Charter to the extent strictly required by the exigencies of the situation, provided that such measures are not inconsistent with its other obligations under international law," the taking of these measures being restricted to "time of war or other public emergency threatening the life of the nation."

It has been objected that these possibilities of derogation seriously weaken the binding force of the undertakings contained in Part II and that while a similar provision is to be found in Article 15 of the Human Rights Convention, its presence in the latter is mitigated by the fact that certain articles cannot be the subject of derogation and that moreover both the Commission and the Court of Human Rights may examine whether or not the measures taken under Article 15 are justified.

In reply to these remarks, it is necessary to recall, in the first place, that the articles of the Human Rights Convention in respect of which no derogation may under any circumstances be made, relate essentially to torture or inhuman and degrading treatment, slavery or servitude and punishment on the basis of retrospective criminal legislation. While this is not the place to attempt to establish a hierarchy of rights, it is, in the opinion of the writer, arguable that the specific cases mentioned in Article 15 represent certain fundamental principles of Western society and that they may therefore justifiably be accorded exceptional treatment.

As regards the suggested absence of any possibility for an objective verification to be made as to whether in a particular case the measures taken in application of Article 30, para. 1 are justified by the facts, it is indeed the case that no provision is made for communication by the Secretary-General of the Council of Europe of notification by Contracting Parties to either the Committee of Independent Experts or the Committee of Governmental Experts. However, it is not unreasonable to assume that such information would be communicated in the two-yearly reports by the Contracting Parties which are submitted to the two Committees mentioned above and that in these circumstances, some comments might be made in the conclusions of these two bodies. Admittedly, some form of jurisdictional control would be preferable but it will be recalled that the power of the European Commission and Court of Human Rights to examine whether derogations under Article 15 of the Convention are justified cannot be exercised *in abstracto* but only in the context of a specific case.

Apart from the exceptional situation contemplated in Article 30, para. 1 of the Charter, provision for further possible restrictions on the effective exercise of the rights and principles enunciated in the Charter is made in Article 31 in the following terms:

"1. The rights and principles set forth in Part I when effectively realised, and their effective exercise as provided for in Part II, shall not be subject to any restrictions or limitations not specified in those Parts, except such as are prescribed by law and are necessary in a democratic society for the protection of the rights and freedoms of others or for the protection of public interest, national security, public health, or morals.
"2. The restrictions permitted under this Charter to the rights and obligations set forth herein shall not be applied for any purpose other than that for which they have been prescribed."

While this provision is in essence an article concerning reservations it refers in fact only to restrictions on the exercise of the rights as provided in Part II which have been accepted by the Contracting Parties. The customary reservation clause has in effect been replaced by the system provided for in Article 20 which grants to Contracting Parties considerable latitude in deciding which undertakings they will accept.

Criticism has been expressed of the combined effect of these two articles.[18] However, if, as some writers have maintained, the quasi-totality of the undertakings contained in Articles 1 to 19 of the Charter were already in fact applied by the majority of the member States of the Council of Europe, it is difficult to understand why these safeguards were considered necessary. Part of the answer must surely lie in the fact that at the time of the signature of the Charter in 1961 many States were uncertain as to whether they were in a position to satisfy all the standards set out in Part II. As has been pointed out by Pugsley, the caution felt by States and expressed not only in the adoption of the mechanism set out in Article 20 but also the subsequent hesitations felt by States of the Council of Europe who have ratified the Charter seems "more than justified since none of these States was able to show to the satisfaction of the Committee of Independent Experts that it satisfied all the provisions which it had accepted."[19] Despite the fact that the system set up by the Charter is far from representing the ideal, it has at least permitted eight States, only Italy having accepted the Charter as a whole, to ratify it, which they would presumably not have been able to do had they been required to accept all the provisions of Part II immediately, or even, as an earlier draft required, to accept all the provisions within five years of ratification.

Furthermore, the dynamic aspect of the Charter should not be overlooked since not only does Article 20, para. 3 make provision for acceptance of articles or numbered paragraphs of Part II of the Charter not already accepted at the time of ratification but the possibility, hitherto regrettably not used, for the Committee of Ministers to request Contracting Parties to furnish reports on provisions of Part II which they have not accepted, would in effect permit a State to obtain an "advisory opinion" on the compatibility of its law with the provisions of the Charter.[20]

These considerations lead naturally to the third principal ground of criticism of the Charter, namely the procedure for its supervision. As has been stressed already in this essay, the machinery applicable is substantially different from that set up under the Human Rights Convention, it having been felt by the drafters of the Charter that a system of control more similar to that used in connection with the Conventions prepared within the framework of the International Labour Organisation would be more appropriate.[21] Since most of the literature concerning the supervisory machinery was written before it was possible to evaluate its effect in practice, it is not proposed to examine in detail the different arguments but rather to concentrate on the first cycle of supervision, on the basis of which it will be possible to draw some general conclusions concerning the efficacity of the Charter and its future.

Without wishing to diminish the importance of the work of the other bodies involved in the procedure, it is, in the first place, necessary to pay tribute to the quite extraordinary achievement of the Committee of Independent Experts whose first conclusions concerned the first reports submitted by Italy, Sweden, Norway, the United Kingdom, Denmark, the Federal Republic of Germany and Ireland, the reports covering the period from the date of entry into force of the Charter in respect of each State concerned, to December 31, 1967.[22]

The magnitude of the task facing the Independent Experts will be appreciated when it is recalled that they were in effect called upon to create a jurisprudence relating to all paragraphs of all Articles contained in Part II of the Charter, Italy it will be recalled having accepted all these provisions. On the basis of its examination of the reports, the Committee, after making a number of general observations concerning its interpretation of the provisions and its findings, dealt in detail with the extent to which each Contracting Party was fulfilling its obligations, concluding in each case whether the undertakings were being fulfilled, not fulfilled or whether no clear judgment could be formed in the absence of supplementary information. The upshot was that the Committee felt itself able in fifty-seven cases to state that Contracting Parties were not fulfilling their undertakings, the breakdown by States being Ireland sixteen, Italy twelve, the Federal Republic of Germany and the United Kingdom each eight, Sweden six, Norway four and Denmark three.[23]

Although it is well beyond the scope of this brief essay to enter into a discussion of the merits of the conclusions of the Committee of Independent Experts, one point should be made. The Committee has been accused in some quarters of undue severity in its interpretation of the provisions of Part II of the Charter and it has been suggested that, from a purely tactical standpoint, it might have been advisable during this first cycle of supervision to adopt a more prudent approach. Such a course of action was not open to the Committee for not only would it have thereby compromised its integrity but moreover it would have bound the Committee for the future, since although it may be possible for a court with a specific set of facts before it to overrule a whole line of cases on the grounds that they were wrongly decided, it is much more difficult, after first deciding that a State's legislation is in conformity with internationally binding standards, subsequently to decide that this is no longer the case, unless, of course, the content of the provision may itself be regarded as being subject to dynamic development.[24]

In any event, the Committee of Governmental Experts, when called upon to examine the conclusions of the Independent Experts, urged that none of the fifty-seven Recommendations suggested by the latter should at this stage be sent to Governments. In some cases, it was felt that the information on which the Independent Experts based their judgments was incomplete or out of date, in others that there had been perhaps certain misunderstandings, and in yet others that the interpretation of the Independent Experts of certain provisions of the Charter was incorrect.

To this already voluminous file to be examined by the Committee of Ministers of the Council of Europe was then added Opinion 57 (1971), adopted by the Consultative Assembly of the Organisation on May 14, 1971, which strongly supported the findings of the Independent Experts and requested the Committee of Ministers, *inter alia*, to "forward the Independent Experts' conclusions to the States concerned *in toto*, commending the comments contained therein as well as the proposals for recommendations to their attention, and calling up on them to take full note of them."

The reaction of the Committee of Ministers is to be found in Resolution

(71) 30, adopted by the Ministers' Deputies on November 12, 1971, in which the Committee of Ministers, after expressing its satisfaction with the way in which the bodies called upon to participate in the application of the Charter had carried out their functions and recalling that this was the first complete cycle of supervision which had taken place, considered that "it would not be opportune for it to make a judgment at this stage on the different observations formulated in this context." The Ministers also decided on the following three points of principle:

> "I. in accordance with the Report of the Governmental Committee, not to address at this stage any recommendations to the Contracting Parties to the European Social Charter;
> II. to transmit to the governments of the Contracting Parties the Report of the Governmental Committee and the Opinion of the Assembly;
> III. to transmit also to the same governments the Conclusions of the Committee of Independent Experts including the analysis made by that Committee, offering useful guidance which may assist in achieving the full application of the principles enshrined in the European Social Charter."

An assessment of this first cycle of supervision is not easy. It might, of course, cynically be argued that since the Governmental Experts are in fact a sub-committee of the Social Committee, a committee of governmental experts which advises the Committee of Ministers on social questions, it was hardly to be expected that the latter committee would reach solutions different from those of the Governmental Experts. This argument is however open to objection, for in the context of the supervisory machinery for the European Code of Social Security, recommendations have, in fact, been addressed to Governments by the Committee of Ministers.[25] Furthermore, the attitude adopted by the Committee of Ministers in connection with the Social Charter was essentially one of "wait and see" and while the recommendations of the Independent Experts were not addressed by the Committee of Ministers to the Contracting Parties, they were in fact brought to their attention inasmuch as the Conclusions of the Experts were transmitted to them.

Only the outcome of the second cycle of supervision will enable us to see how the Committee of Ministers will carry out the unenviable role conferred upon it by the Charter which has in effect made it *iudex in causa sua* and this in a far more political context than in that of the Social Security Code which is a much more technical and precise instrument than the Social Charter.

Ultimately, and this is a point which is sometimes overlooked, the primary purpose of the Social Charter is not the indictment of the Contracting Parties but an attempt to raise the standard of living and promote the social well-being of their populations. It should, therefore, be a source of satisfaction and sufficient evidence that the Charter is fulfilling a useful role to recall that in their conclusions on the second cycle of supervision, the Independent Experts were able to state that "in some cases legislative provisions and administrative practices have been altered to bring them into conformity with the obligations accepted under the Charter," but more important still, that "the system of supervision set up within the framework of the Social Charter constitutes an important dynamic factor for the social evolution of Europe and that its influence is particularly fortunate because the standards to be attained are sometimes of a very high level."[26]

NOTES

*The views expressed in this article are those of the writer and are in no way to be regarded as those of the Council of Europe.

1. European Treaty Series, No. 35.
2. Preamble to the Charter.
3. Pugsley, "The European Social Charter," (1969) 39 Yearbook of the A.A.A. 97.
4. Document 238 of the Consultative Assembly of the Council of Europe (1954).
5. For an account of the history of the Social Charter up to its opening for signature, see Van Asbeck "La Charte Sociale Européenne: sa portée juridique, la mise en oeuvre," *Mélanges offertes à Henri Rolin*, (1964), pp. 427–431, and Janssen-Pevtschin, "Les Engagements des parties contractantes et la mise en oeuvre de la Charte Sociale Européenne" (1966) 39 R. Ins. Soc. 9–15.
6. The Committee consists of seven members, elected by the Committee of Ministers of the Council of Europe from a list of persons proposed by the Contracting Parties to the Social Charter.
7. The Social Committee was set up under Resolution (54) 17 of the Committee of Ministers, as a permanent advisory body composed of senior government officials of the member States of the Council of Europe.
8. Art. 27, para. 2 of the Charter also provides that the Sub-Committee "shall invite no more than two international organisations of employers and no more than two international trade union organisations as it may designate to be represented as observers in a consultative capacity at its meetings. Moreover, it may consult no more than two representatives of international non-governmental organisations having consultative status with the Council of Europe, in respect of questions with which the organisations are particularly qualified to deal, such as social welfare, and the economic and social protection of the family." In its Opinion No. 57 (1971) on the application of the Social Charter, the Consultative Assembly of the Council of Europe drew attention to the fact that none of the national organisations of employers and trade unions referred to in Art. 23 and 24 of the Charter had made any comments on the governmental reports during the first cycle of supervision and in consequence it invited governments to promote the effective application of those articles. Similar regret was expressed by the Committee of Independent Experts, Conclusions I, 7 and again in Conclusions II, xvi.
9. For examples, see those cited by Pugsley, *op. cit.*
10. Tennfjord, "The European Social Charter—an instrument of Social Collaboration in Europe" (1961), IX *European Yearbook* 80.
11. The limited space permitted does not allow a comparison of the provisions of the Social Charter and the Covenant. Although adopted and opened for signature, ratification and accession by General Assembly Resolution 2200 A (XXI) of December 16, 1966, the Covenant has yet to obtain the thirty-five ratifications or instruments of accession necessary under Art. 48, para. 5 for its entry into force. It would, however, seem to be the case that the supervisory machinery for which the Covenant makes provision is both on paper and, in practice after its entry into force, weaker than that of the Social Charter. For detailed information concerning the extent to which the national law of a number of States conforms to the standards laid down in various international conventions see *Cahiers de droit comparé*, 2–3, Strasbourg, 1971.

12. For a good general discussion on this point, see "The European Social Charter and International Labour Standards" (1961) LXXXIV *International Labour Review* 354–375 and 462–477.
13. Schoetter, "La Charte Sociale Européenne: considérations critiques," (1966) 39. R. Ins. Soc. 111.
14. Janssen-Pevtschin, *op. cit.*, p. 18.
15. It should, in this context, be noted that the Governmental Social Committee of the Council of Europe is at present engaged on the task of preparing a draft European Convention on the Social Protection of Farmers. This question has been a source of constant concern for the Consultative Assembly as is shown by its Recommendations 456 (1966) on the social protection of independent farmers and members of their families working or living with them and 577 (1970) on a European Agricultural Charter, the latter containing the text of a draft Statute of the European Farmer.
16. The text of a draft European Convention on the Legal Status of Migrant Workers is at present under study by the Committee of Ministers of the Council of Europe.
17. The limitation of the enjoyment of the rights set out in the Charter to the nationals of the Contracting States is indicative of a traditional approach based on reciprocity, although of course the principle of reciprocity does not apply as between the Contracting States in respect of the articles or paragraphs by which they have accepted to be bound.
18. For example, Schoetter, *op. cit.*, p. 111.
19. *Op. cit.*, p. 99.
20. It is to be noted that this procedure has not yet been invoked, a fact regretted by both the Consultative Assembly in its Opinion (57) 1971 and by the Committee of Independent Experts, Conclusions I, 9–10 and Conclusions II, xv.
21. It should be recalled that the absence of any judicial control at international level in connection with the fulfilment by the Contracting States of their obligations under the Charter is complemented at the municipal level by the provision in the Appendix to the Charter concerning Part III thereof, where it is made clear that "the Charter contains legal obligations of an international character, the application of which is submitted solely to the supervision provided for in Part IV thereof." In other words an individual cannot invoke the provisions of the Charter before national courts. The reasoning advanced by Janssen-Pevtschin, *op. cit.*, pp. 25–26, to refute this conclusion is scarcely convincing although if a Contracting Party to the Charter were in fact to make provision under its municipal law for the possibility of individuals invoking the Charter before national courts, it is difficult to see on what principles of international law such a decision could be attacked. The hypothesis is, however, admittedly somewhat unlikely.
22. The first report from the Government of Cyprus was examined by the Independent Experts during the second cycle of supervision; see Conclusions II, 175–209. The first biennial report from Austria, which ratified the Social Charter on October 29, 1969, is due for submission in 1972 and will be examined by the Independent Experts in the context of the third cycle of supervision.
23. It is of interest to note that 18 of the recommendations related to paragraphs 1, 2 and 3 of Article 18 concerning the right to engage in a gainful occupation in the territory of other Contracting Parties.
24. On the other hand, a provision requiring, for example, equality of pay between the sexes is clearly not subject to such development.
25. See, for example Resolutions (70) 27 and (72) 10 of the Committee of Ministers relating to the application by the Netherlands and by Luxembourg of the European Code of Social Security and the Protocol thereto. These Resolutions were adopted in consideration of Art. 75, para. 2 of the Code, which provides that "if the Committee of Ministers considers that a Contracting Party is not complying with its obligations under this Code, it shall invite the said Contracting Party to take such measures as the Committee of Ministers considers necessary to ensure such compliance." For the full supervisory machinery set up under the Code, see Arts. 74–76 thereof.
26. Conclusions II, xv.

20. FUNDAMENTAL RIGHTS IN THE EUROPEAN ECONOMIC COMMUNITY

J. W. BRIDGE

I—Introduction

"CIVIL rights," Disraeli observed on one occasion, "partake, in some degree, of an economical and, in some degree, certainly of a political character. They conduce to the comfort, the security, and the happiness of the subject; and, at the same time, are invested with a degree of sentiment which mere economical considerations do not involve."[1] The rights of the people are not only "economical" in that sense, but also in the sense that they may be affected by economic policy. Thus the regulation by the European Economic Community (EEC) of the economic and social policies of the member states is inherently likely to impinge on the rights of the citizens of those states under their own national laws.

The uncertainty of the impact of Community law on the law of the United Kingdom coupled with an innate suspicion and distrust of continental institutions has fostered a fear that as a result of British membership of the Communities English law and the English legal system will be forced to undergo changes of such a fundamental nature as to threaten our traditional liberties.[2] In White Papers published in 1967 and 1971[3] Her Majesty's Government made a point of scotching such suggestions and allaying such fears.

> "The Six," we are told, "have not lost any of their national identities or their national institutions and points of view, nor shall we lose our national identity. They retain their own ways of life: as any tourist knows, France and the French are no less French, Holland and the Dutch are no less Dutch, after twenty years of Community life."[4]
>
> "The English and Scottish legal systems will remain intact. Certain provisions of the treaties and instruments made under them, concerned with economic, commercial and closely related matters, will be included in our law. The common law will remain the basis of our legal system, and our courts will continue to operate as they do at present. . . . All the essential features of our law will remain, including the safeguards for individual freedom such as trial by jury and *habeas corpus* and the principle that a man is innocent until proved guilty, as well as the law of contract and tort (and its Scottish equivalent), the law of landlord and tenant, family law, nationality law and land law."[5]

We are also reminded of the European heritage which the United Kingdom shares with the Six in, *inter alia*, matters of political, legal and social framework.[6]

It is the basic aim of this essay to investigate these claims. The following questions in particular will be considered. On the basis of the EEC Treaty and the case law of the Court of Justice of the Communities to what extent does Community law concern itself with fundamental rights? What are the Community "rights, powers, liabilities, obligations and restrictions" referred to in the European Communities Act 1972?[7] To what extent do these concepts give expression to the common heritage of the Member States?

II—*Fundamental Rights in the EEC Treaty*

On a preliminary view the EEC Treaty, unlike other treaties constituting European organisations, does not appear to be much concerned with fundamental rights.[8] The Statute of the Council of Europe 1949 boldly includes amongst its aims "the maintenance and the further realisation of human rights and fundamental freedoms."[9] The Draft Statute for the proposed European Political Community, 1953 went even further and would have made Part I of European Convention on Human Rights and Fundamental Freedoms an integral part of the Statute.[10] There is no such general provision concerned with fundamental rights to be found in the EEC Treaty; not even a provision to the effect that the Community in the performance of its functions shall act in the manner least likely to conflict with the fundamental rights of individuals.[11] The nearest the EEC Treaty comes to matters of general principle concerning fundamental rights is in the Preamble. There references may be found to the determination of the Member States to achieve "the constant improvement of the living and working conditions of their peoples," the reduction of "differences existing between the various regions and the backwardness of less favoured regions," "the development of their prosperity, in accordance with the principles of the Charter of the United Nations"[12] and "by pooling their resources to preserve and strengthen peace and liberty." Thus the EEC and its constituent Member States are clearly concerned not only with increasing their material prosperity but also with ensuring that it is more equitably shared by their citizens with the overall objective of safeguarding peace and liberty. Whilst it is clear that such vague allusions are not creative of any substantive fundamental rights they do provide some insight to the approach of the EEC Treaty to this question.

Upon closer analysis the EEC Treaty is found to take up the theme sketched in its Preamble and to contain numerous specific provisions relating to fundamental rights which are in some cases supplemented by the terms of the Statute and Rules of Procedure of the Court of Justice and the Protocol on Immunities and Privileges. In general terms these provisions fall into two main categories: those which create fundamental Community rights and those which safeguard certain existing national rights of the Member States.

Although the individual Community rights in essence form a unified mosaic of rights, for the purposes of descriptive classification they may be arranged into seven groups. In the first place there are a number of Treaty provisions concerned with the social well-being of the citizens of Member States where the assumption seems to be that they have a right to a certain standard of living. The Treaty seeks to achieve this by two means: by raising the general standard of living and by social security. Thus Article 2 states that one of the tasks of the Community is to promote "an accelerated raising of the standard of living" in the member states. Article 3(i) provides that a European Social Fund shall be set up, one of the purposes of which is to contribute to the raising of the standard of living of workers. Article 39(1) is concerned with ensuring a fair standard of living for the agricultural community in particular and the availability of supplies at reasonable prices to consumers in general. Article 117 pledges the Member States "to promote improved working conditions and an improved standard of living for workers, so as to make possible their harmonisation while the improvement is being maintained." In the field of social security Article 118 is concerned with the promotion of closer co-operation between Member States whilst Article 51 makes provision for the social security of migrant workers and their dependants.[13]

Secondly, the Treaty is concerned with rights of free movement of persons and employment. Article 3(c) includes among the activities of the Community "the abolition, as between Member States, of obstacles to freedom of movement for persons, services and capital." Article 48 provides that "freedom of movement for workers shall be secured within the Community." Article 52 gives a right of establishment to individuals or corporate bodies of one Member State in any other Member State. Article 57(1) provides for the mutual recognition as between Member States of diplomas, certificates and other evidence of formal qualifications in the case of self-employed persons. Under the terms of Article 123 the European Social Fund "shall have the task of rendering the employment of workers easier and of increasing their geographical and occupational mobility within the Community." More specifically on the question of employment Article 118 charges the Commission with the task of promoting close co-operation between Member States in a number of fields. These include employment, labour law and working conditions, vocational training, prevention of occupational accidents and diseases, occupational hygiene, and the right of association and collective bargaining between employers and workers. It is clearly the aim of these provisions to establish a right to free movement and employment under as favourable conditions as possible.[14]

Thirdly, in numerous provisions the Treaty prohibits discrimination, thus according a right of equality of treatment to the citizens of the Member States. Article 7 lays down the basic principle: "Within the scope of application of this Treaty, and without prejudice to any special provisions contained therein, any discrimination on grounds of nationality shall be prohibited." Therefore pursuant to that obligation Article 37(1) requires Member States to adjust State monopolies of a commercial character so as to prevent discrimination in connection with the procurement and marketing of goods as between the nationals of member states. Article 48(2) calls for "the abolition of any discrimination based on nationality between workers of the Member States as regards employment, remuneration and other conditions of work and employment." The Right of establishment provided by Article 52 includes the right to be subject to the same conditions in the country where establishment is effected as are laid down for the nationals of that country. It is also provided by Article 220 that so far as is necessary Member States shall negotiate with each other so as to secure for the benefit of their nationals "the protection of persons and the enjoyment and protection of rights under the same conditions as those accorded by each State to its own nationals."

The prohibition on discrimination is not, however, limited to matters of nationality. Article 119 is concerned with sexual discrimination and requires Member States to "maintain the application of the principle that men and women should receive equal pay for equal work." One of the aims of Article 177 which permits, and in some cases requires, the municipal courts to submit disputed points of Community Law to the Court of Justice of the Communities for a preliminary ruling is to ensure that within the legal systems of the Member States Community Law shall be applied uniformly without discrimination. Similarly, potential litigants before the Court of Justice shall not be discriminated against on grounds of poverty for Article 76 of the Court's Rules of Procedure and Articles 4 and 5 of the Supplementary Rules of Procedure make provision for free legal aid out of the Court's funds. Nor are litigants discriminated against because they customarily reside at some distance from the Court's seat for Article 1 of Appendix II to the Rules of Procedure permits the extension of time limits on account of distance from Luxembourg.

Fourthly, the Treaty recognises a right to the due observance of law in the activities of the Communities. The Court of Justice plays a central role in guaranteeing this right and it is expressly required by Article 164 to ensure "that in the interpretation and application of the Treaty the law is observed." This right imposes a corresponding duty on the institutions of the Community to act at all times in accordance with the Treaty. Under the terms of Article 173 the Court of Justice has jurisdiction to review the legality of the law-making acts of the Commission and Council "on the grounds of lack of competence, infringement of an essential procedural requirement, infringement of the Treaty or any rule of law relating to its application, or misuse of powers."[15] The servants of the Community also have the right for their relations with the Community to be regulated subject to law; Article 179 gives the Court of Justice jurisdiction in such matters.

Fifthly, the Treaty recognises the right of those who have suffered damage as a result of the activities of the Community to receive compensation. Article 215 provides that "in the case of non-contractual liability, the Community shall, in accordance with the general principles common to the laws of the Member States, make good any damage caused by its

institutions or by its servants in the performance of their duties."[16] Thus
the right to compensation under Community Law is in accordance with
standards of liability fundamental to the laws of the Member States.
Jurisdiction in such cases is given to the Court of Justice of the Communities by virtue of Article 178.

Sixthly, the Treaty recognises, albeit in a rudimentary form, the right
of the citizens of the Member States to exercise democratic control over
the activities of the Community. Article 137 states that the Assembly
(commonly referred to as the European Parliament) "shall consist of
representatives of the peoples of the States brought together in the Community." Article 138(3) makes provision for the members of the Assembly
to be elected "by direct universal suffrage in accordance with a uniform
procedure in all Member States."[17] Article 144 authorises the Assembly to
censure and to require the resignation of the entire Commission.[18] And,
Articles 8, 9 and 10 of the Protocol on the Privileges and Immunities of
the European Communities guarantee to members of the Assembly the
rights and privileges necessary to enable them freely to exercise their
functions. These include no restriction on movement to and from the place
of meeting of the Assembly and an immunity from legal proceedings in
respect of the performance of their duties as members of the Assembly.

Lastly an important corpus of procedural rights is guaranteed in relation
to proceedings before the Court of Justice of the Communities. It has
already been pointed out that it is the task of the Court of Justice to ensure
that the law is observed; the various procedural rights ensure that that
task may be performed effectively and in accordance with fundamental
principles of justice. Article 170 of the Treaty extends the *audi alteram
partem* rule to Member States when one alleges that another has failed to
fulfil an obligation under the Treaty. An expression of the same rule in
the general context of proceedings before the Court of Justice is to be
found in Articles 39 and 40 of the Rules of Procedure. There are various
provisions designed to guarantee the right to trial by a qualified, independent and impartial court. Article 167 of the Treaty requires the judges to
be chosen "from persons whose independence is beyond doubt and who
possess qualifications required for appointment to the highest judicial
offices in their respective countries or who are jurisconsults of recognised
competence." Further safeguards are to be found in the Statute of the
Court which render the judges immune from legal proceedings in respect
of their official acts and forbids them from holding any other office or
engaging in any other occupation during their membership of the Court.[19]
The security of tenure of the judges is protected by giving the governments
of the member states no voice in their removal from office which may only
be done by a unanimous decision of all the other judges.[20] The impartiality
of the judges is also preserved by forbidding them from taking part in the
disposal of any case in which they have previously been involved in any
other capacity.[21] Both the Statute of the Court and its Rules of Procedure
recognise the right to be legally represented, indeed it is obligatory[22] and
the Supplementary Rules of Procedure enable the Court to assign counsel

to a party, where the party has not chosen counsel himself, and to pay counsel's expenses and fees.[23] Legal representatives are entitled to enjoy "the rights and immunities necessary to the independent exercise of their duties."[24] These include an immunity from suit in respect of words spoken or written in connection with legal proceedings, facilities and privileges in relation to documents and papers, adequate foreign currency and freedom of movement.[25] The right to a public trial is provided by Article 28 of the Statute of the Court which requires that "the hearing in Court shall be public, unless the Court, of its own motion or on application by the parties, decides otherwise for serious reasons." The right to a reasoned judgment is also guaranteed.[26] Provision is also made for the payment of costs.[27]

In addition to specifying a number of Community rights as described above, the Treaty also contains provisions safeguarding certain rights of the individual Member States. In some cases these national rights permit derogations from the strict terms of the Treaty, in other cases they are concerned with matters which are regarded as essentially subject to the prerogative of individual Member States. Article 48(3) falls into the first of these categories and provides that the right of free movement of workers may be "subject to limitations justified on grounds of public policy, public security or public health." Similarly in relation to the right of establishment Article 56 states that that right "shall not prejudice the applicability of provisions laid down by law, regulation or administrative action providing for special treatment for foreign nationals on grounds of public policy, public security or public health." In the last resort these provisions enable Member States to take precautionary measures in their own interests. In somewhat the same way Article 75(3) permits derogations from the common transport policy where such policy would be liable to have a serious effect on the standard of living and on employment in particular areas. The restrictions on aids granted by states are also relaxed by Article 92(2)(b) and (3)(a) where aid is necessary "to make good the damage caused by natural disasters or other exceptional occurrences" or "to promote the economic development of areas where the standard of living is abnormally low or where there is serious underemployment."

Of those matters which are essentially subject to national control Articles 223, 224 and 225 are perhaps the prime examples and are concerned with questions of security and the maintenance of order. Article 223 authorises Member States to withhold any information the disclosure of which would be contrary to the essential interests of their security and they are also permitted to take necessary measures in connection with "the production of or trade in arms, munitions and war material." Article 224 is concerned with the "measures which a Member State may be called upon to take in the event of serious internal disturbances affecting the maintenance of law and order, in the event of war or serious international tension constituting a threat of war, or in order to carry out obligations it has accepted for the purpose of maintaining peace and international security." Thus subject to an obligation to consult with its fellow members[28] a Member State retains the sovereign right to act in the interests of its security and the maintenance of order and retains control over the means of executing such action. For comparable reasons Article 55 exempts from the operation of the right of establishment any activities in a Member State which "are connected, even occasionally, with the exercise of official authority." Of a similar order are the provisions of Article 36 which permit Member States to deviate from the prohibition on quantitative restrictions on imports and exports between Member States. The grounds on which such deviations may be made are stated to be "public morality, public policy or public security; the protection of health and life of humans animals or plants; the protection of national treasures possessing artistic, historic or archaelogical value; or the protection of industrial and commercial property." Lastly, Article 222 provides that the Treaty "shall in no way prejudice the rules in Member States governing the system of property ownership."

It can be seen from the above that the EEC Treaty and its related documents are considerably concerned with what may be properly called fundamental rights. Some of these, particularly those concerned with questions of legality and judicial protection, are similar to those traditionally found in Bills of Rights, others are less familiar and owe their inspiration to the economic nature of the objects and aims of the Community. In many cases the rights which are but briefly outlined in the Treaty have been further defined and implemented by Community secondary legislation.[29]

III—Fundamental Rights and the Court of Justice of the Communities

The Court of Justice of the Communities plays a central and vital role in the interpretation and implementation of the rights mentioned above. The exigencies of space preclude a comprehensive treatment of this aspect of the Court's work, but the following instances are given by way of illustration.[30]

Under the terms of Article 173 the Court of Justice is given jurisdiction to review the legality of the law-making acts of the Council and the Commission. One of the grounds of review is the "infringement of an essential procedural requirement" and on this the Court has developed a considerable body of case law. A common basis for challenging a Community act on this ground is that the act is not "fully reasoned." The justification for such an allegation is Article 190 which provides that "regulations, directives and decisions of the Council and of the Commission shall state the reasons on which they are based. . . ." A leading case is *Re Tariff Quota on Wine: German Federal Republic* v. *Commission of the EEC* where a decision of the Commission was challenged on the ground of lack of adequate supporting reasons.[31] In his submissions Advocate-General Roemer indicated the essential nature of reasons in this context: "one must not forget the useful function which is ensured by the obligation to give reasons, having regard to the reasonable reinforcement of legal protection, in so far as it forces the Executives, when they formulate the grounds of a decision, to have a clear picture of the conditions giving rise to the decision."[32] The judgment of the Court made the matter quite clear:

> "By imposing upon the Commission the duty to give reasoned decisions, Article 190 does not merely fulfil a formal function but seeks to give the parties an opportunity of defending their rights, the Court an opportunity of exercising its control and the member-states, as well as interested parties, an opportunity of ascertaining the conditions in which the Commission applies the Treaty. To attain these objects, it would be adequate for the decision to set out, in a concise and relevant manner, the principal points of law and of fact upon which it is based and which are necessary in order to clarify the reasoning which led the Commission to its decision."[33]

Thus in that case since the Commission merely stated that it had relied on "the information available," the reasons were clearly inadequate, if not non-existent, and so the decision in question was annulled.

In more recent cases the Court has sought to define the nature of the obligation to give reasons even more precisely. It has held, for example, that "the duty to provide a statement of reasons for . . . a decision must be interpreted in the light of the practical realities and the time and technical facilities available for making such a decision."[34] Thus, in an emergency situation, in which the Commission only had three days in which to act, a comparatively brief and succinct but otherwise adequate statement of reasons would satisfy Article 190.[35]

A further illustration is provided by the jurisdiction of the Court to determine the liability of the Community to pay compensation for damage "in accordance with the general principles common to the laws of the Member States." This has involved the Court in undertaking a comparative analysis of the legal systems of the member states so as to arrive at a common core of legal principle in the light of which liability can be assessed. As far as the general categories of conduct for which damages can be recovered are concerned the Court distinguishes between *fautes de service* and *fautes personnelles*. In the case of the former where damage results from the malfunctioning of Community institutions or Community servants, the Community is liable; in the case of the latter where damage results from some act of a Community servant which is in no way connected with his official position, the wrongdoer alone is personally liable.[36] Among the specific types of conduct for which the Community has been held liable are conduct which would lead an experienced layman to an erroneous and detrimental interpretation of his rights[37]; a negligent failure to exercise proper control over a delegated body[38]; and wrongful dismissal from employment with the Community.[39]

The Court of Justice of the Communities has not merely contented itself with developing Community fundamental rights on the basis of the express terms of the Treaty, but it has also interpreted its task of observing the law as permitting it to apply a body of unwritten legal principles which are common to the national legal and political systems of the member states. In the words of Advocate-General Dutheillet de Lamothe the function of the fundamental principles of national legal systems in Community law is to "contribute to forming that philosophical, political and legal substratum common to the member-states from which emerges through the case law an unwritten Community law, one of the essential aims of which is precisely to ensure the respect for the fundamental rights of the individual."[40] When the Court invokes and applies such principles it relies not on Article 215 (which in this context is limited to non-contractual liability), but on Article 164 which requires it to observe the law in the interpretation and application of the Treaty as a whole.

A striking example of the Court being concerned with such general principles is provided by *Stauder* v. *City of Ulm*.[41] There was a surplus of butter in the Community and it was decided to provide cheap butter to those in receipt of social assistance. The Commission addressed a decision to each Member State specifying that those entitled to the butter should be provided with personal coupons for that purpose. The coupons issued in Germany were only valid if the name of the beneficiary appeared on them, whereas in other Member States other forms of identification (*e.g.* by number) were employed. Stauder, a German beneficiary, objected to the German form of the coupons on the grounds that it was discriminatory and violated his right to dignity and equality under German Constitutional Law.[42] Stauder instituted proceedings before the *Verwaltungsgericht* of Stuttgart and that court requested the Court of Justice of the Communities, under Article 177, to give a preliminary ruling on the compatibility of the Commission's decision with the general principles of Community Law. Advocate-General Roemer submitted that

> "common conceptions of value in the national constitutional law, in particular, national basic rights, must be established by a comparative evaluation of the law and these common conceptions must be observed as unwritten components of Community Law in the formulation of secondary Community Law. Consequently, the Court may quite properly be requested to test the validity of a decision of the Commission against this criterion."[43]

The Court ruled that it was necessary for all these Decisions to be applied uniformly. The Commission's aim was to have individualised coupons and in such cases "preference must be given to the least onerous interpretation if it suffices to achieve the purposes served by the decision in question."[44] Although the decision addressed to Germany, unlike the decisions addressed to the other Member States, specified individualisation by name this was not intended and the Court indicated that the Commission should amend the decision addressed to Germany so as to require individualisation in general terms whilst leaving the choice of method to each Member State.[45] "Thus interpreted," the Court said, "the decision in question does not contain any element which might jeopardise the fundamental rights of the individual contained in the general principles of law of the Community of which the Court must ensure the observance."[46]

Although the *Stauder* case contains one of the clearest statements of the function of general principles in Community Law, it is by no means an isolated example. Among other general principles which have been recognised is the principle of legality[47]; the principle of good faith[48]; and the principle of proportionality,[49] *viz.* that citizens may only have imposed on them for a public interest purpose, obligations which are strictly necessary for that purpose to be achieved.

IV—Community Rights and National Rights

Whilst the written and unwritten law of the Community clearly includes a corpus of fundamental rights, it is equally clearly a corpus of rights which is by no means identical, either in terms of content or scope, with classic Bills of Rights whether national or international. Using the classic Bill of Rights as a yardstick the corpus of Community rights is clearly incomplete in that the content of such rights is finally determined by the Treaty and not by any external notions of what is or is not a fundamental right. The Court of Justice has recognised this limitation on its powers. In *Marga Schlieker* v. *High Authority*[50] the defendant argued that the plaintiff's action should be dismissed on the simple ground that the Treaty did not enable her to bring it. In reply the plaintiff argued that on general principles the Court had a residual jurisdiction to ensure that justice was done. Advocate-General Roemer submitted that "the Treaty system is distinguished from national law in just this point, that it does not in a general clause guarantee legal protection without any gaps . . . for the Court can define the limits of its supranational legal protection only by using the text of the Treaty and not by following national law."[51] The Court agreed and held that in the light of the express wording of the Treaty "whatever may be the consequences of a factual situation of which the Court may not take cognizance, the Court may not depart from the judicial system set out in the Treaty."[52]

Not only is the range of rights guaranteed by the Treaty less extensive than that in the case of a national legal system, but the scope of such rights, whether written or unwritten, is also limited. Throughout the Treaty it is provided, either expressly or by implication, that Community rights are to be guaranteed subject to the aims of the Treaty. The prohibition on discrimination on grounds of nationality in Article 7 is "within the scope of application of this Treaty." The right of free movement of workers is only a right to the extent that it furthers the freedom of the Community labour market[53] and the meaning of the term "workers" in Article 48 is subject to Community law and not to national law.[54] The co-operation between Member States in the social field under the terms of Article 118 shall be in conformity with the general objectives of the Treaty. Similarly, where the Treaty safeguards national rights, such rights are not, in general, to be exercised in a way which is incompatible with the objects of the Treaty. Thus, whilst Article 222 preserves the system of property ownership in the member states it is only the *system* of property which is protected; Article 222 does not guarantee that Community law will not interfere with individual rights of property where the interests of the Community requires it.[55]

The Court has taken an identical line in connection with rights resulting from the unwritten law of the Community. Whilst the inspiration and model of such rights is the national legal systems, the rights themselves must be found within Community law itself. "Respect for fundamental rights has an integral part in the general principles of law of which the Court of Justice ensures respect. The protection of such rights, while inspired by the constitutional principles common to the Member States *must be ensured within the framework of the Community's structure and objectives.*"[56] Therefore while the rights guaranteed by national constitutions are likely to be comprehensive in number and are guaranteed in accordance with traditional, if not objective, standards, the number of rights guaranteed by Community law is limited by the objectives of the Community and the standards by which they are guaranteed are subjective Community standards. This is inevitable since the Community system, as conceived by the Treaty, is not a universal system of national government but has limited economic and social aims.

The fact that Community rights differ from national rights in this way has brought them into conflict in cases where the standard of protection afforded by a Community right (and *a fortiori* the lack of a Community right) falls short of the standard of protection afforded by national law. The problems raised by such conflict have been particularly acute in Germany and to a lesser extent in Italy since in both of those countries fundamental rights are guaranteed by the Constitution.[57] These problems have also been aggravated by the doctrine of the supremacy of Community law over national law.

The nature of the problem is well illustrated by the recent conflict between German courts and the Court of Justice of the Communities in the case *Internationale Handelsgesellschaft mbH* v. *Einfuhr- und Vorratsstelle für Getreide und Futtermittel.* Under Community agricultural regulations import and export licences could be obtained subject to the payment of a security which would be forfeit if the permitted quantity of product was not imported or exported during the relevant period. The validity of those regulations was challenged before the *Verwaltungsgericht* of Frankfurt on the grounds, *inter alia*, that the payment of the security violated a fundamental right guaranteed by the German Constitution. The right in question, derived from Articles 2 and 12 of the Constitution, is that of *Verhältnismässigkeit* or proportionality by which the state for a public purpose may only impose upon citizens such obligations as are strictly necessary for the realisation of that purpose. The Frankfurt Court held that the principle of proportionality was not only a principle of German law but also of Community law on the basis that "it must be assumed that the German legislator agreed to enter the EEC only on condition that the law governing the relations between the Community States is equivalent in value to German constitutional law."[58] It therefore asked the Community Court to give a preliminary ruling on the validity of the regulations in question on the ground that the payment of a security was not strictly necessary to regulate the market in the products in question and so violated the principle of proportionality.

The Community Court agreed that the principle of proportionality was part of Community Law both as an unwritten general principle and as an express provision of Article 40(3) of the Treaty. But the Court pointed out, in accordance with its *jurisprudence constante*,[59] that

> "Recourse to legal rules or concepts of national law to judge the validity of instruments promulgated by Community institutions would have the effect of harming the unity and efficacity [*sic*] of Community law. The validity of such instruments can only be judged in the light of Community law. In fact, the law born from the Treaty, the issue of an autonomous source, could not, by its very nature, have the courts opposing to it rules of national law of any nature whatever without losing its Community character and without the legal basis of the Community itself being put in question. Therefore the validity of a Community instrument or its effect within a member-state cannot be affected by allegations that it strikes at either the fundamental rights as formulated in that State's constitution or the principles of a national constitutional structure."[60]

Thus the Community principle of proportionality is to be evaluated in the light of Community and not national law. The Community Court held that the system of securities was not excessively burdensome and was a necessary consequence of the Community's market organisation system and so did not violate the Community principle of proportionality.[61] There was clearly a conflict between the principle of porportionality known to German constitutional law and the similar but distinct principle known to Community Law; in such a situation by virtue of its inherent superiority, Community Law prevailed.

The *Verwaltungsgericht* of Frankfurt declined to let the matter rest there and requested the *Bundesverfassungsgericht* to rule on the constitutionality of the Community regulations in issue.[62] That Court has declined to give a ruling on the ground that EEC Regulations are not part of German national law and so fall outside the powers of review conferred by Article 100 of the German Constitution,[63] thus, apparently, confirming the supremacy of Community law in practice within the German Constitutional and legal system.[64]

V—Conclusion

It is clear that Community law recognises a body of fundamental rights which derive their inspiration from and in large part reflect the common legal and political heritage of the Member States. In those fields which do not impinge on the economic and social objectives of the Community national rights and the means of enforcing them remain intact. But there is clearly an important area in which Community rights and national rights overlap. In that area Community rights prevail because of the inherent superiority of Community Law, even though, from a national constitutional standpoint, the standard of protection of Community Law may in some cases fall short of that customarily afforded by national law.

To date the extent of such conflict has been very limited and has in practice only been felt in those Member States in which fundamental rights *per se* are justiciable issues. Thus in the United Kingdom where there is no doctrine of guaranteed fundamental rights few problems are immediately foreseeable. The limited extent to which our rights may be affected by Community Law can be regarded as one of the prices we have to pay for participation in an established Community which has been set up and developed without reference to the United Kingdom.

Looking to the future, however, the picture may change. As the Community widens its terms of reference and progresses from an economic union to some form of political union the impact of the Community on traditional fundamental rights will necessarily increase. The Community is already actively considering a programme concerned with environmental pollution which, while laudable in itself, will have implications as far as fundamental rights are concerned. As the Community moves into such new areas, a re-examination of fundamental rights and the Community will be necessary in order to ensure an adequate level of protection and to avoid dangerously enlarging the constitutional and legal vacuum which results from a divergence between Community rights and national rights. A possible solution to these problems would appear to lie in linking Community law in some way to the European Convention on Human Rights and Fundamental Freedoms so as to provide a generally acceptable and adequate guarantee of fundamental rights in the developed Community of the future.

NOTES

1. In a speech made on July 12, 1839 during a debate on the Chartists' National Petition; reproduced in Emden (ed.), *Selected Speeches on the Constitution* (1939), vol. 2, p. 47.
2. *Cf.* the Bow Group pamphlet *Britain into Europe* (1962), p. 58.
3. Legal and Constitutional Implications of United Kingdom Membership of the European Communities, Cmnd. 3301 and The United Kingdom and the European Communities, Cmnd. 4715.
4. Cmnd. 4715, para. 30.
5. *Ibid.*, para. 31; an almost identical statement is made in Cmnd. 3301, para. 25.
6. Cmnd. 4715, para. 32.
7. s. 2(1).
8. Throughout this essay references to the EEC Treaty are to the authentic English version published in 1972 as Cmnd. 4864.
9. Art. 1(b); available in many sources, *e.g. Manual of the Council of Europe* (1970), Appendix I.
10. Arts. 2 and 3; reproduced in Kitzinger, *The European Common Market and Community* (1967), p. 54.
11. For an example of such a provision see the Treaty for a European Defence Community 1952, Art. 3(1) reproduced *ibid.*, pp. 41, 42; this Treaty has not been ratified.
12. This reference to the Charter of the United Nations is less significant than might be supposed for unlike the Purposes of the United Nations (Art. 1) the Principles of the United Nations (Art. 2) contain no direct reference to human rights and fundamental freedoms.

13. The EEC is also concerned to further the interests and prosperity of those non-European countries and territories associated with it, see Art. 131.
14. Art. 135 envisages an extension of the right of free movement to workers from those non-European countries and territories associated with the Community.
15. Also see Art. 184.
16. Contractual liability of the Community is governed by the law applicable to the contract in question, see Art. 215.
17. This provision has not yet been implemented and the members of the Assembly are still appointed by the national Parliaments of the Member States from their own members in accordance with Art. 138(1).
18. This has been threatened on one occasion, see Palmer, *et al.*, *European Unity* (1968), p. 182; and actually attempted on another, see *The Times*, November 17, 1972 and December 13, 1972.
19. Statute of the Court, Arts. 3 and 4.
20. *Ibid.*, Art. 6.
21. *Ibid.*, Art. 16.
22. Statute of the Court, Art. 17.
23. Supplementary Rules, Arts. 4 and 5.
24. Statute of the Court, Art. 17.
25. Rules of Procedure, Title 1, Chap. 9.
26. Statute of the Court, Art. 33 and Rules of Procedure, Art. 63.
27. Rules of Procedure, Title 2, Chap. 5.
28. See Arts. 224 and 225.
29. It is not practicable to discuss such secondary legislation within the scope of this essay; the reader is advised to consult, in the first instance, Campbell, *Common Market Law* (1969) and Supplements.
30. For further information consult Campbell, *op. cit.*
31. Case 24/62: [1963] C.M.L.R. 347; although this case was concerned with decisions it is equally applicable to regulations and directives.
32. *Ibid.* at p. 352.
33. *Ibid.* at p. 367. Also see *Cassella Farbwerke Mainkur AG, et al.* v. *EC Commission*, Cases 55 and 56/69: [1972] C.M.L.R. 644 at p. 646.
34. *Firma C. Schwarze* v. *Einfuhr-und Vorratsstelle für Getreide und Futtermittel*, Case 16/65: [1966] C.M.L.R. 172 at p. 188.
35. *Rewe-Zentrale des Lebensmittel-Grosshandels GmbH* v. *Hauptzollamt Emmerich*, Case 37/70: [1971] C.M.L.R. 238 at pp. 248–249, 253.
36. See for example *Firma E. Kampffmeyer et al.* v. *EEC Commission*, Cases 5, 7, 13–24/66: 13 *Recueil* 317.
37. *Société des Aciéries du Temple* v. *High Authority*, Case 36/62: [1964] C.M.L.R. 49.
38. *Société Fives Lille Cail et al.* v. *High Authority*, Cases 19 and 21/60 and 2 and 3/61: [1962] C.M.L.R. 251.
39. *Willame* v. *Euratom Commission*, Case 110/63: [1966] C.M.L.R. 236.
40. *Internationale Handelsgesellschaft mbH* v. *Einfuhr- und Vorratsstelle für Getreide und Futtermittel*, Case 11/70: [1972] C.M.L.R. 255 at p. 271.
41. Case 29/69: [1970] C.M.L.R. 112.
42. Basic Law of the Federal German Republic, Arts. 1 and 3.
43. [1970] C.M.L.R. at p. 115.
44. *Ibid.* at p. 118.
45. See Decision 69/244/CEE at [1970] J.O.C.E. L.200.
46. [1970] C.M.L.R. at p. 119.
47. *Société Nouvelle des Usines de Pontlieue Aciéries du Temple* v. *High Authority*, Cases 42 and 49/59: 7 *Recueil* 99 at pp. 159, 160.
48. *Eva von Lachmüller et al.* v. *EEC Commission*, Cases 43, 45 and 48/59: 6(2) *Recueil* 223 at p. 242.
49. *Loc. cit.* in note 40 *supra*. For examples of other general principles see Pescatore, "Les droits de l'homme et l'intégration européenne," (1968) 4 Cah. dr. europ. 629 at pp. 642 *et seq.*
50. Case 12/63: [1963] C.M.L.R. 281.
51. *Ibid.* at p. 285.
52. *Ibid.* at p. 288. The Court reached the same conclusion in *Marcelle Sgarlata et al.* v. *EEC Commission*, Case 40/64: [1966] C.M.L.R. 314 at pp. 322, 324.

53. *Cf. City of Wiesbaden* v. *Barulli* [1968] C.M.L.R. 239 (*Landgericht* of Wiesbaden).
54. See *Unger* v. *Bestuur der Bedrijfsvereniging voor Detailhandel en Ambachten*, Case 75/163: [1964] C.M.L.R. 319.
55. See *Etablissements Consten S.A. and Grundig-Verkaufs-GmbH* v. *EEC Commission*, Case 56 and 58/64: [1966] C.M.L.R. 418 at pp. 443, 476.
56. *Internationale Handelsgesellschaft mbH* v. *Einfuhr- und Vorratsstelle für Getreide und Futtermittel*, Case 11/70: [1972] C.M.L.R. 255 at p. 283; italics added.
57. See Pescatore, *op. cit.*, pp. 632 *et seq.*
58. [1970] C.M.L.R. 294 at p. 295.
59. *e.g. Friedrich Stork et Cie* v. *High Authority*, Case 1/58: 5 *Recueil* 42 at p. 63 and *Comptoirs de vente du charbon de la Ruhr* v. *High Authority*, Cases 36–38 and 40/59: 6 *Recueil* 857 at p. 890.
60. *Loc. cit.* in note 56 *supra*.
61. *Ibid.* at pp. 283–286.
62. [1972] C.M.L.R. 177.
63. The writer is indebted to Professor P. D. Dagtoglou of the University of Regensburg for this information since the report of the *Bundesverfassungsgericht's* judgment was not available at the time of writing. *Cf.* the judgment of the *Bundesverfassungsgericht* of October 18, 1967, 22 B Verf. G.E. no. 28, p. 293.
64. But see *Einfuhr- und Vorratsstelle für Getreide und Futtermittel* v. *Wasaknäcke Knäckelbrotfabrik GmbH* [1972] C.M.L.R. 841 at p. 845 (*Hessischer Verwaltungsgerichthof*).

21. THE RIGHT TO FREE MOVEMENT IN THE EUROPEAN COMMUNITIES

R. O. PLENDER

I—The Programme in Outline

THE freedom to enter and settle in one's own country is among the liberties most consistently included in the otherwise fluctuating group of facilities known as fundamental rights. According to the Universal Declaration, everyone has the right to return to his country.[1] The Covenant on Civil and Political Rights echoes this proclamation,[2] and the Convention on Racial Discrimination asserts that the right to enter one's country should be respected without distinction as to race.[3] Indeed, this right is often seen as the very hallmark of citizenship.[4] It finds expression in domestic constitutions from Switzerland[5] to Syria[6]; from Pakistan[7] to Peru.[8] Seen in this light, the free movement programme of the European Communities constitutes more than an adjunct to the process of economic integration. Rather, "it represents . . . an incipient form . . . of European citizenship."[9]

Article 48 of the EEC Treaty provided that freedom of movement for workers should be established by March 1969. It envisaged that this freedom would encompass the abolition of discrimination between Community nationals as regards employment, remuneration and conditions of employment, the right to accept offers of employment, the right to move freely within the territories of member states for the purposes of employment, and the right to remain in those territories not only for the duration of the employment, but also after its determination. To these principles exceptions were to be made only on the grounds of public policy, public safety or public security, or in the case of employment in the public service.[10] The principles enunciated by Article 48 were to be implemented by means of regulations or directives of the Council.[11] Member states agreed that they would actively encourage the exchange of young workers.[12] By Article 51 the Council received the power and duty to facilitate the free movement of workers by the adaptation of social security laws, including provisions for the aggregation of contributions paid into the social funds of the several Member States, and for the distribution in one Community country of benefits arising from contributions paid in another.[13].

At this stage it is proper to reiterate the fundamental, if elementary observation that the Council is empowered to act by way of regulation and directive, rather than by mere recommendation or decision. The programme for the free movement of workers is thus to be achieved by devices designed to supervene over inconsistent domestic laws.[14] In pursuance of this power, the Council on August 15, 1961 adopted the first of three regulations dealing with the progressive establishment of the scheme for free mobility of labour. The 1961 regulation began with the statement of principle that: "*Tout ressortissant d'un État membre est autorisé à occuper un emploi salarié sur le territoire d'un autre État membre.*"[15] However, the principle was qualified, since it was to apply only "*si aucun travailleur approprié n'est pas disponible pour l'emploi vacant parmi la main d'oeuvre appartenant au marché régulier de l'emploi de l'autre État membre.*"[16] The same regulation dealt with the equal treatment of Community workers, including the adoption of equal criteria in their recruitment, without discrimination on the ground of nationality.[17] Special provision was to be made for the ready admission of workers' families into the country of their employment.[18]

Three years later the Council adopted a further regulation which maintained the principles established in 1961, but reduced the preferences given to members of the domestic labour market.[19] Provision was made under this regulation for free access to employment, the admission of workers' families and equality of treatment in respect of working conditions. By a proviso to the first article of this regulation, employment exchanges in the country of immigration had to be notified of any vacancy before a national of a Community country might obtain the right to fill it. Under Article 2, Member States were allowed to restore the priority of the domestic labour market in certain well-defined situations. These two concessions to national economic and social sovereignty were abandoned in 1968 when the Council's third regulation came into effect. The 1968 regulation was designed to abolish restrictions on the assumption of paid employment in other Member States. True, Article 20 of the 1968 regulation ensures that if in any Member State the labour equilibrium is upset, the Commission and other Member States will be so informed, and will take precautions to publish the situation; but if the country of immigration wishes to impose legal restrictions on the admission of other Community nationals, it must submit the matter to the Commission, which alone has the decisive power. The Commission's decisions on such matters are subject to annulment or amendment by the Council, but even when it acts in this supervisory capacity the Council must intervene within two weeks. Moreover, following the Luxembourg *Accords* it is by no means certain that the Council could exercise its supervisory function by a simple majority vote.

Under the 1968 regulation work permits are no longer required for Community nationals seeking to take paid employment in other Community countries.[20] Migrant workers in this category are entitled to bring with them their spouses and minor children, and any of their parents or grandparents who may belong to their household, provided that they are able to furnish these dependents with accommodation considered normal in the country of immigration.[21]

Certain of the Association Agreements concluded between the European

Communities and third states contain provision for the extension of freedoms of movement to nationals of countries outside the European Communities. In particular, Turkish nationals will enjoy freedom to settle within the European Communities by 1986, and similar facilities will be extended to Greek nationals if the Association Agreement with that country ceases to be suspended.[22] The Treaties of Yaoundé and Arusha (which deal with the associated status of certain former colonies and other territories in Africa) do not envisage the extension of freedoms of movement. Rather, the EEC Treaty stipulates that separate agreements shall be required to govern this liberty, and that such agreements shall require the unanimous approval of the member states.[23]

II—The Consequences of the Programme

Although the Communities' programme for freedom of movement has been conceived in grandiose terms, and is of immense symbolic significance, the practical consequences of the programme have hitherto been less than dramatic. In the first place, intra-European quasi-migration[24] falls mainly beyond the purview of the EEC Treaty, with the result that the casual visitor will not normally derive immediate benefit from Community Law. Rather he will rely on bilateral arrangements, or on one or more of the treaties concluded under the aegis of the Council of Europe.[25] In the second place, the administrative procedures employed by the Communities remain cumbersome, so that companies in search of employees from other Member States tend to rely on the old national recruitment missions rather than on the central machinery. Under the present system the employment services of the several Member States submit monthly returns to one another and to the Coordination Bureau in order to report vacancies that cannot be filled nationally, together with the names of prospective migrant workers.[26] There is the possibility of direct exchanges of information between the employment exchanges of separate countries, but this procedure applies only in the case of adjacent states and subject to the approval of their central authorities.[27] Moreover, the latter process had been used before the establishment of the Common Market, and it continues to be useful principally for frontier workers.[28]

An analysis of the consequences of the Communities' programme leads us to make a third qualification to our preliminary remarks about its significance: the principle of the priority of the Community labour market is adopted in Community law, but is curtailed and limited both in law and in fact. Article 19(2) of the governing Regulation specifies that Member States will take appropriate measures to ensure that preferences are extended to the Communities' labour reservoir. However, Article 16 not only envisages the recruitment of workers from third states, but actually authorises employers in Member States to dispense with the principle of the priority of the Community labour market when nationals of third states are required for "reasons connected with the smooth running of the operation."[29] Thus, the Community system accounts only for a proportion of the transnational migrations within the EEC, and immigrations from beyond the Common Market play a very significant part in satisfying the Member States' demands for labour. Apart from Italy, all of the original Member States have relied heavily on immigrant labour. In Luxembourg about one-quarter of the population of 340,000 consisted of foreigners at the beginning of 1971, and immigrants probably accounted for an even greater proportion of the work-force. In the larger Member States, as in Britain, immigrants account for more than 5 (but less than 10 per cent.) of the populace.[30] In these countries migrants from other Member States of the EEC are always outnumbered by migrants from third states.[31] No doubt, the British Government had these facts in mind when it observed that "The movement of labour within an enlarged Community will probably continue to be dominated by economic and social factors, rather than by regulations."[32]

The principal significance of the Communities' programme for the free movement of labour does not, therefore, lie in the demographic consequences which have been experienced so far. Rather, the significance of the programme is to be found in the unique character of Community Law, and in its impact on domestic laws and practices. It is a cardinal (if elementary) principle of Community Law that provisions of domestic law must normally be subordinated to any directly applicable Community provisions with which they are in conflict.[33] This principle has been recognised by national courts not only with respect to conflicts between Community laws and previous domestic rules, but also with respect to certain conflicts between Community laws and subsequent domestic ones. In 1965 the *Finanzgericht* of Münster observed that

> "the organs of the Community were given powers of legislation in matters pertaining to the Community and that legislation is binding on the Member States. If those powers are to mean anything Community legislation must have the effect, within its sphere of competence, of amending or repealing by implication national legislation which is repugnant to it."[34]

In the *Shell-Berre* case the French *Conseil d'Etat* proceeded on the basis that certain French regulations would have been void if they had been in conflict with a prior Community law.[35] The assumption made by the *Conseil* is explicable in the light of the decision made by the European Court of Justice in *Van Gend en Loos* v. *Tariefcommissie*. In that case the Court emphasised that Community law not only creates a new legal order, but also demonstrates that member states have limited their own competence to govern unilaterally matters which they have remitted to the Community organs for central or collective government.[36] It is thus manifest that domestic laws and practices must normally defer when they conflict with Community rules governing the freedom of movement in the EEC.

It is the superiority of Community Law, and the enforceability of that law in domestic courts,[37] which distinguishes the Community's programme for free movement from the similar schemes which preceded it. In October 1953, for example, the Council of the OEEC agreed that Member States would guarantee work permits and equality of treatment to each other's nationals migrating to fill vacancies which could not be filled from the local labour pool.[38] In 1954 the governments of Sweden, Norway, Denmark and Finland concluded an agreement to establish a common labour market.[39] The Benelux Union operated a similar arrangement.[40] However, in each of these cases the international treaty dealt principally with procedural matters: it did not entail the abolition of labour permits, nor grant to the individual a legally enforceable right of migration.[41]

III—The Scope of the Programme

Granted that Community Law is in principle superior to domestic law, and granted that it must be enforced in domestic courts, we are entitled to test domestic immigration laws against the Community's yardstick. The principal criterion which Community Law on free movement now maintains is to be found in Article 1 of Regulation 1612/68. According to that article,

> "Any national of a Member State, irrespective of his place of residence, shall have the right to take up an activity as an employed person, and to pursue such activity within the territory of another Member State. . . ."

Unfortunately, neither the Regulation nor the EEC Treaty expressly defines the term "national," with the result that the task of definition has in fact been remitted to the domestic authorities. In most cases the definitions adopted by the Member States have been unexceptionable. The German Federal Republic, for example, made a Declaration whereby the term "German nationals" was identified with all persons who are German nationals according to the Basic Law. In the case of the United Kingdom a unilateral declaration proclaims that the term "national" relates only to those who fall within either of two categories. The first category consists of citizens of the United Kingdom and Colonies or British subjects without citizenship who have the right of abode in the United Kingdom, and are therefore exempt from United Kingdom immigration control. The second category consists of any person who is a citizen of the United Kingdom and Colonies by birth or by registration or naturalisation in Gibraltar, or whose father was born, registered or naturalised there.[42]

According to W. R. Böhning, the United Kingdom's declaration contravenes Community Law, since "a Member State's right to define whom he considers a national does not include the competence to exclude certain nationals from the benefits of EEC membership".[43] This argument invites three comments: the first concerns the relationship between Community Law and public international law; the second deals with the term "United Kingdom national"; and the third involves the status of Member States' Declarations.

As a matter of public international law, it is clear that each state has, in principle, the right to determine whom it will consider as one of its nationals.[44] While it is no less clear that public international law imposes certain limits on the state's exercise of this competence,[45] it is important to realise that the limitations most clearly established in international law are those designed to discourage the making of expansive claims to citizenship.[46] Rarely does public international law positively require a state to confer its nationality on an individual or group.[47] For these reasons we would hesitate to argue that *international* law requires the United Kingdom to define her nationals more broadly than she has done under the 1972 declaration. However, we cannot presume that the Community Court will be no more assiduous than international tribunals in protecting individuals' claims to the rights flowing from citizenship of appropriate states. Moreover, even a tribunal of public international law might infer from the principle of good faith an obligation not to frustrate the objectives of the EEC Treaty by adopting an unusually narrow definition of the term "United Kingdom national."[48]

We cannot, of course, describe the definition as "narrow" unless we establish that the term is commonly used in some wider sense. Nor can the Community court impugn the definition in order to protect any individual other than one who can substantiate on other grounds his claim to be regarded as a national of the United Kingdom. The term "United Kingdom national" is notorious for its imprecision. The British Nationality Acts not only fail to define nationality, but eschew the very use of the word, other than in their titles. It appears that the definition most commonly employed in international treaties dealing with the protection of United Kingdom nationals abroad comprises four groups. The first group is of citizens of the United Kingdom and Colonies. The second consists of British protected persons. The third includes all British subjects without citizenship. The fourth encompasses citizens of Eire, who, under United Kingdom legislation, were British subjects immediately before the commencement of the 1948 Act, and who could establish association with the United Kingdom or any colony.[49] The adoption of such a definition for the purposes of free movement under the EEC Treaty would not avail citizens of other Commonwealth countries who have settled in the United Kingdom. On the other hand, such a definition would not be popular with those who are reluctant to permit the immigration into the United Kingdom of non-patrials bearing citizenship of the United Kingdom and Colonies. It is, however, well-founded in practice, and for these reasons it may be preferred to the formulation suggested by Böhning. The latter envisaged that the Court of Justice of the European Communities might adopt a definition extending to "every British subject resident in the United Kingdom free of immigration controls."[50]

Any suggestion that the Court of Justice of the European Communities might impugn the United Kingdom's Declaration presupposes that the Declaration is normatively inferior to Regulation 1612/68, and certainly inferior to the EEC Treaty. Neither the EEC Treaty nor the Treaty of Accession specified the legal status of such Declarations,[51] and several distinguished commentators have been extremely reticent in their remarks on the point.[52] It seems impossible to lay down any universal rule govern-ing the legal status of all such Declarations but some general propositions may be offered with confidence. Where a Member State appends a Declara-tion of its own understanding of a point of Community Law, that Declara-tion will have an authority comparable with that of *travaux préparatoires*. That is to say, it will constitute useful evidence of Community Law, but will not be binding *proprio motu*. Where the Member State's Declaration purports to describe objectively the internal law of that state on a point touching on Community affairs, the Declaration will have particular evidential value; but it will remain open to the litigant to disprove the Declaration by introducing contrary evidence. Where the Member State's Declaration does neither of these things, but amounts in fact to a deroga-tion from principles of Community Law, it is invalid. In such circum-stances it may be impugned by the Court of Justice, acting under Articles 169 to 171 of the EEC Treaty.

The United Kingdom's Declaration scarcely amounts to a statement of that country's understanding of Community Law, since it can hardly be maintained that it is in the first instance for Community Law to determine whether an individual qualifies as a "national" of a Member State.[53] Nor does the United Kingdom's Declaration amount to a description of a point of British nationality law, since the formulation contained in the Declaration is entirely novel. Rather, it appears to be analogous to a reservation to the Treaty. In public international law, reservations to multilateral treaties are normally permissible whenever they are not expressly forbidden in the text, or are "incompatible with the object and purpose of the treaty."[54] In Community Law, however, a different rule must apply. Since the object of the founding treaties is to ensure the fusion of certain essential state interests, and to place them under a single administration, there is an absolute prohibition on formal reservations.[55] This prohibition must surely extend to unilateral statements which in fact amount to reservations, though they are not expressed as such.[56] The Court of Justice has therefore affirmed that since Member States have engaged in identical ratifications of the treaties, they are contractually bound to an equal extent, save only for the exceptions expressed in the protocols. Hence, "the participation of any Member State in Community institutions, and the part it takes in the consequential rights and obliga-tions, exclude, in effect the possibility that its nationals might escape the integral and uniform application of the treaty, and thus receive treatment different from that accorded to other Community nationals."[57]

Even if we were to conclude that the United Kingdom's Declaration conforms with Community Law, we might still be able to establish that the Community right to free movement extends to certain citizens of the United Kingdom and Colonies who do not qualify as "nationals" of the United Kingdom. This is so because Article 48(1) of the EEC Treaty requires the establishment of freedom of movement for "workers," rather than for Community nationals.[58] Campbell[59] and Böhning[60] have both expressed the view that the word "worker" is *deliberately* juxtaposed with the word "nationality" in Article 48. This interpretation appears correct. Its consequence is that the Treaty requires the establishment of free movement for all workers, but that it abolishes discriminatory employment controls only among Community nationals.

IV—Safeguards Against the Programme

According to a Joint Declaration appended to the Act of Accession, the enlargement of the Community could give rise to "certain difficulties for the social situation in one or more Member States as regards the application of the provisions relating to the free movement of workers."[61] In such an event, Member States declare that they reserve the right to bring the matter before the institutions of the Community in order to obtain a solution. It is difficult to see what significance (if any) attaches to this vague formulation. Clearly it does not constitute an amendment to the founding treaties, for those agreements may be altered only in accordance with the procedures specified therein.[62] In any case, the EEC Treaty states that freedom of movement will be established subject to limitations justified on grounds of public safety or security, public health or *ordre public*.[63] Should a "difficulty for the social situation" become sufficiently grave, it would surely justify the imposition of limitations on the programme of free movement. According to the circumstances of the case, the limitations might be imposed in defence of public health or *ordre public*. If the Joint Declaration is intended merely to emphasise a principle contained in the EEC Treaty, it is unobjectionable, other than on the ground that it is otiose.

It is possible, however, that the Joint Declaration is intended to supplement Article 20 of Regulation 1612/68. According to that Article, if any Member State experiences or foresees disturbances in its labour market, it may inform the Commission, which may then take steps to suspend the Community's balancing machinery.[64] Conceivably, the Joint Declaration is designed to ensure that the procedures specified in Article 20 may be invoked not only in the case of a disequilibrium in the domestic labour market, but also in cases of social unease. If the framers of the Declaration had this object in mind, their action was incompatible with Article 49 of the EEC Treaty, which necessarily implies that any amendment to the pertinent regulations shall be made by the Council, on a proposal from the Commission, and after consultation with the Economic and Social Committee. The use of a Joint Declaration to amend a regulation would be analogous with a "violation of a substantial procedural requirement"; it might become the subject of proceedings under Article 169 of the Treaty.[65] If the Commission, purportedly acting under Article 20 of Regulation 1612/68, were to suspend the balancing machinery for social rather than industrial reasons, its action might well become the subject of proceedings for *détournement de pouvoir*.[66]

It is precisely because Community Law offers opportunities of this kind to the individual litigant that we are justified in regarding as significant the Community's programme for free movement of workers.[67] Indeed, though Community law consists principally in a code for commerce, it retains, through its uniquely supranational characteristics, openings for the individual to vindicate rights which, on occasions, are not protected elsewhere—even by the European Convention on Human Rights.[68] To the extent that Community Law offers these opportunities, it constitutes a legal foundation for some of those rights which we regard as fundamental.[69]

NOTES

1. Universal Declaration of Human Rights, art. 13(1).
2. Art. 12.
3. Convention on the Elimination of All Forms of Racial Discrimination, art. 5(d)(ii).
4. Van Panhuys, *The Role of Nationality in International Law* (1959), p. 56.
5. Federal Constitution of 1964, art. 45.
6. Constitution of 1964, art. 14(2).
7. Constitution of 1962, art. 5.
8. Constitution of 1933, art. 67.
9. Sr. Lionelli Levi Sandri, Bulletin of the EEC No. 6, June 1961. Bulletin of the European Communities, Vol. I, No. 11, November 1968, pp. 5–6.
10. Art. 48(2).
11. Art. 49.
12. Art. 50.
13. A French court in *Nani* v. *Caisse d'Assurance Vieillesse des Travailleurs Salariés de Paris* correctly affirmed that regulations made under Art. 51 supervene over domestic laws and even over provisions of a bilateral treaty concluded between members of the European Communities. However, the court's interpretation of the regulation appears questionable, inasmuch as it resulted in the migrant worker's deprivation of a right previously enjoyed: [1965] C.M.L.R. 334. See *Moebs.* v. *Bestuur der Sociale Verzekeringsbank* [1964] C.M.L.R. 338 and *Kalsbeek van der Veen* v. *Bestuur der Sociale Verzekeringsbank* [1964] C.M.L.R. 548.
14. On the superiority of regulations and directives over domestic laws, see Treaty of Rome, Art. 189 and *infra*, p. 309.
15. In this paper we are concerned only with freedom of movement for workers. "Workers" include all employees: Case 61/65, *Vaassen Göbbels* v. *Beambtenfonds voor het Mijnbedrijf* [1966] C.M.L.R. 508. Persons migrating for work on their own account are liable to benefit from the freedom of establishment under Art. 52 of the Treaty of Rome.
16. Regulation 15 of August 15, 1961, J.O. C.E., p. 1073/1961, Art. 1.
17. Art. 9 and 10.
18. Art. 11.
19. Regulation 38 of March 25, 1964, J.O. C.E. p. 965/1964.
20. Regulation 1612 of October 15, 1968, J.O. p. 295/12 (L). See generally Lewin, "The Free Movement of Workers," 2 C.M.L. Rev., 1964–65 300; ter Heide, "Free Movement of Workers in the Final Phase," 6 C.M.L. Rev., 1968–69, 466; Böhning and Stephen, *The EEC and the Migration of Workers* (1971).
21. Art. 8.
22. Agreement of Association with Turkey of November 1, 1964, J.O. C.E. p. 3685/64, Article 60; Agreement of Association with Greece of November 1, 1962, J.O. C.E. p. 293/63, Arts. 44–50.
23. Art. 135.
24. "Quasi-migration" refers to the movement of a person to a country other than his own, for purposes other than permanent settlement.
25. European Agreement on Regulations Governing Movement of Persons between the Member States of the Council of Europe, E.T.S. 25; European Agreement on Travel by Young Persons on Collective Passports between

Member Countries of the Council of Europe, E.T.S. 37; European Convention on Establishment, E.T.S. 19. See Robertson, *The Council of Europe* (1961), pp. 206–209, and Smithers (ed.), *Manual of the Council of Europe* (1970), pp. 245–246.

26. Regulation 1612/68, Art. 15.
27. Art. 17(b).
28. ter Heide, *op. cit.*
29. In such a case it is necessary that the relevant employment service must have intervened for the purpose of securing the employment of a national worker or one from another Member State, and must have formed the opinion that there are justifiable reasons for subordinating the principle of priority of the Community labour market.
30. The approximate relevant statistics are as follows: Belgium, 7 per cent. (*Vu* No. 12, 1970, p. 3, *L'institut belge d'information et de documentation*) France: 5 per cent. (based on 1958 sample census, *Hommes et Migrations* No. 113); Germany: 6 per cent. (Böhning, "Immigrant Workers in West Germany" (1971 I(1) *New Community* 21); Netherlands: 7 per cent. (Central Bureau for Statistics, *Annual Statistics of the Nertherlands,* 1971).
31. In Luxembourg, however, the overwhelming majority of immigrants are from the EEC. Thomas, "Immigrants in Belgium and Luxembourg," (1971 I(1) *New Community*, 11, 14).
32. The United Kingdom and the European Communities, Cmnd. 4715, p. 35.
33. This is the principal lesson to be drawn from *Costa* v. *E.N.E.L.* [1964] C.M.L.R. 425. See Hay, "Supremacy of Community Law in National Courts," (1968) 16 Am. J. Comp. L. 524; Garron, "Reflexions sur la primauté du droit communautaire" (1969) 5 Rev. trim. de droit europ. 28–47; Pescatore, "Droit communautaire et droit national selon la jurisprudence de la cour de justice des communautés européennes" (1969) 27 *Recueil Dalloz Sirey* 179.
34. *Re Import Duties on Sunblind Cord,* [1966] C.M.L.R. 485. For purposes of brevity we will ignore the special difficulties which may arise in the case of conflicts between Community Law and domestic constitutional provisions akin to art. 79(3) of the German Basic Law.
35. [1964] C.M.L.R. 462. Campbell, *Common Market Law* (1969), Vol. 1, p. 54.
36. [1963] C.M.L.R. 105 at p. 118.
37. For the enforceability of Community law in domestic courts, see *F.I.V.A.* v. *Mertens* [1963] C.M.L.R. 141.
38. 7 *Keesing's Contemporary Archives* 13218.
39. 199 U.N.T.S. 20.
40. Meade, *Negotiations for Benelux* (1957), p. 80.
41. Beever, *Trade Unions and Free Labour Movement in the EEC* (1969), p. 26.
42. Declaration appended to the Act of Accession, Cmnd. 4862–I, p. 118.
43. "Rejoinder: The Scope of the EEC System of Free Movement of Workers" (hitherto unpublished). Statements to similar effect were made by the same author in *The Migration of Workers in the United Kingdom and the European Community* (1972), p. 136; "No Entry to Europe for Non-Patrials," *Race Today,* July 1972, pp. 236–237.
44. *Advisory Opinion on Nationality Decrees Issued in Tunis and Morocco,* P.C.I.J. Ser. B, No. 4 (1923) 24.
45. *Georges Pinson Case,* (1928) V U.N.R.I.A.A. 326, *per* Professor Verzijl.
46. Harvard Draft, I.L.C. Yearbook (1952–II) 3, 6 (art. 1); *Flegenheimer Claim,* 25 I.L.R. (1958–II) 91: *Nottebohm Case,* I.C.J. Rep. (1955) 6.
47. See the writer's comments and references in *International Migration Law,* (1972) pp. 29–35.
48. In practice, the question is not likely to be considered by a tribunal of public international law, since Art. 219 of the EEC Treaty provides that "Member States undertake not to submit a dispute concerning the interpretation or the carrying out of this Treaty to any method of settlement other than those provided for therein." The Court of Justice of the European Communities will take note of public international law, but is not bound by permissive rules of the public international legal order: *Fédération Charbonnière* v. *High Authority* (1956) 2 *Recueil* 199.
49. See, for example, the Anglo-Japanese Treaty of 1962, 478 U.N.T.S. 29,

together with the comments of Joseph in *Nationality and Diplomatic Protection: The Commonwealth of Nations*, (1969), p. 179.

50. "No Entry to Europe for Non-Patrials," *Race Today*, July 1972, pp. 236–237.

51. However, Art. 3(3) of the Act of Accession (appended to the Treaty of Brussels) states that the new Member States are in the same position as the Six in respect of Declarations of the Council.

52. Reuter observes that even in the case of *travaux*, "their precise juristic meaning is arguable": *La Communauté Européenne du Charbon et de l'Acier*, (1953), p. 30; Wortley writes that "derogations indicate that the principles of the Treaty are applied pragmatically, and that allowances are made for the particular circumstances of Member States": *An Introduction to the Law of the European Economic Community* (1972), p. 96; Lasok and Bridge comment that in tracing the intention of the Member States the Court of Justice is free to consult materials extraneous to the Treaty of Rome: *Introduction to the Law and Institutions of the European Communities* (1973), p. 86.

53. But Edens and Patijn argue that "the competence to give a definition of the purport of the concept "national of a member state" in Community Law rests with the Institutions of the Community, one of which is the Court of Justice": "The Scope of the EEC System of Free Movement of Workers," 9 C.M.L. Rev. 1972, 322.

54. Vienna Convention on Treaties, Cmnd. 4140, 8 I.L.M. (1969) 679, art. 19(c); Grieg, *International Law* (1970), p. 365; O'Connell, *International Law* (1970), Vol. I, pp. 229–239.

55. "L'interdiction absolue des réserves est manifeste dans le Traitée CEE": Lesguillons, *L'Application d'un Traité Fondation: le Traité instituant la C.E.E.* (1968), p. 87.

56. The principle whereby the European Court will have regard to substance rather than form is a familiar theme in its judgments. See Cases 56 and 58/64, *Consten and Grundig* v. *EEC Commission* [1966] C.M.L.R. 418, 468; Cases 16 and 17/62 *Confédération Nationale des Producteurs de Fruits et Légumes* v. *H.A.* [1963] C.M.L.R. 160; Case 28–30/62, *Da Costa en Schaake* v. *Nederlandse Belastingadministratie* [1963] C.M.L.R. 224.

57. *Merisider* v. *H.A.* (1965) I(3) Rev. trim. de droit europ. 483, 485.

58. For the meaning of the word "worker," see Reg. 3/58 on the Social Security of Migrating Workers, Art. 19(1), J.O. C.E. 1958, p. 561 and *supra*, n. 15.

59. *Common Market Law*, Supplement No. 2, (1971), p. 226.

60. "Rejoinder: the Scope of the EEC System of Free Movement of Workers" *supra*, n. 43.

61. Cmnd. 4862–I, p. 117.

62. For amendment of the EEC Treaty, see Arts. 235 and 236, and Lasok and Bridge, *op. cit.*, pp. 24–25.

63. Art. 48(3). *Ordre public* is to be understood in the wide sense generally accepted in Continental countries: Protocol to E.T.S. No. 19 section III. It is a very imprecise conception covering the body of legislation enactments made for the purpose of ensuring the moral and material protection of the nation, and it is often best translated by the terms "public order" or "law and order." See International Institute for Legal and Administrative Terminology, *European Glossary of Legal and Administrative Terminology*, Vol. XII, p. 46.

64. The Community's balancing machinery is the administrative code used to correlate vacancies unfilled or unlikely to be filled by labour from the national employment market with applicants for employment who have declared themselves ready and able to accept employment in another country.

65. For violations of substantial procedural requirements, see Art. 173 of the EEC Treaty which deals with supervision of the legality of certain acts of Community organs.

66. "There is a *détournement de pouvoir* when an administrative act is objectively in accordance with the rule of law, but substantively vitiated by reason of the aim being pursued by the administrative authority": *Féderation Charbonnière* v. *H.A.*, 2 *Recueil* (1955–56) 197, 211. See also Case 1/54, *French Government* v. *H.A.*, 1 *Recueil* (1954) 7; Case 56 and 58/64, *Consten and Grundig* v. *EEC Commission*, 12 *Recueil* (1966) 429 and *supra*, n. 56.

67. On the significance of the programme generally, see EEC Publication No. 1862 of 1966; Fitzgerald, *The Common Market's Labor Programs* (1966); Turak, "Freedom of Movement and Travel Documents in Community Law" (1968) 17 Buffalo Law Rev. 435; Schiefer, *Marché du Travail Européen: Libre Circulation et Migration des Travailleurs* (1961).

68. The writer has expressed elsewhere his view that certain fundamental migratory rights are left unprotected by the European Convention on Human Rights. See "The Exodus of Asians from East and Central Africa: Some Comparative and International Law Aspects" (1971) 16 Am. J. Comp. L. 287 at pp. 321–323.

69. The European Court has recently affirmed its view that it is charged with the duty to protect certain fundamental rights: Case 29/69, *Stauder* v. *City of Ulm* [1970] C.M.L.R. 112. For protection of fundamental rights under Community Law in general see the essay by J. W. Bridge in this book, together with the sources cited there, and Lorenz, "General Principles of Law: Their Elaboration in the Court of Justice of the European Communities" (1964) 13 Am. J. Comp. L. 1. For the rule of non-discrimination in the employment laws of the several member states of the European Communities, see the symposium in 21 Rev. de Droit Int. Comp. (1969).

INDEX